The Cruise Ship Phenomenon
in North America

As passenger travel by sea transformed itself from basic transportation to leisure-oriented cruising in the final decades of the twentieth century, a wonderful symbol of the transition was a
vessel that was built in 1961 for transatlantic service as French Line's *France* and later enjoyed
an extended career in the new order as Norwegian Cruise Line's *Norway*.

The Cruise Ship Phenomenon
in North America

BRIAN J. CUDAHY

CORNELL MARITIME PRESS
Centreville, Maryland

Library of Congress Cataloging-in-Publication Data

Cudahy, Brian J.
    The cruise ship phenomenon in North America / Brian J. Cudahy.
      p. cm.
    Includes bibliographical references and index.
    ISBN 0-87033-529-4
    1. Ocean travel. 2. Cruise lines—North America. I. Title.

  G550 .C85 2000
  910'.2'02—dc21   00-065579

If not otherwise credited, photographs were taken by the author.

Manufactured in the United States of America
First edition, 2001

To Mary Lou, my steady cruise companion—and more

*F*rom the early years of the nineteenth century when steamships were first equipped with funnels to enhance combustion in their boilers, these tall devices became a perfect billboard for decoration in distinctive company designs and colors. The practice remains a maritime tradition to this day, even though funnels themselves have evolved into structures that enclose and contain a variety of vessel exhaust ducts and are no longer the tall, thin stacks of yesteryear. The contemporary cruise industry is replete with examples of wonderfully distinctive funnels, many of which are shown at the start of sections in this book.

Radisson Seven Seas

Contents

Princess Cruises

Foreword

A couple of years ago, I was a passenger aboard *Grand Princess* when the vessel tied up at Naples. Berthed astern of us was *Sunbird*, which I recognized at once as *Song of America* in her post-RCCL guise.

Two things sprang immediately to mind. First, I recalled so clearly seeing *Song of America* under construction in Helsinki over the summer of 1981. Displacing 37,000 tons, she was a company one-off as well as a substantial new-building advance over her trio of predecessors. *Song of America*, Wartsila's hull number 431, was big time. In fact, I took the opportunity, in the yard's Building Hall, to walk beneath the length of her unfinished hull, stooped and splashing through rust-colored pools in the bowels of that drydock. What a marvel she was and how huge!

But second, seen from *Grand Princess*'s stern, *Sunbird/Song of America* now looked like a toy. My hastily readjusted perception was a potent reminder of what Brian Cudahy titles so accurately "the cruise ship phenomenon" in this admirable and much-needed volume.

For the cruise ship industry, mind-boggling growth has proved pandemic. None of us involved with these extraordinary ships could have guessed, in the early eighties, what giant hulls lay over the horizon. The construction of ever-larger vessels in dizzying profusion bears witness to the industry's astonishing vigor. To monitor—no less than savor—that splendid proliferation, it is essential we have a source that keeps us not only abreast of the times but also plugged into cruising's misty origins. Mind you, we are talking about nothing more remote than the 1960s. But if I may be forgiven a quote from my most recent book: "Shipboard history remains fragmented and incomplete, because the industry remains irrevocably fixated on the future." That pervasive myopia about the past comes with the owners' territory.

But Brian Cudahy has filled that lamentable void to perfection. His book tells all and tells it beautifully. We are privy to the first tentative voyages of *Sunward, Song of Norway*, and *Mardi Gras;* we encounter the visionary owners and designers as they hone a radically new shipboard; we are made aware of the accelerated, global expansion of markets and itineraries no less than the nuts and bolts of newbuilding; and, perhaps most significantly, we learn to appreciate cruising's heady appeal to a new generation of passengers.

Indeed, even if Cudahy had done nothing more than publish his invaluable Appendix A—a track chart of cruising tonnage with building records, specifications, and all prior names—he would have performed a noble service. Copies of his book should be mandatory equipment on every cruise ship, one chained down within the library and another chained atop the wheelhouse's navigational console, chained because otherwise they will certainly walk.

The Cruise Ship Phenomenon in North America is not only a good and fascinating read, it is also an unrivaled work of reference. The subject the author deciphers so adroitly is what I describe as near history, not yet distant enough to be accorded the reverence we assign to North Atlantic immortals. Now, we have an invaluable and well-written record of what the industry has achieved thus far.

As for the future, who knows? But at least Brian Cudahy has rewarded passengers, cruise line personnel, and maritime historians alike with a splendidly evocative and unique benchmark.

—John Maxtone-Graham, maritime historian and author

Costa Crocieri

Acknowledgments

Many individuals have provided assistance in the preparation of this work. Among cruise ship officers, I would like to mention, in no special order, Captain Jacob Dijk and Hotel Manager Fekko Ebbens of *Rotterdam* (6); Captain Haakon Gangdal of *Norway;* Captain Einar Lindrupsen and Staff Captain Jostein Kalvoy, who I encountered aboard *Dreamward;* Captain Zissi Koskinas of *Millennium;* Captain Rick Sullivan and Hotel Manager Fred De Cosse of *Legend of the Seas;* Captain David Chrystie of *Star Princess;* Captain Gerassimos Andrianatos of *Infinity;* Captain Henry Andersen of *Crown Jewel;* and Captain John Ikiadis and Staff Captain Kosta Nikolis of Celebrity Cruises.

Among cruise company executives must be mentioned Bruce Nierenberg of Premier Cruise Lines, Bob Dickinson of Carnival Cruise Lines, and Richard Sasso and Demetrios Kaparis of Celebrity Cruises. Other individuals in the industry who deserve a special word of thanks include Fran Sevcik of Norwegian Cruise Line, Mary Schimmelmann of Windstar, Lucette Brehm of American Classic Voyages, Marios Stergiou, Melody Chiron, and Maria Soler of Celebrity Cruises, Julie Benson and Denise Stanley of Princess Cruises, Heidi Kopf of Premier Cruise Lines, Alyssa Bushey of Disney Cruise Line, Janis Goller and Carrie Croom of Holland America Lines, Timothy Beede of American Cruise Lines, Jimmy Quadros of Royal Caribbean, Paul Rhodes of P&O Cruises, Antje Borstel of Hapag-Lloyd, and Aly Bello of Carnival Cruise Lines.

A very special "thank you" is due to Captain Carl Netherland-Brown, a man whose heroism and seamanship were responsible for the saving of many lives on the unfortunate night in 1965 when *Yarmouth Castle* caught fire and sank. The captain was patient and kind in the extreme in sharing his thoughts and recollections with me not only from that tragic night but also from the many years he served as a Biscayne Bay pilot in the port of Miami.

Others who deserve sincere thanks include Linda Horkitz and Rod Musem of OnBoard Media; Louis Pereira of Louis Pereira Associates; Catherine Swallow Swift; Gabriella Eschleman of Wilson Butler Lodge; and Peter T. Eisele, John H. Shaum, Jr., Frank Duffy, and Frank Manwell, colleagues in the Steamship Historical Society of America.

Finally, Monsieur and Madam Raymond, owners of the Hotel du Berry in St. Nazaire, France, merit a special word of thanks and appreciation.

Introduction

During the twentieth century, every sector in the world of transportation witnessed remarkable change and transformation. Automobiles evolved from casual curiosities into omnipresent necessities, while airplanes—which had yet to be invented when the twentieth century began—were routinely carrying millions of people on perfectly ordinary trips by century's end. Perhaps the most remarkable transformation of all, though, involves passenger travel aboard oceangoing ships.

From 1900 through the late 1950s, ocean liners were first the only and then the principal way that people traveled across the sea. This era saw the construction of some altogether marvelous vessels whose names have become part of our common culture—*Mauretania, Ile de France, Queen Mary, United States*—even, and perhaps especially, the forever tragic *Titanic.*

Commercial aviation doomed the magnificent ocean liners. In July 1937, a decade after Charles Lindbergh's epic solo flight between New York and Paris, a Sikorski S-42B flying boat named *Clipper III* and operated by Pan American Airways left the New York suburb of Port Washington on Long Island's north shore, taxied into the wind toward the waters of Long Island Sound, and, once aloft, headed eastward across the North Atlantic on the first commercial flight to England. Simultaneously, a Short S-23 flying boat, the *Caledonia,* working for Imperial Airways of Great Britain (a predecessor of today's British Airways) was completing the first westbound commercial flight across the same hostile ocean.

These were "survey flights," so-called, designed to pave the way for subsequent revenue service. The first transatlantic flight with mail and passengers aboard left New York for Southampton, England, on June 17, 1939. The Pan Am Boeing 314 flying boat *Yankee Clipper* did the honors. Within a time frame of a mere dozen years, transatlantic flight had advanced from Lucky Lindy struggling to stay awake in a single-seat airplane to uniformed cabin attendants serving meals aloft in a plane that offered sleeping accommodations not unlike those available aboard Pullman cars on land.

Further advancement in commercial aviation was put on hold by the Second World War, but once hostilities were over, four-engine propeller planes with pressurized cabins became common crossing the North Atlantic. A one-way flight from New York to Shannon, Ireland, could now be managed in as little as fourteen hours, with a fueling stop in Gander, Newfoundland, thrown in for good measure. Unlike their prewar predecessors, these postwar airliners were land-based craft. The era of the flying boat on the North Atlantic route proved to be an all too brief one.

While transatlantic air travel grew during the postwar era, ocean liners largely managed to hold their own when the aviation competition was limited to piston-engined DC-7s and Super Constellations. Travel by sea enjoyed a measure of growth in the postwar 1940s and through most of the 1950s, with the capstone being, certainly, the 1952 entry into service of the SS *United States,* a vessel that established a new North Atlantic speed record on her very first crossing.

It was the advent of jet-powered commercial aircraft at the end of the 1950s, though, that turned the tide with both startling rapidity and seemingly irreversible finality. The company that had pioneered transatlantic flying boats in the 1930s became the first U.S. carrier to operate jet-powered airliners. In the fall of 1958, Pan Am took delivery of a fleet of Boeing 707 jetliners and was poised to dispatch the first scheduled jet-powered flight to Europe. On October 4, 1958, British Overseas Airways Corporation—also a predecessor of British Airways— stole Pan Am's thunder and began the commercial jet era by sending one of its de Havilland Comet IVs on a commercial flight from London to New York a few days before Pan Am's 707s entered regular service over the same route.

Onward from 1958, the story of transatlantic travel is best told by cold statistics, not by citing dramatic and pioneering events of a one-time nature. In prejet 1955, over 700,000 passengers crossed the North Atlantic by ship through New York. By 1960—only two years into the jet era—this total had fallen to 645,000. Five years later in 1965, it would be 507,000, and in 1974, a mere 85,000 passengers crossed the North Atlantic by sea via the port of New York. In place of an ocean voyage that took six or more days to reach Southampton, Le Havre, or Bremerhaven, 707s—and later, 747s and DC-10s—delivered passengers to virtually any major city in Europe before those traveling aboard ship would have turned in for their first night at sea after sailing away from the Hudson River piers in New York that afternoon.

New York, in fact, was doubly impacted by this shift in travel behavior. Not only did its waterfront lose its traditional role as North America's principal gateway to Europe, the advent of jet-powered airliners eventually turned such diverse cities as Chicago, Los Angeles, Atlanta, and even Raleigh, North Carolina, into departure points for nonstop flights to Europe.

As early as 1965, a consultant's study prepared for the Trans-Atlantic Passenger Steamship Conference—a major trade association of the industry—reached this conclusion: "The trends in trans-Atlantic passenger steamship travel are such as to point inexorably to the death of the industry, or, at best, its stabilization at far lower volume levels than today."

To cope with this decrease in transatlantic passenger business, the steamship companies turned to a style of service that had long been recognized as a useful way to earn a few extra dollars. Capitalizing on the inherent charm that a voyage by sea can offer, vessels that had been designed and built to provide basic transportation across the world's oceans were dispatched, instead, on leisurely cruises to out-of-the-way destinations. The whole experience would be a vacation, not a purposeful trip from one place to another. The Cunard–White Star Line attempted to promote transatlantic travel by sea in the years following the Second World War with the slogan "Getting there is half the fun." A cruise went this one better: when an ocean liner was deployed in cruise service, getting there became all the fun—and nothing *but* fun.

To a certain degree, the strategy was successful. Consider, for example, February 14, 1975. Italian Line's nine-year-old *Michelangelo* steamed into New York that day after a transatlantic crossing from Genoa. With a capacity of 1,775 passengers, the 45,911-ton vessel was carrying only 200 paying customers, indicative of the state to which North Atlantic travel by sea had fallen especially in winter. *Michelangelo*'s crew outnumbered her passengers by a ratio of roughly five-to-one on that trip in February 1975.

The next day, February 15, *Michelangelo* left New York for a cruise to the Caribbean. This time there were 850 passengers aboard—close to, if not exactly, the number Italian Line chose to carry when the vessel sailed a leisure-oriented cruise.

Less than a year later, Italian Line would withdraw *Michelangelo* from all service, cruising as well as transatlantic crossings, as the state-controlled company began a protracted exit from the passenger steamship business. The complete and total departure from the scene of so important a company as the Italian Line underscores a theme that this book will explore. In the final decades of the twentieth century, travel by sea evolved from an activity whose purpose was basic transportation into one that was undertaken as a recreational activity—*Crossing & Cruising*, to cite the title of John Maxtone-Graham's delightful book on the subject—but it was not the old-line steamship companies that managed the transformation. Rather, the popularity that cruising achieved was orchestrated primarily by a group of new companies formed over approximately the past thirty-five years that have little, if any, direct relationship to the transatlantic steamship companies of yesteryear.

It is common today to speak of a trio of cruise companies as constituting the "big three" of the contemporary industry—Carnival, Royal Caribbean, and Princess. Some would include Norwegian Cruise Line and refer to a "big four." But whether the correct number is three or four, not one of these companies ever operated transoceanic steamship service of a point-to-point nature. Each was founded specifically to serve the cruise market, although various mergers and acquisitions over the years have developed certain corporate linkages between the new order and some elements of the old.

Holland America Line, for example, dates its founding to 1873 in Rotterdam and does not hesitate to emphasize the continuity of its current product with the transatlantic passenger services it once proudly offered. Today's Holland America Line, though, operates cruise and tour service exclusively. It is no longer headquartered in the old-world seaport of Rotterdam, but in the high-tech environment of Seattle, Washington, and it is a wholly-owned subsidiary of Carnival Corporation besides.

Another traditional name still active in the contemporary cruise industry is Cunard Line. While its flagship, *Queen Elizabeth 2*, still flies the red ensign of Great Britain, the majority of its cruise vessels in recent years have been registered in such countries as the Bahamas or Panama, and its corporate offices are located amid the palm trees of south Florida, a world away from the streets of London and the docks of Liverpool. Furthermore, like Holland America, by the end of the twentieth century Britain's fabled Cunard Line had also become a subsidiary of Carnival.

Whether it involves totally new companies or the corporate descendants of older ones, the cruise industry today is experiencing an era of tremendous growth and popularity. In 1965, 330,000 passengers boarded cruises that originated in North American ports. By 1990, a quarter-century later, this total had grown to 3.6 million. At the turn of the century it was approaching 7 million. A business activity whose origins involved finding part-time work for under-utilized ocean liners has clearly evolved into an important and freestanding industry all its own.

To understand the scope and the implications of this evolution and to set the stage for the story that will follow, consider something that happened on June 21, 1999, six months and a few days before the long-awaited New Year celebration that ushered in the year 2000.

On that day, a press release was issued jointly in London and Los Angeles. The Peninsular and Oriental Steam Navigation Company, a venerable British maritime institution, and its American subsidiary Princess Cruises had executed agreements for the construction of five new cruise ships. The documents also included options for three additional vessels.

Maritime historians can debate the qualitative impact of this 1999 vessel order for as long as they may choose and argue where it should stand in the history of travel by sea. What is beyond debate, however, is that in quantitative terms, this action in June of 1999 represented the largest single order for new passenger vessels *of all time.*

Two of the vessels will be turned out in St. Nazaire, France, at the Chantiers de l'Atlantique shipyard and will be 88,000-gross-ton cruise ships of a new design that will sail for Princess Cruises. Two more Princess vessels will be built in Japan by Mitsubishi Heavy Industries; they will measure 113,000 gross tons each and will be the first cruise ships built for the North American market by a Japanese shipyard. Finally, the fifth ship in the five-vessel order will be built in Italy by Fincantieri; it will sail for Britain's P&O Cruises and will measure 109,000 gross tons. Five vessels, 511,000 gross tons, with capacity for 11,700 passengers—and all ordered at the same time.

The contemporary cruise industry for which these five new vessels are intended to sail is the subject matter that *The Cruise Ship Phenomenon in North America* will explore. The book will endeavor to trace the development of this new industry, but not as a travel guide for prospective passengers. Readers will look in vain in its pages for comparative information about cruise ship cuisine, details about the ports of call encountered aboard a particular vessel, advice on how to secure discount prices for a cruise vacation, or what kind of gratuities to leave for dining room personnel or cabin attendants. Rather, the book will tell the story of how today's cruise ship industry evolved. It will describe some of the vessels that fly the house flags of various companies, and it will also provide a brief look behind the scenes to show how a complex operation like a contemporary cruise ship company is managed and run, including everything from ensuring that vessels do not run out of strawberry jam between St. Thomas and San Juan to deciding what kind of propulsion system should be installed aboard a brand-new cruise ship.

Chapter 1 sets the stage by talking about several incidents that happened in the 1960s. Chapter 2 provides a general characterization of the contemporary cruise industry. A series of parallel chapters then trace the history of a number of different cruise companies. Additional chapters discuss the management of a cruise ship company, the design and construction of new cruise ships, and the regulatory apparatus that represents the role of government in the industry.

Appendix material provides a roster of cruise vessels from 1965 through 2000 and a table that shows the location of the industry's vessels at high noon on July

4, 2000, as well as the itineraries they were sailing. Bibliographical material is also provided.

The gangway has been pulled in; lines are being let loose fore and aft; the ship's officers are on the bridge; engines are ready for maneuvering; passengers are lining the rails—another adventure is about to begin.

The Cruise Ship Phenomenon
in North America

CHAPTER 1

Early Days

Festival Cruises

In 1965, two unrelated events in the maritime world—one occurring in April and the other in November—helped to establish the context out of which the contemporary cruise industry evolved. Both set the stage for the developments that followed.

THE MAIDEN VOYAGE OF *OCEANIC*

Home Lines, an international shipping company with roots in both Italy and Greece, entered the transatlantic passenger business following the Second World War, operating a number of secondhand vessels between Italy and South America. A strong flow of postwar refugees from Europe was the principal market the new company initially served. Later, Home Lines ran between Italy and New York or ports in Canada, although it was never regarded as a top-of-the-line transatlantic operator in the manner of, say, Cunard or French Line. From the outset its vessels flew "flags of convenience," either Panamanian or Liberian, although most onboard personnel were Italian and the company had a definite Italian flair about it.

As business improved in the 1960s, Home Lines saw the need for a "newbuilding" of its own. (Newbuilding is a common maritime term for a newly constructed vessel.) In 1965, the 39,241-gross-ton *Oceanic* was delivered by Cantieri Riunite dell'Adriatico in Monfalcone, Italy. Originally intended for summer transatlantic service between Italy and the St. Lawrence, and off-season cruising to the Caribbean out of New York, by the time the new vessel was ready for her maiden voyage in the spring of 1965—six years into the era of commercial jet airliners on the North Atlantic—Home Lines had made the corporate decision to forsake transatlantic service entirely and convert itself into a cruise-only steamship company. Claims have been advanced that *Oceanic* may thus be regarded as

3

the very first vessel built exclusively for North American cruise service. Like many such claims, this one must be qualified with the proverbial pinch of salt.

By every measure, though, the $35-million *Oceanic* was handsome in a contemporary sort of way, not as a throwback to older forms and concepts. Steam-turbine powered and with a streamlined stack positioned well aft, her initial voyage was, ironically enough, a transatlantic crossing to move her from Genoa to New York where the majority of her cruises would originate. The *New York Times* regarded the event as sufficiently newsworthy that it dispatched a reporter to Europe to travel aboard the newcomer and file stories as *Oceanic* made her way westward, something the newspaper routinely did when important new ocean liners entered service.

Reporter Virginia Lee Warren drew this assignment. One day she noted that emergency language classes were being conducted between meals in the dining room for the ship's staff of Italian waiters. The men were required to master the English names of nineteen kinds of cereals, eighteen different fruit juices, six varieties of syrup, and eighteen preserves and jellies that were popular with American travelers. On April 10, 1965, as *Oceanic* was nearing Halifax, Nova Scotia, where she would make a brief stop, the ship's theater screened a Hollywood film that may have been inappropriate given the circumstances. Debbie Reynolds starred as *The Unsinkable Molly Brown.* It was during an earlier April in these very same North Atlantic waters that the original Molly Brown had earned her unusual nickname. Heading for Halifax, *Oceanic* was in fact on a course somewhat north of the 1912 ice field where *Titanic* went down and passenger Molly Brown survived.

Finally, on Wednesday, April 14, 1965, *Oceanic* steamed into New York where a traditional harbor welcome was given for her—fireboats shot streams of water skyward, airplanes circled overhead with news photographers aboard, tugboats escorted the new liner up the Hudson, and lusty whistle salutes came from the other ocean liners that were in port that day, including Italian Line's *Leonardo da Vinci* and the Norwegian-registered *Viking Princess.* French Line's *France* had arrived in New York that same day, several hours ahead of *Oceanic.*

Despite the enthusiasm of the welcome, there was a distinctly discordant note in the air. Among the harbor craft accompanying *Oceanic* were two picket boats of the National Maritime Union (NMU) that bore signs protesting the loss of American jobs to foreign-flag cruise ships. Overhead a Stearman biplane dragged a long banner through the sky that read "Runaway Flag Ship." On shore, 3,200 NMU pickets lined Twelfth Avenue opposite North River Pier 84 where the new liner docked at 1:00 P.M. to demonstrate their displeasure at the notion of the foreign cruise ships operating regularly and permanently out of U.S. ports and employing foreign nationals, not NMU members, in every onboard job category.

When the 1965-built *Oceanic* ran under the house flag of Home Lines, she featured an all-white hull. Many feel this vessel deserves to be called the first newbuilding to serve the North American cruise market. Courtesy Premier Cruise Lines.

The NMU correctly saw the shape of the future and it clearly did not like what it saw. In subsequent months, the union would attempt to use its not inconsiderable political muscle to try to prevent the event they were merely protesting on April 14, 1965, from becoming an accepted and common maritime routine. Union president Joseph Curran would testify frequently before Congress in support of this or that piece of legislation designed to retain jobs for American mariners and thwart foreign-flag vessels from carrying cruise passengers out of U.S. ports.

The efforts would not be successful. The new cruise industry that the likes of Home Lines was pioneering in North America in the mid-1960s would become an industry composed almost entirely of foreign-flag vessels, although a most aggressive U.S. regulatory apparatus would be established to enforce safety and public health standards aboard passenger ships calling at U.S. ports, irrespective of their country of registry.

Oceanic's master that day, Captain Giovanni Ruffini, was perplexed by all the protesting. "We don't know what they are complaining about," Ruffini said. "Our crew is all Italian—they all belong to the Italian seamen's union under a contract approved by international agreement."

Several days later, *Oceanic* left New York on her first cruise, a seven-night voyage to Nassau in the Bahamas, and she went on to become one of the most popular cruise ships ever to serve North America. In later years she would be sold to Premier Cruise Lines and renamed *StarShip Oceanic*, one of the "Big Red Boats" that added a dramatic and colorful touch to the cruise industry in the

In later years *Oceanic* ran for Premier Cruise Lines as *StarShip Oceanic*. She featured a dramatic red hull and was marketed as the Big Red Boat. The vessel was eventually formally renamed *The Big Red Boat I*.

1980s, the 1990s, and beyond. Indeed in early 2000, *StarShip Oceanic* was formally renamed *The Big Red Boat I*.

THE *YARMOUTH CASTLE* DISASTER

Seven months after *Oceanic* steamed into New York Harbor on her maiden voyage from Italy and was met by pickets from the National Maritime Union, a different kind of drama played itself out in the waters off south Florida. The passenger steamer *Yarmouth Castle* had been built in Philadelphia in 1927 as *Evangeline* for summer coastal service between Boston and Yarmouth, Nova Scotia, and winter trips out of New York to places like Bermuda and Nassau. In her early days, she was owned and operated by Eastern Steamship Lines, one of the last companies to specialize in short-haul ocean voyages with U.S.-flag vessels.

Following service as a troopship during the Second World War—peregrinations that took her as far as Casablanca in North Africa and Bora Bora in the South Pacific—*Evangeline* was reflagged first as a Liberian-registered vessel, then Panamanian, and eventually put to work on cruises out of Miami as *Yarmouth Castle* for a company called Yarmouth Steamship Company. Her specialty was something that would later become a staple of the North American cruise industry—two cruises each week between south Florida and the nearby Bahamas, one of three nights duration and the other of four. Her running mate out of Miami was her own sister ship from Eastern Steamship days, a vessel called *Yarmouth* that had likewise been reflagged in Panama.

As if foreshadowing troubles to come, *Yarmouth Castle* had garnered some unfavorable publicity for herself during the summer of 1964. Scheduled to operate a series of seven-night cruises out of New York for a tour company called Caribbean Cruises, on two separate occasions she was unable to sail, leaving hundreds of angry and disappointed passengers stranded on the pier. As a result of these problems the vessel was arrested, for a time, at Todd's Erie Basin shipyard in Brooklyn.

The other vessel sailing for Yarmouth Steamship in 1965, *Yarmouth*, had managed to make an interesting contribution to the evolution of the North American cruise industry three years earlier, during the summer of 1962. Acquired by West Coast businessman Stanley B. McDonald, she sailed from San Francisco to the Pacific Northwest carrying passengers on package tours to the Seattle World's Fair that year. When the fair closed, *Yarmouth* returned to Florida, but McDonald, enthusiastic over his first maritime venture, went on to found Princess Cruises, one of today's big three cruise companies.

The 5,002-ton *Yarmouth Castle*, Captain Byron Voutsinas in command, left Pier 1 at the old seaport in downtown Miami at 5:00 P.M. on Friday, November 12, 1965.

(Miami's current cruise terminal, located on Dodge Island east of downtown and between Miami and Miami Beach, was still under construction in 1965 and

The old seaport in downtown Miami, circa 1965. The two passenger vessels in the foreground are *left*, Eastern Steamship's *Ariadne* and *right*, *Bahama Star*. Vessel in the middle is P&O's *Florida*, while at the far pier are *left*, Yarmouth Steamship's *Yarmouth Castle* and *right*, *Yarmouth*. Courtesy Captain Carl Netherland-Brown.

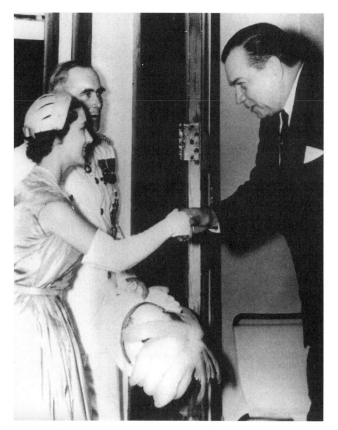

Frank Leslie Fraser greets Her Royal Highness, Princess Margaret, at the Titchfield Hotel in Jamaica in 1955. Courtesy Captain Carl Netherland-Brown.

would not dispatch its first ship until 1966.) The weather was clear; midday temperatures had been in the mid-80s. Recently drydocked in Tampa and inspected there by the U.S. Coast Guard as well as by technical experts from the American Bureau of Shipping, the thirty-eight-year-old *Yarmouth Castle* was bound for the city of Nassau on New Providence Island in the Bahamas, a comfortable overnight sail of some 186 nautical miles that she had made many times before. Aboard were 376 passengers plus a crew of 176.

Following *Yarmouth Castle* as she sailed away from downtown Miami and headed for Nassau that November evening was a vessel of a rival line bound for the same place. This was the 7,114-gross-ton *Bahama Star*, Captain Carl R. Brown in command, that departed from Pier 3. The Panamanian-flagged *Bahama Star*, built in Quincy, Massachusetts, in 1931, was operating for a company with a familiar maritime title, Eastern Steamship. But this was not the same Eastern Steamship Lines that *Yarmouth Castle* had originally worked for as *Evangeline;* it was an unrelated company that was called Eastern Shipping Corporation when it was founded before the Second World War by a Scottish-Jamaican businessman, F. Leslie Fraser. It was renamed Eastern Steamship after Fraser's death in 1962.

Originally, Eastern Shipping hauled cargo and passengers in conventional fashion between Florida and various points in the Caribbean. After the Second World War, however, it was Fraser more than any other individual who first saw the potential that passenger cruise ships sailing out of south Florida represented, and it was Fraser's Eastern Shipping Corporation that deserves to be called the first true Miami-based cruise company. Ironically, between 1954 and the time they were acquired by Yarmouth Steamship in the early 1960s, both *Yarmouth* and *Yarmouth Castle* had sailed for Fraser's Eastern Shipping.

Bahama Star's Captain Brown, incidentally, later enjoyed a distinguished career as a Biscayne Bay pilot in the Port of Miami. He is also a maritime historian. In 1956 Brown wrote an article for *Steamboat Bill,* the quarterly journal of the Steamship Historical Society of America, describing another U.S. coastal steamship company, Peninsular and Occidental (P&O). This should not be confused with a different P&O, Great Britain's Peninsular and Oriental Steam Navigation Company, although it frequently is. Once the principal link between Florida and Cuba, the North American P&O turned to cruise service out of south Florida for a few seasons after Miami-Havana service was suspended in the late 1950s. Brown has also written a history of the Biscayne Bay pilots.

Once a vessel reaches open sea after transiting Government Cut out of Miami, the standard route to Nassau, then as now, involves a northeast heading on a course of 68 degrees, almost as if bound for Freeport on Grand Bahama Island. But after several hours of steaming, a change of course to the southeast at Great Isaac Light would bring *Yarmouth Castle* and the following *Bahama Star* into the

Eastern Steamship's *Bahama Star*. In the early morning hours of November 13, 1965, with Captain Carl Netherland-Brown on the bridge, the vessel came to the rescue of *Yarmouth Castle.* Courtesy Captain Carl Netherland-Brown.

Northeast Providence Channel, putting them on course for a morning arrival in Nassau. Two middle-of-the-night changes in course are involved, the first to 101 degrees, the second to 173.

Captain Brown had retired to his cabin immediately below the bridge on *Bahama Star* with standard orders to be awakened in case of any irregularities or when the officer on the bridge first sighted Great Stirrup Light. When the call came that the light was in view, Brown looked out his cabin window, and while he saw the light, he also saw something else—a strange orange glow.

At first, Brown thought that floodlights were illuminating the red/orange funnel of Cunard Line's *Carmania*, a vessel *Bahama Star* often passed at this point on the overnight journey to Nassau. Further examination, though, revealed the chilling fact that the orange light was nothing so benign as an illuminated funnel; it was fire! Brown, now on the bridge, ordered *Bahama Star* to full speed and steered for the blaze, which he estimated was about fifteen miles away.

As his vessel drew near to the fire, the flames were leaping skyward so vigorously that Captain Brown initially thought a relatively small vessel was fully involved. But when *Bahama Star* encountered the first lifeboat from the stricken

Yarmouth Castle ablaze at 2:20 A.M. on November 13, 1965, as *Bahama Star* maneuvers close to rescue passengers. Flames are most severe behind the pilothouse near the vessel's forward stairwell. Courtesy Captain Carl Netherland-Brown.

vessel, Captain Brown recognized its unusual shape and realized instantly that the burning vessel was *Yarmouth Castle*, a ship Brown himself had earlier served aboard.

Later, Brown learned what happened. At some point close to midnight, fire broke out aboard *Yarmouth Castle* in an area near her forward stairwell. The blaze was discovered around 12:45 A.M., but was not reported to the bridge for another twenty-five minutes. The ensuing minutes—and even hours—were marked by a terrible breakdown of proper marine safety procedures and protocols. The failure of *Yarmouth Castle*'s crew to immediately inform the bridge of the fire allowed the flames to engulf the radio room, and this prevented the vessel's captain from notifying potential rescue forces of the peril his vessel was facing. The first radio message to the United States Coast Guard was not received until 2:01 A.M., and it came not from *Yarmouth Castle* but from a nearby freighter, the *Finnpulp*. (Ironically, *Finnpulp* was in New York Harbor earlier in the year on April 14, the day *Oceanic* made her first landfall in the United States.)

Four fixed-wing Coast Guard aircraft plus a U.S. Navy helicopter were dispatched to the scene. Evacuation of passengers did not begin until 2:20 A.M. and when *Yarmouth Castle* eventually sank in 1,800 feet of water at 6:03 A.M., ninety passengers and crew lost their lives. It is believed that the majority of the victims were trapped in the bow area forward of the stairwell and had no way of reaching safety. Almost 60 percent of those who were lost aboard *Yarmouth Castle* were residents of Florida, emphasizing the fact that cruises out of Miami around 1965 were primarily marketed to local residents.

Captain Brown's rescue work aboard *Bahama Star* was later cited by the United States Coast Guard as heroism "in the highest traditions of the sea." At one point when a lifeboat from *Yarmouth Castle* approached *Bahama Star* and Brown saw that it contained only crewmembers from the doomed vessel, he shouted through a bullhorn, "Return to your ship and pick up more passengers." The 4,049-ton *Finnpulp* took on 92 survivors; Captain Brown's larger *Bahama Star* rescued 367 and brought them to Nassau, where he docked at about two o'clock in the afternoon. Injured passengers had been air-lifted off *Bahama Star* by helicopter earlier and flown directly to hospitals. Among the survivors taken aboard *Bahama Star* was Captain Voutsinas, the master of *Yarmouth Castle*. He spoke briefly with Captain Brown, then went belowdecks and stayed there until *Bahama Star* reached port.

In the investigation that followed the disaster, the U.S. Coast Guard had serious criticism for *Yarmouth Castle*. "The magnitude of loss of life stemmed from failure of early use of the general alarm or the public address system and failure of windows and shutters on outside staterooms to be maintained in a condition so they could be easily opened," a Coast Guard review board concluded several months later. The Coast Guard determined that the most likely cause of the fire

Built in 1927 at the famous William Cramp and Sons shipyard in Philadelphia, the ill-fated *Yarmouth Castle* was typical of passenger steamships that specialized in short-haul coastal voyages from North American ports. Several such vessels were among the first to be converted into full-time cruise ships.

was faulty wiring, more specifically certain temporary lighting arrangements that the investigation described as jury-rigged. The Coast Guard also held out the possibility that stray sparks from a boiler might have been a factor, or even human carelessness.

Interestingly, in the years since the accident, stories continue to suggest that the fire may have been deliberately set by a disgruntled crewmember. A factor that supports such speculation is that the blaze originated in what was absolutely the most vulnerable portion of *Yarmouth Castle*, an area adjacent to the forward stairwell and next to a vent from the below-deck kitchen. More than likely, the Coast Guard's conclusion that the fire was an accident is correct, but it will never be known with certainty whether the loss of *Yarmouth Castle* was accidental or the result of something more sinister.

As to the location of the disaster and the place where *Yarmouth Castle* went down, it was in the Northeast Providence Channel at 25°55′ north latitude, 74°04′ west longitude, thirteen miles off Great Stirrup Cay, an uninhabited island in the Bahamas' Berry Islands. A dozen years after the sinking of *Yarmouth Castle*, a company called Norwegian Caribbean Line—a firm that did not even exist in 1965—purchased Great Stirrup Cay and converted it into the first of several private "out-islands" that contemporary cruise companies use to give passengers aboard their vessels a chance to spend a pleasant day at a very private beach.

This, of course, would be in the future. The more immediate reaction to the loss of *Yarmouth Castle* was an increase in calls for more regulatory control over the cruise industry. In reporting about these various initiatives, the *New York Times* remarked that "some of the proposed regulations indicate attempts to drive foreign-flag cruise ships out of the American market."

The protest by organized labor over *Oceanic*'s arrival in New York in April 1965 was easy to brush aside as mere self-interest, even though members of the National Maritime Union did not hesitate to express their views that passenger safety would be seriously compromised by a large-scale expansion of foreign-flag ships operating cruise service out of U.S. ports. What happened aboard *Yarmouth Castle* several months later, however, could not be shrugged off on the basis of any organization seeking its own interest. Ninety people were dead and less-than-optimal safety conditions aboard a thirty-eight-year-old steamship registered under the flag of Panama clearly contributed to the disaster. The NMU frequently cited the loss of *Yarmouth Castle* in continuing its opposition to the idea of foreign-flag cruise ships operating out of U.S. ports. In delivering a message to Congress in 1966 calling for the creation of a cabinet-level U.S. Department of Transportation, President Lyndon Johnson alluded to the *Yarmouth Castle* tragedy and the need for improved safety at sea.

Yarmouth Steamship Company did not survive the tragedy; it was liquidated within months of the fire. The company's surviving vessel, *Yarmouth*, was scheduled to make a cruise out of Miami on the afternoon following the disaster. It was cancelled, and while *Yarmouth* eventually resumed service, the memory of the tragedy was too great to generate any kind of customer confidence in the company. Promotional materials and brochures that the company routinely used featured pictures of both *Yarmouth* and *Yarmouth Castle* sailing together under the slogan "twin fun ships," a claim that had suddenly become as distasteful as it was macabre. *Yarmouth* was sold to Greek interests the following year and renamed *Elizabeth A.* She never operated under this name, however, and was scrapped in 1979 after a long layup.

With the company's liquidation, members of the management cadre that had been running Yarmouth Steamship found themselves out of work. One of them, general manager Edwin Stephan, learned a good deal from the tragedy. It helped reinforce in his mind what an ideal Miami-based cruise company should be like: smart new vessels, well-planned operations, attractive itineraries, aggressive marketing and, most of all, adequate capitalization. His ideas would be brought to fruition less than a decade later with the creation of Royal Caribbean Cruise Line, another of the big three of the contemporary industry. (Stephan and Royal Caribbean are profiled in chapter 4.)

ANOTHER FIRE

Less than a year after the loss of *Yarmouth Castle*, another Miami-based cruise ship came to grief. The sixteen-year-old *Viking Princess*, operating for a company

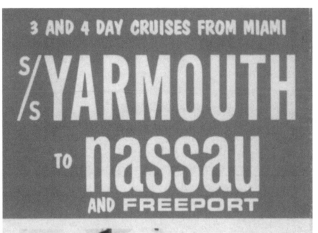

3 AND 4 DAY CRUISES FROM MIAMI

S/S YARMOUTH
TO nassau
AND FREEPORT

YARMOUTH

4 GALA SAILINGS WEEKLY ABOARD
THE FUN SHIPS
100% AIR CONDITIONED • EFFECTIVE JUNE 15, 1965

Brochure issued by Yarmouth Cruise Line to promote its three- and four-night cruises from Miami to the Bahamas. The company's twin vessels, *Yarmouth* and *Yarmouth Castle*, were referred to as "the fun ships." Courtesy Captain Carl Netherland-Brown.

called Flagship Lines, left Miami on Saturday, April 2, 1966, on a seven-night cruise to Aruba and Curacao. The Norwegian-flagged vessel, which had greeted Home Lines *Oceanic* on the day she first steamed into New York the previous year, was in command of Captain Otto Thoreson. Early in the morning on Friday, April 8, *Viking Princess* was swept by fire as she was steaming through the Windward Passage between Cuba and Haiti en route back to Miami. Unlike Captain Voutsinas aboard *Yarmouth Castle*, Captain Thoreson and his crew were widely praised for their courage and seamanship in the face of this disaster, and while 2 people did lose their lives in the fire, the more important fact is that 494 people were safely evacuated, taken first to the United States Naval Base at Guantanamo Bay, Cuba, and then quickly air-lifted to Miami.

One of those rescued is worthy of mention: Lucian P. Smith, a fifty-five-year-old resident of Venice, Florida. Smith's parents had honeymooned in Europe in early 1912 and booked passage for their return to America aboard a brand-new ocean liner, White Star's *Titanic*. Smith's father was lost in the disaster; his then-pregnant mother survived, and Lucian was born several months later.

That the North American cruise industry was able to overcome the pall cast by these early disasters is nothing short of remarkable. While the notion of cruise ships flying foreign "flags of convenience" represented an economic imperative that was not to be denied, the safety shortcomings underscored by the fires aboard *Viking Princess* and more pointedly *Yarmouth Castle* were rectified by action on several fronts. The United States Congress expanded the reach of the federal government's regulatory control, and agencies from the Coast Guard to the Centers for Disease Control and Prevention were given new responsibilities for inspecting ships calling at U.S. ports. International conventions began to specify technical requirements passenger vessels were required to meet, establish protocols for the launching of lifeboats, and so forth. Safety of Life at Sea (SOLAS) is such a treaty. It was adopted in London in 1948, has been periodically updated, and is now managed by the International Maritime Organization, an agency of the United Nations.

What was undoubtedly the most important contribution to the long-term safety of the nascent cruise industry, though, was the purely economic self-interest of the companies themselves. In plain and simple language, it is not to a steamship company's benefit to have its vessels catch fire and its passengers killed or injured.

So while companies will never hesitate to cite their compliance with this or that regulatory requirement imposed by officialdom, the overriding dynamic that brought a new measure of safety to the cruise industry was the economic imperative of profit versus loss. If the tragic fires that doomed *Yarmouth Castle* and *Viking Princess* ever came to be regarded as routine and ordinary, few passengers would be willing to risk their lives traveling aboard such vessels. In 1965, the year of the *Yarmouth Castle* disaster, a grand total of 267,000 passengers boarded cruise ships in the port of Miami. By century's end, the figure would be closer to 3.5 million, clear and convincing evidence that the general public has a solid degree of confidence in the cruise industry, irrespective of what flag is flying from a vessel's mast or what home port is showing on her stern.

CHAPTER 2

Renaissance Cruises

The Industry Today

The cruise industry today is both international and multinational. Its vessels fly the flags of many nations, its workers hail from countries the world over, and whether a cruise ship is departing from Port Klang, Malaysia, from Barcelona, Spain, or from Miami, Florida, the passengers who will be occupying the cabins and ordering meals in the dining room will almost universally be citizens of many countries.

Despite this international dimension, it remains possible to discuss an element of the worldwide cruise industry that is basically North American in its orientation. This North American element, though, cannot be separated from the global industry in any sharp or absolute fashion, or even with the same degree of confidence that was possible as recently as 1990. Increasingly, cruise companies that maintain corporate headquarters in Florida or on the West Coast and whose vessels sail primarily from Florida to the Caribbean during the North American winter and from Vancouver, British Columbia, to Alaska in the summer will also dispatch a vessel or two to the Baltic and Mediterranean each summer and perhaps another to Australia or South America in the winter.

The following table with its data from the year 1998 provides a generally useful perspective on what share of the worldwide industry is oriented around the North American market, although identifying a cruise company as North American does not preclude the possibility that some of its vessels work European or even Asian itineraries during the course of a year's time.

It is possible to specify with some precision the number of passengers who board cruise ships in North American ports each year: 5.4 million in 1998 and 5.9 million in 1999. The worldwide totals for the same years were 7.4 million and almost 8.0 million. By this measure, North American cruise passengers represent approximately 75 percent of world totals, a ratio that is consistent with the data shown in the table for passenger capacity.

17

It is also possible to identify the number of cruise vessels that call at ports of U.S. jurisdiction in any given year since they are subject to inspection by the Coast Guard and the Public Health Service and thus can be counted. In 1999, for example, the Vessel Sanitation Program of the U.S. Centers for Disease Control and Prevention reported the results of inspections that took place on 121 different cruise ships.

These numbers, though, do not address the basic issue that while there is an element of the worldwide cruise industry that is primarily North American in its service and its orientation, it is increasingly difficult to define without some degree of ambiguity.

THE CRUISE INDUSTRY AT A GLANCE (1998)

	North America	Europe	Asia	World Total
Cruise lines	29	33	14	76
	(38%)	(44%)	(18%)	(100%)
Number of ships	122	82	19	223
	(55%)	(37%)	(8%)	(100%)
Berths	123,100	51,612	15,670	190,382
	(65%)	(27%)	(8%)	(100%)
Passenger capacity	6.5 million	1.7 million	1.3 million	9.5 million
	(68%)	(18%)	(14%)	(100%)

Source: *Cruise Industry News*

PUTTING THE COMPANIES IN CATEGORIES

In approaching a multifaceted commercial activity like the cruise industry, it is helpful to begin with some distinctions that place the various cruise companies in categories. The easiest system for such categorization involves the related concepts of quality and price.

A number of cruise companies market their product to a decidedly upscale clientele. The product itself is the last word in cruise ship luxury and is, not surprisingly, priced accordingly. The vessels these companies operate tend to be uncrowded; they range in size from small to medium, feature an extraordinary level of personal attention and service, and wander the globe in search of exotic itineraries and destinations. Such upscale cruise companies rely heavily on business from repeat customers year after year. Hence the need to find new and different destinations and not to sail the same itinerary season after season. Cruise lines such as Seabourn, Radisson Seven Seas, Crystal, and Silverseas had become major players in this upscale market by the late 1990s, while in earlier years, a company like Royal Viking Line not only merited such a designation, it virtually invented this entire cruise category. There are those who claim, for example, that the now-common expression "world class" was coined by marketing personnel at Royal Viking some years ago to emphasize the luxury of its cruise product. As noted in chapter 6, Royal Viking Line passed from the scene in 1994.

As a general rule, cruise lines serving this upscale market segment are more difficult to identify as "North American" in their orientation and service than are companies that fall within the other categories. In rough numbers, these companies own and operate about 10 percent of the industry's overall fleet. Because their vessels are not among the industry's largest, they carry a slightly smaller percentage of the overall total of cruise ship passengers.

The most dominant segment of the industry is composed of what are often called mass-market cruise companies. These include the major lines such as Carnival, Princess, Royal Caribbean, and Norwegian Cruise, plus a number of others. Mass-market cruise lines generally operate new vessels of medium to large size; furthermore, they assign their ships to repetitive routes for long periods of time. This does not rule out seasonal variation—winter in the Caribbean, summer in Alaska, for example. But unlike the pricey and often yachtlike upscale cruise ships that may never repeat the same cruise twice in a year's time, many mass-market vessels may not vary their routine for a period of many years. "If today is Tuesday, we must be in Charlotte Amalie." About 75 percent of the industry's overall passenger capacity falls into this mass-market category, although because its ships are larger, a percentage based on the number of ships is slightly less.

Within the broad category called mass market there is room for a good deal of variation. For instance, a mass-market operator with a vessel working a combination of three- and four-night cruises out of south Florida to the Bahamas each week is likely charging fares for this service that are little different from those charged by the "bargain-basement" companies that shall be discussed presently. The same mass-market company, though, may also have vessels assigned to longer European cruises or even to an annual around-the-world voyage, trips whose overall costs on either an absolute or a per-diem basis begin to approach what one might expect to pay for a cruise with a more upscale company. The category called mass market is the industry's largest tent, and there is much variety under it. The mass-market category is also the easiest one in which to identify companies that are North American in their overall orientation, although the caution must be repeated that few cruise companies are as rigidly or as exclusively North American as they were just a few years ago.

Before talking about the bargain-basement operators, mention should be made of a third category, the various niche-market cruise companies. These operators shy away from such fundamental fare as seven-night Caribbean cruises out of Miami or Port Everglades, for instance, and concentrate instead on more specialized, exotic, and sometimes even adventuresome itineraries.

As an example, admittedly an extreme one, a post–Cold War niche-market operator that has recently appeared on the scene is represented in the United

States by a Seattle tour company called TCS Expeditions. Its specialty is taking about a hundred daring souls at a time aboard an atomic-powered icebreaker that once belonged to the former Soviet Union for cruises to such decidedly out-of-the-way places as the North Pole or the continent of Antarctica. Measured by brochure cost alone, a twelve-night cruise to "ninety degrees north" aboard the 23,445-gross-ton *Sovetskiy Soyuz* is more expensive than a cruise of similar length in anything but a top-of-the-line suite aboard an upscale cruise ship. A twelve-night cruise in the least expensive cabin was advertised at $16,950 per person in 1999, with passengers being required to pay for transportation to and from Norway's Spitsbergen Island besides, in order to board the icebreaker. Spitsbergen is about as far north as one might ever expect to sail aboard a mass-market cruise ship. Yet it is the southernmost port for *Sovetskiy Soyuz*'s cruises to the North Pole.

Niche-market cruises do not have to be this exotic or this expensive. The four gingerbread-bedecked riverboats of the Delta Queen Steamboat Company, for instance, that sail America's inland rivers—*Delta Queen, Mississippi Queen, American Queen,* and *Columbia Queen*—represent a niche-market cruise operation, as do any number of largely U.S.-flag mini cruise ships that ply inland and coastal waterways from New England to the Caribbean and from the Gulf of California to Alaska. These are smaller vessels that accommodate 50 to 200 passengers, feature a more informal ambience than one usually finds aboard oceangoing vessels, and specialize in unique itineraries that larger vessels cannot sail. The niche-market category also includes cruise companies that operate various kinds of sailing ships.

Because their vessels are not large, niche-market cruise companies account for a small, single-digit percentage of the industry's overall passenger capacity, although they do bring a welcome measure of variety to the table in the way of the unique and interesting cruises they offer.

Finally, there are the bargain-basement cruise lines that play a very important role in the industry. By their use of less costly older ships, they are able to offer a variety of cruises at prices that are at least a little—and sometimes a lot—less than the fares normally charged by the mass-market companies. What they can do, therefore, is enable more people to take that all-important first cruise, so that, perhaps, they will then become regular cruise customers and move up the ladder to sample itineraries in other market categories. Bargain cruise lines provide about 15 percent of the industry's overall capacity. Like the mass-market companies, bargain-basement cruise lines ordinarily operate their vessels on repetitive itineraries.

Bargain cruise lines have sometimes been called "bottom feeders" in the industry, a rather inelegant and even demeaning term that is largely undeserved. One of the more memorable cruises I ever took was on a bargain-basement line.

It was aboard Premier Cruises *OceanBreeze*, a steam-powered veteran that was forty-three years old when I sailed aboard her in 1998 out of Montego Bay, Jamaica, on a cruise that included a partial transit of the Panama Canal, a day's visit to Gatun Lake in the middle of the canal, and shore excursions to watch Gatun Locks in operation from up close. Passengers aboard *OceanBreeze* were also invited to take a swim in the Panama Canal (specifically, in Gatun Lake) from the grounds of the Gatun Yacht Club, if they were so inclined.

Was *OceanBreeze* the equal of cruise ships higher up on the price scale? No, she certainly was not. But she gave an honest seven days worth of service on an out-of-the-ordinary itinerary at a very good price.

Something else that must be said of the bargain-basement category is that it often represents the only way one can travel aboard passenger vessels that predate the recent growth of the cruise industry and that reflect styles and decor from an older age of ocean travel. Premier's *OceanBreeze*, for example, was built in 1955 as Shaw, Savill's *Southern Cross* and long worked a route from Great Britain to Australia.

Placing too much emphasis on any scheme for categorizing cruise companies can result in sometimes severe distortions, as operators are seen not for their individuality but merely as representatives of a general category. Furthermore, the industry is replete with examples of companies that began years ago in one category and then upgraded into another as their business grew and improved. Carnival Cruise Lines, the industry's largest and the epitome of a mass-market company, does not hesitate to describe itself as a one-time bargain-basement line, for instance. The general notion that cruise companies fall into categories—with upscale, mass-market, niche-market, and bargain-basement being one such set of categories—has some measure of validity and can be useful for understanding the scope and dimension of the contemporary industry.

CONTEMPORARY CRUISE SHIP DESIGN

The design of today's typical cruise ship is unlike that of the classic ocean liners of yesteryear. While some cruise ships at work at the start of the twenty-first century were originally designed and built decades ago as ocean liners, their numbers grow fewer year after year, and the great majority of vessels that constitute the contemporary fleet were laid down from the outset to meet the unique needs of cruising.

Classic ocean liners were, in virtually all cases, combination passenger-cargo ships. Consequently, room had to be provided both forward and aft for deck hatches, cargo booms, and other associated equipment. For instance, an early scene from James Cameron's film *Titanic* shows a four-door sedan being hoisted aboard the about-to-depart liner and lowered into its hold. Requirements for such equipment meant that a vessel's superstructure had to be positioned back

from the bow and forward of the stern, creating an altogether balanced and attractive relationship between hull and superstructure. As decks within the superstructure were "stacked" one atop the other, each was slightly smaller than
the one below, in both length and breadth, creating what has often been called a
"wedding cake" profile.

In designing a contemporary cruise ship, naval architects have no need to include provisions for cargo handling. As a result, a vessel's superstructure can begin much closer to the bow than on a classic ocean liner and can extend all the
way aft to the stern. This has created what some decry as very "boxy looking"
vessels. Curiously, it is a development that has a parallel in urban architecture.

Classic skyscrapers from the first half of the twentieth century taper gracefully as they extend upward. Buildings of a more contemporary design, though,
often retain the same profile from ground level to roofline. They, too, are criti-
cized in some quarters because of their boxy look, granted that changes in sky-
scraper design are largely a function of more liberal urban building codes, and
not, obviously, an absence of cargo-handling capability.

What contemporary skyscrapers and contemporary cruise ships do share are
designs that seek to create the most usable, revenue-generating space within a
given envelope. To this extent, while a brand-new cruise ship may lack the
graceful lines and form that characterized, say, Cunard-White Star's RMS *Queen
Mary* of 1936, the fact that must not be ignored is that the cruise ship industry is
flourishing today at least in part because contemporary cruise ships have pioneered new standards of design efficiency and cost-effectiveness. There is more
revenue-generating space aboard a boxy-looking contemporary cruise ship than
on a gracefully-tiered ocean liner with the same overall dimensions.

Another comparison between oceangoing passenger vessels of yesterday and
cruise ships of today is that the hulls of the older ships were designed with graceful and subtle curvature, from the vessel's sharp, knifelike prow all the way to its
carefully rounded stern. Contemporary cruise ships eschew such design princi-
ples and are built with hulls that, except for some minimum curvature at the
bow, are about as squared off and boxy—that word again—as a hull can possibly
be. Several reasons may be advanced to explain why.

The most important dimensional difference between an ocean liner of the
1940s or 1950s and a similar-sized cruise ship of today involves something that is
quite hidden and unseen—its draft, the distance between the waterline and the
bottom of the keel. Both vessels might have comparable length and width, but
while the older ship could easily have a draft of thirty-five feet, today's cruise
ship might draw only twenty.

In the final years of the great transatlantic ocean liners, routine crossing
speeds had to be in the thirty-knot range to remain competitive. To maintain
such speed, hulls had to be graceful and streamlined. One little secret of the

A classic transatlantic steamship of yesteryear, Cunard-White Star's RMS *Queen Mary* of 1936.

cruise industry today is that many itineraries can be successfully sailed at speeds between ten and fifteen knots. If a cruise ship leaves port A at six o'clock in the evening and is scheduled to arrive at port B, 150 nautical miles away, at six o'clock the next morning, a speed of twelve and a half knots is all it takes to arrive on time. Going any faster serves no useful purpose, since arrival at port B must be coordinated with the availability of line handlers, customs inspectors, and dockworkers. (The only ports where cruise ships often seek to arrive as early as they can—in the middle of the night, if possible, irrespective of any additional costs this might entail—are ports where cruises will end, and extensive work will be required to off-load luggage, disembark and embark passengers, take on fuel and provisions, and so forth.) In any event, one factor that influenced the shift away from sleek and deep-draft hull designs was that higher speed capability was no longer a requirement.

Another factor influencing hull design is that contemporary cruise ships rely on stabilizers to ensure smooth travel; a stabilized hull can provide a comfortable passenger environment with much less draft than a nonstabilized one. Stabilizers are finlike devices set into a vessel's hull below the waterline. They extend outward to counteract any tendency of the hull to roll in less-than-placid seas. They are not static, however. Stabilizers are dynamic and equipped with sensitive gyroscopes that quickly detect a potential roll and then adjust the pitch of the fins to counteract the pending motion.

Couple these two factors together—maximum speed in the twenty-knot range and hulls that include stabilizers—and naval architects are able to avoid the gentle hull curvature of the classic ocean liner and design cruise ships with hulls that are far more bargelike, and have considerably less draft, than the likes of French Line's *Normandie* or Cunard's *Queen Mary*. True enough, the cruise industry is currently beginning to develop passenger vessels that are able to operate a little faster than twenty knots, permitting them to sail more diverse routes and schedules. As a general matter, though, cruise ships are not designed to be speed merchants. Furthermore, in a contemporary context, "faster" means speeds approaching twenty-five knots, not thirty or thirty-five. The hull, power-plant, and fuel-capacity alterations needed to advance a vessel to twenty-five-

The look and line of a typical contemporary cruise ship, *Silver Cloud,* which operates for Silverseas Cruises. Note how the pilothouse is located much closer to the bow than is *Queen Mary*'s.

knot-speed capability from twenty are significant and quite costly. But cruise ships are able to achieve twenty-five-knot speed with adaptations of the boxy hulls that were adequate to sustain twenty-knot speed. A return to the deep-draft and knifelike hulls of yesteryear has not been necessary. Like the shift away from wedding-cake design in the superstructure, the use of squared-off and boxy-looking hulls generates opportunities for design efficiencies.

Aboard a ship, the uppermost deck that extends all the way from the bow to the stern is called the strength deck, or main deck. Everything below the strength deck is hull, everything above the strength deck is superstructure. Viewed from the side, a modest curvature away from the horizontal in the strength deck is the vessel's sheer. Contemporary cruise ships, however, have little if any sheer.

In a classic ocean liner, the corridor that contains passenger cabins would have a gentle up-and-down slope from bow to stern, reflecting the sheer. Between this corridor and the hull sides, the area where outside cabins are constructed, dimensions would vary, reflecting subtle curvature of the hull as well as the sheer. It might be a slight exaggeration, but one can almost say that no two cabins on a vessel like *Ile de France* or *Aquitania* were built to exactly the same dimensions. The less graceful and boxy hulls of contemporary cruise ships feature corridors that are virtually as straight as any in a land-based hotel, and with the exception of a small area immediately behind the bow, passenger cabins can be much more identical, one to the other, introducing major cost savings. Some shipyards even prefer to prefabricate cabins away from the vessel and install the finished products. One major shipyard where contemporary cruise ships are built even has a separate subsidiary company that specializes solely in the prefabrication of passenger cabins.

With respect to the evolution of exterior design in contemporary cruise ships, several other factors are worth mentioning. Initially, cruise ships followed the traditional ocean liner concept that called for lifeboats and their associated davits to be positioned on an upper deck. Typically this would also be where outdoor promenades were located. More recently, the trend has been to place lifeboats on a lower deck, closer to the waterline and inside a large cutout of the superstructure. Outdoor promenades are generally located here as well.

From a safety perspective, it is easier to launch lifeboats from a lower deck than from an upper one. Furthermore, having lifeboat muster stations situated closer to the decks where most passenger cabins are located—above some, but below others—can also facilitate matters should passengers be called to their muster stations. Finally, removing lifeboats from positions higher up in the vessel gives designers additional flexibility and room for laying out such important cruise ship facilities as swimming pools and various outdoor areas where passengers congregate and enjoy themselves during a cruise.

An early pioneer of this concept of lifeboats and muster stations on lower decks was *Canberra,* a classic Belfast-built ocean liner–turned–cruise ship that was built in 1961 and long worked for Great Britain's Peninsular and Oriental Steam Navigation Company. It is a design feature that became popular only in more recent years, however.

Another change in cruise ship design has been an extraordinary growth in the number of passenger cabins that include outdoor balconies. As recently as the early 1990s, newly built cruise ships might feature a few dozen balconies, and these were only for a vessel's most expensive suite accommodations. By the end of the 1990s it was not unusual to find new mass-market cruise ships being turned out with more cabins with balconies than without them, while some up-scale vessels featured outdoor balconies on every one of their passenger cabins. To permit more cabins to include balconies, naval architects recently returned to a version of the wedding-cake design that was once so characteristic of ocean-going passenger ships. By narrowing some of a ship's upper decks, designers are finding they can add an additional deck without compromising stability, thus providing a greater percentage of exterior cabins to which balconies can be added.

By far the most dramatic development in recent cruise ship design has been the construction of larger and larger vessels. Not all that many years ago, the cruise industry remained totally confident that 20,000 gross registered tons rep-resented not only the ideal size for a cruise vessel, but a practical upper limit as well. This limit was expanded through an interesting series of stages until, in the late 1990s, the world's first passenger vessels to exceed 100,000 gross tons were designed and built; by the turn of the century, three different cruise companies were welcoming passengers aboard such vessels. How much larger cruise ships will get in the twenty-first century remains to be seen, although it would clearly be folly to impose any a priori limits and declare, dogmatically, that cruise ships will never exceed any specified limit, be it 200,000 gross tons or even 300,000.

There are many additional aspects of cruise ship design—issues associated with engines and propulsion systems, for example, as well as interior design and appointments—that will be explored as individual cruise fleets are examined in subsequent chapters.

CRUISE MARKETS

Using the term market to identify the places where cruise vessels sail (not the passengers who travel aboard them), the principal market for the North American cruise industry is the Caribbean. It is here that the contemporary industry had its beginnings; it will likely always remain its base, even if it no longer generates the same percentage of overall trips that it once did as companies venture forth and deploy their vessels in new and different markets. Add to the Caribbean the nearby islands of the Bahamas just over the horizon from the cruise ports of south Florida and one has an extended chain of island ports that are perfect for the kind of leisure-oriented travel the cruise industry provides. Besides the availability of so many interesting ports of call, sea conditions in the Caribbean are normally calm and placid, thus adding to its reputation as an ideal cruise venue.

Unfortunately, between June and November the Caribbean is prone to visitation by tropical hurricanes. While severe, such storms are very localized and usually avoidable. A hurricane's forward movement is normally less than ten miles per hour; cruise ships with top speeds of twenty knots and access to up-to-the-minute weather information rarely have trouble keeping out of their way. The larger fact is that, hurricanes aside, the Caribbean enjoys climate and sea conditions that are made to order for the needs of the cruise industry.

The paradigm of a Caribbean cruise has long been a seven-night voyage out of either Miami or Port Everglades that includes a day or more at sea in each direction, plus port calls at St. Maarten, Charlotte Amalie on St. Thomas in the U.S. Virgin Islands, or possibly San Juan, Puerto Rico. A brief half-day stop at Nassau or a private out-island in the Bahamas is also common. So ordinary has this general itinerary become that within the industry it has long been called the "milk run." In the more formal world of cruise brochures and advertisements intended for the general public, what the industry internally calls the milk run is generally referred to as an eastern Caribbean cruise.

The principal seven-night variation out of south Florida would be a cruise that encircles the island nation of Cuba and includes calls at Grand Cayman Island, a port in Jamaica, a stop at the Mexican island of Cozumel, and an additional visit either to Nassau, a private out-island, or even Key West, Florida. Such an itinerary is generally called a western Caribbean cruise. Between them, eastern Caribbean and western Caribbean cruises constitute the vast majority of seven-night departures from south Florida, and seven-night cruises are the industry's most basic and important product, especially for mass-market companies. Some vessels sail one or the other of these exclusively, while others alternate between eastern and western Caribbean itineraries and in doing so provide the possibility of a passenger's booking a two-week cruise with little or no repetition of ports of call.

Miami and Port Everglades are the principal ports of departure for such cruises. There, bunkering (fueling) and provisioning usually take place. In addition, many cruise lines have their corporate and operational headquarters in south Florida, facilitating interaction between personnel on shore and aboard ship. Seven-night cruises typically depart on either Saturday or Sunday, a scheduling factor that respects the concept of a passenger's enjoying a weeklong cruise while taking only a single week off from work. Longer cruises out of south Florida to the lower Caribbean normally require more than a week to accom-

The city of Nassau in the Bahamas is a short overnight sail from the popular cruise ports of south Florida, and it welcomes many cruise ships and cruise ship passengers. The vessel to the right is Royal Caribbean's *Nordic Empress;* the vessel on the left is Premier Cruise Lines' *StarShip Oceanic.* The twin-stack vessel in the background is Chandris Fantasy's *Britanis.*

plish, and they call at some of the exotic islands that stretch from Puerto Rico all the way to the South American mainland: Barbados, Martinique, St. Lucia, Grenada, and others.

To allow passengers to visit these lower Caribbean islands within the limits of a seven-night cruise, many companies now schedule cruise departures out of San Juan, Puerto Rico. The distance between Miami and San Juan—almost a thousand statute miles—requires up to two full days for a cruise ship to transit but it can be managed by a jet airliner in a little over two hours.

One near-universal feature of San Juan cruise departures is an accommodation to the usually longer flights required to reach Puerto Rico from interior mainland cities. Where south Florida cruises inevitably sail between four and six o'clock in the afternoon, cruises departing from San Juan normally cast off closer to ten o'clock at night. Whether they are seven-night itineraries departing from Puerto Rico or longer cruises originating in south Florida, cruises that visit these more distant islands are generally referred to as southern Caribbean itineraries.

While nearby islands of the Bahamas are often visited en route by ships sailing longer itineraries, they are the principal destination of the many vessels working two-a-week cruises out of south Florida, just as they were when *Yarmouth Castle* and *Bahama Star* offered them in 1965. A three-night cruise usually involves a full day in Nassau and another at sea or perhaps at a private out-island where the cruise company maintains a beach and associated facilities. Three-night cruises typically depart on Friday and return to port on Monday, keeping the ships out of south Florida on the days seven-night voyages normally originate. Monday sees the start of the four-night cruises, which return to south Florida on Friday. Four-night cruises can visit the Bahamas, but a more popular itinerary involves a trip to Cozumel, Mexico, with a half-day stop at Key West in one direction or the other. Tuesday through Thursday are the days when cruise ships working longer and nonrepetitive itineraries usually set sail from the cruise ports of south Florida.

Miami has long been a popular port for three- and four-night cruises; although Port Everglades has not. Port Everglades, incidentally, is often thought to be just another name for Fort Lauderdale, but that is a little imprecise. Twenty-five miles north of Miami, Port Everglades is actually a facility that is owned and maintained by three adjacent Florida cities—Fort Lauderdale, Hollywood, and Dania.

A Florida port that absolutely specializes in three- and four-night cruises is found 175 miles north of Miami. This is Port Canaveral, located just south of the NASA facility at Cape Canaveral. Five major companies have operated from here—Carnival, Premier, Royal Caribbean, Canaveral, and, more recently, a new cruise company founded by the Disney organization. Among them, these five lines ran six vessels, and since each made two trips a week, this added up to a dozen weekly departures. Very little about the cruise industry remains static, however. Early in the new century a few of the companies serving Port Canaveral were experimenting with seven-night cruises from there in addition to those of three- or four-night duration, while two of the companies—Premier and Canaveral—were forced to suspend operations.

For a variety of reasons, cruise lines have been anxious to explore alternative ports of origin for their Caribbean itineraries, and the recent growth of Port Canaveral is a good example of this. Crowding at both Port Everglades and Miami is one reason for such a strategy. Also a factor is that as the cruise industry continues to grow and expand and as its ships get larger and larger, the demand for space aboard commercial airliners into and out of south Florida airports is becoming a limiting factor.

On a typical Saturday afternoon in high season, it is not unusual for over 12,000 cruise passengers to be embarking from the Port of Miami, with another 10,000 or more leaving from Port Everglades. Combined, that means 22,000 outbound cruise passengers, coupled with an equal number of inbound passengers. Assuming that all 22,000 outbound passengers fly into south Florida on Saturday, that represents the equivalent of fifty-five jumbo-jet airplanes carrying nothing but cruise passengers.

In fact, of course, all 22,000 will not be flying into south Florida on Saturday. Some will arrive by other transport modes, others will have booked a precruise stay for a night or two in a nearby Florida hotel and arrived a few days prior to departure. Cruise lines promote such options for both the cash flow and profit they generate as well as the airline space freed up on departure day. But the fact remains that airlift capacity is as much a constraint on the growth of the cruise industry as are the number of available cabins aboard its vessels.

Carnival, Holland America, and Regal already base vessels in the Tampa Bay area on Florida's west coast, and Celebrity is about to do the same. A number of companies have recently established Houston/Galveston as a port where cruises to the western Caribbean originate. Cruise ships can also work seven-night Caribbean itineraries from New Orleans, and both Carnival and Commodore have been doing so for some years. Such cities as Mobile, Alabama; Gulfport, Mississippi; Corpus Christi, Texas; and Palm Beach, Florida, continue to explore the potential for having a cruise company use their port facilities to originate Caribbean cruises.

A major imponderable for the future of Caribbean cruises involves Cuba. Will it soon—or will it ever—become a lawful and routine port of call for the various cruise lines operating out of south Florida? If it does, it will effectively "add" a new island to the Caribbean and provide additional options for cruise-ship itineraries.

Actually, for some years it has been possible to visit Cuba during a seven-night Caribbean cruise. Greta Cruise Line's 15,614-gross-ton *Italia Prima*, registered in Italy, made several visits to Havana in the late 1990s. The cruises originated in Mexico and did not call at any U.S. ports. Built in 1948, *Italia Prima* was not only a former ocean liner, she was a very special ocean liner. On July 25, 1956, while known as *Stockholm*, she collided with Italian Line's *Andrea Doria* off Nantucket Island and sent her to the bottom. Clearly, there is a certain irony to the fact that the vessel that sank *Andrea Doria* later sailed under the Italian flag. Over the winter of 1999–2000, *Italia Prima* was renamed *Valtur Prima* and began to offer winter Caribbean cruises out of Havana itself.

Costa Lines and First European Cruises also dispatched a few trips to Cuba from Mexican ports in the 1990s, and during the summer of 2000, the upscale cruise ship *Deutschland*, operating for Peter Deilmann Cruises, included a port call in Havana on a one-way cruise from New York to the west coast of South America. (As matters turned out, it proved to be a singularly tragic voyage. An Air France Concorde bound for New York with cruise passengers on board crashed while taking off from Charles de Gaulle Airport in Paris, killing everyone on the plane.)

Although cruises aboard *Deutschland* are primarily marketed to residents of Germany and not to North Americans, an asterisk next to the Havana arrival time in one of the company's promotional brochures said this: "U.S. citizens need to check with the U.S. Department of State to determine restrictions on visiting Cuba." It is not unlawful for a cruise ship to visit Cuba following a port call in the United States, but it does preclude the vessel's return to a U.S. port for a period of several months. In late 2000, a Canadian tour operator, Blyth and Company Travel Limited, planned to initiate four- and five-night cruises to Cuba from Nassau aboard the four-hundred-passenger vessel *La Habana*. Plans were canceled before they could be implemented when the company began to receive bomb threats against its cruise vessel.

The future of Cuban calls, and the question of whether they will have a substantial impact on the Caribbean itineraries of the major cruise lines, must wait upon a change in diplomatic relations between Cuba and the United States. It must also be determined if Cuba, after decades of political and social isolation, retains some measure of the magic that once made it such a popular tourist attraction.

Another important East Coast cruise market can be found in New York, which was America's premier seaport during the days of the great ocean liners. At one point when the transition from crossing to cruising was underway, it was thought that New York would emerge as an all-year cruise port. For reasons that will be touched upon in subsequent chapters, this did not happen; instead New York has evolved into a largely seasonal cruise port, primarily for warm weather voyages to Bermuda and to Canada.

At the start of the twenty-first century, the North American cruise industry was experiencing its greatest growth in markets away from the Caribbean and away from the East Coast. Cruises from southern California to various ports in Mexico, while never rivaling the Caribbean in terms of number of ships or passengers, have created a steady market since the earliest days of the contemporary industry. A second West Coast market, although active only for a relatively short May-through-September season, is Alaska. By the turn of the century, as many as two dozen major cruise ships plus another dozen or so smaller cruise ships were deployed in Alaska service each season, and Alaskan service was experiencing steady and healthy growth.

Larger vessels in Alaskan service ordinarily work one of two different seven-night itineraries. The first departs from Vancouver, British Columbia, and returns seven nights later after visiting such southeast Alaskan cities as Ketchikan, Juneau, and Skagway plus spending a day or two cruising past some of Alaska's magnificent glaciers. Such out-and-back Alaskan cruises are often called Inside Passages voyages.

The second option is a seven-night one-way cruise between Vancouver and Seward, Alaska, with a return cruise the following week in the opposite direction. The one-way distance between Seward and Vancouver is about 1,700 nautical miles—it varies depending on the precise itinerary a vessel follows. Because Seward is about a two-hour motor coach ride south of Anchorage, passengers beginning or ending a cruise in Seward can arrive or depart through Anchorage International Airport. Others use Seward as a jumping off point for extended vacations to inland points in central Alaska.

Vancouver-Seward cruises visit many of the same Alaskan ports as Inside Passage itineraries plus an extra glacier or two; they are generally called Gulf of Alaska voyages. Both Gulf of Alaska and Inside Passage cruises include a transit of an extraordinary body of water called Seymour Narrows in British Columbia, approximately 200 miles north of Vancouver. Cruise ships can make their way through Seymour Narrows only during times of slack water, and a ship's captain must take measures to ensure that his vessel is in position and ready to proceed during a thirty-minute window that occurs every six hours when the tide shifts. Given its location with respect to Vancouver, cruise ships often transit Seymour Narrows in the wee hours while passengers are sound asleep, but being on deck for this portion of the cruise is well worth the sacrifice of a little shut-eye.

One or two cruise ships offer different Alaskan fare—for example, longer cruises that originate in San Francisco. In 2000 one company, Norwegian Cruise Line, began offering seven-night Inside Passage cruises out of Seattle, Washington. As is the case with south Florida departures for the Caribbean, finding alternative ports of departure for Alaskan cruises is dictated by a desire to avoid overcrowding at the principal port of embarkation, Vancouver, and to spread the pattern of arrivals and departures by air over a broader assortment of airports.

Europe, Asia, and to a lesser extent South America were important growth areas for the North American cruise industry at the dawn of the twenty-first century. Both Europe and Asia have indigenous cruise companies that are at various stages of development, with all of them harboring desires of becoming "another Carnival," "another Princess," or "another Royal Caribbean" in and for their home market. This might well have come to pass had not something else happened—namely, the older and more experienced North American companies moved into many of these overseas markets and did so with a vengeance.

South America is not yet that large a cruise market and involves little more than a dozen vessels offering seasonal service there. A popular South American itinerary is a fourteen-night cruise between Valparaiso, Chile, on the Pacific and Buenos Aires, Argentina, on the Atlantic, often including a port call in the Falkland Islands. Some niche-market companies offer cruises that sail up the Amazon River deep into the Brazilian rain forest. Thus far there are no indigenous cruise companies operating in the South American market, although as North American and European cruise companies continue to send vessels there, it is certainly possible that one or more such companies will emerge.

Passengers line the rails as a cruise ship moves into Alaska's College Fjords for an up-close look at the glaciers.

Asia is a definite growth area and is also where local companies such as Sun Cruises of Malaysia and Hyundai Merchant Marine of South Korea have made strong efforts to exercise dominance in local markets. Star can lay claim to some especially impressive achievements. Despite short-term reversals in the general Asian economy during the late 1990s, this company has been designing and building new vessels, expanding itineraries, and in early 2000, even becoming an investor-owner of one of the major North American cruise companies, Norwegian Cruise Line, a development that will be discussed in more detail in chapter 6. Mere weeks after orchestrating this takeover, Star turned around and bought out one of its Asian competitors, Sun Cruises.

Europe, though, is where the growth of the cruise industry has recently been nothing less than explosive. Smaller companies have been offering specialized cruises to such places as the Greek islands and the fjords of Norway for many decades. In more recent years, the entire Mediterranean, the British Isles, Scandinavian waters, and the Baltic Sea have seen more vessels offering more and more cruises each year. Political developments that improved east-west relations have also helped the cruising industry by opening seaports in countries that were formerly part of the Soviet block to western cruise lines, thereby expanding the itineraries such vessels may sail.

While there are some mass-market cruise companies that are European-based and promote their cruises primarily to European customers—Festival Cruises and a British company called Airtours/Sun Cruises are two such lines—they tend to operate small fleets of older vessels and bear a haunting similarity to the North American cruise industry of a quarter century ago. While there are also more than a few upscale cruise lines that are basically European in their orientation, the truly dominant force in this market has become one-time North American–oriented companies, cruise lines operating the newest and the latest of cruise ships and backed up by marketing and sales forces that are perfectly comfortable selling their product to customers the world over.

Although North American companies continue to market their product primarily to customers who live in the United States and Canada, they are expanding into overseas areas. Starting in 2001, Royal Caribbean International will promote cruises aboard its 1996-built *Splendour of the Seas* exclusively to Europeans. Cruises aboard this vessel—European itineraries in summer, South American during the winter—will not even be listed in brochures distributed in North America, and even more tellingly, English will no longer be the sole language used for onboard announcements. Other fine-tuning of the company's cruise product aboard *Splendour of the Seas* will involve menu changes and entertainment that does not rely on knowledge of any single language to be enjoyed.

Cruise markets, of course, can experience fluctuations and are sensitive to both real and perceived political instabilities. The NATO military action in Kosovo in 1999, for example, resulted in a serious reduction in cruise bookings for itineraries that included the Adriatic, while earlier, the Gulf War of 1990–91 saw many prospective passengers cancel reservations for cruises throughout the Mediterranean. Because a good number of these displaced cruise passengers are thought to have booked Alaskan cruises in lieu of planned Mediterranean itineraries, it has often been said that the individual most responsible for the rapid growth of the Alaskan market in the early 1990s was Saddam Hussein. In 1985, Mediterranean cruising was dealt a positively frightening blow when the *Achille Lauro* was seized by terrorists between Alexandria and Port Said and an American passenger was brutally murdered, an episode that resulted in the swift implementation of more rigorous security arrangements aboard cruise ships the world over.

The following table displays in rounded numbers the percentage share that various cruise markets represent, showing how values have shifted between 1995 and 1999. The data reflect only cruises of two or more nights in duration.

CRUISE MARKETS: 1995 AND 1999

1995	Market	1999
43%	Caribbean	36%
8%	Bahamas	6.5%
14%	Europe	20%
8.5%	Alaska	9%
6%	Panama Canal	6.5%
5%	Mexico (West Coast)	5.5%
3%	Bermuda	3%
4%	Asia, South Pacific, etc.	3%
2%	Transatlantic	2%
1.5%	Hawaii	2%
1%	Canada/New England	1.5%
1%	South America	1.5%
3%	Other	3.5%
100%		100%

Source: Cruise Lines International Association

A final consideration with respect to the cruise market is this: it relates not to where passengers want to go, but when they choose to travel.

In the industry's early days, the average passengers were older, more often than not people who were enjoying their retirement years. For such a market, time was not a factor; a winter cruise to the Caribbean was made to order, and January through March quickly developed as the peak cruise season.

As the industry has grown and expanded, its customer base has shifted. Now the average age of a cruise passenger is much younger than it once was, and a cruise is not something that can be taken any time, but only during vacations from work. Since people usually take their vacations in the summertime, the peak season for the cruise business has, not surprisingly, shifted to the summer months.

CORPORATE EVOLUTION

Because they are part of a healthy and growing industry, cruise companies are subject to the same kind of mergers and consolidations that are dominating other sectors of the world economy. While this book will chronicle major developments in this area, a preliminary caution is in order. The industry will continue to experience corporate alignments in future months and years, and thus anything that is said and reported here is subject to revision and updating by the unyielding forces of the real world.

The realignments that have happened over the past quarter century are nothing short of remarkable. Carnival has emerged as a major force in the industry, for instance, not merely on the strength of the performance of the cruise

A classic piece of maritime equipment—an old-fashioned engine room telegraph—is reading "full ahead" aboard Premier's *OceanBreeze.*

ships that fly the red, white, and blue house flag of Carnival Cruise Lines, but also because of the many corporate mergers and takeovers that have been engineered by its parent, Carnival Corporation. And mergers and acquisitions are not merely the province of companies at the high end of the size scale. There have been consolidations among smaller companies as well. For example, Commodore Cruise Line and Bermuda Star Line merged into an expanded Commodore operation in 1989, while as recently as 1997, three relatively small cruise companies—Dolphin, Premier, and Seawind—came under the management of a single holding company and were formally merged into one operation under a revamped Premier brand name. Home Lines—once a strong and stable force in the industry—was taken over by Holland America in 1987, while other once-common fleets such as Sitmar and Royal Viking have long since been absorbed into larger cruise companies.

Nor is out-and-out failure unknown in the industry. Regency Cruises, established in 1985 and thought to be on the road to long-term success, hauled down its house flag in 1995 and exited the business entirely, while such once-considered stable operations as Swedish-American Line, Royal Cruise Line, and, more recently, Premier Cruise Lines are no longer active players.

Aspects of these developments will be seen in subsequent chapters. For now, the point to be made is that the cruise industry—precisely because it is strong and healthy—will undoubtedly always be subject to continual mergers, further consolidations, and even an occasional corporate failure.

CHAPTER 3

Carnival Cruise Lines

Carnival Cruise Lines is, surely, the best-known name in the contemporary cruise industry. It owns and operates more vessels than any other company, it actively promotes its product with catchy television commercials, and it has been a leader in seeking to expand not only its own customer base, but that of the entire industry. Oddly, the Carnival story begins with a man who is more identified with a competitor of the company than with Carnival itself.

Knut U. Kloster, Jr., was born in Norway in 1929. He studied marine engineering and architecture at the Massachusetts Institute of Technology and became the third-generation head of the Oslo-based maritime business founded by his grandfather in 1905. Unlike his predecessors, Knut Kloster sought to expand the family business from the cargo hauling it had traditionally performed into the area of passenger travel by sea.

In 1966, Kloster took delivery of an 8,666-gross-ton combination passenger cruise ship and open-water ferry that had been built for him in Bergen, Norway, by A/S Bergens. His idea was to run the new vessel, which he christened *Sunward*, between Great Britain and Gibraltar. *Sunward* would haul lorries and automobiles on its lower decks between the two points to earn basic revenue, but would also provide a leisure-oriented luxury cruise service for passengers on her upper decks.

Sunward was both conventional and exceptional. She was conventional to the extent that passenger-carrying car ferries had become an important element in Europe's postwar transportation network. But she was exceptional in that her passenger facilities were designed to make the voyage pleasant and enjoyable, not just something to be endured.

For a variety of largely political reasons that remain less than clear decades after the fact, Kloster was never able to sustain his Britain-Gibraltar service. This is where fate intervened in a way that would have a substantial impact on the development of the North American cruise industry.

At the same time Kloster was running into difficulties inaugurating a new cruise service in Europe, across the North Atlantic in Florida forty-two-year-old Ted Arison was harboring vague dreams of early retirement. But Arison was not destined to spend his days on the shuffleboard court. A veteran of the Second World War as well as Israel's 1948 War for Independence and with a strong family background in the shipping business—Arison's father was an executive with M. Dizengoff and Company, a leading shipping agency in the Middle East—Ted Arison established a Miami-based company, Arison Shipping, and in early 1966 took over the operation of a chartered Israeli car ferry, the *Nili*, that was running winter cruises out of Miami under the flag of a company called Pan American Cruise Lines.

Launched in Glasgow in 1965, the newly built *Nili* was more practical than luxurious. Few of her staterooms had windows or portholes, most had upper and lower bunks, and as many as half featured toilet facilities that had to be shared with the cabin next door.

Despite the awful specter generated by the loss of *Yarmouth Castle* in 1965, Arison's operation was doing well and enjoying modest success. It was, that is, until the first mortgage holder of the vessel—which happened to be the Israeli government—foreclosed and demanded that *Nili* be returned to home waters. There was talk the government felt that *Nili* and another car ferry that had been chartered for use in North America, *Bilu*, had strategic value as troop and equipment transports in the event of future hostilities. And such hostilities would indeed come to pass. In June 1967 Israel fought—and won—the famous "six-day war" against its Arab neighbors.

The year is 1966 and *Nili*, Ted Arison's first cruise ship, is docked in Nassau. The vessel to her port is Eastern's *Ariadne*. Courtesy Captain Carl Netherland-Brown.

Back in Florida, Arison was left with the remnants of a cruise company infrastructure—marketing and ticketing capability as well as some operations-oriented personnel—but no vessels. At this point, while paging through a professional travel journal, Arison read that Kloster's *Sunward* was unable to operate over the Britain-Gibraltar route.

Arison contacted Kloster, told him that *Sunward* seemed to be similar to *Nili* in many ways, and suggested that Miami was the perfect place to send his new ship to take advantage of the advance bookings that he, Arison, was still holding. Kloster was receptive and agreed to meet with Arison. While the advance bookings were legitimate, when Kloster asked for documentation, Arison had none available, and it has been said that he put his people to work and just plain made them up. But the two men negotiated an agreement and Kloster dispatched *Sunward* across the Atlantic to Miami, where she arrived on December 18, 1966, thirteen months and some days after the loss of *Yarmouth Castle*. *Sunward*'s docking in Miami was delayed for an hour or so as workers scurried to find a proper gangway that would match up with the new vessel's landing areas. Tied up adjacent to her was Arison's former vessel, *Nili*, delayed in her return to Israel by some kind of protracted court proceeding.

The very next day, December 19, 1966, *Sunward* departed from Miami's recently opened Dodge Island terminal on her first North American cruise. Owned and operated by Kloster's company and marketed by Arison's, the joint venture soon came to do business under the trade name Norwegian Caribbean Line (NCL). The first cruise brochure produced to promote the new service, though, did not use the NCL name but referred simply to the "Norwegian MS *Sunward*." Klosters Rederi A/S of Oslo was identified as the vessel's owner and operator and Arison Shipping Company of Miami as agent.

The new *Sunward* was a different kind of vessel, one that took Miami by storm. While converted ocean liners or out-of-work coastal steamers like *Yarmouth Castle* that attempted to find a place in the newly developing south Florida cruise business were old ships, *Sunward* was brand spanking new. Fully air-conditioned, she had a rakish profile and seemed to offer an enticing hint of what the developing cruise industry could become, if only given half a chance. Florida, "the sunshine state," quickly became the perfect home for Kloster's *Sunward*, even though when the vessel was christened, it was Mediterranean sunshine, not the Florida variety, that her name sought to evoke.

More important than her new and modern appearance was that from the very outset, *Sunward*'s cruises proved to be commercially successful. The enthusiastic booking reports that Arison initially showed Kloster might not have been factually accurate at the time, but they proved to be a valid projection of future performance. Initially, *Sunward* sailed only three-night and four-night cruises to Nassau. In subsequent years she worked such split-week cruises

Sunward, the first cruise ship to work for the company that was later called Norwegian Caribbean Line. Courtesy of The Mariners' Museum, Newport News, Virginia.

three weeks a month, while during the fourth week she operated a seven-night cruise on the milk run to St. Thomas and San Juan. During her first season of service, a three-night cruise to Nassau aboard *Sunward* cost $59 per passenger for the least expensive interior accommodations and $225 for a top-of-the-line suite.

Success naturally led to expansion; in 1968 Kloster supplemented the two-year-old *Sunward* with the larger *Starward*, also a combination car ferry/ cruise ship. *Skyward* followed in 1969 and *Southward* in 1971. All were newly built vessels in the range of 16,000 gross tons and 525 feet long. *Sunward* measured 8,666 gross tons and was 457 feet from bow to stern.

Southward, incidentally, was the first cruise ship to pioneer a new style of public relations that would later become very common in the cruise industry. She was not christened at the European shipyard where she was built, but rather in Miami later, after sailing across the Atlantic to her new operating venue. Why christen a new cruise ship intended for the North American market in a faraway city like Helsinki, Finland, or Monfalcone, Italy, and merely get a story in the local paper there, if one can create a "photo opportunity" in a major U.S. market where large numbers of potential passengers live?

By this time, the trademark of the NCL fleet was a pair of flared funnels positioned aft, and each ship's hull was decorated with a stylized orange sunburst, all of which had been pioneered by *Sunward*. And while departures from Miami were nominally departures of passenger-carrying cruise ships, in fact NCL took advantage of the ferry capacity built into its earliest vessels. Passenger revenue was supplemented with fees paid by trucking companies who dispatched trailers full of groceries, construction materials, and other goods to various Caribbean and Bahamian locations aboard the same ships. Advocates of cruise travel were quick to call attention to NCL's success. The more skeptical never failed to point out that much of the new company's good fortune was attributable to income generated belowdecks by those trucks and trailers. NCL even ran a pure cargo ship out of Miami during its early years to help haul such trailers, a vessel that was called *Trailer Express*.

While the NCL enterprise flourished commercially, the Kloster-Arison relationship proved to be less durable. In 1971, as the fourth vessel, *Southward*, was about to join the growing NCL fleet, Kloster decided to cancel the contract under which he and Arison were doing business. Kloster had the legal authority to do so, but Arison felt the action was unjustified and sought to protect himself by isolating and retaining certain financial resources that represented, essentially, cruise deposits paid by future NCL passengers, a sum of money that added up to approximately $1.5 million. Kloster and Arison would litigate for several years over this money; eventually the matter was settled through an out-of-court compromise in 1974. What is of interest to the story of the North American cruise industry is what each of the two men, Knut Kloster and Ted Arison, did in the years after their joint working agreement came to an end in 1971.

Kloster's not inconsiderable contribution to the cruise industry will be treated in chapter 6 where Norwegian Caribbean Line is explored in greater detail. Arison's activities in the years after 1971, however, are the stuff of pure and unabashed legend.

With NCL now being managed by Kloster's people, Arison found himself in 1971 in a position that was not unlike his situation in 1966, when the car ferry *Nili* was called back to Israel and he was in Florida with the capability to run a cruise service, but without any vessels. While some of Arison's old employees chose to remain with Kloster and NCL, the majority elected to stay with Arison, confident the man would be able to pull something out of his hat that would keep their paychecks flowing.

After an effort to acquire two Cunard Line vessels, *Franconia* and *Carmania*, proved unsuccessful, what Arison eventually did pull out of his hat was a 27,284-gross-ton ocean liner that had recently been taken out of transatlantic service by her owner, Canadian Pacific, and laid up in Liverpool, England, to await a buyer. Built by Vickers-Armstrongs at Newcastle in 1961, she was the

Early brochure used to promote cruises aboard *Sunward*. Courtesy Captain Carl Netherland-Brown.

Empress of Canada, one of a trio of vessels that Canadian Pacific had ordered after the Second World War to replace older ships. While basically ocean liners, CP's postwar vessels were designed to be equally at home in summer transatlantic service between Europe and the St. Lawrence and winter cruise service to the Caribbean. With but ten years of service and only 121 transatlantic crossings under her belt, *Empress of Canada* was an attractive buy for Arison and would allow him to start up yet another new south Florida cruise venture, his third in a little more than five years.

To finance the acquisition, Arison turned to an old friend, Meshulam Riklis, a principal in a Boston-based travel company known as American International Travel Service (AITS). One of the trade names AITS used for various package tours it operated was "Carnival," and so what Arison and Riklis set up was a new subsidiary of the Boston company that was called Carnival Cruise Lines. Riklis and AITS put up $6.5 million to finance the acquisition of *Empress of Canada;* Arison used the million-plus he had retained from NCL as working capital to get the new Carnival Cruise Lines into operation. AITS would market and promote the new venture.

Empress of Canada was renamed *Mardi Gras*, a name that clearly suggested a "carnival-like" spirit, and she was hastily refurbished for her new service. Converting an out-of-service transatlantic liner, even a relatively new and small one like *Empress of Canada*, into a full-time Caribbean cruise ship took a bit of work. Because the vessel's previous owner, Canadian Pacific, was a member of the Trans-Atlantic Passenger Steamship Conference, its vessels necessarily had to feature accommodations in at least two separate classes. While cabins designed for first-class transatlantic passengers were appropriate for passengers anxious to take a Caribbean cruise, tourist-class cabins were not and Carnival had to undertake extensive remodeling of the vessel's tourist facilities. In transatlantic tourist accommodations, total strangers were often expected to share four-berth cabins that often lacked their own shower facilities. When Canadian Pacific ran the vessel in occasional cruise service, it only sold space in *Empress of Canada*'s first-class accommodations. Arison, however, needed all the ship's potential carrying capacity to sustain his new cruise venture, and so workers traveled aboard *Mardi Gras* for the better part of her first two years of service under the new Carnival house flag completing this transformation. Which is to say, the vessel's initial capacity was limited because her full and complete transformation into a cruise ship was still a work in progress.

While not important from a business or operational perspective, one "short cut" Arison took in transforming *Empress of Canada* into *Mardi Gras* is rather interesting. In 1968, Canadian Pacific had adopted completely new and different corporate identifications for the various arms of its worldwide operations. Canadian Pacific Railway was renamed CP Rail, Canadian Pacific Airlines became CP

Air, and the ocean liner service provided by the likes of *Empress of Canada* was re-named CP Ships.

A new logo was developed that would be used across the entire system. Called the multimark, it was a geometric design showing a triangle and crescent inside a square, rendered in colors appropriate for the service in question. When used on the locomotives and passenger cars of CP Rail, the multimark was rendered in red, white, and black. When applied to the funnels of CP Ships, the multimark was green, white, and black. Previously, Canadian Pacific ocean liners had featured buff-colored stacks with a white and red checkerboard design near the top.

When Arison's people got a look at *Empress of Canada*, they decided that the multimark was a nearly perfect outline for a new logo of their own. With a few straight lines turned into curves, CP green became Carnival red, black became blue, and the one-time decoration that was originally developed for multimodal application across the entire Canadian Pacific transportation system became the signature for Arison's new Carnival Cruise Lines, not only on the funnel of the renamed *Mardi Gras*, but on luggage tags, letterheads, business cards, and pro-motional brochures. What is doubly interesting is that while Canadian Pacific has since abandoned the 1968 multimark as its own corporate logo, the succes-sors of *Mardi Gras* that continue to sail for Carnival Cruise Lines retain a version of the design, one of the most distinctive funnel decorations among contempo-rary cruise companies, and equally distinctive in the larger universe of ocean lin-ers from all eras.

Something else that changed when *Empress of Canada* became *Mardi Gras* was the vessel's gross registered tonnage. Under Canadian Pacific ownership, the vessel measured 27,284 gross tons. When she went to work for Arison, her gross tonnage was listed as 18,261. It was later revised back to 27,250.

Mardi Gras entered cruise service out of Miami for Carnival on March 11, 1972. An earlier cruise scheduled for March 4 had to be canceled until a mil-lion-dollar financial responsibility bond was posted, but everything was ready a week later on March 11, and the new vessel cast off and headed for sea. As she was clearing Government Cut on the ocean side of Miami Beach, *Mardi Gras* ran hard aground on a sandbar. There she stayed for over a day; the 530 passengers who were on board—several hundred of whom were travel agents whose good-will the new company was hoping to cultivate—continued to enjoy themselves, even though the vessel was making no progress. Wire services sent photos of the grounded vessel to newspapers and television stations from coast to coast. Hoping this was not an omen to suggest how the new venture was going to fare, Arison must have asked himself what could possibly be worse than having his new company's only vessel run aground on her very first cruise?

The following day five tugboats managed to free *Mardi Gras*, and she contin-ued her seven-night cruise to San Juan and St. Thomas. Writing of this first

The first cruise ship to sail under the Carnival Cruise Lines house flag was *Mardi Gras*. The vessel was built in 1961 as *Empress of Canada* for Canadian Pacific's transatlantic service.

voyage of Carnival's first cruise ship some years later, Bob Dickinson—who would later become president of the company—told how Ted Arison had to collect money from cash registers in several cocktail lounges aboard *Mardi Gras* to help pay for necessary refueling in San Juan. The new company had yet to establish its credit, and fuel dealers in Puerto Rico were demanding payment in advance before *Mardi Gras* could bunker for the return trip to Miami.

Mardi Gras remained on the seven-night Miami–St. Thomas milk run during her early years with Carnival, although to help celebrate the twenty-fifth anniversary of the founding of the State of Israel in 1973, the vessel made a special forty-day transatlantic round trip between Florida and Haifa that year. Unlike NCL's *Sunward*, which was a solid financial success from its very first trip, *Mardi Gras* seemed unable to turn the elusive corner of profitability. Losses mounted, AITS began to grow concerned over its investment, and the need to coordinate decision-making between Miami and Boston was proving difficult. Then, when the Nevada Gaming Commission requested that AITS divest itself of Carnival—a request that involved the fact AITS was also the owner of a licensed Las Vegas casino—AITS sold its interest in the vessel to Arison and two fellow investors in 1974 for the munificent sum of one whole dollar. Included in the transaction, however, was full and complete "ownership" of what was then $5 million worth of *Mardi Gras* debt. The "one whole dollar," in other words, may not have been as big a bargain as it seemed.

Except it was. With a new marketing team aboard, Carnival began to promote its cruise product to a different and more diverse type of customer, younger people whose idea of a good time was playing silly games around the pool during the day, then singing and dancing on into the night, not sitting quietly in a deck chair all afternoon watching flying fish jump out of the water and capping the day off by turning in early. A promotional program, complete with television advertisements, was developed around the concept "the Carnival fun ship," and new relationships were developed with independent travel agents. Less than a year later *Mardi Gras* was posting steady profits. During 1975, for example, *Mardi Gras* was able to claim a full-year occupancy rate of 109 percent.

Incidentally, such a statistic—one that appears to exceed perfection itself—is not uncommon in the cruise industry. "Full occupancy," by definition, means two people occupying each of a vessel's cabins. Many cabins, though, can actually accommodate a third, or sometimes even a fourth, passenger. Thus an occupancy rate in excess of 100 percent does not imply either stowaways or people sleeping on deck.

Arison was hardly one to rest on any laurels. Once the balance sheet began to show positive numbers, he supplemented *Mardi Gras* with a running mate, a vessel that Carnival called *Carnivale*.

Carnivale was also a former Canadian Pacific vessel—the *Empress of Britain*—but one that CP had disposed of some years earlier; she then worked for the Greek Line as *Queen Anna Maria,* largely in North American cruise service. Greek Line abandoned all of its oceangoing passenger services in early 1975 and *Queen Anna Maria* was laid up in Greece awaiting a buyer. New York's Chase Manhattan Bank was also in the picture since it had been involved in the financing of the vessel's purchase from CP by Greek Line and was thus happy to help Carnival put together a financing package for the acquisition as a way of protecting its own interest. *Carnivale* made her first sailing out of Miami for her new owners on February 7, 1976, following a $2.5-million refurbishing at Newport News Shipbuilding. *Mardi Gras* had been soldiering alone for Carnival for almost four years before *Carnivale* entered service.

The new company did not remain a two-ship fleet for very long. In May of 1978, the one-time Union-Castle mailboat *Transvaal Castle,* more recently running as South African Marine's *S.A. Vaal,* was acquired. Because she was in need of more extensive conversion work than either of the ex-CP ships, Arison negotiated a contract with Kawasaki Heavy Industries in Japan for a refurbishing that was to have cost in the vicinity of $16 to $18 million. Meanwhile, Arison was also quietly negotiating with Kawasaki to build a totally new cruise ship for Carnival, a 30,000-gross-ton vessel that was to have been called *Carousel* and whose price was expected to be in the $56 million range.

International currency fluctuations impacted both transactions. The conversion work on *S.A. Vaal* wound up costing closer to $30 million before she was returned to Carnival as *Festivale* and ran her first cruise out of Miami on October 28, 1978; the contract for *Carousel* was never executed because the price for such a newbuilding had escalated to almost $100 million. It would be another quarter-century before a North American cruise company would place an order with a Japanese yard for a new cruise ship.

Although *Mardi Gras, Carnivale,* and *Festivale* were reasonably similar in overall profile—a classic ocean liner look topped off by a single stack amidships—*Festivale* was, by far, the largest of the trio. Over a hundred feet longer than either of the one-time CP vessels, when she joined the Carnival fleet, her 26,632 gross tons made her the sixth largest cruise ship in the world. Carnival operated all three vessels out of Miami on seven-night cruises exclusively.

While Arison's deal with Japan's Kawasaki for a new vessel failed to materialize, Carnival did order such a ship from a European yard, a decision that Arison announced in 1978 to an utterly shocked Miami convention of Cruise Lines International Association, a trade association of the industry. With a firm called Technical Marine Planning of London serving as naval architects for the project, Denmark's Aalborg Vaerft turned out the 35,190-ton *Tropicale* in 1981, and Carnival took delivery of its first newbuilding. It would not be the company's last. Unfortunately, the price escalation that caused Arison to sour on his pending deal with Kawasaki proved to be all too real. Like the never-built *Carousel, Tropicale* also came with a price tag of $100 million. (Vessel costs cited here and elsewhere are not necessarily precise. While there is no overt effort to confuse or deceive, cruise companies tend to express the cost of their new vessels in numbers that are often severely rounded.)

Tropicale pioneered a new and dramatic design that Carnival would repeat over a dozen times in the ensuing two decades. The principal visual effect of this design on the outside was a large winged funnel positioned more aft than amidships and rendered in an appropriate evolutionary version of the multimark from CP Ships that *Mardi Gras* had introduced a decade earlier.

Winged funnels had been used earlier on French Line's *France*. But while *France*'s two funnels were more or less perpendicular, *Tropicale*'s stack was set at a rakish angle and quickly became a strong and distinctive symbol of Carnival Cruise Lines itself. The basic concept of the winged funnel was first suggested by Miami designer and architect Joseph Farcus, who was also responsible for interior work on *Tropicale*. His talents would continue to be reflected in subsequent Carnival newbuildings, all of which would feature red, white, and blue winged funnels.

Since she was designed as a cruise ship from the very beginning, *Tropicale* began to evidence many of the features that would become commonplace not only on Carnival ships, but in the industry as a whole. Her superstructure extends well forward since there is no need to provide for cargo hatches and the open deck space they require. Following upon designs then evolving among European naval architects in the construction of new car ferries there, she was laid down with a squared-off stern, or a transom stern as it is sometimes called. Her hull thus featured a rather constant width for most of its length, a characteristic that greatly facilitated the design of passenger cabins. With the exception of a small area near the bow where the hull narrowed, all cabins of any given category were exactly the same size. Based on the usual standard of double occupancy in all cabins, *Tropicale*'s capacity was 1,022 passengers. Her staff numbered 550, her registry was Liberian, she could cruise at twenty knots, and she was powered by two 7-cylinder Sulzer diesel engines that were mechanically geared to a pair of controllable-pitch propellers. A bow thruster helped her maneuver in close quarters.

Tropicale ran counter to a piece of conventional wisdom in the newly developing industry, namely the idea that the ideal cruise ship was one in the 20,000-gross-ton size range, not unlike the early NCL fleet that Arison once operated in conjunction with Knut Kloster. *Tropicale*'s 36,674 gross tons put her in a class apart from other new cruise ships of her day, a much larger class. But a little more than a decade after she was built and introduced into cruise service, *Tropicale* would become—by default—the *smallest* ship in the growing Carnival fleet as newer and even larger vessels were designed and built.

As another contrast, when *Tropicale* was new, her interior decor was regarded as new, unconventional, even flamboyant. Today, she can be described as rather restrained when compared with some of her younger Carnival fleetmates and the decorative themes that Joseph Farcus has executed for them.

Carnival used the occasion of *Tropicale*'s joining the fleet to expand into a new market. Instead of operating her to the Caribbean out of Miami, *Tropicale* headed through the Panama Canal to the West Coast and established a Carnival presence in Los Angeles, where she offered seven-night cruises to Mexico. The 36,674-ton *Tropicale* was just the start, though. She was followed in 1985 by the 46,052-ton *Holiday*, and in 1987 by the sister ships *Jubilee* and *Celebration*, both of which measured 47,262 gross tons. Like *Tropicale*, *Holiday* was also turned out in Denmark by Aalborg Vaerft, while the other two were products of Kockums Shipyard in Malmo, Sweden. The three new vessels that followed *Tropicale* represented an investment by Carnival of almost half a billion dollars.

As the Carnival fleet began to expand, in 1984 *Carnivale* was taken off the company's basic seven-night itinerary and redeployed into a market that Carnival had not previously served, combination three- and four-night cruises each week from south Florida to the nearby Bahamas. In 1986, *Mardi Gras* joined *Carnivale* in operating such a split-week schedule. At first these shorter cruises operated out of Miami. Later, as the Carnival fleet continued to expand and docking space at Miami's Dodge Island cruise terminal became scarce, they were transferred to Port Canaveral, 175 miles north and adjacent to such tourist attractions as Walt Disney World and the NASA facility at Cape Canaveral. If a space shuttle is poised on its launch pad, it is visible from the deck of a cruise ship docked at Port Canaveral. Similarly, if an early morning space launch happens to take place while a Port Canaveral–based cruise ship is returning to port, early-rising passengers are treated to a sight they will not soon forget.

Carnival's fleet expansion reached an important milestone in 1990 with the delivery of a vessel the company called *Fantasy.* Larger than any of the company's earlier newbuildings, *Fantasy* measured an impressive 70,367 gross tons, was 855 feet from bow to stern, and had a passenger capacity of 2,048. She entered service out of Miami on March 2, 1990, and in doing so became the very first newly built passenger vessel to serve the popular split-week, three- and four-night itinerary that had long been a staple of the cruise industry.

(This seemingly simple factual assertion requires a minor qualification. *Fantasy* was the first newly built cruise vessel to serve the split-week market, although she was not designed specifically for such service. As shall be seen in the following chapter, a Royal Caribbean vessel, *Nordic Empress,* was purposefully designed and built for such service. Her maiden voyage did not take place until several months after *Fantasy* entered service.)

Over the next decade, Carnival would add seven additional Fantasy-class ships to its fleet. One could argue that *Fantasy* and her sister ships represent the largest single class of oceangoing passenger vessels of all time, provided one is willing to use the total gross registered tonnage as the standard of comparison, not the number of hulls. There were sixteen vessels in the U.S. Shipping Board's "535-foot class" of the 1920s, each approximately 15,000 gross tons, while North German Lloyd's Barbarosa-class, built between 1896 and 1901, included twelve passenger ships in the 10,000-gross-ton range. More recently, Renaissance Cruises has ordered an eight-ship fleet of cruise ships that will equal the Fantasy class in number of vessels, but, at 30,200 gross registered tons each, will fall far below Carnival's eight in overall size.

All of Carnival's Fantasy-class vessels are similar, not to say identical, on the outside, although each boasts its own unique interior treatment, designs that rely heavily on neon-like lighting, vivid colors, unusual reflecting surfaces, and other components that could never be called conventional, much less classic, and certainly not restrained.

Going back to a pre-Fantasy class, the *Celebration* of 1987, one finds a cocktail lounge called The Trolley Bar that includes a replica of a New Orleans streetcar, painted in the authentic colors of New Orleans trolley cars. Perhaps the most unique artifact on any Carnival cruise ship, though—and maybe on any vessel ever—is to be found aboard *Holiday*, also a pre-Fantasy ship. Here there is a real 1934 bus, the *Bette Astrup*, that once made regular trips between Astrup and Hjorring in Denmark and was carefully restored by Carnival for its new role aboard *Holiday*. In the next-stop window on the bus, a sign reads Coney Island. This, it may safely be assumed, is not an authentic leftover from the days when the bus operated in the Danish countryside.

The second Fantasy-class vessel, *Ecstasy*, includes a marvelously restored 1934 green and gray Rolls Royce saloon car that is "parked" at the Rolls Royce Cafe along an indoor promenade called City Lights Boulevard. Like finding the bus *Bette Astrup*, locating a Rolls of the correct style and vintage was not easy. It was eventually discovered at a small antique car dealer in northern Wales and painstakingly rebuilt for its new role.

Carnival turned to the Wartsila shipyard in Helsinki, Finland, for the first two Fantasy-class vessels, *Fantasy* and *Ecstasy*. But Wartsila was experiencing financial difficulties of a serious sort in the late 1980s and in October 1989, the company went bankrupt. To protect its newbuildings, Carnival helped finance a reorganization of the yard that was spearheaded by Martin Saarikangas, a man who had been managing director of the yard under Wartsila. Renamed Masa-Yards, a shortening of Saarikangas's two names, the one-time Wartsila facility was able to continue work on the Carnival vessels without missing a beat. Not a single Wartsila shipwright missed so much as a single day's work or a single day's pay.

Masa-Yards was eventually taken over by Kvaerner, a Norwegian company, and Carnival sold off its stake in the company. What is interesting to reflect upon, of course, is that a cruise company that once had to raid onboard cash registers to find money to get its only vessel refueled in San Juan for the return trip to Miami was now able to "buy the shipyard," so to speak, when financial problems of the previous owner threatened the timely delivery of its new vessels. The remainder of the Fantasy-class ships were also built in Helsinki, but with Kvaerner Masa-Yards as the contractor.

As new Fantasy-class vessels continued to arrive in Miami from Helsinki in the 1990s, Carnival decided that its original trio of secondhand vessels—*Mardi Gras*, *Carnivale*, and *Festivale*—no longer had any role to play. An attempt by Carnival to use *Carnivale*, renamed *FiestaMarina*, in a subsidiary company that would market its product primarily to Hispanic passengers proved unprofitable and eventually all three of the company's original "fun ships" were sold off to cruise companies in the bargain-basement category of the industry. *Festivale* was leased to Dolphin/Premier Cruises for a number of years before being sold to the same company, with a provision written into the contract that the vessel could not be operated in direct competition with any Carnival vessel for a specified period of time.

As the Carnival fleet grew, so did the choice of itineraries, but more than other contemporary mass-market cruise companies, Carnival remained wedded to the Caribbean. Even now, few of its vessels are dispatched elsewhere. Two ships are typically assigned to Los Angeles, one working a seven-night Mexican itinerary, the other offering a combination of three- and four-night cruises. A single Carnival vessel is normally sent north to Alaska each summer—through 2000 this was the 1987-built *Jubilee*—but as a general rule it remains correct to say that Carnival continues to regard the Caribbean as its principal cruise market. Over the years, few of Carnival's vessels have been dispatched on cruises that are longer than seven nights in duration. In fact, as the twentieth century was coming to an end, Carnival was experimenting with additional styles of cruises that were less than seven nights long. Keeping vessels assigned to some kind of repetitive cycle remains important in the cruise industry. Over a two-week period, a vessel can run two five-night cruises and one four, or during a week's time, one five-night cruise and one two-night. Split-week three- and four-night cruises also remain popular.

Fantasy and her sister ships included a style of vessel propulsion that was new for Carnival but was becoming popular in the industry, particularly for larger vessels—electric drive. Instead of diesel engines being geared to propeller shafts and effecting propulsion through purely mechanical linkages, with electric drive, the diesel engines turned electric generators, and the propeller shafts were rotated, in turn, by large electric motors. Fantasy-class cruise ships are powered by six big diesel engines manufactured by Wartsila under license from Sultzer Diesel, STD. The six diesels drive generators that produce the electricity which, in turn, powers everything on board Fantasy-class vessels, from the motors turning a ship's propellers to the reading lamps at each passenger's bed. Heat recovered from the diesel engines and from such other sources as onboard refuse incinerators provides energy to evaporate freshwater from seawater in sufficient quantities for all onboard needs.

Although it is an ordinary feature of cruise ships, the ability to turn seawater into fresh drinking water is worth dwelling on for a moment. While in port, cruise ships often supplement their supplies of freshwater from sources ashore, since it is usually less expensive to purchase water than to run the machinery needed to produce it on board. But contemporary cruise ships are fully capable of providing all their freshwater needs from the sea. Cruise ships avoid purchasing freshwater, of course, from any port whose water supply is felt to be suspect in any way, and cruise companies maintain up-to-date intelligence about water quality in the various ports their vessels visit.

Elation and *Paradise*—the seventh and eighth Fantasy-class vessels, both delivered by Kvaerner Masa-Yards in 1998—took the concept of electric drive one important step further. Known as pod propulsion, the idea was a logical follow-up once the propellers were driven by electric motors.

The initial use of electric drive involved motors positioned deep inside the hull and connected to conventional propeller shafts there. But electric motors can be sufficiently small and compact in size that they need not be placed inside the hull at all. They can be attached directly to the propeller on the hull exterior, thus obviating the need for cumbersome mechanical shafts and other hardware. The energy that drives the motors is transmitted from the engine room inside the hull to the propellers outside, not by rotating shafts but by electric cable. Motors outside the hull must obviously be protected from the sea, and the watertight enclosures that house them are called pods. Both motor and pod can swivel, much like the propeller on an outboard motor. Thus a pod-propelled vessel is steered not by moving a rudder but by moving the pod and the propeller in one direction or the other. In addition to eliminating the complexity of propeller shafts and rudders, pod propulsion is also far less likely to generate onboard vibration than is a more conventional propulsion and steering system.

Naval architects quickly determined that with a pod drive, propellers work more efficiently if they face forward, not aft. With conventional steering, aft-facing propellers are needed to ensure proper water flow over the rudder, but ships with pod propulsion are not equipped with rudders at all. Thus, one might say that with pod propulsion, the propellers "pull" a vessel through the water rather than "push" it. The form of pod propulsion Carnival selected for *Elation* and *Paradise,* known by the trade name Azipod, was built by a joint venture of ABB Marine, Kvaerner Masa-Yards, and the Italian shipyard Fincantieri. *Elation* and *Paradise* are each equipped with two pod-propulsion units built by Azipod.

The "azi-" in Azipod is derived from the fact that pod-propulsion units are "fully azimuthal." That is to say they are capable of turning through 360 degrees, and they can exert full power in any direction while turning. Various forms of fully azimuthal vessel propulsion systems gained an early maritime foothold from applications aboard harbor craft such as tugboats. When they proved successful there, the cruise industry became understandably interested.

As with new technical developments in many areas, there appears to be a risk that the word "Azipod" will be treated as a generic term for any make or manufacture of pod-propulsion unit. It is not; it is one manufacturer's contribution. (See chapter 11 for a discussion of a different manufacturer's pod-propulsion unit that was installed aboard a new cruise ship. It should definitely not be called an Azipod, although it has been already.)

Pod propulsion has another advantage: because the pod drive itself can provide thrust at the stern in any direction, the need for separate stern thrusters is avoided. *Elation* and *Paradise* are equipped with three bow thrusters just like other members of the Fantasy class, but they have no stern thrusters, since they have no need for them. (Thrusters are electric-powered propellers that assist vessels during close-quarter maneuvering such as docking. They are mounted inside "tunnels" that extend through the hull below the waterline from one side of the vessel to the other.)

Elation and *Paradise* are also equipped with slightly different engines than their Fantasy-class predecessors. The first six ships of the class are powered by four 12-cylinder Sulzer diesels and two 8-cylinder models. *Elation* and *Paradise* feature six 12-cylinder Sulzer engines.

If specifying pod propulsion for *Paradise* and *Elation* was a major change in naval architecture, the novelty for which *Paradise* quickly earned the more public notice was the fact she is a completely smoke-free vessel. Large images of the familiar "no smoking" pictograph—a red circle with a diagonal line crossed through a cigarette—are displayed on her sides and her stern. Indeed they may well be the largest "no smoking" symbols in the world.

Individuals who book passage aboard *Paradise* are warned that failure to observe the vessel's smoke-free status will not only bring a $250 fine, but they will be put ashore at the next port and must arrange and pay for their own passage home. Passengers are required to sign a very explicit and plain-language agreement to this effect before boarding. The policy does not merely prohibit the use of tobacco products, it equally enjoins mere possession. In the language of the day, Carnival calls the whole business a "zero tolerance" policy.

In the vessel's first eight months of service, Carnival claims that fourteen *Paradise* passengers were disciplined for failure to observe the new requirements, including one woman who was put off the vessel on Grand Cayman Island because "a cabin steward found a package of cigarettes in her cabin." The woman claimed she had purchased the contraband in Cozumel as a gift for someone back home; the cigarettes were clearly visible inside the cabin and were not

Inspiration, one of Carnival's eight Fantasy-class cruise ships. Courtesy John Whittel.

discovered as the result of any kind of intrusive search. Presumably, most of the other violators were people who felt—incorrectly, as it sadly turned out—that a week's cruise aboard the smoke-free *Paradise* would be their ticket to "kicking the habit."

Paradise offers seven-night cruises out of Miami that alternate between the eastern and western Caribbean. Another Carnival vessel—one that allows smoking—is paired with *Paradise* and travels east when she goes west, and vice versa, meaning there is no itinerary from which Carnival excludes passengers who smoke. Carnival is quite pleased with the noble experiment that *Paradise* represents and has promised to introduce additional smoke-free cruise ships in the future. *Elation,* the first of the company's Azipod-propelled vessels, was initially dispatched to Los Angeles to work seven-night cruises to the "Mexican Riviera" from there.

Paradise features an interesting decorative theme that is unrelated to the vessel's smoke-free status or its pod-propulsion system. Many of her public rooms are named after classic transatlantic ocean liners of yesteryear, with appropriate artwork, displays, and treatment. The Blue Riband Library, for example, includes a carefully executed replica of the Hales Trophy that was traditionally awarded to the vessel with the fastest transatlantic crossing time, while the America Bar recalls the 1940-built SS *America* of United States Lines, including floor-to-ceiling re-creations of that vessel's distinctive red, white, and blue funnels. Aboard *Paradise,* passengers take in stage shows in the Normandie Lounge, relax in the Queen Mary Lounge, trip the light fantastic in the Rex Dance Club, and play the odds in the Majestic Casino.

In 1997, before either *Elation* or *Paradise* joined the fleet, Carnival did something that no other operator of oceangoing passenger ships had ever done before but which several have done since. It took delivery of a passenger vessel whose gross registered tonnage could only be written in six figures—with no decimal points.

Built in Monfalcone, Italy, at the Fincantieri yard, the 101,353-gross-ton *Carnival Destiny* was the largest passenger ship in the world, a record previously held by Cunard–White Star's *Queen Elizabeth* of 1940. The 83,673-gross-ton *Queen Elizabeth* held the world record from the time she first took to the sea in the early days of the Second World War until long after she was destroyed by fire in Hong Kong Harbor in 1972. Indeed *Queen Elizabeth* held the title, posthumously, to be sure, until the advent of *Carnival Destiny.*

Carnival Destiny, however, would not hold the record quite so long as RMS *Queen Elizabeth* did. She was eclipsed by the 108,806-gross-ton *Grand Princess* less than a year later, and *Grand Princess,* in turn, gave up the title to Royal Caribbean's 137,276-gross-ton *Voyager of the Seas* before the end of the century. Uneasy, it seems once again, lies any head that wears a crown.

Carnival Destiny will always and forever be the world's first passenger ship to exceed 100,000 gross tons. Like *Fantasy* before her, she has given rise to an entire class of vessels built to similar specifications—*Carnival Triumph* of 1999, *Carnival Victory* of 2000, *Carnival Conquest* due out in 2002, *Carnival Glory* in 2003, and *Carnival Valor* in 2004. The last three vessels, in fact, will be even larger than the first three: sixty feet longer with capacity for almost two hundred additional passengers.

Carnival followed up on the Destiny-class and the eight-ship Fantasy-class with a new design in the 80,000-gross-ton range, the first unit of which will be *Carnival Spirit* in early 2001, followed by *Carnival Pride* later in the same year and *Carnival Legend* due out in 2002, and *Carnival Miracle* in 2004. *Carnival Spirit* and her sisters spring from an entirely new design called Project 8000 that will be adapted for use by subsidiary cruise lines controlled by Carnival in addition to Carnival Cruise Lines itself. Indeed the first newbuilding to exemplify the general look and line of *Carnival Spirit*—and Project 8000—is not a Carnival vessel at all, but a ship owned by Costa Cruise Lines, the *Costa Atlantica* that entered service in 2000 (see chapter 10).

Carnival Destiny accommodates over 2,600 passengers. At 2,112 passengers, *Carnival Spirit* and her sisters will have slightly lower capacities. Unlike their larger fleetmates, they are capable of transiting the Panama Canal, even though it will be a tight fit. (Vessels that just barely qualify for the canal are referred to as Panamax, while ships that are too big for the canal, like the Destiny-class, are known as post-Panamax vessels.) The Destiny-class eschewed the novelty of pod propulsion and each of the 101,000-gross-ton vessels is powered by four 16-cylinder and two 12-cylinder Sulzer diesels. The engines generate electricity, and electric motors positioned inside the hull turn a pair of controllable-pitch propellers. Carnival's Spirit-class vessels, on the other hand, will be equipped with Azipod propulsion units as pioneered on *Elation* and *Paradise*, while their diesel engines are of a new design that promises to reduce noxious emissions to previously unachievable low levels. To capitalize on *Carnival Spirit*'s environment-friendly performance, the company plans to deploy her in the Alaska trade starting in the summer of 2001.

As Carnival's newbuilding program advanced from the 1,022-passenger *Tropicale* of 1981 to the 2,642-passenger *Carnival Destiny* in 1997, it was interesting to follow the escalation in the cost of new vessels. Equally important now is to compare the capital cost of newbuildings on a per-passenger basis, since this underscores a fundamental fact of cruise industry economics. *Tropicale* was reported to be a $100 million investment for Arison and Company in the early 1980s. When *Fantasy* joined the fleet almost a decade later, her price tag was said to be $200 million, twice as much as *Tropicale*, and that is expressed in simple dollars, with no effort to factor the impact of inflation.

What is important is that *Fantasy* accommodates twice as many passengers as *Tropicale*. This means that on a per-passenger basis, the two vessels cost Carnival the same number of dollars, $97,847. If one also factors a decade's worth of inflation into this calculation, though, it becomes obvious that in terms of Carnival's real investment on a per-passenger basis, *Fantasy* was considerably less expensive than *Tropicale*. Even *Carnival Destiny*'s $151,400 cost per passenger in 1997 works out to be substantially below that of *Tropicale*'s in 1981 if costs are adjusted to reflect inflation. The following table displays some Carnival vessel costs in both whole dollars and on a per-passenger basis from 1981 through 1997, with the final column adjusting the per-passenger cost to 1981 dollars.

CARNIVAL VESSEL COSTS, 1981–1997

Year	Vessel	Cost	Passenger Capacity	Cost per Passenger	Cost per Passenger 1981 $$
1981	*Tropicale*	$100 million	1,022	$ 97,847	$97,847
1987	*Jubilee*	$140 million	1,486	$ 94,212	$70,779
1990	*Fantasy*	$200 million	2,044	$ 97,847	$65,035
1997	*Carnival Destiny*	$400 million	2,642	$151,400	$79,737

Carnival's growth in the final quarter of the twentieth century was nothing short of extraordinary. The company grew from a single ship in 1972 to the largest fleet in the industry by the 1990s, and this does not even begin to address the fact that Carnival also became a major player in the high-stakes world of cruise-line mergers and acquisitions, expanding its reach into new markets by this strategy.

Initially, Carnival planned to compete in the upscale market by creating a new and separate cruise brand, an effort that was known within the company for many years as Project Tiffany to signify its luxury orientation. As matters turned out, plans for the project were shelved and Arison supplemented the mass-market offerings of Carnival Cruise Lines by acquiring existing cruise companies with established reputations for serving the higher end of the market.

The first cruise companies that Carnival acquired were Holland America Line and its subsidiary, Windstar Cruises, a transaction that was announced in November 1988 and completed in January 1989. Carnival owns these two lines fully and outright. Carnival also fully owns Cunard Line, Seabourn, and Costa Crociere, and is a part-owner of Airtours, a British retailer of package tours as well as the operator of a small fleet of vessels doing business under the name Sun Cruises. (Carnival's takeover of these various cruise companies will be treated in more detail in subsequent chapters.)

Under Ted Arison's leadership, Carnival "went public" in 1987, thus generating a considerable source of fresh investment capital for subsequent expansion.

The first passenger vessel in the world to exceed 100,000 gross registered tons was *Carnival Destiny*, shown here sailing out of New York in the summer of 2000 on a cruise to Canada.

Ted Arison   Micky Arison

In 1990, Arison stepped down as chairman of the corporation, to be succeeded by his son, Micky Arison, a man who, as a young student, worked aboard *Sunward* during the days when his father and Knut Kloster were jointly involved in Norwegian Caribbean Line. The Arisons, both father and son, were also instrumental in the founding and the ongoing management of the Miami Heat, that city's entry in the National Basketball Association.

In 1993, a corporate reorganization was effected at Carnival to recognize its new role as a direct cruise operator itself and also as the owner of other cruise companies. Carnival Corporation was established to serve as an overall holding company, while Carnival Cruise Lines and the acquired properties became subsidiaries of the larger corporation.

After his retirement in 1990, Ted Arison remained active in Carnival affairs. But he also reclaimed his Israeli citizenship and moved back to his birthplace, Tel Aviv. Like his earlier "retirement" in Florida in the 1960s, though, Arison had no intention of taking things easy; he quickly became active in business, civic, and philanthropic affairs in Israel.

On Friday, October 1, 1999, at the age of seventy-five, Ted Arison quietly passed away. On the day he died, the Carnival house flag proudly flew from the masts of fourteen active cruise ships, and construction continued in shipyards on five additional Carnival vessels. This does not count the many additional vessels—in active service and under construction—of Carnival's various subsidiaries. It represented a legacy nobody could have predicted on the afternoon of March 11, 1972, when the United States Coast Guard was called in Miami and told that a secondhand ocean liner named *Mardi Gras* had gone hard aground on a sandbar off Miami Beach at the start of her very first cruise.

The winged funnel of Carnival Cruise Lines atop the very first vessel to feature the now-classic design, *Tropicale*. In 2001, *Tropicale* is scheduled to be shifted to Costa Crociere, a subsidiary company of Carnival Corporation.

CHAPTER 4

Royal Caribbean International

To understand how the cruise company known today as Royal Caribbean International came to be, one must go back to south Florida and November 1965, when *Yarmouth Castle* tragically caught fire and sank. Edwin Stephan was the general manager of Yarmouth Steamship Company, and the days following the disaster must have been especially difficult for him. Half the company's fleet was on the bottom of the ocean and its remaining vessel, *Yarmouth*, was a sister ship of the lost vessel; her very appearance could not help but recall the awful disaster.

Edwin Stephan, though, was a man of vision. Born in Wisconsin and a veteran of the Korean War, Stephan had been making a name for himself in the Florida hotel business when he decided to shift careers and move into the cruise industry. Following the demise of Yarmouth Steamship, Stephan joined a new company, Commodore Cruise Line, and helped that agency introduce a vessel called *Boheme* to the Florida cruise market.

Boheme had been built in Finland in 1968 as the open-water car ferry *Aida*, but she was converted into a full-fledged cruise ship before entering service. *Boheme* would remain in Florida service for Commodore for over twenty years and the company would become a small but stable component of the North American cruise industry. Edwin Stephan, on the other hand, left Commodore after supervising the entry of the new vessel into service. (For more on Commodore Cruise Line, see chapter 9.)

Stephan had a much grander idea he wanted to pursue, one that dated back to his days with Yarmouth Steamship and which far transcended the limited scope of operation Commodore Cruise Line had in mind. Stephan saw a new company, adequately capitalized, that would operate a fleet of new and imaginatively designed cruise ships out of Miami on steady Caribbean itineraries all year round. His planned marketing strategy would not confine its customer base primarily to Florida residents, as companies like Yarmouth Steamship did, but would tap the virtually unlimited market made possible by jet airliners, selling cruise vacation packages that included air travel to and from Miami. Jet airplanes may have been responsible for destroying the economic viability of oceangoing passenger ships as basic transportation, but Stephan felt they were critical to the development of a new style of ocean travel—leisure-oriented cruises out of Miami.

In late 1967, while he was still associated with Commodore, Stephan traveled to Norway, that land of seafarers located diagonally across the North Atlantic from Miami, in search of investors who might see merit in his ideas. The scope of Stephan's proposal was so far reaching that it took the combined backing of three Norwegian investors to finance and launch what soon came to be called Royal Caribbean Cruise Line (RCCL).

The first of the trio of investors was I. M. Skaugen, S/A, a second-generation maritime company then controlled by the sons of its founder, Isak Martinius Skaugen. Because the Skaugen company had considerable experience building and operating oceangoing vessels, its role in Stephan's new cruise company—besides providing a one-third share of necessary investment capital—involved vessel design, construction, and operation. For example, a Skaugen professional, Martin Hallen, served as naval architect for Royal Caribbean's first vessels and became a fixture with the new cruise company for many years.

The second investor was the Oslo firm of Anders Wilhelmsen and Company. Founded by Anders Wilhelmsen just before the Second World War and run in the late 1960s by his two sons, Arne and Gjert, the Wilhelmsen firm supplemented its financial investment in Stephan's new venture with hands-on accounting and management expertise.

The third partner was Gotaas-Larsen Shipping Corporation. Originally a joint venture of Trygve Gotaas and Harry Larsen, the company later became a subsidiary of the Toronto-based International Utilities Corporation and grew into a maritime conglomerate of international dimension. Gotaas-Larsen owned one of the world's largest bulk cargo fleets, for instance. In July 1969, shortly before it joined Skaugen and Wilhelmsen as an investor in Stephan's new Royal Caribbean operation, Gotaas-Larsen added to its corporate holdings by acquiring an existing cruise company, Eastern Steamship, whose cruise ship *Bahama Star* came to the aid of *Yarmouth Castle* on the night that vessel caught fire and sank in the Northeast Providence Channel.

What was then called Eastern Shipping Corporation made its entry into the south Florida cruise business in 1954. When its founder, Frank Leslie Fraser, passed away in 1962, the company was sold to Florida businessman W. R. Lovett. The new owner changed the company's name to Eastern Steamship and replaced the "F" (for Fraser) on the vessel's funnels with an "L" (for Lovett), but after the loss of *Yarmouth Castle* he grew concerned that a similar disaster to an

Eastern vessel could impact his other Florida business interests, which were substantial. Thus when Gotaas-Larsen offered to purchase Eastern in 1969, Lovett was more than willing to sell.

There are two conflicting interpretations of this transaction. One holds that Gotaas-Larsen's acquisition of Eastern was independent of the creation of Royal Caribbean and that Gotaas-Larsen was sought out as a potential investor in Stephan's new venture simply because additional capital was required. A different view suggests that Gotaas-Larsen acquired Eastern solely as a bargaining chip to gain access to the new Royal Caribbean enterprise and that it was potential competition from an expanded Eastern Steamship that forced the other partners to bring Gotaas-Larsen aboard, even though doing so was not their original intent.

In any event, once Gotaas-Larsen signed on with the other Royal Caribbean investors later in 1969, it was agreed that its Eastern Steamship subsidiary would never expand beyond two ships. Unlike Skaugen and Wilhelmsen, who both played active roles in the management of Royal Caribbean, Gotaas-Larsen would be an investment partner only.

Because Stephan had such a lofty vision of the kind of cruise company he wanted to establish, there was no aspect of Royal Caribbean's initial business and operational plans that did not require extensive work to lay out, develop, and implement: marketing, reservations, ticketing, corporate identification, staffing, training, uniforms, routes and schedules, onboard food and beverage services, plus ways to deal with the many contingencies that can bring instant chaos to any well-crafted plan. No single aspect of the company's early work, however, was quite as important as designing and building a fleet of new cruise ships.

Stephan was adamant that the new Royal Caribbean needed three vessels from the outset, or, if not from day one, then as quickly as they could be built. One would be assigned to seven-night cruise service between Miami and St. Thomas—the milk run—while the other two would sail fourteen-night itineraries from Miami to islands farther down the Caribbean chain. This way, each weekend would see two Royal Caribbean departures from Miami, one of seven-nights duration, the other of fourteen.

The three vessels were built in Helsinki at the Wartsila yard. While most European shipbuilders had turned away from the construction of passenger ships by the late 1960s, Wartsila had retained expertise in this area by virtue of orders for car ferries of various kinds over the years. The first of Stephan's new ships was christened *Song of Norway,* the second *Nordic Prince,* and the third *Sun Viking,* names chosen to evoke the Norwegian heritage that Royal Caribbean would always seek to maintain. *Song of Norway* inaugurated the Royal Caribbean era when she carried her first revenue passengers out of Miami on November 7, 1970.

Nordic Prince entered service several months later in mid-1971, and *Sun Viking* arrived in 1973. Officers from the Norwegian merchant marine commanded all three vessels; each ship showed Oslo as its port of registry and proudly flew the Norwegian postal banner, a swallow-tailed version of Norway's traditional national ensign that was long used by vessels carrying the country's mail.

The design of *Song of Norway* and her two sister ships can be seen as a transition between the classic ocean liners of yesteryear and a typical cruise ship of the early twenty-first century, although the new Royal Caribbean vessels are far closer to contemporary cruise ships than to ocean liners. *Song of Norway*'s prow had a very pronounced rake and her hull was compounded with far more curvature than would later be common in the cruise industry. There was a perceptible degree of sheer to her hull and she also had a gracefully rounded stern, a design feature that RCCL not only included in its first cruise ships, but retained long after more boxy transoms became common in the industry.

The new Royal Caribbean vessels reflected the conventional wisdom of the day as to the ideal size for a cruise ship. *Song of Norway* was 552 feet long and

One of Royal Caribbean's original trio of vessels was the 1971-built *Nordic Prince*, shown here following a 1980 "stretching" procedure that added 85 feet to her original length of 552 feet. Royal Caribbean's Viking Crown Lounge can be seen on the aft end of the vessel's funnel. The stack visible on the left is that of Celebrity's *Meridian*.

could accommodate 754 passengers under the usual assumption of two passengers to a cabin, 876 if all available berths were occupied; she required a crew of 325 and had a gross registered tonnage of 18,416. *Song of Norway* could make twenty-one knots and was powered by four 9-cylinder Sulzer diesels that were mechanically geared to a pair of controllable-pitch propellers. *Nordic Prince* and *Sun Viking* were identical to *Song of Norway* in most measurements and specifications, ever-so-slightly different in others.

Clearly, the most visually distinctive feature of *Song of Norway* and her sisters was something that came from the imagination of Edwin Stephan—a glass-enclosed, circular lounge that was built right into the funnel of the ship and was called the Viking Crown Lounge. Stephan first developed the idea for this unusual feature after a trip to the Seattle World's Fair in 1962. There, he saw the unique Space Needle, a structure that included a revolving circular lounge at its top. The Viking Crown Lounge on Royal Caribbean cruise ships is stationary and does not revolve, but ironically enough, the Seattle World's Fair also played a role in the early development of another major North American cruise company, Princess Cruises (see chapter 5).

Viking Crown Lounges will become a distinctive identification for this company. On *Song of Norway,* only two dozen passengers could comfortably occupy the lounge at one time, while aboard the 1999-built *Voyager of the Seas,* the lounge accommodates 335 people. Viking Crown Lounges will be incorporated into every cruise ship RCCL builds or acquires. Most will be fabricated into and around the funnel itself, but in a few cases, the lounge will be built as a separate structure adjacent to the funnel.

The three new Royal Caribbean cruise ships proved to be popular and profitable as they turned Edwin Stephan's vision into a functioning reality. One deviation from the original plan resulted from the recognition of a substantially stronger market for seven-night cruises and a lesser demand for the fourteen-night voyages. RCCL revised its schedules, and seven-night cruises assumed a much larger role in the company's cruise offerings.

After less than a decade of successful and profitable operation, the new cruise company was ready for its first dose of expansion. Business was good, but so was the competition. Standing pat was not a reasonable option.

RCCL's initial expansion involved something that had never been done before with an oceangoing passenger ship. *Song of Norway* and *Nordic Prince* were sent back to Helsinki. Wartsila proceeded to cut the vessels in two and splice a new prebuilt hull section into each ship, adding more passenger cabins. This was a common enough thing to do with cargo ships, but the added complexity of a passenger vessel made it a far more exacting procedure. Wartsila came through with flying colors, and following RCCL's lead many other cruise companies have since expanded fleet capacity in a similar fashion. The original engines were ca-

When Royal Caribbean's *Song of America* was built in 1982, she featured the first Viking Crown Lounge, which completely encircled the vessel's funnel.

pable of powering the vessel in its stretched configuration, although to assist with maneuvering, a second bow thruster was added as part of the overall project.

Song of Norway's overall length was thus increased from 550 to 635 feet, and her passenger capacity was expanded from 754 to 1,082. The vessel was out of service for this work from August 19 through December 16, 1977, and most observers felt the lengthened *Song of Norway* had a more graceful profile than did the original. *Nordic Prince* underwent similar surgery between March and June of 1980, and while RCCL never sent *Sun Viking* back to Helsinki to increase her capacity, it was not because the company no longer needed to expand its fleet. It was, rather, because Royal Caribbean had decided to pursue its expansion plans in a different and more dramatic fashion.

In December 1979, before *Nordic Prince* traveled to Helsinki for stretching, the company ordered its fourth vessel, a 31,000-gross-ton cruise ship that would accommodate 1,400 passengers, fully one-third more than the capacity of the stretched *Song of Norway* or *Nordic Prince*, twice as much as the unstretched *Sun Viking*. Built once again at Wartsila's Helsinki yard, the newbuilding was christened *Song of America* and joined the fleet in Miami in early December of 1982.

Royal Caribbean was now a robust twelve-year-old cruise company, one that thanks to this new vessel and the stretching of two older ones had doubled its passenger capacity from the days its initial three cruise ships entered service.

Growth continued in ways that had seemed implausible just a few years earlier. New vessels that joined the fleet were much larger than the original trio, even exceeding the size of *Song of America*. *Sovereign of the Seas* was ordered in 1985 and handed over to RCCL in late December of 1987. She steamed into Miami to begin revenue work in early January 1988. She was christened by Rosalynn Carter, the wife of former president Jimmy Carter, but perhaps more important than the vessel's formal name was the new generic term coined to describe her and similar vessels of all companies that would shortly sail in her wake. *Sovereign of the Seas* was quickly referred to as Royal Caribbean's first megaship.

What makes a ship "mega"? *Sovereign of the Seas* accommodates 2,276 passengers assuming double occupancy, several hundred more, of course, if three- and four-berth capability is considered. *Sovereign* has a gross registered tonnage of 73,129, a measurement that made her the largest passenger ship in the world when she was built in the late 1980s. More tellingly, *Sovereign of the Seas* was the fourth largest passenger vessel of all time, trailing only *Queen Mary*, *Queen Elizabeth*, and *Normandie* in this regard.

Sovereign of the Seas is 880 feet long and 106 feet wide, dimensions adequate to permit passage through the Panama Canal. She was built not in Helsinki by Wartsila (contractor for all previous RCCL vessels) but in St. Nazaire, France, by Chantiers de l'Atlantique, a legendary shipyard whose defining vessel, surely, was French Line's *Normandie* of 1935, one of three historic passengers vessels to exceed *Sovereign* in gross tonnage.

In more recent years, the cruise industry generated considerable publicity as the world's first passenger vessels to exceed of 100,000 gross tons were built and introduced into service. No recent size increment, though, was quite so dramatic as that which *Sovereign of the Seas*, the cruise industry's first megaship, represented when she appeared in late 1987. A new passenger ship had been designed, built, and placed in service that was at least in some respects comparable to, and legitimately able to be discussed in terms of, *Normandie*, *Queen Mary*, and *Queen Elizabeth*. Ten years earlier, the most optimistic advocates of the cruise industry would have been hard pressed to predict that such a development would ever come to pass.

Sovereign of the Seas brought one modest decorative change to the RCCL fleet. Previous ships, from *Song of Norway* through *Song of America*, had featured white hulls with modest blue trim. *Sovereign* has much less trim, and what she has is green to match the tint of her many windows. The only blue decoration is a large illuminated graphic of the company's crown and anchor logo placed just be-

Royal Caribbean's *Sovereign of the Seas* heads down the River Loire from the Chantiers de l'Atlantique shipyard in St. Nazaire, France, where she was built. When the vessel took to the seas in 1987, her 73,129 gross registered tons made her the largest passenger ship in the world.

low her funnel. This would become standard for subsequent RCCL-designed newbuildings.

Despite the entry of *Sovereign of the Seas* into service in early 1988, Royal Caribbean's year would be marked by developments in a very different area. These posed a serious threat to the existence of the company and threatened the three-way financial partnership that was the very foundation of the company.

Gotaas-Larsen not only continued to control Eastern Steamship, it combined this operation with a California service it established in 1980 called Western Steamship. Western's specialty was three- and four-night cruises out of Los Angeles to Ensenada, Mexico. A veteran ocean liner that had been launched in Belfast in 1954 as *Southern Cross* worked for Western Steamship as *Azure Seas.*

In 1968, the year before it was taken over by Gotaas-Larsen, Eastern had retired *Bahama Star* and replaced her with a vessel initially called *New Bahama Star*, although she soon reverted to the simpler name *Bahama Star.* A second vessel that long worked for Eastern Steamship was called *Ariadne.*

In 1972, the 6,644-gross-ton *Ariadne* was sold to Chandris, while at the same time Chandris transferred a much larger ship to Eastern, a vessel that Eastern christened *Emerald Seas*. The second *Bahama Star* was withdrawn in 1975 when she was no longer able to meet applicable international safety standards. *Emerald Seas* began life as a U.S. troop transport during the Second World War and worked for a number of different steamship companies afterward.

Eventually, Gotaas-Larsen combined Eastern Steamship and Western Steamship under the banner of a new company called Admiral Cruises. *Emerald Seas* continued to work the new company's Florida service. The one-time *Southern Cross* was replaced on the West Coast by a vessel which had been built in 1981 for DFDS Seaways as the open-water car ferry *Scandinavia*, but which proved singularly unsuccessful when DFDS attempted to establish a New York–Florida car ferry service in the early 1980s. Prevailing U.S. law prohibited the foreign-flag *Scandinavia* from operating directly between New York and Florida. Passengers and their automobiles were required to change vessels in the Bahamas.

Scandinavia was renamed *Stardancer* and after a short tenure working on the West Coast for a company called Sundance Cruises, she was used by Admiral in split-week service between Los Angeles and Ensenada in the winter and on longer cruises to Alaska in the summer. This service put her capability as a car ferry to good use hauling campers, travel trailers, and other kinds of recreational vehicles. In fact, Gotaas-Larsen's combining of Eastern and Western Steamship to form Admiral was actually a three-way merger, with Sundance Cruises and *Stardancer* also being a party to the arrangement.

Because of Gotaas-Larsen's interests in both Admiral and Royal Caribbean, in early 1988 a merger, of sorts, was proposed and consummated. The smaller Admiral and the larger Royal Caribbean would continue to operate as separate cruise brands, but a new company called Royal Admiral Cruises would coordinate the operations of its two subsidiaries. Admiral had even contracted with Chantiers de l'Atlantique to replace the veteran *Emerald Seas* with a newbuilding, a vessel that was to bear the name *Future Seas*. This would be the first vessel designed and built specifically for three- and four-night split-week cruise service. Admiral, in other words, was anxious to move out of the bargainbasement category of cruise operations and carve a niche for itself in the growing mass market. Before all parties could begin to sort out the implications of the creation of Royal Admiral, something unexpected happened.

In *Under Crown and Anchor*, a marvelous 1995 book commemorating the twenty-fifth anniversary of Royal Caribbean, authors John Maxtone-Graham and Bard Kolltveit refer to a forty-day period in the summer of 1988 as "an unforeseen seismic upheaval" in the life of the company. Royal Caribbean Cruise Line—successful, innovative, and pioneering as it surely had been—found itself under a threat that was as serious as it was sudden. A future that was rosy and optimistic one day became uncertain and insecure the next, at least from the perspective of Royal Caribbean Cruise Line.

Royal Caribbean's *Nordic Empress,* a vessel that was designed by Admiral Cruises.

The financial backing that Edwin Stephan had secured to start the company in 1970 came from three separate sources: Anders Wilhelmsen and Company, I.M. Skaugen S/A, and Gotaas-Larsen Shipping Corporation. Of the three partners, Gotaas-Larsen was the only publicly traded company, a fact that served to make important financial information about the company matters of common knowledge. Once his people had reviewed Gotaas-Larsen's fiscal position in detail, Carnival's Ted Arison felt the time was right to advance a proposal to acquire the company's stake in Royal Caribbean. After reviewing Arison's offer, Gotaas-Larsen agreed to sell for $260 million, a decision that was made public on August 6, 1988.

By virtue of the contractual instruments that had been crafted in 1970 to create Royal Caribbean, the investment partners enjoyed a right of first refusal should any of them choose to entertain a purchase offer. That is to say if Wilhelmsen and Skaugen could match Carnival's $260 million bid for the Gotaas-Larsen stake in Royal Caribbean, either together or separately, they would retain full control of the company and keep the interloper at bay. Except Skaugen was itself in a weakened financial position and just days after RCCL was shocked by the news of the proposed Carnival buyout of the Gotaas-Larsen share of the company, Skaugen announced that it, too, had agreed to sell its share of Royal Caribbean to Carnival for $232 million. The unequal offer to each of the partners reflected the fact that following the Admiral–Royal Caribbean merger, the three-way partnership was no longer an equal one.

Two partners raising $260 million to thwart the proposed buyout of the Gotaas-Larsen share was one thing. But one partner having to raise virtually twice that much—over half a billion dollars—to forestall Carnival's initiative was quite another matter. To make matters even more difficult, the contractual agreement provided a very narrow window for any partner to convert this right of first refusal into an alternative purchase—thirty days to arrange the deal and forty days to complete the financing. The Wilhelmsens clearly had their work cut out for them.

As Maxtone-Graham and Kolltveit describe in wonderful detail, the Wilhelmsens were able to raise the needed capital and exercise their right to match Carnival's twin offers to purchase both the Gotaas-Larsen and the Skaugen interests in Royal Caribbean. The money came from two sources. The Pritzker family of Chicago, founding owners of the Hyatt hotel chain, became one of the new RCCL investors, while Israeli shipowner Sammy Offer became the other. It was a complicated transaction involving various borrowings and the transfer of equities. But on November 4, 1988, both Skaugen and Gotaas-Larsen received payment in full for their share of Royal Caribbean and the crisis was over. RCCL thus was able to remain an independent company and not become affiliated in any fashion with Arison's Carnival operation. Those forty days in the summer of 1988 before the Carnival offer was matched represented a rare period of uncertainty for Royal Caribbean, a proud company that had developed a unique and distinctive presence in the North American cruise industry. Thanks to the Wilhelmsens' faith in the company, Royal Caribbean was able to retain its independence.

Arison and Carnival quickly demonstrated, though, that their plans for expansion through the acquisition of other cruise properties were both real and serious, one might even say inevitable. Later in November 1988, Carnival announced a $625 million purchase of Holland America Line, a transaction completed on January 16, 1989, that will be discussed in chapter 7. Gotaas-Larsen, on the other hand, turned around and in that same November promptly negotiated a merger with a British firm, GL Acquisition Corporation, to strengthen its position in the bulk carrier trade.

For RCCL, the ability of the Wilhelmsens to put together a new group of investors to take over both the Gotaas-Larsen and the Skaugen interests in the company was critical to the company's survival and subsequent growth as an independent force in the industry. Following Gotaas-Larsen's departure, earlier plans to retain separate Royal Caribbean and Admiral operations under a combined Royal Admiral Corporation were dropped and Admiral was wholly absorbed into RCCL. Admiral's *Stardancer* was transferred to RCCL, renamed *Viking Serenade,* and rebuilt with more cabins and, of course, a Viking Crown Lounge. The Admiral newbuilding planned as *Future Seas* was completed as RCCL's *Nordic Empress.* She, too, had a Viking Crown Lounge added to her upper deck, but because design and construction work was too far along, the trademark lounge had to be positioned behind and adjacent to the vessel's funnel, not interlocked within it. *Viking Serenade*'s lounge is of a similar design. Both *Viking*

Serenade and *Nordic Empress* reverted to the decorative scheme in use before *Sovereign of the Seas:* white hulls with modest blue striping.

With both *Viking Serenade* and *Nordic Empress* now in the fleet, Royal Caribbean, for the first time, began to offer shorter cruises, those of less than a week's duration. On the West Coast, *Viking Serenade* ran three- and four-night cruises out of San Pedro/Los Angeles to Ensenada, Mexico, with additional stops at San Diego and Catalina Island. *Nordic Empress* took over the three- and four-night Bahamas routes that *Emerald Seas* had been operating for Admiral: these included the out-island stop at Little Stirrup Cay in the Berry Islands, which Admiral had established in 1983. RCCL renamed this destination Coco Cay.

Coco Cay, incidentally, is adjacent to Great Stirrup Cay, the original private out-island developed by Norwegian Caribbean Line in 1980. Both islands are but a short distance from the spot in Northeast Providence Channel where *Yarmouth Castle* caught fire and sank in 1965.

Following the delivery of *Sovereign of the Sea,* in 1987—and the resolution of the company's ownership status the following year—Royal Caribbean embarked on a newbuilding program that was nothing short of breathtaking in its scope.

Legend of the Seas calls at the port of Olbia on the Mediterranean island of Sardinia.

Viking Serenade is the former car ferry *Scandinavia* that was built in 1981 to inaugurate a New York–Florida service. The vessel joined the Royal Caribbean fleet in 1988 when RCCL acquired the assets of Admiral Cruises.

Two additional Sovereign-class vessels were delivered by Chantiers de l'Atlantique: *Monarch of the Seas* in 1991 and *Majesty of the Seas* in 1992. Then, over a period of three years, six new megaships would be delivered from two builders, Chantiers de l'Atlantique in St. Nazaire and Kvaerner Masa-Yards in Helsinki, the successor of Wartsila. Within RCCL, the sextet of newbuildings were referred to as Project Vision, a term that referred to the extensive use of glass in each vessel's superstructure.

The six new ships are slightly smaller than the three Sovereign-class vessels and include interesting differences between and among them. They can be thought of as three sets of two sister ships. Tellingly, two of the Project Vision vessels include twenty-four-knot speed capability to permit their serving more extended cruise itineraries. Royal Caribbean was poised to emerge from the Caribbean of its origin and deploy its fleet in such faraway venues as the Baltic Sea, the Mediterranean, even the South Pacific, and the company needed vessels with more robust speed to do so successfully.

Project Vision vessels were the first in the Royal Caribbean fleet to feature diesel-electric power, a propulsion system that was quickly becoming the industry's new standard, especially for larger vessels. The Chantiers-built *Legend of the Seas* and *Splendour of the Seas*—the two vessels with twenty-four-knot speed capability—feature engines that are positioned amidships. The reason for this is technical, but it produced a fortunate combination of circumstances that allowed something altogether remarkable to be incorporated into the design of passenger facilities aboard the two vessels.

The engines could be placed amidships because with diesel-electric propulsion they no longer had to be aligned and positioned delicately and precisely with respect to the propeller shafts; rather they could be placed virtually anywhere, and electricity would be routed to the driving motors from the generators attached to the diesel engines by flexible cable. In point of engineering fact, the heftier engines required to achieve higher speed were placed amidships because of balancing factors associated with their heavier weight, plus the added fuel and water capacity that such speed capability demanded.

The three Sovereign-class vessels—as well as the one-of-a-kind *Nordic Empress*—had earlier introduced the concept of a large multideck atrium aboard RCCL cruise ships. (This elegantly decorated open central area within the vessel functions as a crossroads for passengers as they make their way from one section of the ship to another. On RCCL ships, this atrium is called the Centrum.) The engines on *Legend* and *Splendour* were positioned amidships, so each ship's funnel was necessarily positioned above the engines. This meant the funnel was also atop the Centrum. And as the Viking Crown Lounge incorporated within the funnel wound up over the Centrum, the glass elevators that ran up and down within the atrium were able to continue upward to provide access to the trademark lounge.

This was quite an evolution from *Song of Norway* and her two sister ships, where the only way to reach the Viking Crown Lounge was by means of a steep outdoor stairway that bore more than a little similarity to a ladder. So pleased was Royal Caribbean with the notion of a Viking Crown Lounge atop the atrium that on the four "slower" Project Vision vessels that feature a more conventional arrangement with engines and stack located aft—*Vision of the Seas, Rhapsody of the Seas, Enchantment of the Seas,* and *Grandeur of the Seas*—the lounge was left amidships atop the Centrum, even though this meant it could not be incorporated within the stack, as had long been RCCL practice and preference.

The two twenty-four-knot Project Vision ships—*Legend* and *Splendour*—are products of Chantiers de l'Atlantique; Chantiers also turned out two of the twenty-one-knot Project Vision ships, *Rhapsody* and *Vision*. The third pair, *Grandeur* and *Enchantment*, were built in Helsinki at Kvaerner Masa-Yards.

As these new vessels joined the fleet, RCCL expanded its itineraries away from the steady Caribbean routes that Edwin Stephan had originally developed. Seasonal service between New York and Bermuda as well as Alaskan routes out

Legend of the Seas makes her way into Juneau amidst a low-lying Alaskan mist. Note how the vessel's Viking Crown Lounge has been incorporated into the funnel.

of Vancouver had previously been added to the company's offerings. In the early 1990s, RCCL began deploying the smaller *Sun Viking* on winter cruises in the Far East. In later years, *Sun Viking*'s pioneering cruises in Asian waters would be expanded and handed over to the larger and faster vessels from Project Vision. Eventually, something the company called Royal Journeys would be implemented: longer, nonrepetitive cruise itineraries to far corners of the world that are more akin to upscale cruise company offerings than to mass-market routes. Meanwhile, other Royal Caribbean ships began to show the company flag in the Mediterranean, on Baltic cruises, around the British Isles, through the Panama Canal, and elsewhere.

Understandably, the company's older ships ultimately became a liability and Royal Caribbean began to look for opportunities that would allow it to sell off vessels like *Nordic Prince* and *Song of Norway* to other cruise operators. *Sun Viking* went to Star Cruises in the Far East and became *SuperStar Sagittarius,* while her two sister ships, along with *Song of America,* were sold to Airtours, a British tour operator that was eager to build up a cruise fleet of its own, rather than book tour passengers aboard cruise vessels of independent companies as had been its previous practice.

Interestingly enough, Airtours is partially owned by Carnival Corporation, so in a sense it can be said that the acquisition of Royal Caribbean and its vessels that Carnival attempted to engineer in 1988 was partially achieved in the late 1990s when three secondhand RCCL cruise ships were sold off to Airtours. When RCCL first began to dispose of its vessels, a contractual requirement was incorporated into the sales agreements, stipulating that the trademark Viking Crown Lounge had to be removed and dismantled. More recently, though, the company has been less demanding and both *Sun Viking* and *Song of America* left the fleet with their distinctive lounges intact. On a vessel that Airtours calls *Sunbird*—the former *Song of America*—the lounge is called the Chart Room. (Other equipment from *Song of Norway* was removed and has been incorporated into the Wilhelmsen family's summer complex on an island outside Oslo.)

In 1999, Royal Caribbean took delivery of the first vessel of a truly radical class of newbuildings that were initially designated Project Eagle. Built in Turku, Finland, at the Kvaerner Masa-Yards, a ship called *Voyager of the Seas* measured an almost impossible to comprehend 137,276 gross tons, with stateroom accommodations for 3,114 passengers. *Voyager* exceeds the size of the previous world record holder, the year-old *Grand Princess*, by an amazing 28,000 gross tons. *Voyager of the Seas*, all by herself, is more than twice as large as all three of the vessels that inaugurated RCCL service in the early 1970s. Not twice as big as any one of the three ships, but twice as big as all three put together. Needless to say, *Voyager of the Seas* has been built to post-Panamax dimensions. With her arrival, Royal Caribbean decided to drop the Project Eagle name and call the new class of superships, appropriately enough, Project Voyager.

Press releases issued by Royal Caribbean at the time *Voyager of the Seas* entered service stressed such unusual features as the first ice-skating rink ever built aboard a cruise ship and also the first rock-climbing wall. (The wall is affixed to the after end of the vessel's funnel.) Apart from the marketing value of a cruise company's being able to boast that it owns and operates the largest passenger vessel of all time, there is a tremendous economy of scale at work in the cruise industry. It costs less money to carry 3,000 passengers aboard one vessel than it does to carry 1,500 aboard two, and much less than to carry 1,000 aboard three. Even the enormous capital investment such massive vessels require—*Voyager of the Seas* was said to have cost $500 million—is less on a per-passenger basis than it would be for equivalent carrying capacity in multiple hulls. Indeed it is the continued validity and reaffirmation of this fundamental economic truth that is the root of all the growth and development Royal Caribbean has experienced over the years, everything from the decision to stretch *Song of Norway* to the construction of *Song of America*, *Sovereign of the Seas*, and, ultimately, *Voyager of the Seas.*

When she entered service out of Miami's Dodge Island on November 21, 1999, from a brand-new multimillion cruise terminal built especially for Project

Enchantment of the Seas lies at anchor in the Caribbean while passengers are transported to shore by tender. Courtesy Roger J. Cudahy.

Voyager vessels, *Voyager of the Seas* was placed on a steady, year-round western Caribbean itinerary. Her Viking Crown Lounge is located within the ship's funnel and, like the vessels of Project Vision, it is accessible by glass elevators that run up and down inside the Centrum, which in this case is fourteen decks high.

Project Voyager vessels—eventually there will be as many as five—have not only a Centrum in the area directly beneath their funnel and a Viking Crown Lounge, they also have a second Centrum located further forward. In addition, what may be the most dramatic single feature of *Voyager* is a "horizontal atrium" that is four decks high. This connects the forward atrium to the after one and is nothing less than a stylish indoor boulevard. At the "street level" of this thoroughfare, which is called Royal Promenade, are found shops and sidewalk cafes. And just as along a real urban thoroughfare, looking down on the streetscape from above are three decks of bay windows on passenger cabins. Though technically "interior" cabins, on this magnificent vessel they are able to command a view, not of the sea, to be sure, but of the action along Royal Promenade.

In addition to their extraordinary size, Project Voyager vessels have other unique features. They are diesel-electric powered, and propulsion is achieved by a set of three Azipod units. The central Azipod is fixed and does not rotate, while port and starboard units are fully-azimuthal and provide directional control for the vessel in addition to propulsion. During her 1999 sea trials in the Gulf of Finland, *Voyager of the Seas* was able to record these impressive performance achievements: forward speed, twenty-five knots; speed astern, seventeen knots; speed *sideways,* three knots. (It might be suggested that *Voyager of the Seas* now holds the world speed record for sideways travel by an oceangoing passenger vessel!) Technical experts believe that were it not for the flexibility provided by her pod-propulsion system, *Voyager of the Seas* would never be able to enter many of the Caribbean ports where she now calls regularly. One feature of *Voyager of the Seas* is a throwback to *Song of Norway* and other early RCCL cruise ships: she sports blue striping along her sides.

As Edwin Stephan quickly found back in the 1970s after he had successfully introduced Royal Caribbean's first three vessels into service out of Miami, growth and development are continuous necessities in the cruise industry. In 1997, a merger was announced. Royal Caribbean had acquired a smaller company, Celebrity Cruises. Rather than merge its operations into the larger company, Celebrity was retained as a separate cruise brand, even though certain management and overhead functions were combined in the interests of efficiency. (See chapter 9.)

The design of new cruise ships was one area where Royal Caribbean and Celebrity achieved important benefits of a cooperative sort. Consequently, what Celebrity calls its Millennium-class vessels—and Royal Caribbean dubbed Project Vantage—includes two designs with many common features. Compared to Project Voyager, Project Vantage involves a smaller vessel. Smaller in this case means approximately 85,000 gross tons, vessels that will still be larger, for example, than almost all of the famous transatlantic ocean liners of yesteryear.

Celebrity's Millennium-class and Royal Caribbean's Project Vantage vessels will have hulls with common dimensions. They will feature gas turbine power and pod propulsion, and they will include an abundance of cabins with balconies as well as a variety of other novel features. Royal Caribbean's first of the new breed, *Radiance of the Seas,* will be built at Meyer Werft in Papenburg, Germany. This is Royal Caribbean's first newbuilding from this shipyard, and she is scheduled to enter service in 2001. Celebrity's *Millennium* was the first of either class to be completed. She was built in St. Nazaire at Chantiers de l'Atlantique and ran her initial cruise out of Rotterdam in the summer of 2000.

Royal Caribbean Cruise Line has followed an interesting path from the day in 1970 when the 18,416-gross-ton *Song of Norway* entered service with a capacity of 754 passengers, to the 1999 arrival of the 137,276-gross-ton *Voyager of the Seas,* with a capacity of 3,114 passengers. The company has successfully introduced sixteen vessels into cruise service, all but two designed and built by Royal Caribbean itself, and it plans to continue to upgrade and expand its fleet in the

Form the small, semicircular facility found on its original vessels, Royal Caribbean's signature Viking Crown Lounge evolved into a larger and more dramatic design feature on later ships.

early years of the twenty-first century by taking delivery of additional new-buildings.

In early 2000, Royal Caribbean announced expansion of a different sort. It acquired an interest in a European-based cruise-tour company called First Choice and plans to move a renamed *Viking Serenade* to Europe to work in conjunction with its newest acquisition.

To emphasize its new and expanded dimensions, the cruise operating company is now called Royal Caribben International (RCI). The parent company of both RCI and Celebrity Cruises calls itself Royal Caribbean Cruise, Ltd., thus preserving the familiar RCCL abbreviation that Edwin Stephan inaugurated many years ago.

CHAPTER 5

Princess Cruises

While cruises were growing in popularity in south Florida in the mid-to-late 1960s, there was little equivalent service available on the West Coast of the United States. True, each summer passenger vessels headed north from Vancouver, British Columbia, to explore the southeast coast of Alaska, but these were more ferry services operated by the likes of Canadian Pacific and Canadian National, not the kind of luxury cruise operations available in the Caribbean. People sailing to Alaska in the 1960s usually packed sleeping bags and hiking boots, not tuxedos and evening gowns.

Something that later proved to be important happened in 1962. With the Seattle World's Fair scheduled to open that summer, Canadian businessman Stanley B. McDonald had an idea. Since hotel and motel reservations were likely to be at a premium in the Seattle area, why not find a passenger vessel of some kind—a ship that people could sleep aboard—and run ten-day package tours to the fair, perhaps from San Francisco? And that is exactly what McDonald did.

The ship he acquired was the coastal steamer *Yarmouth*, sister ship of the ill-fated *Yarmouth Castle*. Because *Yarmouth* no longer flew the U.S. flag but was registered in Panama, McDonald had to include a stop en route at Victoria, British Columbia, to respect relevant provisions of the Passenger Vessel Services Act of 1886 prohibiting foreign-flag vessels from carrying passengers between U.S. ports exclusively.

It all worked out reasonably well and while McDonald sent *Yarmouth* back to Florida at the conclusion of the 1962 summer season, the experience whetted his appetite for the passenger cruise business. Two years later he was ready for another venture.

In the fall of 1964, McDonald chartered one of the coastal vessels that Canadian Pacific operated between Vancouver and Alaska in summer months and brought her south, together with her Canadian crew, to work from Los Angeles to ports along the Pacific Coast of Mexico in the winter. The vessel CP agreed to lease McDonald was the four-hundred-passenger coastal steamship *Princess Patricia,* and because of this happenstance of nomenclature McDonald decided to call his new venture Princess Cruises. Ironic in the extreme is the fact that two of today's major North American cruise companies—Princess and Carnival—began their respective services with one-time Canadian Pacific vessels. (Carnival's *Mardi Gras,* formerly the *Empress of Canada,* was part of CP's oceangoing steamship division. *Princess Patricia,* a coastal steamboat, was operated by Canadian Pacific Railroad. When the new CP multimark form of corporate identification was applied to *Princess Patricia,* it was in the railroad's colors, not those of the steamship division.)

Princess Pat, as she was popularly called, had her share of teething problems when she went to work for McDonald. Onboard air-conditioning, unnecessary for summer service to Alaska but important in Mexican waters, had to be provided. McDonald installed small "window" units in individual cabins but failure to include proper drainage for the moisture they wrung out of the humid Mexican atmosphere caused havoc with passengers' belongings. Perhaps the funniest story from the first year of service by Princess Cruises involved an effort to send out several bundles of laundry to a facility in Acapulco, Mexico, in the middle of a cruise. When the company picked up the dirty laundry at the pier, it was prop-

Canadian Pacific's *Princess Patricia* of 1949, a vessel designed for seasonal coastal service between Vancouver, British Columbia, and Alaska, became the first ship to sail for the new Princess Cruises. Courtesy of The Mariners' Museum, Newport News, Virginia.

erly segregated—ship's laundry in large bags, the laundry of individual passengers in a number of smaller bags. When the finished laundry was returned to *Princess Patricia*, however, it was all neatly combined into one huge shipment.

It probably never happened again in the history of the cruise industry, but passengers aboard *Princess Pat* gathered in the dining room that evening for a most unusual onboard game—Sort the Laundry. One can just hear the cruise director asking, "Does anyone recognize this little . . . ah, whatever it is?"

During its first two years, Princess Cruises was a seasonal operation only; *Princess Patricia* and her crew returned to Canadian Pacific for summer service to Alaska after both the 1964–65 and 1965–66 winter seasons. Anxious to convert his cruise operation into a year-round business, McDonald went shopping for a vessel to replace *Princess Pat*. What he found was a sleek, new, and almost yachtlike cruise ship whose intended owner had run into financial difficulty. The vessel, the 12,218-gross-ton *Italia*, was then in the hands of an Italian bank, and in 1967 McDonald leased her from the bank. Called *Princess Italia* and brought to California, she set sail on her first cruise for McDonald on December 15, 1967. The lease agreement included not only the vessel but also her Italian crew.

The following year, 1968, saw McDonald arrange the lease of a second ship, the 19,975-gross-ton *Carla C.*, a vessel that began life in 1952 as French Line's transatlantic liner *Flandre* but had recently been acquired by Costa Line. She was called *Princess Carla* for her service with McDonald's company. The Costa people must have been surprised when they learned that the family member who was the vessel's namesake had suddenly entered the ranks of royalty. *Princess Carla* worked her way to Los Angeles and her new assignment on what was called a coronation cruise. She left Nassau on December 4, 1968, and departed from Los Angeles on her first Princess cruise to the Mexican Riviera on December 19. As *Princess Carla* began her new career, her funnel was adorned with the corporate logo that McDonald's company had recently adopted, a stylized image of a woman whose blowing hair resembled ocean waves. The logo has since become permanent and today adorns the funnel of every Princess vessel.

With these two Italian-registered vessels and their Italian crews thus comprising the Princess fleet, McDonald was able to supplement his winter service from southern California to Mexico with itineraries through the Panama Canal, as well as summer sailings to Alaska. On June 3, 1969, *Princess Italia* set sail from San Francisco on the company's very first Alaskan cruise, for example, an itinerary that in later years would become a mainstay for Princess Cruises. The Italian crews on these early Princess vessels would also become a hallmark of the company and to this day there is a distinctly Italian presence among the officers and dining room personnel on many Princess cruise ships.

While Princess referred to the two vessels as *Princess Italia* and *Princess Carla*, they were never formally renamed and remained officially enrolled as *Italia* and

Carla C. For example, *Carla C.* had a large name board positioned on her top deck amidships that read *Princess Carla.* On the vessel's stern, however, her true name showed in much smaller letters as *Carla C.,* home port, Roma.

No sooner had the new vessels been acquired than McDonald was given the proverbial "offer he couldn't refuse." In 1968, the same year *Carla C.* joined the fleet, the Boise-Cascade Corporation, anxious to diversify and expand its holdings, purchased Princess Cruises from McDonald. But the cruise company did not remain in the Boise-Cascade corporate family for long. Two years later in 1970 McDonald repurchased the company and began to upgrade and expand its operations.

A company called Flagship Cruises had designed and built two new vessels in the early 1970s that McDonald thought were simply the last word in contemporary cruise ship design. Indeed McDonald was among the people Flagship had consulted while the two vessels were being designed. This latter-day Flagship Cruises had no corporate relationship with Flagship Lines, the company whose *Viking Princess* caught fire off Cuba in 1966. Flagship Cruises was a joint venture of Olvind Lorentzen and the Norwegian firm of Fearnley and Eger doing business as Norwegian Cruiseships.

Flagship Cruises twin vessels—the 19,903-gross-ton *Sea Venture* and the 19,907-gross-ton *Island Venture*—had been built in West Germany and worked New York–Bermuda and other East Coast cruise itineraries for Flagship. For some reason, the new company was never able to find a comfortable or profitable niche for itself. An option for a third vessel was never exercised and in early 1972, McDonald was able to negotiate a lease for *Island Venture* from Flagship. Brought to the West Coast, renamed *Island Princess,* and later purchased by McDonald, she would reign as the unofficial flagship of the Princess fleet for over a quarter century. The arrival of *Island Princess* in 1972 proved to be fortuitous, though. In 1970 Costa Lines had canceled the charter agreement for *Carla C.,* brought the vessel back to its own fleet, and left McDonald with only *Princess Italia.*

The more success Princess achieved in southern California, the more competitive companies began to feel that this was a cruise market they themselves should be able to penetrate. In early 1973, Great Britain's fabled P&O Lines— the Peninsular and Oriental Steam Navigation Company—dispatched their recently built *Spirit of London* to Los Angeles to compete with McDonald. Originally designed by Knut Kloster for his expanding cruise operation, *Spirit of London* never joined Norwegian Caribbean Line but was purchased instead by P&O.

Nor was P&O the only competitor Princess faced. An Italian-based company called Sitmar—short for Societa Italiana Transporti Marittimi, S.p.A.—had shifted its focus from transoceanic passenger service to cruises in the early 1970s. The company was founded in 1938 by Russian engineer Alexandre Vlasov and managed in later years by his son Boris; the funnels of Sitmar vessels were

Island Princess, a vessel that served as the unofficial flagship of the Princess fleet for many years. Courtesy Garwood Whaley.

decorated with a large blue V. Among the cruise markets Sitmar chose to serve were itineraries to Mexico out of Los Angeles, summer sailings to Alaska, and in later years, winter service to the Caribbean from Port Everglades, Florida. Much of this was in direct competition with Princess. Sitmar also operated cruise service out of Sydney, Australia; that hardly impacted Princess, although it was a service that competed directly with P&O.

Sitmar operated an extraordinarily diverse fleet of passenger vessels over the years, including a pair of ships that were converted from World War II aircraft carriers—small escort carriers, though, not full-size flat tops. By the 1970s, the vessels Sitmar primarily used in its North American cruise service—*Fairland* and *Fairsea*—were the one-time Cunard Line ships *Carinthia* and *Sylvania.*

When the lease of *Italia* reached its term in 1973, McDonald attempted to purchase the vessel outright. He could not reach a satisfactory agreement with the Italian bank that owned the ship, however, and extending the lease was apparently not an option. The Princess "fleet" was again reduced to a single vessel, *Island Princess,* and she was still sailing under the terms of a charter, not yet owned by McDonald. *Italia* was later acquired by Costa, where she joined her one-time Princess fleetmate, *Carla C.*

By the end of the twentieth century, a cruise vessel bearing the name *Flamenco* was working in the fleet of a European company called Festival Cruises. *Flamenco* has an interesting history. Launched in 1972 as P&O's *Spirit of London*, she was later conveyed to Princess and operated for a number of years as *Sun Princess.*

Like many cruise lines, Princess was hit hard by the petroleum crisis of 1973. The company was in need of investment capital to replace *Italia* and expand its operations. Instead, the company was having trouble making payments to fuel dealers whose prices were increasing, often quite literally, hour by hour.

At this potentially troubling moment in the history of Princess Cruises, something very unexpected, yet very fortunate, came to pass. Britain's P&O Lines had been competing with McDonald and with Princess in the Los Angeles market, but the company decided it would make more sense to join forces with its competitor and forge a larger and stronger presence in the southern California cruise market. P&O had ready access to world capital markets and after negotiating the purchase of Princess in 1974, the British company followed up by converting the lease of *Island Princess* into an outright purchase, and also by acquiring, in 1975, the second Flagship vessel that McDonald had always wanted, *Sea Venture. Sea Venture* became *Pacific Princess* and P&O also transferred its own *Spirit of London* to its new subsidiary where she was renamed *Sun Princess.* Princess was now a bona fide fleet of three new vessels.

One thing that P&O's acquisition of Princess did not change was the chief executive officer at Princess Cruises. The purchase agreement included a provision that McDonald would continue to run the company he had founded, and he did so until 1980. The Princess brand name was also retained, although the company's vessels soon came to be decorated with a modest P&O logo below the bridge wing. Princess vessels also flew the P&O company flag.

During the early days of P&O ownership—onward from 1974, in other words—McDonald's company concentrated on a core business of cruises to Mexico out of southern California, summer itineraries to Alaska, and gradual expansion through the Panama Canal and into the Caribbean. Circumstances that involved Princess in 1975, though, may have had more impact on the later growth of the North American cruise industry than anything associated with the core business of Princess Cruises.

Television producer Douglas Cramer approached McDonald with an idea. How would the cruise company feel about using one of its vessels as the setting for a weekly television show? Because its ships were sailing with close-to-capacity passenger loads at the time, Princess could easily have justified saying no to Cramer's proposal. But McDonald did not and thus was born something called *The Love Boat*, a television series that remained in production for nine full seasons, was syndicated for many years after that, and is widely credited with helping to popularize the whole idea of cruising among people who otherwise might have felt that a vacation aboard a ship was not their cup of tea.

Such claims may be more self-serving exaggeration than verifiable fact, but even if they are, they are perfectly innocent. It remains true that Princess Cruises and *The Love Boat* will forever enjoy a linkage that brings discredit to neither.

Just for the record, the first broadcast aired as a pilot in May 1977; the series itself began that fall and continued through 1986. The episodes were primarily, but not exclusively, filmed aboard *Pacific Princess*. An undocumented Hollywood legend suggests that producer Cramer first got the idea of a shipboard television series while cruising out of Los Angeles aboard a Sitmar vessel, not one of the Princess fleet. While actor Gavin MacLeod in his role of Captain Merrill Stubing undoubtedly is the best known member of the cast of *The Love Boat*, Fred Grandy, who played the role of Yeoman Purser Burt "Gopher" Smith, later shifted his celebrity status from television to electoral politics and was elected to the U.S. House of Representatives for two terms from Iowa. To this day, the musical theme from *The Love Boat* wafts from the loudspeakers aboard Princess vessels when they set sail on a cruise.

While the combination of Princess and P&O operating jointly provided stiff competition for Sitmar in the southern California market, Boris Vlasov responded aggressively. His company initiated a vigorous program of newbuilding, beginning with the delivery of the 46,314-gross-ton *Fairsky* in 1984. Two years later in 1986, Sitmar executed orders for three more newbuildings—three large vessels that were at the cutting edge of cruise ship design and size.

None of the three would ever sail for Sitmar, however, because on November 2, 1987, Boris Vlasov passed away. He was seventy-four. The following year, a trust that Vlasov had created put Sitmar Cruises up for sale, and in July of 1988 the company was acquired by P&O for a reported $210 million. Sitmar's North American cruise services were incorporated into the Princess operation, while itineraries in and around Australia were placed under the wing of P&O. The three newbuildings were completed as Princess vessels.

The acquisition of Sitmar had a major impact on the Princess fleet. Older Sitmar ships that were absorbed into the newly combined company—the two former Cunard ships *Carinthia* and *Sylvania* that were renamed, respectively, *Fair Princess* and *Dawn Princess*—would not remain in the Princess fleet for very long. The first of the three vessels that was under construction for Sitmar was to have been called *Sitmar Fair Majesty* and was in the final stages of construction at Chantiers de l'Atlantique in St. Nazaire, France, when the merger was consummated. She never formally bore the name *Fair Majesty* but was completed as *Star Princess* in 1989, and while she was transferred to P&O Cruises to sail as *Arcadia*

What will likely be the last oceangoing passenger vessel to be designed and built with steam turbine engines as its principal power sailed for many years as *Sky Princess*. Originally Sitmar's *Fairsky*, the vessel was later transferred to P&O Holiday Cruises for service in the Far East as *Pacific Sky*.

at the conclusion of the 1997 summer cruise season, as a one-of-a-kind design she is worth more than a passing mention.

She is an interesting vessel of 63,524 gross tons with a distinctive circular lounge situated above the pilothouse. During builder's trials out of St. Nazaire, *Star Princess* was painted in her ultimate cruise-ship white, but the lounge high atop the vessel was coated only by a brown-colored primer. Color photography of the vessel during these trials creates the mistaken impression of a style of passenger-vessel decoration popular before the Second World War but uncommon since, that of a white superstructure with the pilothouse rendered in natural wood.

But if the Sitmar vessel that was to have been *Fair Majesty* can be called conventional, the other two newbuildings that Princess took over from Sitmar were anything but. Completed as *Crown Princess* in 1990 and *Regal Princess* in 1991, the sister ships feature an unusual forward treatment that has sometimes been described as "dolphinlike." A product of the Genoese designer Renzo Piano, the area both above and below the pilothouse is composed of many compound curves and appears to be part of a single sculpted, or perhaps molded, surface. The look of these two new Sitmar/Princess vessels caused quite a stir in the industry when they were completed and placed in service; it is a look, however, that no cruise company, including Princess, has yet seen fit to emulate.

Interestingly, while the forward end of the two vessels was new and different—even radical—the funnel at the aft end was simply a straight stack set perpendicular to the vessel's long dimension, recalling an earlier era. Several recent Costa vessels feature similar stacks as do Holland America's *Rotterdam* (6) of 1997 and *Amsterdam* (3) of 2000. (With Holland America ships, successor vessels of the same name are sometimes identified using sequential numerals.) Renzo Piano had originally suggested a streamlined aft treatment that would have matched the dolphin look forward. It was supposedly rejected as too costly, thus creating the marvelous anomaly of two vessels whose forward treatment is totally futuristic, while the aft end is a throwback to older concepts. All three of the Sitmar newbuildings that joined the Princess fleet in the years after the acquisition are driven by diesel-electric propulsion systems.

As new and different as was the exterior appearance of the Sitmar-designed vessels that became *Regal Princess* and *Crown Princess*, the shipyard that Vlasov selected for their construction was equally unusual. The yard he chose was Fincantieri, located in Monfalcone, north of Trieste on Italy's Adriatic coast. The facility had not turned out a major new passenger vessel since it delivered *Eugenio C.* to Costa in 1966, two decades earlier, but it is of interest that Fincantieri would go on from the construction of these two new Sitmar/Princess vessels to become one of the principal suppliers of new ships for the cruise industry, including the construction of the first passenger vessels in the world to

Regal Princess is about to dock at Vancouver's Canada Place after a seven-night Alaskan cruise. She and her sister, *Crown Princess,* feature a unique sculpted treatment that has often been described as "dolphinlike."

Crown Princess and *Regal Princess* were both christened in Brooklyn, New York. Movie actress Sophia Loren served as sponsor for *Crown* in 1990, and former British Prime Minister Margaret Thatcher handled similar honors for *Regal* in 1991.

exceed 100,000 gross tons in size. The question, of course, is how quickly—or even whether—Fincantieri would have returned to the building of passenger ships had not Boris Vlasov selected them for his two newbuildings in the mid-1980s.

Regal Princess and *Crown Princess* share another interesting similarity over and above their unusual appearance and the place they were built. Before entering service, each vessel was christened at Pier 8 in Brooklyn, New York, after crossing the North Atlantic from Monfalcone. The Brooklyn site was supposedly selected because it ensured that photos taken during the ceremony would feature the dramatic lower Manhattan skyline in the background. The two vessels were christened by women of rather dissimilar background and style. *Regal Princess* was christened by Margaret Thatcher, the former prime minister of Great Britain, while actress Sophia Loren did the honors for *Crown Princess.*

Earlier oceangoing vessels that were christened in Brooklyn include, among others, the battleships USS *Arizona* and USS *Missouri* as well as the aircraft carrier USS *Constellation,* all built in the New York Naval Shipyard that is popularly called the Brooklyn Navy Yard. One would be hard pressed, however, to identify

Star Princess was one of three newbuildings that were conveyed from Sitmar to Princess while they were under construction. In 1997, the vessel was transferred to parent P&O Cruises for service as their *Arcadia.*

the last oceangoing passenger vessel prior to *Crown Princess* whose christening took place in Brooklyn. (For the record, the first Sitmar-designed Princess newbuilding, the vessel that became *Star Princess*, was christened in Port Everglades, Florida, in 1988 by movie actress Audrey Hepburn.)

Other than these three newbuildings, the newest Sitmar vessel that was conveyed to Princess at the time of the acquisition was the 1984-built *Fairsky*, a vessel that became *Sky Princess* once it began sailing for its new owner. Of *Fairsky*, this can be said: she will likely stand as the final oceangoing passenger vessel to be built as steam-powered. Exactly why Sitmar specified a steam-turbine power plant for a new passenger vessel in 1984, a time when diesel power had become otherwise universal for new cruise vessels, is a bit of a puzzlement. It was not, certainly, out of any desire to recreate an "old fashioned ocean liner" for marketing purposes, as the Delta Queen Steamboat Company had done in designing and building steam-powered riverboats for its inland fleet of cruise vessels. New steam-turbine engines were not unknown in the mid-1980s and were frequently specified for various oceangoing freighters as well as heavy naval ships. Sitmar's decision can likely be traced to a desire to have maximum mechanical compatibility with the company's older ships, coupled with a strong personal aversion to diesel engines on the part of Boris Vlasov, who felt they produced excessive onboard vibration.

Some years afterward, when Sitmar's *Fair Majesty* was under design (the vessel that was eventually launched as *Star Princess*) a decision was reached quite late in the design process to eschew steam-turbine power for this vessel and substitute a diesel-electric system. Indeed *Star Princess* was the very first contemporary cruise ship to feature diesel-electric propulsion.

For that matter, when Sitmar completed the preliminary general arrangement for the vessels that eventually became *Regal Princess* and *Crown Princess*, they, too, were initially specified as being steam powered. This decision was later changed in favor of diesel-electric systems. ("General arrangement" is an important maritime concept. It refers to the overall and definitive plan of and for a new vessel. As issues develop during construction, they are resolved by consulting the general arrangement, which is regarded as definitive and normative.)

So *Sky Princess* will likely be the world's final cruise ship to be designed and built as steam powered. In 2000, parent P&O shifted *Sky Princess* to its own fleet, renamed her *Pacific Sky*, and put her to work in the Australian market for P&O Holiday Cruises, replacing, oddly enough, another former Sitmar vessel, *Fair Princess*.

A final point about Sitmar: the sale of Sitmar Cruises to P&O/Princess in 1988 did not represent the complete and total departure of the company from the cruise industry. Los Angeles–based Sitmar Cruises was only one element within a maritime and transport enterprise—a conglomerate, really—that was known as the Vlasov Group; only Sitmar Cruises was sold after the death of Boris Vlasov. Onward from 1984, all of the Group's maritime activities were placed under the umbrella of a new Monte Carlo–based corporation called V. Ships. A specialty of V. Ships is providing management services to the maritime industry, including the cruise industry. Such contemporary cruise companies as Radisson Seven Seas and Silverseas are clients of V. Ships, thus keeping the Sitmar traditions alive, even while Sitmar Cruises has long since been absorbed within P&O/Princess. (More about V. Ships in chapter 11.)

A related issue here is that unlike either Carnival or Royal Caribbean, Princess Cruises did not handle expansion in the 1970s and 1980s with new vessels designed and built to its own specifications. Both *Pacific Princess* and *Island Princess* joined the fleet when they could still be regarded as new, and *Spirit of London* was no older in 1974 when P&O conveyed her to Princess to become *Sun Princess*. But none of the trio was the product of concepts and designs developed by naval architects working for Princess Cruises. Because of this plus the later acquisition of Sitmar, for a good number of years it was not possible to identify any vessel design as representing the "Princess look." Winged funnels and high superstructures

Royal Princess was built in Helsinki by Wartsila in 1984. While some feel she is an exceptionally fine-looking cruise ship, her design was never repeated and *Royal Princess* remains a one-of-a-kind vessel.

The 1995-built *Sun Princess* introduced a new look that can now be regarded as the fleet standard of Princess Cruises. The vessel is seen here sailing Alaskan waters. Courtesy Princess Cruises.

are the distinctive marks of Carnival, a rounded stern plus a Viking Crown Lounge clearly show that a ship belongs to Royal Caribbean, and twin flared funnels aft identified the early Norwegian Caribbean Line. There was nothing similar to point out as the characteristic design element of a Princess ship.

The only newbuilding specifically ordered by Princess during the 1970s and the 1980s—the Wartsila-built *Royal Princess* of 1984—is a genuine classic among contemporary cruise ships. Many observers unhesitatingly declare it to be the best-looking vessel in the entire Princess fleet, some might even say in the entire cruise industry. But *Royal Princess* remains a classic that was never repeated, because following her construction, the company focused its growth on merger and acquisition, not additional new construction. *Royal Princess* was christened in Southampton by Her Royal Highness, Princess Diana, and for many years she

Grand Princess was the second passenger vessel in the world to exceed 100,000 gross registered tons. The vessel's two most prominent features are the extended treatment of the pilothouse at the forward end and an elevated lounge called Skywalkers positioned across the stern. Courtesy Princess Cruises.

was one of the few vessels in the Princess fleet that was registered in the United Kingdom. The 44,588-gross-ton *Royal Princess* is also one of the few large cruise ships whose passengers are accommodated in outside cabins only, and it was absolutely the first mass-market vessel that could make such a claim. There are no inside (windowless) cabins aboard *Royal Princess.*

It was not until the delivery of *Sun Princess* from Fincantieri in 1995 that Princess Cruises finally found a design that it would repeat over and over again to give its fleet a sense of design unity. *Sun Princess* was quickly followed by *Dawn Princess, Sea Princess,* and *Ocean Princess.* Then in 1998, the company introduced to its fleet the 109,000-gross-ton *Grand Princess,* a vessel that while significantly larger than the 77,441-gross-ton *Sun Princess* and her sisters, nonetheless featured sufficient design similarities to make it easy to see the larger vessel belonged to the same fleet.

The most obvious unifying design feature of these Princess newbuildings is the funnel—it is not quite symmetrical and when viewed from the side, it exhibits what might be called a semiparabolic shape. Strangely, the funnel is not solid; it is composed of pipes and bars that allow one to see through the funnel from one side to other. In the middle of the funnel, of course, are the various ducts that exhaust everything from diesel fumes to kitchen odors into the atmosphere. In the contemporary cruise industry, Celebrity Cruises has identified itself with somewhat similar "see-through" funnels. When all is said and done, while *Sun Princess* and her sisters have upgraded and expanded the Princess fleet with newly built vessels, they have also allowed a sense to emerge that the company's many vessels are finally part of a single fleet with a defining look of its own.

The Fincantieri-built *Grand Princess*, of course, is a distinctive vessel in her own right. Size aside—although this vessel's size is not something that can easily be put aside—the most distinctive characteristic of *Grand Princess* is a lounge elevated over the stern (150 feet over it, in fact). Called Skywalkers, this lounge has been described as resembling a spoiler on a sports car or, less flatteringly, the handle on a supermarket pushcart. Skywalkers is reached via an enclosed moving walkway called a travelator that carries passengers up to the unique lounge from passenger elevators on the upper deck.

An elevated lounge across the stern that resembles an automotive spoiler could give a vessel an unbalanced look, but *Grand Princess* is certainly not visually unbalanced, and the reason is the very different treatment of the vessel's pilothouse.

A pilothouse is normally recessed within the superstructure of a vessel, with only the bridge wings extending beyond the superstructure to give the ship's officers the perspective they need for navigational purposes. On *Grand Princess* and her 109,000-gross-ton sisters, the entire navigating bridge extends out from the superstructure from one end to the other, so extensively in fact that the bridge wings must be supported by large angled columns reaching out from a point on the superstructure three decks below. The hull of *Grand Princess* has a measured beam of 118 feet precluding her from transiting the Panama Canal, of course, whose locks measure 110 feet across. From the extreme of one bridge wing to the other is a massive 159 feet. In an aesthetic sense, this exaggerated treatment of the navigational bridge provides visual balance to the extraordinarily different treatment that Skywalkers represents at the vessel's stern.

Grand Princess is 951 feet long and each of her two fixed-pitch propellers is turned by a large electric motor built by Siemens. The current needed to power the motors aboard *Grand Princess*, as well as the electricity for all other onboard needs, is generated by six 16-cylinder GMT diesel engines.

(A ship's propellers may be fixed-pitch, or controllable-pitch. Controllable-pitch propellers allow the angle at which the propeller blades attack the water to be adjusted while the propeller is revolving, thus effecting control of the vessel's speed. A controllable-pitch propeller can even shift from power forward to power astern by adjusting the pitch of a propeller's blades, not the direction of its rotation. While fixed-pitch propellers lack this flexibility, thanks to new and advanced forms of electronic motor control, cruise ships equipped with electric drive are able to achieve sufficient flexibility without the added complexity of controllable-pitch propellers.)

When *Grand Princess* entered service in 1999, she wrested the crown of world's largest passenger ship from the 1997-built *Carnival Destiny*. It was a mantle she would not long hold, however. In late 1999, Royal Caribbean's 137,276-gross-ton *Voyager of the Seas* emerged from Kvaerner Masa-Yards, and the reign of *Grand Princess* as the world's largest passenger ship was over. Two 109,000-gross-ton sister ships are scheduled to join *Grand Princess* early in the twenty-first century.

With the advent of larger and larger vessels, many people, even those within the cruise industry, began to voice fears that cruise ships were simply getting too big. With respect to Princess in particular, one man who harbored such feelings was none other than Stanley McDonald, the man who founded the company back in 1964. "I have been a little concerned that 2,000 and 2,500 passengers would be too impersonal," said McDonald, "but my fears were alleviated after a visit aboard *Grand Princess*. It doesn't seem like such a big ship at all." McDonald, who left Princess in 1980 to pursue other business interests, was involved in the creation of Sundance Cruises, one of the companies that later became part of Admiral Cruises and ultimately was merged into Royal Caribbean.

Although Princess Cruises continues to be a strong player in the seasonal Alaskan market, the company no longer bases any vessels in Los Angeles, the port where *Princess Patricia* began service back in 1964 and where the company still maintains its corporate headquarters. Princess will schedule some cruises out of Los Angeles by vessels heading to Alaska in the spring and back to the Caribbean in the fall, but nothing any more permanent than that. Princess remains steady in the Caribbean during the winter, of course, and dispatches vessels to all emerging world markets from Europe to South America to Asia. In the summer of 2000, Princess Cruises was able to deploy *Pacific Princess* in summer service between New York and Bermuda, one of the routes the vessel worked for Flagship Cruises as *Sea Venture* in the early 1970s.

Then in 1999 came the announcement that P&O/Princess was about to order five new cruise ships, vessels with a cumulative gross tonnage in excess of half a million. One of the vessel orders involves picking up an option with Fincantieri for the construction of a fourth Grand Princess-class vessel, although that ship will most likely operate for parent P&O Cruises, not Princess. Two new 88,000-gross-ton ships of a new design will be built for Princess at Chantiers de l'Atlantique in St. Nazaire. These vessels will be powered by a combination of diesel and gas-turbine engines, with the gas-turbine engines mounted aloft, so to speak, inside the funnel. Finally, two new 113,000-gross-ton Princess ships will be built in Japan by Mitsubishi Heavy Industries, the first cruise ships to be

The elevated stern lounge on *Grand Princess* has been likened to a spoiler on a sports car and, less flatteringly, the handle on a supermarket pushcart.

built in the Far East for a North American operator. These Mitsubishi-built vessels will be similar to, but a bit larger than, *Grand Princess*.

In a dynamic and changing world, nothing remains static for very long. Early in the year 2000, an important announcement was forthcoming from the Peninsular and Oriental Steam Navigation Company. P&O is actually a vast transportation conglomerate, including not just cruise ships, but also European ferry lines, port facilities, cargo vessels, intermodal transportation, real estate investments, and more. All the cruise operations are to be separated from the rest of P&O—"demerged" was the verb used in the press releases—and combined to form a separate and independent corporation. At least four separate cruise brands were involved: Princess Cruises, P&O Cruises, Australia-based P&O Holiday Cruises, and Aida Cruises, a small German cruise line that was brought under the P&O umbrella in 1999.

Exactly how this will all play out in terms of brand identification remains to be seen. What is obvious, though, is that within the new corporation, by far the most dominant component will be Princess Cruises. An early impact of this new arrangement was the decision announced in early 2000 to reflag the entire Princess fleet under British registry. Most will be enrolled in Britain proper, but two ships—*Crown Princess* and *Grand Princess*—will have their British registry in Bermuda. The reason for so registering *Crown Princess* is technical, but for *Grand Princess* it is social. An extremely popular and quite profitable facility aboard *Grand Princess* has proven to be the wedding chapel, where the ship's captain regularly presides at nuptial ceremonies. British registry precludes a captain's performing such ceremonies, while Bermuda is open to the idea. And so *Grand Princess* sails the Caribbean with Hamilton, Bermuda, showing as her home port, a British red ensign displayed off her stern whenever she's in port, and a captain whose "job description" includes presiding at as many wedding ceremonies as the ship's chapel can accommodate.

In 1974, when Stanley McDonald's decade-old cruise company was bought out by Great Britain's P&O, the British firm was seen as a salvation for what was then a struggling Princess operation. A quarter century later, P&O's intervention can be called an unqualified success as a new corporation confidently sails into a new millennium.

CHAPTER 6

Norwegian Cruise Line

Knut Kloster and Ted Arison joined forces in 1966 to establish a Florida-based cruise operation that was called Norwegian Caribbean Line (NCL). The venture prospered and its first vessel, *Sunward,* was soon joined by three others: *Starward* in 1968, *Skyward* in 1969, and *Southward* in 1971.

The Kloster-Arison working agreement, however, was dissolved in late 1971. NCL was, effectively, Kloster-owned and operated. Arison had served as marketing and sales agent, but the company's tangible assets—that is to say its fleet of cruise ships—remained with Kloster. On February 1, 1972, Kloster's company, Klosters-Rederi A/S, took over all aspects of NCL from Arison's company, Arison Shipping. Arison, of course, went on to found Carnival Cruise Lines and leave a more indelible mark on the industry than any other individual. But Knut Kloster and NCL also made some remarkable contributions of their own to the growth of the new cruise industry after the partnership with Ted Arison was dissolved. The Kloster-Arison litigation continued through the early 1970s, with decisions favoring one or the other parties issued at various appellate levels. At issue was a sum of money Arison had retained after the working agreement was dissolved in 1971. Finally, in late 1974, the parties reached an out-of-court settlement, with Arison and Carnival getting approximately one-third of the disputed $1.7 million, Kloster the rest.

FROM "CARIBBEAN" TO "CRUISE"

As cruising began to grow and prosper in the 1970s and on into the 1980s, there can be little arguing with the proposition that Kloster's Norwegian Caribbean Line was the industry's true pacesetter, particularly with respect to cruises originating in the warm waters of south Florida. When Royal Caribbean Cruise Line's first vessel, *Song of Norway,* carried her first passengers out of Miami on November 7, 1970, NCL was already a thriving operation with three active vessels and a fourth under construction. By contrast, Carnival's first newbuilding, *Tropicale*, did not enter service until 1981, a full decade later, and RCCL would not equal NCL by introducing its fourth brand-new vessel until *Song of America* came on the scene in 1982. By this time, though, Knut Kloster had done even more to enhance his role as industry pacesetter.

It took Kloster and NCL about a year to regain equilibrium after the split with Arison. Operational matters were always under the control of Kloster's people in Norway and there were no problems in these areas. But marketing and reservations had been Arison's responsibility, and it was difficult for Kloster, located in Oslo, to put together a new team in Miami to carry out these important functions. After he did, though, NCL once again became the "big fellow on the block." Its vessels sailed what are now typical eastern, western, and southern Caribbean itineraries, with *Sunward* holding down three- and four-night cruises from Miami to the Bahamas. Indeed it was NCL that pioneered the idea of western Caribbean cruise itineraries.

In the mid-1970s, Kloster began looking for a cruise ship to replace the 1966-built *Sunward*, NCL's pioneer vessel, and in February 1977 the company purchased the six-year-old *Cunard Adventurer*, a hull the venerable British company was anxious to dispose of because it was bringing newer and slightly larger cruise ships into its fleet. A $5 million refit, with some of the work done in Rotterdam and some in Jacksonville, Florida, and the one-time Cunarder was fitted out with a pair of typical NCL twin-flared funnels and christened *Sunward II*. She made her first NCL cruise out of Miami on May 30, 1977, picking up her namesake's three- and four-night split-week cruises to the Bahamas. The original *Sunward* was sold and ran for a number of different companies over the next two decades or more, but she left behind many fond memories at NCL, especially among Norwegian officers whose early work for NCL was aboard the company's very first vessel. Years after she had departed, nothing could spark a spirited conversation with an NCL officer who once served aboard her quite like posing a question or two about "the old *Sunward*."

In 1980, NCL became the first cruise line to purchase its own island in the Bahamas, where vessels could anchor and tender passengers ashore for a quiet day at the beach. In late 1987, the company changed its name from Norwegian Caribbean Line to Norwegian Cruise Line to reflect the fact that *Southward* was being dispatched away from the Caribbean to the West Coast to work three- and four-night cruises out of Los Angeles. (By way of contrast, Royal Caribbean has since expanded into a truly worldwide cruise operation, yet feels perfectly comfortable retaining the word Caribbean in its title.)

In the early 1970s, Kloster had intended to add to the NCL fleet another vessel that would have been a true sister ship to the company's fourth vessel, *Southward*, and quite similar to *Skyward* and *Starward*. Construction was actually well along on the vessel at Cantieri Navali del Tirreno e Riuniti in Italy, the same builder that had turned out *Southward*, when the shipyard ran into financial difficulties and was taken over by the Italian Government, who promptly cancelled the contract with Klosters Rederi A/S. Kloster prevailed upon the Norwegian Government to lodge a formal protest with Italy and demand that the original contract be honored, but it proved unsuccessful. The ship, which would have been christened *Seaward* had she joined the NCL fleet, was eventually completed and sold to P&O as its *Spirit of London*. She retained a distinctly "NCL look," however, save for the fact a more conventional single funnel was installed instead of NCL's signature twin flared funnels.

Following this setback in the early 1970s, Kloster toyed with other ideas. One was to build a different kind of cruise ship, a 20,000-gross-ton, semi-catamaran called *Elysian* that would see passengers and crew eating in the same dining room and have both navigating bridge and engine room visible to curious passengers from behind plateglass windows. Nothing ever came of this idea, but by the end of the 1970s, Knut Kloster had decided to expand NCL in an altogether different direction.

Not to put too fine a point on matters, but Kloster would expand Norwegian Caribbean Line with what can probably be called the most dramatic and unex-

Twin flared funnels, as on *Southward*, were a signature design feature of early NCL vessels.

pected development the growing cruise industry had ever seen, would ever see, and, quite possibly, ever will see. First, though, some background for an announcement Knut Kloster would make in 1979.

If anything had emerged as a piece of conventional wisdom in the developing cruise industry in the 1970s, it was this: the perfect Caribbean cruise ship was one in the 20,000-gross-ton range. As one author put it in 1976: "Within the industry today, there is only one style of ship to be considered: a vessel of about 20,000 gross tons, 600 feet in length and 80-feet wide." Any smaller and a vessel could not carry enough passengers to make it profitable, at least profitable within the limits of the fares that competitive companies were charging for similar service. Any larger, and a vessel would be unable to visit many popular Caribbean ports of call. In addition, keeping a larger vessel fully occupied year-round seemed an impossible dream and, more importantly, a senseless risk.

Cruise ships would get larger, of course, and the 20,000-gross-ton range would soon become nothing more than a quaint reminder of the industry's early days. And while the 20,000-ton limit was starting to fall in gradual increments as companies such as Carnival, Holland America, and Royal Caribbean designed and ordered vessels that were in the 30,000-gross-ton range in the early 1980s, nothing—absolutely nothing—did more to render the 20,000-ton cruise ship functionally obsolete than an announcement Knut Kloster made at a news conference in New York's Hotel Pierre on June 28, 1979.

Five years earlier in 1974, a marvelous ocean liner had been removed from North Atlantic service and laid up. She was the 1961-built *France*, once the flagship of the French Line, *La Compagnie Generale Transatlantique*. After little more than a decade of service that included 377 transatlantic crossings, the economics that doomed the North Atlantic ocean liner generally caught up with *France*. While her retirement was bitterly fought by French seafarers and their unions, their protests were insufficient to convince the French Government that a continuation of the vessel's extensive annual operating subsidy was a wise use of scarce national resources.

France had actually been sold by French Line some months earlier to Akram Ojjeh, a Paris-based financier from the Middle East who had vague plans to use her as a stationary shoreside hotel or perhaps even a gambling casino. What Kloster told the press at the Hotel Pierre in 1979 was that NCL had purchased *France* from Ojjeh for $18 million, and following an upcoming rehabilitation at Lloyd Werft's shipyard in Bremerhaven, Germany, she would be put into Caribbean cruise service out of Miami. It was an idea that was first suggested to Kloster by a young man working for him in Miami, Bruce Nierenberg, whose fascination with oceangoing passenger ships began when he would look out the window of his parents' home in the Sea Gate section of Brooklyn's Coney Island and watch the likes of *Queen Mary* and *Ile de France* sail in and out of New York Harbor.

The refit in Bremerhaven was initially estimated at $42 million; in fact, it wound up costing closer to $65 million. In her new role, the former *France* would sail as *Norway* and in one fell swoop the idea that 20,000 gross tons was somehow a limit that a cruise ship should not exceed was blown to smithereens. *France* had a registered gross tonnage of 66,348. Furthermore, her 1,035 feet of length made her the longest passenger vessel of all time, although not by much. At 1,031 feet, *Queen Elizabeth* of 1940 was only 48 inches shorter. (During her years with NCL, *Norway* would be refitted and renovated any number of times and her gross tonnage increased to 76,049.)

To convert a North Atlantic *France* into a Caribbean *Norway* involved towing the big vessel to Bremerhaven, West Germany, and removing two of her original four screws (the outboard two), shutting down two of her four steam-turbine engines, and opting for a more leisurely paced vessel. During her days with French Line, *France* never won the fabled transatlantic Blue Riband, nor even tried to, but she did manage thirty-five-knot speed during her sea trials and regularly pushed thirty knots on transatlantic crossings. She was not exactly at the cutting edge in the way of ocean liner speed, but she was no tramp steamer, either. As a cruise ship and with half of her original power plant out of service, the vessel's top speed would be twenty-one knots (she actually made twenty-five knots during postconversion trials) although she would rarely exceed sixteen knots in routine cruise service.

Norway was to be given an upgraded air-conditioning system during the refit for her new role in the tropics, and countless other adaptations and changes were made throughout her interior spaces. She was also fitted out with a set of five thrusters, three at the bow and two at the stern, to assist when maneuvering in

France, in the classic livery of her first owner, the French Line.

close quarters. Hull plating had to be reinforced in several places to handle the additional stress the thrusters generated. The conversion work was performed under the overall management of naval architect Tage Wandborg of Denmark, with interior design largely the province of Angelo Donghia of New York.

When *Norway* was scheduled to leave Bremerhaven in the spring of 1980 for a transatlantic journey to New York and then south to Miami, the conversion was not yet complete and a crew of five hundred shipyard workers remained aboard to finish the job as the ship steamed westward. George Taylor, a designer with the Miami firm of Tom Graboski Associates that was responsible for developing and installing a new system of signs and graphics aboard the big ship, later described the spring crossing as rather rough, and noted there were days at sea when his team was able to do no work at all.

Before heading west, however, *Norway* first sailed north from Bremerhaven and paid a special ceremonial visit to Oslo, the city that would be her new home port. Then, on May 16, 1980, she steamed into New York harbor, her western terminal when she was in transatlantic service as *France*. Her once-black hull had been repainted a medium-to-dark blue and her twin funnels, formerly dark red with black topping, had been redone to resemble the design on NCL's other cruise vessels. *Norway*'s dark hull, though, was in obvious contrast to the typical white hulls of both her own fleetmates—the "white fleet," as they were often called—and most other cruise ships of the day. "It's the biggest blue thing I've ever seen," one observer remarked when *Norway* steamed into New York in May 1980. It was clear at the time that here was a ship that was special. And that is exactly what she has always been: special, very special.

One further touch that was retained from her days with French Line was a rendering of her new name in large letters above the top deck and amidships. This distinctive bit of decoration had adorned such earlier French Line ships as *Ile de France, Normandie, Liberte,* and, of course, *France.*

Once *Norway* reached Miami, NCL put her to work on the most basic of Caribbean itineraries, the seven-night milk run to St. Thomas. With only occasional variations, that would be her steady assignment for the next two decades. She towered over other cruise ships when she was tied up along Government Cut on the north side of Miami's new Dodge Island cruise terminal, and she instantly became the new standard by which to measure the plans other companies were making for expanding their fleets. NCL, on the other hand, had increased the capacity of its Caribbean fleet by an impressive 70 percent in one dramatic move, and *Norway* was in service and carrying passengers out of Miami less than a year after Knut Kloster called reporters to the Hotel Pierre in New York to tell them what he had in mind.

Within a decade of *Norway*'s entry into service, other cruise lines would be ordering newbuildings with gross tonnages—and passenger capacities—that exceeded those of the one-time French Line flagship. The imponderable question, though, is whether such large cruise ships would ever have been built, or, at the very least, would have been built as soon as they were, had Knut Kloster not taken the bold step in 1979 of buying the ocean liner *France* and converting her into the cruise ship *Norway*.

With *Norway* in service, there was continual talk of additional newbuildings for NCL during the 1980s. There were also plans to stretch the company's original vessels to expand their capacity, as RCCL had successfully done with *Song of Norway* and *Nordic Prince*. The degree to which the rehabilitation of *France* into *Norway* exceeded its projected cost estimates put a crimp in NCL's plans to stretch its older vessels, and nothing concrete materialized in the way of newbuildings until the 42,276-gross-ton *Seaward* was delivered by Wartsila's Turku yard in 1988. Speculation in the trade press suggested that, as an economy move, *Seaward*'s design owed much to *Royal Princess* of 1984, also a Wartsila product, and the two vessels are not totally dissimilar. Unlike *Royal Princess*, though, *Seaward* cannot boast that none of her cabins are interior-facing and windowless.

Bearing the name *Norway*, the one-time *France* heads down the Hudson River past the World Trade Center and out to sea from New York. In 2001, the vessel is scheduled to leave North America and begin a new career in the Far East for Star Cruises, the parent corporation of Norwegian Cruise Line.

Norwegian Cruise Line's *Seaward*, built in Helsinki in 1988, was later renamed *Norwegian Sea*.

In the way of new services, Norwegian Cruise Line moved a vessel to San Juan to allow seven-night cruises to the southern Caribbean and eventually the company earned one of the coveted spots in the highly competitive New York–Bermuda market. But for NCL, despite the arrival of *Norway* and the construction of *Seaward*, the 1980s became a decade that saw its competitors making more dramatic strides in the way of fleet expansion and upgrading of services than the industry's one-time leader was able to manage. Norwegian Cruise Line was about to give up its position as front-runner and fall behind the pack for a period of years.

ROYAL VIKING LINE

Knut Kloster was never without plans—sometimes bold and grandiose plans—that he was attempting to realize. He developed a concept called Project Phoenix, an effort that would have seen the construction of a huge 5,000-passenger, 250,000-gross-ton cruise ship, a vessel so big it would rarely, if ever, enter any conventional ports but would transfer embarking and disembarking passengers to and from shore aboard a fleet of tenders, vessels that would be described with only slight exaggeration as not much smaller than the original *Sunward*. A group of investors was actually put together for Project Phoenix and preliminary plans and specifications were developed. When shipyards were approached and asked for quotes on the effort, however, they mentioned prices in the range of $650 million and the effort was, if not abandoned, at least deferred.

Kloster continued to explore new and different avenues. In August 1984, he bought out a trio of Norwegian investors who had formed an upscale cruise company called Royal Viking Line back in the early 1970s. It was on December 2, 1970, in fact, during a press conference at the Plaza Hotel in New York, that Royal Viking's president, Warren S. Titus, first told the world about the new company.

Royal Viking has a number of obvious parallels with Royal Caribbean. It began in the 1970s with investment capital from three Norwegian backers, Nordenfjelske, Klaveness, and the Norwegian coastal ferry company known as Bergen Line. Like RCCL, Royal Viking quickly grew to a fleet of three new Wartsila-built cruise ships, and while two of Royal Caribbean's three vessels were sent back to Finland for stretching, all three Royal Viking ships were so expanded, although the work was not done in Helsinki where the vessels were built but in Bremerhaven, West Germany, by A. G. Weser. Their initial length of 583 feet became 674, gross tonnage rose from 21,848 to 28,000, and an original passenger capacity in the mid-500s was increased by approximately 200 passengers each. The work was done between 1981 and 1983.

Where Royal Caribbean was aiming at what would later be called the mass market, Royal Viking saw its clientele as those passengers who were willing to spend a few more dollars—perhaps many more dollars—for their cruise vacations, a decidedly upscale market. The early Royal Caribbean prided itself on vessels that sailed the same repetitive Caribbean itineraries all year round. Under the careful management of the talented Warren Titus, Royal Viking sent its three cruise ships on worldwide itineraries that visited dozens of different ports with very little in the way of repetition over a year's time.

Royal Viking's three original vessels, *Royal Viking Sea, Royal Viking Star,* and *Royal Viking Sky,* developed extraordinarily loyal passengers, people who insisted on traveling aboard nothing except their favorite Royal Viking ship, even though the other two were its equal in every technical respect and specification. Royal Viking featured an interesting duality of management: maritime operations were handled out of Oslo, while marketing and ticketing were headquartered in San Francisco.

After one and a half decades of successful operation, by 1984 the original investors were anxious to divest. That was when Kloster stepped in and purchased Royal Viking for $240 million. The deal was a combination of cash and the assumption of existing mortgages. Interests behind Norway's Bergen Line—one of the three original investors—attempted to block the sale. Unlike Wilhelmsen's successful effort to fend off the acquisition of Royal Caribbean by Carnival, Bergen

Line was unsuccessful and Royal Viking became Knut Kloster's second cruise company.

Under Kloster's ownership, first one and ultimately all three of the original Royal Viking ships were transferred to NCL after appropriate renovations to increase their passenger-carrying capacity to mass-market levels. Kloster still wanted to retain Royal Viking as an upscale player in the cruise business, so in late 1988 he took delivery of a newbuilding, a 37,845-gross-ton cruise ship from Wartsila that was christened *Royal Viking Sun*. The same year of 1988 also saw a merger and consolidation of Royal Viking's overhead functions with those of NCL and the closing of Royal Viking's San Francisco offices.

Then, four years later in 1992, a rather unusual vessel joined the Royal Viking fleet, although this was more of a target of opportunity than part of any carefully crafted expansion strategy. The ship was christened *Royal Viking Queen*, but she had been designed to the specifications of another upscale cruise company, Seabourn Cruises. What Royal Viking did was pick up an option for a vessel that Seabourn chose not to exercise, and she was built to the same specifications as Seabourn's other two vessels. *Royal Viking Queen* had a gross tonnage of 9,961, was 443 feet long, and featured deluxe stateroom accommodations for a mere 212 passengers. In both appearance and appointment, *Royal Viking Queen* was identical to *Seabourn Pride* and *Seabourn Spirit*.

Eventually, it was decided that Royal Viking could not be sustained as a separate brand. This was not due to any inherent problems with Royal Viking itself; rather, it was a decision brought on by overall financial difficulties that the Kloster-originated enterprises were experiencing coupled with expanded competition from a number of newer companies for what was a limited upscale cruise market. In 1994, *Royal Viking Sun*, the Royal Viking name, and perhaps most important of all, the mailing list of former Royal Viking customers was sold to Cunard Line. After a short tenure with yet another Kloster-owned cruise company, *Royal Viking Queen* was sold to Seabourn where she joined her two look-alike sisters and was rechristened *Seabourn Legend*.

Royal Viking Sun sailed for Cunard under her original name for about five years. In late 1999 she was sent to Lloyd Werft's Bremerhaven yard and emerged as *Seabourn Sun*. The linkage between Cunard and Seabourn, a function of their both coming under the Carnival umbrella, will be explored in chapter 8.

ROYAL CRUISE LINE

Royal Viking was one of two important cruise lines that Kloster acquired during the days when NCL itself was being eclipsed by its mass-market competitors. In 1989, he purchased Royal Cruise Line, a company that had been founded in Greece in 1971 and during its early years operated but one vessel, the 10,500-gross-ton *Golden Odyssey*.

Royal Cruise Line was one of a number of companies whose initial mission was to cruise the Aegean Sea and visit the many islands located there. Royal Cruise soon grew into a company whose itineraries became more extensive and more expansive. Royal acquired Home Lines *Doric* in 1981 and rebuilt her as *Royal Odyssey*, while in 1988 the company took delivery of a newbuilding, the 34,242-gross-ton *Crown Odyssey*, a vessel built by Joseph L. Meyer in Papenburg, West Germany.

The year after the arrival of *Crown Odyssey*, 1989, saw Kloster's purchase of Royal Cruise Line. This was followed by a rather wholesale shifting of vessels between and among his several companies—NCL, Royal Cruise, and Royal Viking. *Royal Viking Star* became *Star Odyssey* and eventually NCL's *Westward*. Even the yachtlike *Royal Viking Queen* sailed for a season or two as *Queen Odyssey* before eventually being sold off to Seabourn.

Royal Cruise Line continued to see itself as an upscale company and deployed its fleet on appropriate worldwide itineraries both before and after its acquisition by Kloster. As more competition developed within the upscale market in the 1990s, it became painfully apparent that part of the financial difficulties the various enterprises were experiencing could be traced to an overextension of resources and a consequent loss of managerial discipline. The result was the sell-off of Royal Viking in 1994 and the dismantling of Royal Cruise Line in early 1996. The original enterprise, mass-market Norwegian Cruise Line, survived as the sole activity of the once-extensive cruise enterprise begun by Knut Kloster.

BACK AT NCL

Although there was continual talk throughout the 1980s about building new vessels for Norwegian Cruise Line, nothing concrete happened until *Seaward* was turned out by Wartsila in 1988. Two Royal Viking vessels were also transferred to NCL. *Royal Viking Star* became *Westward* for a short time before being sold off to become, eventually, *Black Watch* of the British-based Fred Olson Cruises. *Royal Viking Sky* took over split-week cruises out of Miami for *Sunward II* and assumed the name *Sunward* for a season or two. She later worked for Princess Cruises for a short time and still later moved to the Far East as *SuperStar Capricorn* of Star Cruises. The bewildering pace of these vessel reassignments, as much as anything else, underscores the turmoil that NCL was experiencing in the late 1980s and early 1990s.

When it was announced in 1990 that Kloster's firm had contracted for two 40,000-gross-ton cruise ships from Chantiers de l'Atlantique, at first it was not specified whether the newbuildings would join the upscale Royal Viking fleet or the mass-market NCL. When they were finally delivered as *Dreamward* in 1992 and *Windward* in 1993, they were assigned to NCL and substantially upgraded the company's capabilities. *Seaward* and *Norway* aside, the backbone of the NCL fleet had long remained vessels like *Starward*, *Skyward*, and *Southward* from the early 1970s, while the competition was pursuing vigorous and steady new-building programs. *Starward*, *Skyward*, and *Southward* had given NCL a competitive edge when Carnival was operating nothing but secondhand ships, Princess was hardly a force beyond the West Coast, and the great bulk of departures from Dodge Island were former ocean liners hastily rebuilt for cruise service. *Starward*, *Skyward*, and *Southward* became distinct competitive liabilities for NCL, as Carnival's newbuilding program progressed from *Tropicale* to the Fantasy-class, as Princess grew in size, and as Royal Caribbean began to introduce megaliners into Caribbean service.

The advent of *Windward* and *Dreamward* allowed NCL to dispose of its original vessels, and all of them found interesting second careers with emerging cruise companies in Europe. Shortly after the two new ships joined the fleet, NCL adopted a new corporate identification that, symbolically at least, represented a break with the past. In place of a stylized orange sunburst and flowing lines in light shades of blue that had adorned the fleet from its earliest days, the company switched to a dark blue funnel with a new logo featuring the letters NCL in a rich gold color. It was a simple change, but it made a big difference—in appearance, surely, but perhaps on a more profound level as well.

NCL's 1992-built *Dreamward*. The vessel was later lengthened and renamed *Norwegian Dream.*

Leeward, a vessel NCL chartered for a number of years to work popular split-week cruises out of south Florida, has since been conveyed to Star Cruises in the Far East. In this 1998 photograph, *Leeward* is heading down the Potomac River on a charter cruise out of Alexandria, Virginia.

As NCL began to shake off the problems caused by a protracted period of poor financial performance in the late 1980s and early 1990s and to reclaim a position of strength within the industry in the mid- to late-1990s, three relatively new vessels were acquired from other companies, two by charter, one by purchase.

The 1992-built *Royal Majesty* was purchased in 1997 for $110 million and renamed *Norwegian Majesty.* Together with the vessel, NCL also acquired rights that *Royal Majesty* held to operate summer service between Bermuda and Boston, and she has remained in this service for her new owner. A vessel originally built in 1992 as *Crown Dynasty* was leased for a period of years and worked as *Norwegian Dynasty,* while a one-time European car ferry called *Sally Albatross* was leased specifically to work split-week cruises out of Miami to the Bahamas as *Leeward,* the service pioneered by the original *Sunward* back in 1966. *Leeward* departed from Miami on her first cruise under NCL colors on October 20, 1995.

By the end of 1999, the leases for *Leeward* and *Norwegian Dynasty* had run their course and the two ships left the NCL fleet, *Leeward* to become *SuperStar Taurus* for Star Cruises, a Far Eastern company that would shortly figure even more prominently in the NCL story. *Norwegian Dynasty* reverted to her original name, *Crown Dynasty,* and inaugurated a new service for a new subsidiary of Commodore Cruise Line.

Windward and *Dreamward* proved to be fine vessels for NCL, so much so that the company soon decided to increase their capacity by splicing a 130-foot section into each of them, something that was more or less intended in their original design. The work was done in the spring of 1998 at the Lloyd Werft shipyard in Bremerhaven, Germany.

Windward was first. On January 3, 1998, almost a hundred technicians from Lloyd Werft who had flown from Germany to Puerto Rico boarded the ship at the conclusion of a cruise in San Juan and as *Windward* made her way east across the North Atlantic, the technicians went to work and marked the decks and bulkheads of the vessel for its upcoming surgery. When *Windward* reached Bremerhaven she was drydocked, workers fired up their torches, and the vessel was cut in two. So delicate was this important task that it took fourteen days to complete; in addition to the hull itself, 793 electric cables and 600 pipes of varying shapes, sizes, and purposes had to be cut and carefully labeled for subsequent resplicing.

Next, the freshly exposed interior of the recently cut hull had to be welded closed below the waterline with temporary steel plating so the two sections of the hull could be floated apart. The drydock was flooded, *Windward*'s forward section was pulled out of the way by tugboats, and an already-built new midsection was floated in to mate up with the after end of the vessel. Once in place, the bow section was floated back into the drydock and after all three sections were carefully and painstakingly positioned, the vessel was welded back together. To unite the three sections into a single vessel required the skills of fifty technical specialists working around the clock for five straight days. And that was just the basic welding; splicing all the pipes and wires back together took many additional weeks, as did the restoration of the vessel's interior decorations.

Windward left Bremerhaven in mid-March, two months after arriving. Her dimensions had changed as follows: gross tonnage had been increased from 39,277 to 50,760; passenger capacity from 1,246 to 1,748; and length from 624 feet to 754. (Oddly enough, with an additional section spliced into her middle, the draft of the ship was actually reduced from 23 feet to 22 feet.) The newly stretched vessel, now renamed *Norwegian Wind*, requires 130 more crewmembers in various categories than did the smaller *Windward,* and the stretching effort included additional facilities for their accommodation. The project represented a $69 million investment for NCL.

Two days before *Norwegian Wind* set sail for Miami to resume cruise service, *Dreamward* tied up at the Lloyd Werft yard to undergo similar surgery. Well, not exactly similar. Because *Dreamward,* soon to be renamed *Norwegian Dream,* would be assigned to Baltic summer cruises that NCL planned to operate via the Kiel Canal, both her mast and her funnel had to be fitted with hydraulic hinges so the vessel could navigate under a fixed bridge which crossed that waterway. A trade publication of the cruise industry offered the light-hearted comment that some future operations manager at NCL, thinking *Norwegian Dream* and *Norwegian Wind* to be sister ships in all respects, might, during some summer down the road, assign the latter to the former's itinerary, with devastating effects during her first attempted transit of the Kiel Canal.

Following the successful stretching of both *Windward* and *Dreamward* in 1998, Norwegian Cruise Line decided that its newly acquired *Norwegian Majesty* was a good candidate for similar work, and she paid a visit to Lloyd Werft in early 1999. When she left she was 112 feet longer, and her passenger capacity had been increased from 1,056 to 1,462.

Through all of NCL's ups and downs over the years, *Norway* remained a wonderful symbol of stability. Her profile has been altered, some say slightly, others insist substantially. When she sailed as *France* and during her early years with NCL, the uppermost element of superstructure was the vessel's pilothouse. By the turn of the century, *Norway*'s pilothouse peered out from beneath a large slab of prefabricated superstructure that had been installed atop it. This two-deck addition contains more cabins in the upper price ranges, accommodations de-

The funnel of *Norwegian Dream* includes an unusual hydraulic mechanism that allows the vessel to pass safely beneath low clearances along Germany's Kiel Canal. Courtesy Frederick Kurst.

During her years with Norwegian Cruise Line, various changes were made to *Norway*'s profile. As one instance, a prefabricated cluster of high-priced cabins now overshadows the vessel's pilothouse.

signed to improve *Norway*'s earning capacity. In a sense, these can be regarded as the seagoing equivalent of the pricey "sky boxes" that are now incorporated into sports arenas and baseball fields. In any event, the vessel has a different look, especially from the bow. Belowdecks, diesel engines have been installed, not to replace steam turbines for basic propulsion but in lieu of the vessel's original steam-powered electric generators. As a result, there are now all kinds of new exhaust vents running out of *Norway*'s funnels.

By the end of the 1990s, NCL had regained a measure of the stability it once enjoyed and nearly lost. The summer of 1999 saw the delivery of the company's first newbuilding since *Windward* of 1993, a vessel that bore the name *Norwegian Sky*. This ship's hull had been laid down some years earlier at Vulkan Werft in Bremen, Germany, with the intention of its becoming *Costa Olympia*. The shipyard ran into financial difficulties and defaulted on the order with Costa Cruises. NCL stepped in and acquired the partially completed vessel and had it redesigned and finished at Lloyd Werft's Bremerhaven yard as *Norwegian Sky*. No sooner was *Norwegian Sky* in service in 1999 than NCL contracted with Lloyd Werft for a sister ship, a vessel that will be called *Norwegian Sun*.

The summer that saw *Norwegian Sky* join the fleet was marred by two accidents, however. *Norwegian Dream* was involved in a collision with the Evergreen Line containership *Ever Decent* off Dover, England, in August and was out of service for several weeks. And on one of her early cruises, the brand new *Sky* ran aground while sailing along the Saguenay River in Canada and was also forced to cancel a number of her early cruises, hardly an auspicious beginning.

In terms of service areas, by the late 1990s Norwegian Cruise Line was deploying its fleet on a genuinely worldwide basis, in much the same manner as were other cruise companies. *Norwegian Crown* pioneered fourteen-night cruises from Buenos Aires to Valparaiso during winter in the Northern Hemisphere, and the company's services in Europe experienced excellent growth, as well. *Norwegian Dream* has become a fixture in Europe each summer, and for a number of years in the mid-1990s even the venerable *Norway* was dispatched across the North Atlantic to work various Mediterranean and Baltic itineraries. For one set of cruises that were marketed exclusively to Europeans, the vessel was informally renamed *France* to stress her history and heritage.

There was some speculation in the industry that *Norway* would be withdrawn from service with the onset of more stringent international vessel safety requirements in 1997. Adapting older ships to meet the new requirements was expensive and both Holland America Line and P&O, for example, felt it was unwise to upgrade older vessels in their respective fleets. Holland America's *Rotterdam* (5) was sold to Premier Cruises, who did make the requisite safety investments and kept the vessel in service as their *Rembrandt*. P&O's *Canberra*, on the other hand, was withdrawn from service and summarily scrapped.

NCL felt that *Norway* was worthy of additional investment, though, and during a four-week visit to the King George V drydock in Southampton in late 1996, she was upgraded to meet new and more rigorous safety standards mandated by SOLAS, the International Maritime Organization's International Convention for Safety of Life at Sea. (More on safety standards in chapter 13.)

Norwegian Cruise Line maintains a two-vessel presence in the Alaskan market each summer, with the new *Norwegian Sky* pioneering something new and different in 2000: seven-night Inside Passage Alaskan cruises that originate in Seattle, not Vancouver. The vessel's twenty-four-knot speed capability makes such longer voyages possible and practical, although to satisfy the requirements of U.S. law that prohibit foreign-flag vessels from serving U.S. ports only, a visit must be paid to Vancouver, British Columbia, in one direction or the other.

NCL has even begun to revisit an idea that Knut Kloster once explored with some gusto, the acquisition of specialized cruise companies to serve specialized markets. Orient Lines was acquired toward the end of the 1990s as something of a niche-market provider whose specialty is leisurely cruises to exotic places such as the South Pacific. Orient will continue to be operated as a separate brand, with its own vessel, *Marco Polo* (a former Soviet passenger ship) now joined by *Norwegian Crown,* which reassumed her original name of *Crown Odyssey* when she was transferred to Orient. To establish an indigenous cruise company in the Far East/Australian market, a subsidiary called Norwegian Capricorn Line—conveniently, another NCL—was created and *Norwegian Star* assigned to it.

Prior to her transfer to Norwegian Capricorn Line, *Norwegian Star* became the first deepwater cruise ship to offer year-round western Caribbean cruises out of Houston, Texas, a marketing decision that not only put the vessel within easy reach of the many important population centers in Texas itself, but also closer to even larger markets on the West Coast. One of the growing pains the entire cruise industry must continually face is that there is a limit to the number of commercial airplanes that can land and take off in south Florida on any given day, and originating Caribbean cruises in a place like Houston effectively generates additional airlift capacity in addition to reducing the flying distance and cost between dockside and, for example, California. After *Norwegian Star* was reassigned to Norwegian Capricorn service in the Far East, NCL made *Norwegian Sea,* originally the *Seaward* of 1988, its regular Houston-based vessel for a number of seasons.

As Norwegian Cruise Line reestablished itself as a more stable player in the cruise industry in the late 1990s, the company became an inviting target for acquisition by a larger company. Indeed the fact that NCL became such a target is ample testimony to the fact that the company had righted itself financially. In December 1999, reports surfaced that Carnival Corporation had submitted a $1.7 billion offer to purchase the company's outstanding shares. Then Star Cruises—a new company that was formed in Malaysia in 1993 and whose fleet had quietly grown to make it the fourth largest cruise company in the world— jumped in and began to bid against Carnival. At one point it appeared that Star and Carnival might acquire NCL jointly, but in early 2000 Carnival dropped out and Star Cruises is now the sole owner of the cruise company that Knut Kloster founded in 1966.

NCL figures to retain its identity, despite the fact it is now a subsidiary of another company. The first indication of change under the new order was an announcement that the Norwegian Capricorn operation in Australia would be phased out in late 2000. In addition, *Norwegian Wind* will operate cruises out of Hong Kong during the winter in North America, while *Norwegian Star* will be conveyed to NCL's new parent as *SuperStar Capricorn.* Even the beloved *Norway* will shift her operating venue. In late 2001 she too will be moved to Asian waters.

Additional newbuildings seem to be in NCL's future. In April 2000 it was announced that a 91,000-gross-ton cruise liner that Star had ordered from Meyer Werft and that was to have been called *SuperStar Scorpio* would be completed instead as an NCL vessel and carry an appropriate NCL name. The new ship will include a new style of dining room management aboard a mass-market cruise ship—"freestyle cruising" as NCL is calling it. Instead of passengers' selecting or being assigned a fixed time for taking meals in the main dining room, the new vessel will feature open seating during expanded meal hours. Passengers will be free to dine as the spirit moves them. An early version of freestyle cruising has been introduced aboard *Norwegian Sky* and several other NCL vessels even before the newbuilding enters service. (Some competitive cruise lines see merit in NCL's initiative and are revising their own dining room options accordingly; others feel fixed hours are a shipboard tradition and plan no changes at all.)

Another impact of Star's acquisition of NCL is a plan to shift the former's 1998-built *SuperStar Leo* to the older line and operate her under the new name *Norwegian Leo*.

Knut Kloster was no longer associated with NCL when it fought its way back from the brink of insolvency in the 1990s and then began a new era in partnership with Star Cruises in a new century, but his pioneering spirit and the strong sense of values and ethical standards that he brought to the company—and to the industry itself, really—remain a lasting legacy.

CHAPTER 7

Holland America Line

Although it is today a wholly owned subsidiary of Carnival Corporation, Holland America Line (HAL) is managed independently. The company retains a strong measure of its traditional Dutch heritage, despite the fact that its operational headquarters are now located in Seattle, Washington, a city that is half-a-world away—in more ways than one—from the Dutch seaport of Rotterdam where Holland America Line had its beginnings in 1873.

Holland America Line was an early entrant into the cruise business, although its first such voyage was clearly not an effort to find new markets for its ocean liners in the face of airline competition. The company operated its first leisure-oriented voyage in 1895, eight years before Kitty Hawk. Of course this makes HAL little more than a Johnny-come-lately to the cruise business compared to Great Britain's P&O. That storied company boasts that it operated the world's very first cruise a half-century earlier in 1844 and with no less than British novelist William Thackeray aboard. It took Holland America some time before it ran its second cruise. It did not set sail until 1910, a full fifteen years after the company's first voyage.

The full story of Holland America is both rich and long and has been adequately told elsewhere. For purposes of understanding how HAL transformed itself from a transatlantic steamship company into a mainstay of the contemporary cruise industry, though, reference must be established to two important and classic company vessels, *Nieuw Amsterdam* (2) of 1938 and *Rotterdam* (5) of 1959. (More so than with other steamship companies, Holland America emphasizes the continuity of its operations by identifying successor vessels of the same name with sequential numerals. These numerals are not part of a vessel's formally enrolled name and are commonly used in company documents, but generally not in consumer-oriented publications like cruise brochures.)

Nieuw Amsterdam (2) was a wonderful, two-stack liner of 36,287 gross tons that many regard as nothing less than the most handsome vessel ever to sail the North Atlantic. She contributed to the Allied cause by serving as a troop transport during the Second World War and returned to passenger service afterward as the company flagship, running between a marine terminal in Rotterdam called the Wilhelminakade and piers in New York Harbor that were located across the Hudson River in Hoboken, New Jersey, close by the terminal of the Delaware, Lackawanna and Western Railroad. HAL ships began using Hoboken as their western terminal in 1882; in 1963, they moved across the river to a new facility on the Manhattan side that was designated Pier 40.

From the day *Nieuw Amsterdam* (2) joined the fleet, HAL felt the need for a proper running mate to complement the 1938-built vessel. Such a ship eventually emerged in 1959 in the form of the 38,647-gross-ton *Rotterdam* (5). While classic in every other respect, *Rotterdam* (5) featured as unusual a profile as any North Atlantic liner of her era—she had no funnels in any traditional sense, merely a pair of thin "uptakes," as they were called, positioned well aft to vent exhaust into the atmosphere. *Rotterdam* (5) would develop her own cadre of super-loyal followers over the years, despite the fact that she lacked one of the most important and distinctive characteristics an oceangoing passenger vessel can have, a funnel.

From the outset, *Rotterdam* (5) was designed with the dual needs of crossing and cruising in mind. When operating transatlantic, passengers were segregated into either of two classes, first and tourist. When the vessel was used in cruise service, though, the separations were eliminated and all passengers were able to

The 1959-built *Rotterdam* (5) no longer sails for Holland America Line, but a faithful likeness of her is featured outside the La Fontaine Dining Room aboard her replacement, *Rotterdam* (6).

enjoy near-equal access to the ship's facilities. Older ocean liners that were not designed to make such a transition easily and swiftly, as *Rotterdam* (5) was, had difficulty alternating between the two markets.

Rotterdam (5) departed from her namesake city on September 3, 1959, for her maiden voyage to New York; in HAL terms, the transatlantic crossing was called "Noordreizen." Three months later on December 11 the new vessel left New York on her first cruise, a six-week voyage around South America. *Rotterdam* (5) will serve as Holland America's most important symbol of stability as the company shifts its focus and its operations from Noordreizen to leisure-oriented cruises.

Through the 1960s and 1970s, HAL was not an especially robust company. It had a few smaller combination passenger-cargo vessels that were built after the war to replace older ships on the North Atlantic. They bore traditional company names: *Ryndam* (2) of 1951 and *Maasdam* (3) of 1952 were both in the 15,000-gross-ton range. At 24,294 gross tons, *Statendam* (4) of 1957 was a little larger but was another combination passenger-cargo ship. The mainstays of the fleet throughout this era remained *Nieuw Amsterdam* (2) and *Rotterdam* (5). As demand for space on the company's transatlantic crossings began to wane and jet aircraft assumed a more dominant role, HAL began to deploy its vessels more and more on various cruise itineraries.

But the company's passenger services were proving difficult to manage and were not faring well, either in cruising or crossing. Because of heavy taxes levied by the Netherlands Government on ships registered there, plus the requirement to staff such vessels with Dutch personnel, HAL made a series of important operational changes in the 1970s.

First, it reflagged its passenger vessels from Rotterdam to Willemstad in the Netherlands Antilles. This allowed the ships to continue to fly the red, white, and blue Dutch flag. It also permitted the company to benefit from more lenient maritime tax policies in effect in the West Indies as well as to avoid the need to hire none but Dutch seamen, whose labor unions were placing new and costly demands on Holland America management. As a cost-control measure, HAL decided to replace the Dutch dining room personnel on board its vessels with Indonesian help, Indonesia being a country that enjoys a long relationship with the Netherlands, dating back to the age of exploration when the area was known as the Dutch East Indies. Eventually, Holland America opened its own training institute in Indonesia for such workers, and soon afterward as another economy move, it became company policy to hire only Filipinos in onboard housekeeping departments. The final change—actually it was a series of changes—was to shift the company's corporate and operational headquarters from Rotterdam to New York in 1971, from New York to Stamford, Connecticut, in 1978, and finally from Stamford to Seattle, Washington, in 1983. During the course of these developments, HAL's passenger and cruise business was totally separated from the cargo services that were once central to the company's mission.

By the early 1970s, Holland America also recognized that the cruise market was not merely a revenue-generating supplement to its transatlantic services, it was rapidly becoming the sole passenger market the company could ever expect to serve. *Statendam* (4) was refitted for cruise service exclusively over the winter of 1972–73; she was rebuilt as a single-class vessel, additional passenger cabins were constructed in areas that had previously been cargo holds, and such warm-weather facilities as a lido cafe were added. When *Statendam* (4) rejoined the fleet after this conversion she pioneered a new livery for the HAL fleet. In place of the light gray hull that had long been the company's standard for its oceangoing passenger ships, she emerged with a dark blue hull plus an orange funnel decorated with a completely new company logo, one that featured a series of multicolored stylized ocean waves.

Interestingly, when most steamship companies moved into the cruise business, they repainted the once-black hulls of their ocean liners all white. Holland America painted the hulls of its vessels light gray during its transatlantic era but changed to dark blue to symbolize its shift into cruising.

In any event, soon enough the entire fleet was done in the new color scheme, all except *Nieuw Amsterdam* (2) of 1938. As a gesture to her venerable status, she retained the old color scheme until her retirement in 1974. *Nieuw Amsterdam* (2) had made the company's final transatlantic crossing in September 1971 and spent her final three years in cruise service only, primarily out of Port Everglades. *Rotterdam* (5) made the transition to full-time cruising even earlier. Since 1969—the tenth anniversary of her maiden voyage—the vessel's only assignments were leisure-oriented cruises.

In the years since—and to this day, in fact—it remains possible to book a transatlantic crossing aboard a Holland America ship or a vessel of any number of other cruise companies. But these voyages are simply positioning cruises, necessary to move a vessel from one market to another at the beginning or the end of a season, not purposeful journeys between Europe and North America in direct competition with jet aircraft.

In the early 1970s the company decided it needed some new ships, vessels designed from the outset to serve the unique needs of the new cruise-only markets it was attempting to serve. The initial design the company developed was for a most unusual vessel: a small, almost pocket-size cruise ship that measured a mere 8,566 gross tons in size and was 427 feet long. The contract for the first such vessel from N.V. Scheepswerf in the Netherlands included an option for a second, but the option was never exercised and only *Prinsendam* of 1973 was built to these unusual specifications.

Why the option was never exercised—and more importantly, what HAL did in its place—will be discussed presently. First, though, the brief but sad chapter that *Prinsendam* represents in HAL history must be recounted.

Her assignment was Far Eastern cruises from Singapore to Indonesian ports during the North American winter and journeys from Vancouver, British Columbia, north to Alaska along the Inside Passage in summer. *Prinsendam* was the first Holland America vessel to offer Alaskan cruises; she would not, however, be the last.

On September 30, 1980, the seven-year-old *Prinsendam* left Vancouver on a repositioning cruise back to her winter assignment in the Far East. While steaming through the Gulf of Alaska several days later with 319 passengers and a crew of 204 on board, a ruptured fuel line in the engine room quickly led to a fire that eventually doomed the seven-year-old vessel. Passengers and crew were safely evacuated, and at first it was thought the Canadian tug *Commodore Straits* would be able to tow the damaged ship back to Portland, Oregon, for repairs and rebuilding. It was not to be, though. Water continued to enter the stricken vessel through broken portholes and on October 11, 1980, *Prinsendam* suddenly capsized, and in three minutes she disappeared from view beneath the waves.

In lieu of exercising the option it held to order a sister ship of the diminutive *Prinsendam,* in the early 1970s (even before the loss of *Prinsendam*), Holland America acquired a pair of one-time U.S.-flag ocean liners that had been built in 1958 for Moore-McCormick Line service between New York and South America. Originally christened *Argentina* and *Brasil,* the pair became *Veendam* (3) and *Volendam* (2) for HAL—the V-ships, as they were often called. The company felt their larger capacity was a better alternative for meeting the needs of the evolving cruise market than building more vessels the size of *Prinsendam.*

HAL paid $10 million each for the two ships in early 1971, but the sale was not completed until the summer of 1972 when the U.S. Congress authorized the transfer of the pair to a foreign flag. Refurbishing at the Hapag-Lloyd yard in Bremerhaven, Germany, took the better part of another year, and the two vessels entered HAL cruise service in mid-1973. Less than a year later, though, both ships were taken out of service and laid up. The world petroleum crisis brought on by the Arab Oil Embargo of 1973 rendered fuel costs for the two steam-powered veterans quite prohibitive. In addition, the anticipated demand for cruising that the two ships were acquired to fill never materialized. The same petroleum crisis that increased the cost of fuel so dramatically took a serious toll on the disposable income of potential cruise passengers.

Both vessels went on to enjoy interesting careers over the next two decades, including a brief return to HAL service in 1978 when Holland America absorbed a small company called Monarch Cruises for which they were then operating. Miami-based Monarch Cruises was established in 1974 by Frederick C. Metcalf, a one-time president of Sitmar, and Robert P. Connors, formerly with Norwegian Caribbean Line, and the two former Moore-McCormick passenger ships were put to work for the new company. Holland America acquired Monarch in 1975 with the intention of retaining it as a separate cruise brand in the bargain-basement category of cruise companies, but Monarch did not flourish, and by the end of the decade the two vessels were back in the HAL fleet and Monarch Cruises was nothing but a memory. The two ships would find a home in the fleet of Commodore Cruise Lines in 1990 (see chapter 10).

HAL continued to expand its Alaskan cruise offerings both before and after the tragedy that doomed *Prinsendam.* In 1977, *Veendam* (3) joined *Prinsendam* in offering cruises out of Vancouver. Following the loss of *Prinsendam* and the departure of *Veendam* (3) from the fleet, summer service to Alaska was held down by *Rotterdam* (5) and *Statendam* (4).

Because it saw the emerging Alaskan cruise market as pivotal to its future, Holland America developed a working relationship with a Seattle-based tour company that began life in 1947 as Arctic Alaska Travel Service and by 1954 was known simply as Westours, after its founder, Chuck West. West's original activity was to offer overland Alaskan tours in conjunction with sailings of the Alaska Steamship Company. When Alaska Steamship discontinued its passenger service after the 1963 summer season, West secured two cruise ships of his own, *Polar Star* and *West Star,* to bring passengers north to his hotel and tour enterprises.

Westours, though, experienced difficultes operating the two ships. In 1971, Holland America purchased a 70 percent interest in the company, a share that increased by increments to full ownership in 1977. Initially, HAL attempted to coordinate a three-phase Alaskan operation—its own vessels, vessels of Westours, and Westours hotels and land tours. Eventually matters were simplified with HAL operating its own ships and Westours handling the tour, hotel, and later the railroad excursion side of things, even though all were under the management of a single parent company that was called Holland America Westours. Various cruise ships of other companies—for example, Carnival's *Tropicale* and *Cunard Princess*—were chartered by either Westours or HAL in various years to operate in Alaska service. It was because of this union of HAL and Westours that in 1984 Holland America moved its corporate and operational headquarters to Seattle, Washington, where it has remained ever since.

Chuck West severed his relationship with Westours in 1973, the year HAL increased its stake in the company to 85 percent. He remained active in the Alaskan cruise business, though, and founded a new company that is today known as Alaska Sightseeing/Cruise West, one of several operators of minicruise ships in Alaska each summer (see chapter 10).

With its future firmly linked to the growth of the Alaskan cruise market, Holland America recognized the need for new ships. In 1983 the company took delivery of a new vessel, one whose style and appointments would be in the tradition of the company's finest ocean liners from its transatlantic days. Built in St. Nazaire, France, at the storied Chantiers de l'Atlantique shipyard, a hallowed Holland America name was given to the newbuilding. On July 9, 1983, she was christened *Nieuw Amsterdam* (3) by Princess Margriet of the Netherlands, and the next day she set sail from St. Nazaire on a maiden voyage to New York. As if to emphasize a venerable tradition from the golden age of ocean liners—but one which is not commonly associated with the cruise industry—when *Nieuw Amsterdam* (3) reached New York, two stowaways who had sneaked aboard the ship in St. Nazaire were discovered in one of the lifeboats. They were promptly sent back to France.

As much as any single event can, the arrival of *Nieuw Amsterdam* (3) in 1983 signaled a change in fortunes for Holland America and the beginning of a new era of growth for the company. In fact, the construction of *Nieuw Amsterdam* (3) marked a turnaround not only for HAL. It was also the first new passenger ship to be built at Chantiers de l'Atlantique in well over a decade and the shipyard would go on to become a major supplier of newbuildings as the cruise industry grew and prospered. *Nieuw Amsterdam* (3) was quickly followed by a sister ship from Chantiers de l'Atlantique, *Noordam* (3) of 1984. Reportedly, the financing

Noordam (3), shown here leaving Juneau, Alaska, in 1997, and her sister ship, *Nieuw Amsterdam* (3), were the first modern newbuildings to join the HAL fleet.

of the two newbuildings in part made use of insurance settlements from the loss of *Prinsendam.*

The company's next fleet addition would arrive not as a newbuilding, but as the result of the acquisition by HAL of another cruise line. Home Lines was an early trendsetter in the new cruise industry. It believed in the importance of newbuildings, for example, at a time when many cruise companies were content to operate nothing but older ships. Home Lines *Oceanic* of 1965, a vessel whose maiden voyage was described in chapter 1, was followed by *Atlantic* of 1982. Once *Atlantic* was in service, the company placed an order with the Joseph L. Meyer shipyard in Papenburg, West Germany, for a third new vessel, a ship the company called *Homeric* and placed in service in 1986.

In terms of corporate strategy, though, Home Lines made what in retrospect must be called a major miscalculation. It assumed that the newly developing cruise industry in North America would focus its activity in the Port of New York, the place where the transatlantic liners of yesteryear arrived and departed. This was where Home Lines based its cruise fleet.

While this might have been a reasonable assumption, it proved to be a devastatingly incorrect one. What Homes Lines failed to appreciate was the extent to which south Florida would emerge and prosper as the cruise capital of North America. The Port of New York is certainly proximate to an enormous residential population that represents a ready market for cruises of all shapes and sizes. But a cruise out of New York in wintertime to the sunny and warm environs of the Caribbean had to begin and end with an often foul-weather passage around Cape Hatteras coupled with all the fury for which the North Atlantic was rightly famous. A seven-night Caribbean cruise out of New York took almost two full days to reach warmer latitudes and two more to get back, with a good possibility of weather-related distress along the way.

What emerged as the perfect winter alternative for New Yorkers was to jump aboard a jet airliner for a two-hour flight to south Florida and enjoy a seven-night Caribbean cruise that was sailed on calm seas under warm and sunny skies for its entire duration. New York—the all-year port of embarkation when ocean liners sailed to Europe—was transformed into an important but largely seasonal cruise port, with vessels departing for Bermuda, for Canada, and for an occasional transatlantic crossing, primarily during warm-weather months.

In 1987, Holland America purchased Home Lines. HAL saw no purpose in retaining *Atlantic* and she was quickly sold off to become *StarShip Atlantic* for Premier Cruises, joining there, incidentally, her one-time Home Lines fleetmate *Oceanic. Homeric,* the newest member of the fleet, did fit into HAL's plans, and she was absorbed by Holland America as *Westerdam* (2).

If Holland America's takeover of Home Lines was big news in the cruise industry in 1987, it was totally overshadowed by something that would happen the next year. In November 1988, HAL invited a number of people from the indus-try to a reception to mark the entry of the refurbished *Westerdam* (2) into the company's service. During the festivities, HAL chairman Nico van der Vorm was approached by one of his guests and an extremely important conversation en-sued. The guest was Ted Arison of Carnival Cruise Lines and he asked van der Vorm whether HAL might be open to a negotiated takeover by Carnival. Arison had been rebuffed in a bid to acquire a majority interest in Royal Caribbean ear-lier that same month, and so he had investment capital at his disposal. A deal was worked out several days later and on January 17, 1989, Holland America Line be-came a wholly owned subsidiary of Carnival. The purchase price usually men-tioned for the transaction was $625 million.

Included in the purchase was not only HAL itself, but also HAL's ownership of Westours as well as HAL's interest in a niche-market cruise company called Windstar that it had acquired in two phases in 1987 and 1988. Windstar was founded in the mid-1980s by interests associated with New York's Circle Line Sightseeing Yachts, offering cruises aboard re-created sailing vessels with deluxe stateroom accommodations and fine cuisine (see chapter 10).

Under Carnival ownership, HAL retains a good deal of autonomy. Its head-quarters remain in Seattle, it handles its own marketing and ticketing, its Dutch heritage has, if anything, been enhanced, although decisions of a long-range and strategic nature are obviously made in close coordination with Carnival.

The first activity of an investment nature that HAL made after the Carnival takeover was the stretching of *Westerdam* (2) to expand her capacity. Over the winter of 1989–90 the vessel was sent back to Meyer Werft in Papenburg and her passenger capacity was expanded from 1,132 to 1,476 by splicing a new 130-foot section into her middle. The project increased her gross registered tonnage from 42,092 to 53,872.

Unlike other ship-stretching projects (where a ship is cut in two in a dry-dock, the drydock is reflooded, the separated bow and stern sections are floated away from each other so a fully preconstructed midsection can be floated be-tween, and all three are welded together), *Westerdam* (2) remained in drydock throughout the project. The ship was cut in two and the bow section was pulled forward on rollers. Then, prebuilt modules that would constitute the new sec-tion were assembled in place between the forward and aft sections. That sum-mer, 1990, the entire HAL fleet—*Rotterdam* (5), *Nieuw Amsterdam* (3), *Noordam* (3), and the recently-stretched *Westerdam* (2)—were all deployed in summer service to Alaska.

The previous year, 1989, Holland America had announced nothing less than the largest program of passenger newbuilding in its entire 123-year history. Prior to its being purchased by Carnival, HAL had signed letters of intent with Bre-mer-Vulkan for the construction of two 60,000-gross-ton newbuildings. Once

Carnival was in the picture, though, it was decided to let these preliminary agreements expire and move in a different direction.

Three new 55,000-gross-ton cruise ships were ordered from the Fincantieri yard in Monfalcone, Italy, an order that was later expanded to four. The first was christened *Statendam* (5) and entered service in June 1993, to be followed by *Maasdam* (5) in 1993, *Ryndam* (3) in 1994, and *Veendam* (4) in 1996; all four vessels are generally referred to as the Statendam-class. Some of the early meetings between Fincantieri people and a Carnival–Holland America technical team working on the project were conducted at sea in the Mediterranean aboard Ted Arison's yacht, *Mylin III*. The contract for construction of the first three Statendam-class ships was signed on November 29, 1989; the per-vessel price was estimated to be in the range of $250 million.

The Statendam-class was the last word in cruise ship design, technology, and interior appointment. The four ships do not rival Carnival's Fantasy-class in size, but they do feature diesel-electric propulsion and can be controlled by a computer-linked "joystick" that simultaneously engages the main propulsion motors, the three side thrusters, the controllable-pitch propellers, and the twin Becker rudders, as needed, by a single flick of the wrist. Motors, thrusters, pro-

Veendam (4) has backed away from Vancouver's Canada Place and is about to depart on a seven-night Alaskan cruise. The vessel is one of HAL's Statendam-class cruise ships.

Maasdam (5), built by Fincantieri in 1993 and a member of HAL's Statendam-class, is maneuvering into her assigned berth in the Russian port of St. Petersburg.

pellers, and rudders can, of course, be controlled independently, if a captain should so prefer. But during an intricate docking maneuver, a simple movement of the joystick can engage whatever combination of power sources are needed to move the bow or the stern closer to a berth.

Five medium-speed Sulzer diesel engines—two 12-cylinder and three 8-cylinder models—are each linked to a separate electric generator, and each of a vessel's twin propeller shafts are turned by a large electric motor built by ABB.

As this infusion of new vessels began to join the fleet, Holland America Line was able to dispatch six cruise ships to Alaska each summer, leaving only one behind to work the Caribbean. Then in the late 1990s when the European market began to develop, HAL saw no problem in forsaking the Caribbean entirely in June, July, and August and sending a ship or two across the Atlantic to cruise European itineraries.

The HAL fleet had now grown to seven vessels. All were new, modern, diesel-powered vessels, except for the one that was often referred to as the "Grande Dame" not only of Holland America Line, but of the entire cruise industry—*Rotterdam* (5) of 1959.

Her end would come in 1997 with the implementation of more stringent safety requirements as mandated by SOLAS. She made her final cruise under HAL colors that fall, a positioning voyage from Vancouver to Fort Lauderdale. Rather than invest millions of dollars to bring a forty-year-old cruise ship up to the new international safety standards—and do so in an absolutely first-class fashion—HAL and Carnival decided to replace her with a larger and faster version of the Statendam class, a vessel that was called *Rotterdam* (6) and upon which was bestowed the title of flagship of the Holland America fleet.

The passing of *Rotterdam* (5) was sad. Many people—HAL passengers and HAL employees alike—invested a considerable measure of their emotions in this marvelous vessel, emotions that were not at all assuaged when *Rotterdam* (5) was sold to Premier Cruises and returned to cruise service, with SOLAS modifications, as their *Rembrandt*.

The new *Rotterdam* (6) is a marvelous vessel that is already on the way to developing new loyalties among both old and new HAL passengers. Faster than her Statendam-class predecessors—during early planning sessions, the ship that became *Rotterdam* (6) was often referred to as the *Fast-dam*—hull and power-plant modifications allow her to better the twenty-knot top speed of the earlier quartet and reach twenty-five knots. *Rotterdam* (6) was built by Fincantieri, the same

HAL's 1997-built *Rotterdam* (6) is somewhat larger than the company's four earlier Statendam-class vessels and features more robust speed capability. The vessel is in the port of Copenhagen, Denmark, about to depart on a North Cape cruise.

The stack treatment pioneered here on *Rotterdam* (6) has been repeated on *Amsterdam* (3).

company that turned out the four Statendam-class vessels, and she features, in memory of *Rotterdam* (5), a pair of distinctive side-by-side funnels positioned aft. They are more substantial funnels than the thin uptakes of *Rotterdam* (5); perhaps, one might even say, they compensate for what some feel was a serious design flaw in *Rotterdam* (5), namely, her absence of true funnels. *Rotterdam* (6) quickly picked up a HAL tradition that *Rotterdam* (5) had been handling in previous years, a ninety-day world cruise early in the year. Holland America inaugurated an annual world cruise with *Statendam* (4) in 1958, although the company did not offer such a voyage each and every year since 1958.

Investment in new cruise ships did not stop with *Rotterdam* (6). *Volendam* (3) came out in 1999, followed by *Zaandam* the next year. The two are slightly larger than *Rotterdam* (6), but are still regarded as part of the Statendam class, even though they have a slightly different external profile than other members of the class. The initial itinerary that HAL announced for *Zaandam* was interesting; she became the first company vessel in many years to work the Caribbean on a year-round basis. Then, in late 2000, another newbuilding entered service, one that imitates *Rotterdam* (6) in all external respects, including the twin funnels, and bears the name *Amsterdam* (3). *Rotterdam* (6) and *Amsterdam* (3) have been designated the twin flagships of the HAL fleet.

Initially, when the new name was announced, it was felt that it might lead to some serious confusion in the vessel nomenclature department—a new *Amsterdam* (3) sailing in the same fleet whose oldest vessel was *Nieuw Amsterdam* (3). Confusion was avoided when HAL announced that *Nieuw Amsterdam* (3) would be sold to American Classic Voyages and reflagged to U.S. registry to begin a new career of intra-island service in Hawaii under the name *Patriot*.

While *Amsterdam* (3) is a twin of *Rotterdam* (6) in terms of her general profile, she has one important mechanical difference. *Amsterdam* (3) is the first vessel in the HAL fleet to feature pod propulsion. She has twin Azipod units, similar to those pioneered by Carnival's *Elation* and *Paradise*.

Rotterdam (6) and *Amsterdam* (3) will actually surrender the title of twin flagships in the early years of the twenty-first century as even more newbuildings join the HAL fleet. These vessels will reflect certain features common to cruise ships under design and construction for several subsidiary companies of Carnival, and their gross registered tonnage will be in the 84,000 range, larger than any previous HAL ships. Like *Amsterdam* (3), the new vessels will be Azipod-propelled, and Fincantieri plans to deliver the first of this latest class of HAL cruise ships in 2002, the second in 2003, and three more before 2005.

A company that operated its first cruise in the final years of the nineteenth century is certainly going strong in the early years of the twenty-first. And to give added emphasis to the Dutch maritime traditions the company proudly upholds, in recent years changes in tax policies in the Netherlands have enabled the company to forsake the registration of its vessels in the Netherlands Antilles and restore the home port of Rotterdam to the majority of its fleet.

CHAPTER 8

Cunard Line and Seabourn Cruise Line

Cunard Line

Few would contest the claim that Great Britain's Cunard Line is the best-known steamship company of all time. Founded in 1840 by Sam Cunard, a Canadian from Halifax, the company's distinctive corporate signature—a Cunard red funnel with thin black bands—has graced such important vessels as the *Mauretania* and the *Lusitania,* the *Queen Mary* and the *Queen Elizabeth.* Why the best-known steamship company of all time is appropriately treated in the same chapter with a veritable newcomer like Seabourn Cruise Line will soon become apparent.

CUNARD LINE

This is neither the time nor the place to talk about all the glory that was Cunard; that story has been told often and well. Our purpose is rather to sketch out how an element of once-mighty Cunard survived the decline of transatlantic ocean liners and converted itself into a company whose principal business is cruising. But take careful note of the qualification implicit in the use of the expression "principal business." Because the marvelous fact is that Cunard is the only cruise line to enter the twenty-first century with its flagship, the 1969-built *Queen Elizabeth 2,* still providing a measure of the transatlantic service that was once the company's basic fare. Indeed, Cunard is committed to retaining such service as a permanent option. In 2000 the company executed a contract for the construction of a new transatlantic liner, a vessel that will be called *Queen Mary 2* and will be a proper transatlantic running mate of *Queen Elizabeth 2.*

The advent of jet-powered commercial air service across the North Atlantic in 1959 was the start of a long decline for Cunard. While many are aware that the company's twin superliners, *Queen Mary* and *Queen Elizabeth,* provided weekly departures from each side of the Atlantic for many years, the two vessels were by no means the company's only vessels on the North Atlantic, even during the period after the Second World War. *Mauretania* of 1939 and *Britannic* of 1930 were two

131

lesser vessels, for example, with the comparative adjective "lesser" needed only when the two are contrasted with the company's stately Queens.

Britannic, incidentally, provides an interesting footnote to the overall Cunard story. Cunard vessels traditionally were given Latinized names that ended in the letters "ia"—*Sylvania, Aquitania, Franconia*. Rival White Star Line, on the other hand, identified its vessels with names ending in "ic"— *Olympic, Baltic, Celtic*. (More recently, Home Lines also identified its ships with names ending in "ic." A member of that company's board of directors was said to be enamored of the White Star Line and felt Home Lines should honor the tradition by repeating it.)

The 26,943-gross-ton *Britannic*, built in 1930, was originally a White Star vessel. When Cunard and White Star merged in 1934 to create a company that was known for a number of years as the Cunard–White Star Line, White Star vessels retained their original names and even continued to feature White Star's traditional colors—buff funnels with a black band at the top. *Britannic* survived to be the last former White Star vessel in the combined fleet, an identity she retained until she was retired in late 1960 and broken up the following year.

Cunard Line was always aware of the commercial possibilities that cruising represented. Even so stately a vessel as the original *Mauretania* of 1907 ended her career during the Great Depression with her hull painted white to better acclimate her for frequent cruises out of New York to the Bahamas, to Cuba, or to Haiti. The second *Mauretania* likewise ended her career in 1965 with her once-black hull repainted cruise-ship white. As Cunard rebuilt and refurbished its passenger fleet after the Second World War, a 1948 product of John Brown's Clydebank yard must be mentioned when one talks about the transition from crossing to cruising. This was the 34,172-gross-ton *Caronia*, a vessel that was designed from the outset to meet the specialized needs that cruise service demanded.

Caronia, whose hull and superstructure were painted in several highly distinctive shades of light green, provided a service that was not even remotely like the mass-market cruise operations that would later emerge in the North American market. *Caronia* was upscale from the outset. She specialized in grand cruises to every corner of the world, including an annual around-the-world voyage that set sail each January. One legendary woman supposedly sailed aboard *Caronia* as a passenger for fifteen straight years!

Caronia's final days were sad; in no sense did she participate in the emergence of the contemporary cruise industry. Cunard withdrew her from service in the late 1960s and still a youngster, she was sold to Greek interests and renamed *Caribia*. But she enjoyed no success at all in her new identity. After a long layup in New York, she was sold for scrap in 1974 and was lost in the Pacific en route to a ship breaker in Taiwan.

In the late 1950s Cunard built four ocean liners in the 20,000-gross-ton range. Primarily designed for transatlantic service between the United Kingdom and Canada, *Ivernia, Saxonia, Carinthia,* and *Sylvania* were classic passenger/cargo ships. Tourist class accommodations, for example, did not feature full plumbing in all cabins, and there were no facilities like outdoor swimming pools or lido decks that would later be so important aboard vessels competing for cruise passengers.

The four ships were the right size for the new cruise industry, though, and Cunard soon sent *Saxonia* and *Ivernia* back to John Brown's for conversion into vessels that would be better suited to the needs of cruising. To signify this change in status, *Saxonia* was renamed *Carmania* and *Ivernia* became *Franconia.* The other two vessels, *Sylvania* and *Carinthia,* were eventually sold to Sitmar and refitted for cruise service by that company. (When Sitmar was absorbed by P&O/Princess, the pair became, respectively, *Dawn Princess* and *Fair Princess.*)

The rebuilt *Franconia* operated for Cunard for several years in seasonal service between New York and Bermuda, an unusual market that combines, in a sense, elements of crossing and cruising. Cunard was able to move into this market in the late 1960s when the long-time operator on the route, Furness-Withy, Ltd., withdrew.

Furness-Withy entered the Bermuda market in 1919 and eventually deployed a pair of classic three-stack steamships in the service—*Monarch of Bermuda* of 1931 and *Queen of Bermuda* of 1933. Both were recruited for military service during the Second World War, but only the *Queen* returned to New York–Bermuda service afterward. As a running mate, Furness-Withy built the 1951 *Ocean Monarch,* a single-stack steamship that could well be called the first ship that was purpose-built exclusively for cruise service out of North American ports.

It was during this postwar era, though, that a fundamental change impacted New York–Bermuda service. Initially people traveled from New York to Bermuda by ship and then stayed in a fashionable island hotel for several days or even weeks before returning to the mainland aboard a subsequent sailing. The change saw New York–Bermuda service evolve into "liveaboard" cruises, with passengers never surrendering their shipboard accommodations and a vessel's spending two or three nights docked in Bermuda.

Cunard operated *Franconia* in cruise service—summer to Bermuda, winter in the Caribbean—from 1963 until 1973, when she was sold to the Black Sea Shipping Company for service under the Soviet flag as *Feodor Shalyapin.* Her Cunard sister ship, *Carmania,* became *Leonid Sobinov* for the same company at the same time after spending her cruising days working Caribbean and Mediterranean cruise itineraries.

In addition to adapting *Franconia* and *Carmania* for cruise service, a Cunard vessel that was designed from the outset with the needs of cruise passengers in

Furness-Withy's *Queen of Bermuda*, long a favorite on the New York–Bermuda run.

mind was *Queen Elizabeth 2* of 1969. True, *QE2* would carry the flag (Cunard's as well as Britain's) on transatlantic crossings between New York and Southampton. But she was designed to be at home in leisure-oriented cruises as well as point-to-point travel across the North Atlantic. More recently, for that matter, Cunard has recrafted its transatlantic crossings into more of a cruise experience. In 1997, for instance, speed was reduced and *QE2*'s crossings were expanded from a five-day experience into a six-day one.

Queen Elizabeth 2 would be continually rebuilt and refurbished during her Cunard career, with the most extensive work taking place over the winter of 1986–87. During a visit to the Lloyd Werft yard in Bremerhaven, Germany, her four original steam-turbine engines were replaced by a set of nine 9-cylinder MAN model 9L58/64 diesel engines. The diesels drive electric generators and *QE2*'s twin screws are now turned by large electric motors.

Even with the advent of the new *QE2* in 1969, Cunard felt that to remain competitive, it needed additional ships more in tune with the emerging styles characteristic of the cruise industry. An opportunity came along in the late 1960s when a pair of cruise vessels that had been ordered by a Dutch operator became available even before they were finished. Cunard moved quickly and snapped up the pair, calling them *Cunard Adventurer* and *Cunard Ambassador*. They joined the fleet in 1971 and 1972, respectively. Neither, however, would enjoy a long or a distinguished Cunard career.

Cunard Ambassador caught fire in late 1974. Too badly damaged to warrant rebuilding as a cruise ship, she was converted instead into a livestock carrier, surely not a happy fate for a vessel designed to carry passengers on relaxing Caribbean cruises. *Cunard Adventurer* was sold to Norwegian Caribbean Line in 1976 and became that company's *Sunward II.*

In the mid-1970s, Cunard designed and built another pair of cruise ships, *Cunard Countess* and *Cunard Princess.* Slightly larger that *Adventurer* and *Ambassador*—17,500 gross tons vs. 14,000, approximately—they gave Cunard a steady presence in various mass-market Caribbean cruises for a good number of years.

In the 1980s, Cunard's cruising growth would come primarily by way of acquisition and merger rather than newbuilding. In 1983 the company purchased two vessels that had been designed and built by the Norwegian-American Line, the 1965-built *Sagafjord* and the *Vistafjord* of 1973. Norwegian-American was an old-line transatlantic steamship company that had transformed itself into the epitome of an upmarket cruise operation. By the early 1980s, though, Norwegian-American was ready to leave the business and was receptive to Cunard's offer. To retain the many loyal passengers who regularly patronized Norwegian-American cruise ships over the years, Cunard retained the original "-*fjord*" names of the two vessels, creating the altogether anomalous situation of the world's most obviously British steamship company owning and operating vessels with names that were just as obviously Norwegian in origin and meaning.

Front Street, Hamilton, Bermuda, in the summer of 1970. Cunard's *Franconia* is tied up astern of Greek Line's *Olympia.* Both vessels would enjoy additional years of service for different owners.

Cunard's *Queen Elizabeth 2* heads out of Boston in the fall of 1973 on a transatlantic crossing.

It was a precedent that would soon be repeated. When the cruise holding company established by Knut Kloster decided to divest itself of Royal Viking Line in 1994, Cunard purchased that company as well, together with its principal vessel, *Royal Viking Sun*, and again Cunard retained the vessel's original name. While these three "Scandinavian" vessels sailed for Cunard and were decorated with traditional Cunard-red funnels, none ever flew the British flag. All were registered in the Bahamas.

In 1986, after the acquisition of Norwegian-American but before taking over Royal Viking, Cunard acquired yet another cruise property. This was a small upmarket company that was founded a few years earlier as Sea Goddess Cruises. Its fleet consisted of a pair of yachtlike luxury vessels, the Wartsila-built *Sea Goddess I* and *Sea Goddess II*. Each carried only 120 passengers and included such features as stern platforms that permit passengers to swim and scuba-dive directly from the vessel or to board kayaks and inflatables for further adventures. Cunard retained these original names, too, and deployed the pair on exotic Caribbean, Mediterranean, and South American itineraries, including visits to small ports where larger cruise ships are unable to venture.

A Cunard expansion in the mid-1990s was less an out-and-out acquisition and more a cooperative marketing arrangement that allowed a fleet of three new mass-market cruise ships to have their funnels painted Cunard-red and be promoted as part of the overall Cunard enterprise. Crown Cruise Line was a separate cruise brand that had come under the umbrella of Effjohn International in the early 1990s. While Crown earlier operated such older vessels as the 1967-built *Crown del Mar*, in the late 1980s it ordered a trio of newbuildings, the 15,271-gross-ton *Crown Monarch* plus the 19,000-ton sister ships *Crown Jewel* and

Crown Dynasty. All three were built by a yard not traditionally associated with cruise industry newbuilding, Union Naval de Levante of Valencia, Spain. This arrangement with Crown allowed *Cunard Princess* to be sold off to Festival Cruises in 1995, while *Cunard Countess* joined the three Crown vessels to constitute a four-vessel Cunard presence in the mass-market segment of the industry. *QE2, Royal Viking Sun, Vistafjord, Sagafjord,* and the two Sea Goddess yachts clearly appealed to a more upscale market and were, of course, priced accordingly.

The Cunard/Crown joint arrangement did not achieve any long-term stability. *Crown Monarch* and *Crown Jewel* were soon sold to emerging cruise operators in the Far East, while *Crown Dynasty* was leased first to Majesty Cruise Lines and then to Norwegian Cruise Line in the late-1990s before reverting to her original name and service for Commodore Cruise Line under a newly restored Crown Cruise Line brand.

Cunard/Crown did deploy *Crown Dynasty* in the Alaskan market for several seasons, though, and while her 19,093 gross tons made her a much smaller vessel than competitive ships in the 50,000- and 60,000-ton range then being operated in Alaskan service by companies like Princess and Royal Caribbean, the brilliant

In the fall of 1999, *Queen Elizabeth 2* is preparing to leave New York on yet another crossing to Southampton.

Crown Monarch, one of three Crown vessels that wore Cunard colors for a few seasons.

color of her Cunard-red funnel made her a genuine standout amid the low-lying mists of the Inside Passage.

Despite all these developments, Cunard was not enjoying sound financial health, even while the cruise industry itself was experiencing robust growth. Ownership of Cunard passed from one set of investors to another, and predictions that the company's fabled house flag would soon be hauled down were not uncommon. In 1996, Trafalgar House, the final British owner of the old company that had acquired it back in 1971, was itself taken over by the Norwegian firm, Kvaerner. While Cunard's mass-market cruise operations were dismantled so it could concentrate on its upscale product, the line's financial prospects hardly improved.

The corner was turned in 1998 when none other than Carnival Corporation stepped in and for $500 million acquired Cunard. At first, Carnival merely held a partial interest in the famous company, although at 68 percent it was certainly controlling. By 1999, Carnival had become Cunard's sole owner. "We bought an extremely mismanaged company," Carnival's Micky Arison said after the acquisition when he had a chance to examine the company's books in greater detail. Despite what they found, Carnival quickly took steps to turn the venerable company around and put it on a sound footing.

Because Carnival owned both Cunard and Seabourn, it was able to combine certain management and operational aspects of its two upscale subsidiaries. By the start of the 2000 cruise season, Cunard had been reduced in the scope of its operations but given a very clear brand identification that played to the line's heritage and tradition. *Queen Elizabeth 2* continued her usual itineraries, which involved a January world cruise followed by a combination of cruises interspersed with transatlantic crossings. A typical pattern in summertime would be an east-bound crossing, a seven- or ten-night cruise out of Southampton, then a west-bound crossing followed by a cruise out of New York.

All the other Cunard vessels except *Vistafjord* were transferred to Seabourn. (*Sagafjord* had left the fleet in 1996 after protracted mechanical problems.) *Vistafjord* entered the Lloyd Werft shipyard in late 1999 and emerged as *Caronia,* the name once carried by Cunard's legendary postwar cruise pioneer. Unlike the original *Caronia* with her light green hull, this more recent *Caronia* was given a traditional black hull and white superstructure, all topped off, of course, with a Cunard-red funnel. (The color that has long been called "Cunard red" is perhaps best described as a very vivid shade of orange, while the company's version of a traditional black hull is in reality more of a charcoal gray.) To emphasize Cunard's British heritage, when *Vistafjord* became *Caronia* she was also reflagged to British registry.

The big Cunard news at the turn of the century was not the reassignment or reflagging of existing vessels. It was the fact that in 2000 Cunard signed a contract with Chantiers de l'Atlantique for the construction of an extraordinary new vessel that will be called *Queen Mary 2.* The cost announced for this newbuilding was a staggering $780 million—more than the $500 million Royal Caribbean paid for the 142,000-gross-ton *Voyager of the Seas* and far more than the $325 million Carnival paid for its final Fantasy-class vessel, *Paradise.* Virtually all major European shipyards were considered for this important project, including Harland and Wolff in Belfast, a company that had not turned out a passenger vessel in several decades but was sought out by Cunard in an effort to have *Queen Mary 2* built in a British yard. It was not to be; instead the massive new vessel will be turned out in St. Nazaire, France. Her statistics, post Panamax to be sure, are positively mind-numbing: length, 1,131 feet; breadth, 135 feet; estimated gross registered tonnage, 150,000; passenger capacity, 2,800; number of decks, *seventeen!*

The new liner's engines will include four diesels and two gas turbines and she will be propelled by four electric Mermaid pod-propulsion units, two stationary and two fully azimuthal. To emphasize Cunard traditions, the new *Queen Mary 2* will be equipped with a ship's whistle that will faithfully recreate the deep report that was once an important signature of her namesake, the original *Queen Mary* of 1936.

Building a new passenger ship is not an exercise any shipyard approaches lightly, especially when the vessel in question will be the largest in history. Furthermore, *Queen Mary 2,* irrespective of her record-shattering size, will not be just another cruise ship. She will be a bona fide transatlantic ocean liner, with a hull and power plant designed not for leisurely cruising in the calm waters of the Caribbean but for swift passage across a sometimes hostile ocean.

Carnival does not see *Queen Mary 2* or *QE2*, for that matter, as ships that will impact the popularity of jet aircraft for basic transatlantic travel or reverse market trends that began in 1959. Rather, they see the North Atlantic as a kind of ultimate cruise experience, one that is not merely a casual trip through placid Caribbean waters, but a repetition and a recreation of a voyage that was once at the very heart of world commerce, from the first voyages of exploration by the likes of Henry Hudson to the vast armada of cargo ships that successfully delivered the manpower and equipment to Europe to defeat the Axis powers during two world wars.

A final thought about Cunard Line and *Queen Mary 2* is this: just as the television series *The Love Boat* is widely credited with playing a helpful role in popularizing the new cruise industry in the final decades of the twentieth century, so James Cameron's 1997 award-winning movie *Titanic* may have played an important role in raising interest in transatlantic travel by sea. Despite *Titanic*'s tragic sinking, the movie apparently created a situation where Carnival Corporation could make a hard-headed business decision to invest many hundreds of millions of dollars in building a new transatlantic liner.

SEABOURN CRUISE LINE

Seabourn Cruise Line enjoys nothing even remotely like the distinguished heritage that is Cunard. When it was founded in 1987 by Norwegian industrialist Atle Brynestad, Cunard was a robust 147 years old. Brynestad's goal was to create nothing less than the world's most elegant cruise product. Initially the company intended to call itself Signet Cruise Line, but a copyright issue emerged and a new name had to be coined.

To help achieve his goal, Brynestad was able to hire Warren Titus to run his new cruise line. Titus had been the chief officer at Royal Viking Line for many years and was thought to be the man most responsible for the success of that earlier effort at creating a genuinely upscale cruise company.

Unlike Royal Viking—whose vessels, by the standards of their day, were full-size cruise ships—Seabourn opted for smaller and more intimate vessels. The first of these, *Seabourn Pride*, was built at Schichau Seebeckwerft in Bremerhaven, Germany, in 1988 and measured a modest 9,975 gross tons. She is 439 feet long with accommodations for 204 passengers. A sister ship, *Seabourn Spirit*, was built the following year at the same yard and to the same specifications.

Seabourn held an option for a third vessel, but it was an option Brynestad never exercised. Instead, Klosters Rederi bought the rights to the option from Seabourn, had the vessel completed as *Royal Viking Queen*, and assigned her to Royal Viking Line. *Royal Viking Queen* was not part of the package that was sold to Cunard when Royal Viking itself was liquidated in 1994; instead, she was transferred to Royal Cruise Line and became its *Queen Odyssey*. When Royal Cruise was

Seabourn Pride, one of a trio of smaller cruise ships that were Seabourn's initial vessels.

later dissolved, *Queen Odyssey* was sold to Seabourn and became *Seabourn Legend,* joining her sister ships.

Carnival purchased a 25 percent interest in Seabourn in 1992, with Brynestead staying on as a minority partner. Carnival later increased its stake to that of majority owner. After Cunard was added to the Carnival family in 1997, the Seabourn and Cunard fleets were managed as a quasi-merged entity, although each cruise brand retained an identity of its own. The year 2000, though, saw further change. As noted earlier, Cunard was positioned in a way that emphasized its British traditions while the Seabourn side of the house was expanded by considerable measure and identified as an unabashed upscale cruise company with worldwide itineraries of a genuinely luxurious sort. *Royal Viking Sun* became *Seabourn Sun* while the two Sea Goddess vessels became *Seabourn Goddess I* and *Seabourn Goddess II.* This all served to make the Seabourn brand an extraordinarily large presence within the limited confines of the upscale cruise market, a company that owned and operated no fewer than six vessels.

Royal Viking Sun, a vessel that ran for both Royal Viking and Cunard, has since been conveyed to Seabourn and renamed *Seabourn Sun.*

Many years before, Carnival itself had talked about something it called Project Tiffany, an effort to move into upscale cruise markets without compromising the mass-market position Carnival Cruise Lines itself represented. Carnival's various acquisitions over the years, from Holland America and Windstar in 1987 to Seabourn and more recently Cunard, have given the Tiffany Project a clear and definite shape and form, although it is likely one that is a little different from what Ted Arison had in mind when he first coined the phrase.

CHAPTER 9

Celebrity Cruises

In Greece during the years before the First World War, John D. Chandris founded a shipping line that would soon bear his name. Initially, the new company hauled freight from mainland Greece to islands in the Aegean Sea. Chandris Lines would not make a permanent expansion into passenger markets until after the Second World War. By this time, the company was run by Dimitrios and Antonios Chandris, sons of the line's founder.

The strong outflow of postwar immigrants from Europe to Australia prompted Chandris Lines to try its hand at the operation of passenger ships. The first true passenger liner to fly the company's house flag was built in 1950 in Belfast as *Bloemfontein Castle* for Britain's Union-Castle Line. Sold to Chandris in June 1959 and renamed *Patris*, she sailed away from Piraeus, the seaport of Athens, on her maiden voyage to Sydney on December 14, 1959. This was mere weeks after the first jet airliners entered regular service across the North Atlantic. For a variety of reasons associated with cost and distance, oceangoing passenger vessels would remain commercially viable on such longer routes as Europe-to-Australia for an additional period of years, especially for large-volume markets like the immigrant trade.

Throughout the 1960s and the 1970s, Chandris Lines added many ocean liners to its expanding passenger fleet. The company was able to recondition older ships very economically at its own facility near Piraeus and by the mid-1970s, Chandris was operating fourteen ocean liners that were carrying half a million passengers annually. By most standards, Chandris was then the largest operator of oceangoing passenger vessels in the world, granted that it was a time when the heyday of the great transatlantic steamship companies was over.

A notable Chandris acquisition during this period was the one-time flagship of United States Lines, the 1940-built *America*. Sold to Chandris in November

1964 and renamed *Australis,* she became a mainstay of the company for over fifteen years.

As the 1970s gave way to the 1980s, jet aircraft had become dominant the world over, and even the long run from Southampton to Sydney was more economically made by air than by sea. It was clear to Chandris management that if the company's passenger vessels were to survive, they should be redeployed into cruise service. And so Chandris Lines began to recondition its vessels to serve such markets. The kind of dining and entertainment and sleeping accommodations that economy-class passengers might find satisfactory during a long, one-way voyage to Australia were no longer suitable; more luxurious facilities were needed if customers were expected to select a Chandris cruise over one being offered by the competition.

Two marvelous cruise vessels ran for Chandris Lines during the 1980s as *Britanis* and *Amerikanis.* The latter was built for Britain's Union-Castle Line in 1952 as *Kenya Castle* while the former was a classic-looking vessel with twin stacks that began her career in 1932 as Matson Line's *Monterey* and sailed under the American flag between San Francisco and points in the Pacific. *Britanis* and *Amerikanis* developed strong followings among Chandris cruise passengers and were among the most popular ships of their era. The two were not the only vessels to work cruise itineraries for Chandris, but they enjoyed exceptional careers.

Even as ships like *Britanis* and *Amerikanis* were carrying satisfied cruise passengers year-round, consumer research conducted by what was then the London-based management of Chandris Lines was telling the company in no

A 1932-built vessel that began life as Matson Line's *Monterey* ran for Chandris for many years as *Britanis.* Retired in 1995, the veteran oceanliner sank in the South Atlantic while being towed to a scrap yard in October 2000.

uncertain terms that a major upgrade of its cruise product was necessary if it wished to retain—much less expand—its market share. Other companies were designing and building dramatically new and different cruise ships year after year. Chandris could not expect to compete with such vessels so long as its fleet consisted of nothing but reconditioned ships from an older era.

By the late 1980s, thanks to corporate links with a North American tour operator, the company was trading under the name Chandris Fantasy Cruises. Instead of upgrading its existing service incrementally, management decided to start afresh and create a totally new cruise brand, one that from the very outset would be identified with quality, luxury, innovation, and an absolutely impeccable and uncompromising level of passenger service. Chandris, in other words, was not only shifting itself from bargain basement to mass-market, it planned to position itself at the upper end of the mass-market category. On April 14, 1989, John D. Chandris—son of Antonios Chandris and grandson of company founder John D. Chandris—issued an important statement: Chandris was forming a new operating entity that would be called Celebrity Cruises. (Interestingly, celebrity is a Middle English word meaning distinguished or special. It is thought by many scholars to have been coined by the fourteenth-century poet Geoffrey Chaucer.)

In the 1980s, Chandris Fantasy had secured a toehold in a very important cruise market—seasonal service between New York and Bermuda. Chandris management would launch Celebrity Cruises by substituting its new product for its old one on this route in summer and by developing new Caribbean itineraries during the winter. In the years following the inauguration of Celebrity Cruises, Chandris Fantasy quietly faded from the scene.

To create a dramatic new look for its new service, Celebrity turned to naval architect Jon Bannenberg of London, a man whose maritime reputation had been earned through the design of luxurious oceangoing yachts of a very exciting sort, and commissioned him to create a new cruise ship with a totally different external profile. Bannenberg's efforts, carefully supervised by Celebrity's own professional staff, produced *Horizon*, a $185-million vessel built at the Joseph L. Meyer shipyard, Meyer Werft, located on the banks of the River Ems in Papenburg, West Germany.

Horizon featured strong and angular lines; her hull and superstructure were accentuated by a series of dark blue stripes that conveyed a sense of motion even when the vessel was tied up in port. Yet as new and different as was *Horizon* on the outside, the understated elegance of her interior appointments was even more dramatic and striking. Celebrity assembled a talented design team to develop specifications for the interiors of its new vessels. With a few substitutions along the way, and with Bannenberg in the lead as naval architect, this same team would, over the next decade, design an entire fleet of luxury cruise ships for the new company.

In 1990, Celebrity needed two vessels, not one, for the New York–Bermuda service. Pending the construction of additional new cruise ships, the company decided to upgrade one of the old fleet, a vessel that had been operating for Chandris Fantasy as *Galileo*. Built in 1963 for Lloyd Triestino, she had run for many years under the Italian flag between Italy and South America as *Galileo Galilei*. While she had been modestly reconditioned by Chandris for cruise service in 1983, a more thorough rehabilitation was required to bring the vessel up to the new standards Celebrity was determined to establish. A complete reconstruction was performed at the Lloyd Werft shipyard in Bremerhaven, West Germany, at a cost in excess of $50 million.

Renamed *Meridian* for her new career with Celebrity, the reconditioned vessel entered cruise service to the Caribbean out of Port Everglades, Florida, on April 1, 1990, the very first sailing under the new Celebrity label. Later that spring *Meridian* migrated north to New York, and on May 12, 1990, the new *Horizon* sailed into New York Harbor from Papenburg. The two vessels then worked together between New York and Bermuda during that first Celebrity summer of 1990.

While *Horizon* and *Meridian* were new and different in many ways, there was one dramatic feature of both vessels that emphasized the heritage John D. Chandris began back in 1915. Chandris vessels had long featured a distinctive funnel decoration. Painted medium blue, the company's funnels included a white symbol that most people instinctively called the letter X, even though it was not the letter X at all. It was the upper-case rendition of a letter from the Greek alphabet, "chi," as in Chandris and also Chios, the Aegean island that was the home of the Chandris family.

Meridian, a reconditioned vessel that was built in 1963 as *Galileo Galilei*, joined the Celebrity fleet in early 1990 following a complete reconstruction in Germany.

Horizon, Celebrity's first newbuilding, exhibits the sharp and angular lines that would become an important characteristic of the new company's fleet.

To honor its Chandris origins, the funnels of Celebrity Cruises remained blue, although Bannenberg specified a darker shade to symbolize the start of a new order. The "chi" not only remained, it was rendered more dramatically and more vividly on *Horizon* and *Meridian* than on earlier Chandris ships. In addition, Bannenberg complemented the "chi" on *Horizon*'s funnel with a distinctive white wind deflector that looks like some kind of unusual accent mark attached to the large letter. It would become a unique signature element in the design of all subsequent Celebrity newbuildings.

Another feature that Bannenberg incorporated into *Horizon*'s exterior design was a set of uptakes around the vessel's mainmast that almost appear to be a second, albeit much smaller, funnel. These uptakes—John Maxtone-Graham calls them funnel simulacra—serve no function and are included solely as an aesthetic feature. The uptakes are highlighted by a white wind deflector just like the funnel itself, and the inclusion of such uptakes, along with the wind deflectors, would also become a feature of the Celebrity fleet.

Celebrity's expansion would continue. *Zenith*, a sister ship of *Horizon*, was delivered in April 1992. But even three vessels—the new *Zenith* and *Horizon* plus the reconditioned *Meridian*—were insufficient to achieve the goals Celebrity

Cruises had set for itself. Further newbuildings were needed and the company again called on Jon Bannenberg and the team of interior designers who had given the company such a distinctive initial identity. This time, they were to lay out a trio of even larger vessels, ships that would be called the Century class.

The first was *Century*. She appeared in 1995 and was followed in 1996 and 1997 by *Galaxy* and *Mercury*. *Century* is a bit smaller than the other two in length, gross registered tonnage, and passenger capacity; *Century* accommodates 1,750 passengers, *Galaxy* and *Mercury*, 1,870. *Horizon* and *Zenith*, by comparison, each accommodate slightly fewer than 1,500 passengers.

With the arrival of these three new vessels, Celebrity was able to declare *Meridian*, its first cruise ship, to be surplus. She left the fleet in 1997 and was sold to Sun Cruises, an emerging operator in the Far East. Renamed *Sun Vista*, Celebrity's first vessel unfortunately came to grief in Asian waters. In May 1999 she caught fire in the Strait of Malacca on a six-night cruise out of Singapore. All passengers and crew were safely rescued, but *Sun Vista* herself was not so lucky. She sank.

The sharp and bold lines Bannenberg pioneered on *Horizon* were continued on the Century class. In addition, Century-class vessels feature a totally unprec-

Galaxy, a member of Celebrity's three-vessel Century class, continues many of the design features that were pioneered on *Horizon*.

Millennium under construction at the Chantiers de l'Atlantique yard in St. Nazaire, France.

edented level of onboard technology. A formal partnership between Celebrity the SONY Corporation of America in 1994 prompted the deployment of entertainment and communications equipment that allows passengers to do everything from select movies for in-cabin viewing (in the language of one's choice, in fact), to preview and order shore excursions, not to mention choose the proper wine to accompany dinner.

To help secure the capital required to design and build the Century class, Celebrity sought, and found, an investment partner anxious to move into the passenger cruise business. In October 1992, Celebrity Cruises formed a joint venture with Overseas Shipholding Group (OSG) of New York. While Celebrity had ordered *Century* prior to joining forces with OSG, the expanded access to capital markets the new firm provided enabled *Galaxy* and *Mercury* to be constructed more rapidly than Celebrity could have managed on its own.

With five smartly designed new vessels in its fleet, Celebrity was able to expand into additional cruise markets. In 1997, the company dispatched two ships, *Horizon* and *Galaxy,* through the Panama Canal to offer seasonal Alaskan cruises, and in 1999, *Century* inaugurated the company's first summer season in Europe, working itineraries from the Mediterranean to the Baltic. The next service expansion will take Celebrity Cruises below the equator to itineraries in South America in the new century.

In the summer of 1997, Celebrity Cruises and Royal Caribbean International merged under the banner of a parent corporation known as Royal Caribbean Cruises, Ltd. The two companies—Celebrity and Royal Caribbean—will retain separate identities and operate as separate cruise brands, although in the interests of economy and efficiency, certain overhead and management functions have been combined under the parent corporation at Royal Caribbean's Miami head-quarters. The merger involved a transfer of almost $1.3 billion in cash, equities, and the assumption of debt. Celebrity's chairman John D. Chandris and Morton Hyman, the president of Overseas Shipholding Group, were both added to the Royal Caribbean board of directors as part of the overall arrangement.

With additional investment resources available to underwrite further fleet expansion and a merger partner with a long and successful history in the cruise business, the growth of Celebrity Cruises was accelerated. In 2000, yet another new ship joined the Celebrity fleet, the first of an intended quartet of 91,000-gross-ton newbuildings. Christened *Millennium*, the new ship represented several important milestones not only in the Chandris-Celebrity story, but in the history of the cruise industry itself.

Millennium was the first Celebrity newbuilding that was not a product of Meyer Werft. She was built, instead, at St. Nazaire, France, by the Chantiers de l'Atlantique shipyard. In addition, *Millennium* is the first cruise ship to employ a totally new and different style of power plant. While her propellers are turned by electric motors—a common enough feature in the contemporary cruise indus-try—the current to run these motors is generated not by diesel engines, but by a pair of gas turbine engines built in the United States by General Electric. Gas turbine engines have many advantages over diesels in a marine environment. To generate equivalent output, a gas turbine engine room can be much smaller than one equipped with diesels, thus freeing up space aboard ship for other purposes. Diesel engines require complex systems for both the storage and the subse-quent separation of lubricating oil onboard ship; gas turbines do not. Gas tur-bines emit a small fraction of the noxious emissions that diesels emit, and because they generate energy by rotation instead of reciprocation, gas turbines are less likely to produce unwanted shipboard noise and vibration.

Gas turbines have proven their mettle with many years of dependable per-formance in naval fleets the world over. The more a joint Celebrity–Royal Carib-bean team examined gas turbines as potential power plants for future cruise ships, the better they looked. And so a decision was quickly made to specify such engines in future newbuildings for both companies. (As noted earlier, new ves-sels that Royal Caribbean identifies as Project Vantage share many similarities with Celebrity's Millennium-class ships, including gas turbine engines.)

Other cruise companies besides Celebrity and Royal Caribbean have also be-gun to experiment with gas-turbine power. The 1999 P&O/Princess order for five new ships, for example, includes four vessels that will have some of their electric current generated by gas turbines. *Millennium*, her sister ships, and RCI's Project Vantage vessels, however, will have all of their power produced by gas turbines.

Well, almost. The GE system on board *Millennium* includes two main gas-turbine engines that supply most of the ship's electrical power. Celebrity press releases used the term "aeroderivative" in describing the engines, meaning they are adaptations of the extraordinarily dependable engines that are used to power jet airliners throughout the world. But the overall power plant also includes an auxiliary steam turbine that generates additional electricity from steam generated by the water evaporators, the incinerators, and other sources.

The steam turbine is small compared to the gas turbines: 12,000 horsepower versus 67,000. But its presence in the overall system underscores an important shipboard imperative: energy must be conserved and utilized to the maximum extent possible. GE uses the designation COGES to describe this power plant, an acronym that stands for combined cycle gas turbines and steam turbine integrated electric propulsion system.

In addition to the novelty of gas-turbine power, Celebrity's new Millennium-class cruise ships are driven by a pod-propulsion system built by a joint venture of two European companies, Kamewa and Cegelec, and marketed under the trade name Mermaid. *Millennium*'s two Mermaid pod-propulsion units are fully azimuthal, but they should not be called Azipod units, since, as pointed out earlier, Azipod is the trade name of a competitive pod-propulsion system.

Like all Celebrity newbuilding efforts, the construction of *Millennium* was managed by a senior vice president of the company, Demetrios Kaparis, a man

Above: On November 7, 1999, Celebrity's new *Millennium* was moved out of the drydock and into the River Loire by a fleet of local tugboats. *Left:* Demetrios Kaparis, whose career with Chandris began in 1960, has overseen the construction of all new Celebrity cruise ships.

whose career with Chandris began when he was a young man in 1960 and included such early assignments as the acquisition of the SS *America* from United States Lines in 1964. "Seeing *Millennium* launched is like having a lifelong dream come true," Kaparis told a French television camera crew on November 7, 1999, the day the big vessel was floated out of the drydock where she had been built in St. Nazaire and moved to a fitting-out berth for the final stages of construction.

Cruise passengers aboard *Millennium,* of course, have little occasion to be aware of what kind of engines are driving the vessel or generating the electricity that lights their cabins, cooks their food, and powers the elevators they ride. What passengers boarding *Millennium* will see is a vessel whose looks are markedly different from her Celebrity predecessors. She boasts an all-blue hull, not the white hull of earlier Celebrity vessels. Four middle decks are set back from the outer limits of the superstructure, and the weight and stability advantages that this generates allow the inclusion of an extra deck with additional exterior cabins with balconies. Glass elevators provide a panoramic view of the sea as they travel up and down.

Another new feature cruise passengers will notice aboard a Millennium-class vessel is a specialty restaurant, a small, intimate hideaway that allows passengers to forsake the main dining room once or twice during a cruise and sample specialized fare in a different setting. These are gaining popularity with many cruise companies and customers.

Infinity, the second vessel in Celebrity's new Millennium class, is entering the final stages of her construction at the Chantiers de l'Atlantique shipyard in St. Nazaire, France.

Celebrity's *Zenith* heads out to sea from New York on a summer cruise to Bermuda.

The specialty restaurants on Millennium-class vessels are more than places to eat. They are also rooms that memorialize classic ocean liners from yesteryear. The restaurant on *Infinity*, for instance, is dedicated to the U.S.-flag superliner S.S. *United States*, while *Millennium*'s specialty restaurant not only recalls the one-time White Star liner R.M.S. *Olympic*, it actually includes some authentic hand-carved walnut paneling that once graced the a la carte restaurant on the historic vessel.

The paneling was auctioned off when *Olympic* was withdrawn from service in 1935 and tracked down by Demetrios Kaparis a half-century later for use—or, more correctly, reuse—aboard *Millennium*. No sooner had *Millennium* taken to the sea with her marvelously decorated specialty restaurant from R.M.S. *Olympic* than she managed to merit inclusion on a rather unusual list. On the weekend before Halloween in 2000, a major American television network did a travel story identifying a number of locations that, for one reason or other, have earned reputations for being haunted by ghosts.

According to the story, crewmembers aboard *Millennium* have reported late-night sightings of shadowy figures dressed in early twentieth-century finery dining in the new specialty restaurant.

Millennium entered service in the summer of 2000 and worked several European itineraries before heading transatlantic in the fall for a winter Caribbean assignment out of Fort Lauderdale. New and different as she is, one feature of this vessel is familiar. Her stack is decorated by the large white figure that the uninitiated will undoubtedly call the letter "X." With *Millennium* and her three sister ships, Bannenburg's treatment of this traditional Chandris-Celebrity design feature has reached a new level. The funnel on which it is displayed remains dark blue and the "chi" remains white. But the white letter is outlined in vivid yellow, while the very top of the funnel is finished off with a dramatic dash of red.

The wind deflector Bannenburg pioneered on *Horizon* is retained, and it is repeated on not one, but two separate and parallel uptakes—simulacra—that Bannenburg developed to give *Millennium* its highly distinctive profile. And in a very subtle touch, Bannenburg has replicated the dartlike look of the wind deflectors in the design of the aft end of four decks of the vessel's superstructure.

The following table displays a range of data and information about Celebrity's Millennium-class vessels. Many of these statistics exceed the dimensions of all the famous transatlantic superliners, and yet the vessels they describe are not the largest cruise vessels at work in the industry today.

CELEBRITY'S MILLENNIUM-CLASS CRUISE SHIPS

Chantiers de l'Atlantique yard numbers (and names)	R-31 *(Millennium)*, S-31 *(Infinity)*, T-31 *(Summit)*, U-31 (unnamed)
Gross registered tonnage (estimate)	91,000
Net tonnage (estimate)	56,000
Overall length	964.5 feet
Breadth	105.6 feet
Draft	26.3 feet
Number of passenger staterooms	1,019
Passenger capacity (double occupancy)	2,038
Passenger capacity (total)	2,540
Number of crew	997
Maximum speed	24.8 knots
Number of elevators	10 guest, 7 service
Onboard freshwater production	2 evaporators, 700 tons each per day
Tank capacity: fuel (marine gas oil)	898,185 gallons
Tank capacity: potable water	713,265 gallons
Stabilizers	One pair, folding type
Special feature	Helicopter landing area at bow
Main engines	2 GE LM2500+ gas turbines
Propulsion	2 Mermaid 20,100 kW pod drives
Thrusters	3 at bow
Classification society	Lloyd's Register
Country of registry	Liberia
Home port	Monrovia

In early 2001, Celebrity's second Millennium-class cruise ship, *Infinity*, is expected to join the fleet, with the third and fourth sister ships scheduled to enter service in the fall of 2001 and the spring of 2002, respectively.

From *Meridian*'s initial cruise in April 1990 to the advent of the Millennium class a little over a decade later, Celebrity has established itself as a young and aggressive provider of cruise vacations. It is a fitting development, certainly, to a seafaring tradition that John D. Chandris began on the Aegean Sea in the early years of the twentieth century.

CHAPTER 10

More Choices

Premier Cruise Lines

The industry is enriched by a variety of other cruise companies of varying shapes and sizes that enjoy interesting traditions. Some continue to sail and carry passengers while others have passed from the scene. They are presented in no special order and represent a variety of market categories—mass market, bargain basement, upscale, and niche.

COMMODORE CRUISE LINE

In discussing the origins of Royal Caribbean Cruise Line, mention was made of a short tenure that RCCL's founder, Edwin Stephan, enjoyed at a company called Commodore Cruise Line following the demise of Yarmouth Steamship Company. Commodore inaugurated service in 1968, three years after the *Yarmouth Castle* disaster and two years after Ted Arison and Knut Kloster joined forces to form Norwegian Caribbean Line. The guiding force behind the new venture was a man who, like Stephan, had earlier worked as a Florida hotelier; his name was Sanford ("Sandy") Chobol, and he was very popular in Miami business and social circles.

Actually, Chobol and Commodore first got into the cruise business out of south Florida in 1962 with a chartered Spanish-built vessel, the *Princess Leopoldina*, that was owned by Brasilian Coastal Line. Because of both operational and personnel problems, this operation survived for only a single season, and it was not until 1968 that the company secured another vessel—first by charter, later by purchase—that would be identified with Commodore for the better part of twenty years. This was *Boheme*, a ship under construction in Finland as a Baltic Sea car ferry when Chobol and Stephan learned that she was no longer needed for her intended market and might be available for cruise purposes. Stephan played a major role in redesigning *Boheme* into a proper cruise ship, turning open car decks into deluxe passenger cabins. Powered by a pair of 8-cylinder Sulzer diesels, *Boheme* was a stylish-looking vessel with a pair of tandem funnels aft and a strong and square look that made no effort to disguise the fact she was originally designed to be a car ferry. *Boheme* specialized in seven-night cruises out of Miami and pioneered visits to such unusual Caribbean ports of call as Cap Haitien in northern Haiti and Puerto Plata in the Dominican Republic.

Commodore Cruise Line would never become a large operation. In the mid-1980s the company replaced *Boheme* with a former ocean liner, Greek Line's *Olympia*, which was renamed *Caribe*, then later, *Caribe I*. *Caribe* was also repowered; *Olympia*'s four steam turbines were torn out and replaced by a pair of 12-cylinder Deutz diesels.

There had been an earlier *Caribe* that Commodore once operated, a one-time car ferry that began life as *Freeport I* and became *Scandinavian Sun* after leaving the Commodore fleet in 1980. *Scandinavian Sun* would enter a south Florida cruise trade that has not been mentioned thus far: one-day cruises from Miami to Freeport in the Bahamas, departing early in the morning and returning that same evening. It was also planned to use *Scandinavian Sun*'s car-carrying capability to create a New York–to–Florida car ferry service in conjunction with a

Built on the Clyde in 1953 as *Olympia* for Greek Line's transatlantic service, this vessel ran for Commodore as *Caribe I* and eventually became *Regal Empress*. Originally steam-powered, the ship was later converted to diesel.

newbuilding called *Scandinavia.* Because a foreign-flag vessel could not run directly from New York to Florida, *Scandinavia* would operate between New York and Freeport in the Bahamas, where passengers and their automobiles would transfer to *Scandinavian Sun* for the final leg to Florida. This was hardly an ideal arrangement. This development was touched on briefly in chapter 4 when *Scandinavia* became Royal Caribbean's *Viking Serenade* after the New York–Florida car ferry service flopped.

The biggest changes Commodore Cruises would see, though, happened in the early 1990s. Chobol had passed away in the 1970s and Commodore was then sold to British owners. In the 1990s, the company was acquired by Effjohn International, a maritime holding company that had been formed by the merger of two important Scandinavian shipping concerns, the Effoa-Finland Steamship Company and Johnson Line AB, of Sweden. Effjohn International was anxious to expand its presence in the growing world of cruise ship operations. In 1989, Effjohn had added a company called Bermuda Star Line to its portfolio and later merged it with Commodore. Bermuda Star Line's two vessels thus joined *Caribe* under the Commodore house flag.

The two Bermuda Star Line vessels were no ordinary cruise ships. They served briefly as Holland America's *Veendam* (3) and *Volendam* (2). Under Commodore the two vessels—built in the United States in 1958 as Moore-McCormick's *Argentina* and *Brasil*—were renamed, respectively, *Enchanted Isle* and *Enchanted Seas* and the steam-powered pair would see the dawn of the twenty-first century still in active cruise service for Commodore. While remaining under Commodore ownership and operated by Commodore personnel, *Enchanted Seas* has been renamed *Universe Explorer.* She specializes in educational cruises of various sorts connected with the University of Pittsburgh, and she is used for adventuresome summer cruises in Alaska under the auspices of World Explorer Cruises.

Enchanted Isle, on the other hand, developed an interesting year-round niche in the world of Caribbean cruises. Instead of originating seven-night cruises from either Miami or Port Everglades, *Enchanted Isle* embarks her passengers at the port of New Orleans, a city made to order for extended stays either before or after a cruise. Or before *and* after a cruise.

In 1992, *Caribe I* was sold to a company called Regal Cruise Line. Thus a vessel that was built on the Clyde in 1953 as a transatlantic liner began a new career as *Regal Empress.* She, too, developed an interesting market niche: in winter, she offers Caribbean cruises out of Port Manatee on Florida's Tampa Bay, while in the summer she ventures north to the Port of New York and offers cruises of various lengths—anything from two nights to nine nights—touching at a variety of destinations from Canada to Bermuda. From time to time *Regal Empress* will even include a circumnavigation of the South American continent in her winter schedule.

New York–based JeMJ Financial Services acquired Commodore Cruises from Effjohn in 1995—Effjohn's entry into the North American cruise industry proved to be short-lived—and shortly afterward supplemented *Enchanted Isle*'s year-round cruises out of New Orleans with offerings by a second vessel, *Enchanted Capri*, which specialized in split-week two- and five-night cruises.

Enchanted Isle and *Universe Explorer* were built right down the Gulf Coast from New Orleans in Pascagoula, Mississippi. *Enchanted Capri*, on the other hand, was not. She was built in 1975 at Wartsila's Abo yard in Turku, Finland—the same place, interestingly, where *Boheme* had earlier been constructed—and she spent her first years flying the hammer and sickle of the Soviet Union as the Black Sea car ferry *Azerbaydzhan*.

In 1999 Commodore announced that it had obtained yet another vessel, *Enchanted Sun*, for deployment on short day-cruises to Mexico out of San Diego. But the arrival of *Enchanted Sun* was not the big company news of 1999—Commodore's West Coast day-cruise venture proved to be short-lived. Aware that any cruise company operating forty-year-old steam-powered vessels would never be regarded as offering a top-of-the-line product, Commodore decided to form a new subsidiary that it could position higher up on the scale. Resurrecting a brand name that was once part of Effjohn, Commodore formed a new unit called Crown Cruise Line, and for its first vessel, the company secured a seven-year-old cruise ship that had herself once sailed for Effjohn's older Crown Cruise Line.

Built in Valencia, Spain, in 1993 as *Crown Dynasty*, she later wore Cunard colors, worked for Majesty Cruise Line for a year as *Crown Majesty*, and more recently was leased to Norwegian Cruise Line as *Norwegian Dynasty*. For service with Commodore's new Crown Cruise Line, the vessel reverted to her original name, *Crown Dynasty*, and in keeping with Commodore's specialty of providing unique itineraries, the renamed vessel offered seven-night winter cruises in the lower Caribbean out of Aruba and summer cruises between Philadelphia and Bermuda. The summer itinerary includes interesting distinctions. The ship departs from the mainland at midweek and spends the weekend in Bermuda, something the island government had not sanctioned in recent years. In addition, a portion of her cabins must be reserved for "one-way passengers," people who combine their cruise aboard *Crown Dynasty* with a stay in a Bermuda hotel. This is an effort to placate resort interests in Bermuda who see cruise ships as competitive threats for the same tourist dollars they themselves are seeking to earn.

A similar feeling exists at certain islands in the Caribbean, and it is a dynamic that the cruise industry will undoubtedly find itself facing with more frequency in future years. Some years back, certain Caribbean islands attempted to enforce a ban on the sale of liquor in the lounges of in-port cruise ships in an effort to encourage cruise passengers to slake their thirst ashore in local establishments. Thus far the industry has been able to avoid such situations.

When Moore-McCormick took delivery of *Argentina* and *Brasil* in 1958, the company intended to use the pair on its traditional passenger routes between New York and South America. The two were not regarded as extraordinary vessels at the time, not when the SS *United States* was the reigning queen of the North Atlantic and the notion of six-hour flights to Europe aboard jet-powered airliners was still in the future. But the two Pascagoula-built vessels have proved to be extraordinary indeed, and while Commodore itself faces an uncertain future—the company suspended operations in late 2000—it will always be remembered for allowing these two wonderful vessels to grow old gracefully and serve faithfully for additional years.

REGENCY CRUISES

The rise and fall of Regency Cruises is a sad story. The company was founded in November 1984 by William Schanz, a man who had earlier served as president of Paquet French Cruises, a European-based company that had made modest inroads into south Florida during the early years of the cruise industry.

The company's first cruise ship sailed as *Regent Sea*, a vessel that was built in 1957 as Swedish-American Line's *Gripsholm*, a handsome twin-stack classic. She entered service for Regency in November 1985, offering weekly Caribbean cruises out of Montego Bay, Jamaica. As with San Juan, Puerto Rico, the use of Montego Bay as a point of origin for cruises allows for an expanded southern Caribbean itinerary that can proceed all the way to the South American mainland within the limits of a seven-night cruise.

Regency Cruises grew; additional vessels were added and itineraries were expanded. Indeed Regency seemed intent on not becoming just another company offering basic Caribbean fare. By the early 1990s, it sent as many as three vessels north to Alaska in the summertime and dispatched another to Europe. The company was beginning to take a hard look at the Far East as a potential cruise market. Regency was doing on a small scale exactly what the North American cruise industry itself was about to do on a large scale—expanding beyond the Caribbean into interesting and exciting new world markets.

The Regency fleet grew to a maximum of seven vessels; all had previously worked for other companies with most dating back to the era of transatlantic ocean liners. There was talk of newbuildings, including an unfortunate effort to convert two almost-new containerships into bona fide cruise ships. (Costa Cruises eventually took title to the two hulls Regency intended to convert, went ahead with the conversion, and produced *Costa Marina* and *Costa Allegra*. More on Costa Cruises shortly.)

For one reason or another, though, Regency's efforts were insufficient to the task it had planned. Its debt load was too large and its revenues too small to equal success. The company—by the mid-1990s owned primarily by Antonios

Regent Rainbow, here leaving Key West, Florida, was built in 1958 as Grace Line's *Santa Paula.* The vessel was substantially rebuilt over the years and bears little resemblance to the original design.

Lelakis—made valiant efforts to refinance its outstanding obligations, but by this time some of its vessels had been impounded, thus drying up the revenue streams that might otherwise have been used to help in the refinancing efforts. All of this, of course, took an awful toll in the way of consumer confidence. Travel agents were understandably reluctant about confirming cruise reservations for their clients aboard vessels that were sitting in shipyards guarded by marshals and under the control of various courts.

It ended suddenly on November 1, 1995, when Regency Cruises went out of business. Many of its vessels were eventually picked up by other operators and enjoyed further years of service. The cruise venture that William Schanz began in November 1985 when *Regent Sea* set out from Montego Bay came to a full and complete halt a decade later.

AMERICAN CLASSIC VOYAGES

Although no potential cruise passenger sits down and reads a brochure with the name American Classic Voyages prominently displayed on its cover, four different cruise operating lines are subsidiaries of this important Chicago-based company. Between them they offer customers some interesting cruise opportunities.

Would a passenger like to sail aboard an oceangoing vessel that flies the American flag? American Classic Voyages has not one but two subsidiaries that offer such service. Does a cruise up or down the Mississippi River on a steam-powered stern-wheeler sound more inviting? American Classic Voyages provides this as well. Or perhaps a coastal cruise aboard a smaller vessel—around Chesapeake Bay, for example, or to the offshore islands of Nantucket and Martha's Vineyard—is one's cup of tea. American Classic Voyages has a new subsidiary specializing in this kind of service, too.

At the turn of the twenty-first century, the oldest passenger vessel embarking passengers for overnight cruises in North America was a 1926-built steamboat called the *Delta Queen*. Owned and operated by the Delta Queen Steamboat Company, a subsidiary of American Classic Voyages, she offers cruises of various lengths from cities up and down America's system of inland rivers, northern cities like Minneapolis and Cincinnati and St. Louis during warm-weather months, southern ports like New Orleans during the winter.

That *Delta Queen* is still in service is nothing short of remarkable. She was built in Stockton, California, with a hull and machinery that were prefabricated in Europe and then shipped to the West Coast for final assembly. *Delta Queen*'s wooden cabin work appeared to be a fatal flaw that should have forced her removal from overnight passenger service when more stringent regulations were enacted into law in the wake of the 1966 fire aboard *Yarmouth Castle*.

Post-*Yarmouth Castle* statutes, of course, were drafted to protect passengers from fire at sea, when a vessel would be miles from the nearest landfall. *Delta Queen*'s inland itineraries clearly do not incur the same degree of risk as would a vessel sailing the seven-night milk run from south Florida to St. Maarten, for example. The U.S. Congress was prevailed upon to enact exempting legislation for this classic steamboat; they did, and so she survived.

The name *Delta Queen* seems totally appropriate for a steamboat operating up and down the Mississippi River, but curiously, her name references the delta of the Sacramento River in California where she and a sister ship, *Delta King*, offered overnight service between San Francisco and Sacramento in the years before the Second World War. Following military service around San Francisco Bay during the war, she was purchased by Greene Line in Cincinnati, brought east through the Panama Canal, and put to work on the company's overnight service along the Ohio and Mississippi rivers. Delta Queen Steamboat Company is a direct descendant of Greene Line.

Thanks to the statutory exemption it was able to secure to keep its classic vessel in service, the Delta Queen Steamboat Company was first able to survive. Then as the cruise industry itself began to grow and prosper, it was able to thrive and expand. The smaller *Delta Queen* was soon joined by two newer and larger running mates, the 1976-built *Mississippi Queen* and the 1995-built *American*

Queen. All three are powered by old-fashioned steam engines; all are propelled by a huge stern-mounted paddle wheel. To give a sense of the respective size of the three vessels, *Delta Queen* has a passenger capacity of 174, *Mississippi Queen* accommodates 416, while *American Queen* can carry 436 passengers.

In 2000, Delta Queen expanded to the West Coast. A partially-built passenger vessel that had been laid down as yet another inland gaming ship was purchased, shipped to the West Coast aboard an oceangoing barge, and put into service cruising as the gingerbread-bedecked *Columbia Queen,* out of Portland, Oregon, along the Columbia River. *Columbia Queen* has all the external appearance of an old-fashioned riverboat, but unlike her Mississippi fleetmates, she is not steam powered—she's driven by a pair of 12-cylinder Cummins diesel engines. Nor is she stern-wheel driven; her propulsion comes from a pair of ordinary screw propellers assisted by a pair of Schottel Z-drive units that are powered by a separate and smaller set of Cummins diesels. Fortunately, *Columbia Queen* was not fitted with a faux paddle wheel as many excursion and gaming vessels have been in recent years, a helpless little appendage that does not power the vessel but spins weakly in the vessel's wake.

American Classic Voyages does not restrict itself to inland rivers. In 1993 the company took over a troubled cruise operation in the Hawaiian Islands that was operating two vintage American-built passenger ships on seven-night cruises around the islands. Built in Quincy, Massachusetts, in the early 1950s, *Independence*

Delta Queen Steamboat's new diesel-powered *Columbia Queen* entered cruise service along the Columbia River in the summer of 2000.

In July 1954, American Export Line's *Constitution* is tied up in New York at North River Pier 84, preparing for a transatlantic crossing to various Mediterranean ports. The vessel spent her final years in cruise service under the U.S. flag for American Hawaii Cruise Line. The vintage automobiles parked adjacent to the vessel have a historic character all their own.

and *Constitution* originally ran in transatlantic service between New York and Mediterranean ports for American Export Lines. Displaced by the economics of jet airplanes, the two were transferred to foreign registry but never managed to find a proper market where they might operate profitably.

In 1980 the two vessels were returned to U.S. registry. Like *Delta Queen's* exemption from prevailing fire codes, reflagging *Independence* and *Constitution* required the enactment of special legislation. The law prohibits the return of a vessel to U.S. registration once it has departed, but U.S. registration was necessary for the service the pair would provide. The seven-night cruises around the Hawaiian Islands with no intervening visits to any ports not under U.S. jurisdiction may not be operated legally by foreign-flag vessels. (En route to and from Alaska each summer, vessels of many cruise lines include a Hawaiian trip or two. Trips that begin in Honolulu, visit various islands in the Hawaiian chain, and then end in either Ensenada, Mexico, or Vancouver, British Columbia, are permissible under prevailing legislation. Some companies are even able to offer Honolulu-Honolulu cruises with foreign-flag vessels by including a two-day diversion to Fanning Island in the middle of such a cruise.)

American Hawaii Cruise Line, as the company came to be called, was not an unqualified success from the outset. It was only after American Classic Voyages entered the picture in 1993 that the operation was put on a sound footing. But *Independence* and *Constitution*, built in the 1950s, were hardly the last word in contemporary cruise ships. All manner of business plans and market evaluations suggested that cruises around the Hawaiian Islands had scarcely begun to tap the market potential such service represented, but if the company were to thrive, new ships were necessary. How, though, does one go about securing new cruise ships for intra-Hawaiian service when the law specifies that such vessels must be built in a U.S. shipyard, fly the American flag, and employ U.S. crews?

The solution was found on Capitol Hill in Washington, D.C. In the early 1990s, Congress quietly tacked an amendment onto an annual appropriations measure for the U.S. Department of Defense. American Classic Voyages could, indeed, reflag a foreign-built vessel for U.S. coastwise trade in Hawaii, so long as the company agreed to purchase two or more new cruise ships from a U.S. yard within five years. And if it decided to exercise the statutory exemptions it was being offered, American Classic Voyages would enjoy an exclusive right to operate intra-Hawaiian service for the life of the new ships.

By the turn of the century, the process had begun. Holland America's *Nieuw Amsterdam* was purchased to begin intra-Hawaiian service under the U.S. flag in late 2000 as *Patriot,* and a contract was signed with Ingalls Shipbuilding in Pascagoula, Mississippi, to build two new, 72,000-gross-ton cruise ships, vessels that are expected to enter service in 2003 and 2004. Loan guarantees from the U.S. Maritime Administration of almost a billion dollars were also forthcoming to assist in the overall financing of the effort, and the venture, referred to as Project America, will see the first new oceangoing passenger ships to be constructed in the United States in over forty years. (One could possibly argue that certain car ferries built for the Alaska Marine Highway System over the years represent U.S.-built passenger vessels with oceangoing capability, but that would be a bit of a quibble.) Steel was cut for the first of the new ships in a patriotic ceremony held at the shipyard on July 4, 2000, and the contemporary equivalent of a "laying the keel" ceremony was held on October 10, 2000. A veteran worker at the shipyard, Charlie Overstreet, welded the initials of the company's chief executive officer, Rod McLeod, on to the keel. (Overstreet's career at Ingalls includes work on Moore-McCormick's *Argentina* and *Brasil* in the late 1950s.)

American Classic Voyages has decided to differentiate its newer vessels from the older service provided by *Independence* and *Constitution* under the American Hawaii house flag. (By the turn of the new century, *Independence* was still sailing for the company, *Constitution* having been withdrawn from service in 1996.) As the former *Nieuw Amsterdam* enters service as *Patriot* and the two newbuildings are delivered by Ingalls, they will sail under the name of yet another American Classic Voyages subsidiary, United States Lines.

There is no corporate link between the new Hawaiian operation and the company that once operated such ocean liners as *Leviathan, America,* and *United States* in transatlantic service, although American Classic Voyages did have to pay money to secure the right to use the old name. Such rights were purchased in 1986 by an anonymous buyer whose father worked for the original United States Lines. But to underscore the fact that new state-of-the-art passenger vessels will once again be sailing under the American flag, what name could possibly be more appropriate?

And American Classic Voyages has more new vessels on the way. It recently established yet another subsidiary, Delta Queen Coastal Cruises, and the summer season of 2001 will see *Cape May Light* and *Cape Cod Light,* the first of what will likely become a fleet of five new 226-passenger vessels, providing coastal cruise service. (More on Delta Queen Coastal later in this chapter.)

PREMIER CRUISE LINES

To talk about Premier is to talk about a number of different cruise ventures. The original Premier Cruise Lines came on the scene in 1983 and pioneered three- and four-night cruises out of Port Canaveral in central Florida. The company was founded by Bruce Nierenberg, who, during an earlier tenure with Norwegian Caribbean Line, had advanced the modest proposal to Knut Kloster that he acquire *France* and convert her into *Norway.* With financial backing from Greyhound, one of Premier's aims was to package cruise vacations together with land-based visits to Walt Disney World, the Kennedy Space Center, and other central Florida attractions.

Premier was even able to negotiate with the Disney organization and have itself designated the "Official Cruise Line of Walt Disney World." Its vessels were thus festooned with banners and signs decorated with Disney figures and trademarks, and costumed Disney characters roamed the decks greeting passengers. More importantly, though, the central Florida/Disney affiliation emphasized an important marketing goal that Nierenberg and Premier were attempting to reach. They saw their prime customers not as young couples anxious to spend romantic days at sea, not as senior citizens enjoying the fruits of retirement years, but as active families with kids, sometimes lots and lots of kids.

The marketing surveys that Premier conducted prior to inaugurating service out of Port Canaveral told the new company something else. They told Premier that in-state Florida residents represented an important component of cruise passengers who booked passage aboard three- and four-night cruises out of south

Florida. Many of these Florida residents lived in the central part of the state, though, along the Tampa–Orlando–Cape Canaveral axis, almost two hundred miles north of the Dodge Island and Port Everglades cruise terminals.

Positioning the new cruise venture closer to central Florida thus seemed to make sense on two major counts. It was closer to home for many Florida residents with a demonstrated propensity for taking cruises; and it was also close to major tourist attractions that drew people to Florida from, quite literally, all over the world.

Premier shocked maritime traditionalists when it developed a color scheme for its first vessel, a 21,000-ton former ocean liner called, initially, *Royale*. Most cruise ships feature hulls that are painted all white; some few companies still retain hulls that are black or dark blue. When *Royale* entered service for Premier, she featured a hull that was painted bright red, a decorative scheme that quickly gave the new company a very catchy marketing tag line, especially given the younger clientele the company was seeking to serve. Officially the company was Premier Cruise Lines and its first vessel was enrolled as *Royale* (later *StarShip Royale*). Both company and vessel, though, soon came to be known as "the Big Red Boat."

She inaugurated service for Premier Cruise Lines in 1983 as *Royale*, was later acquired by Dolphin and renamed *SeaBreeze I*, and finally returned to Premier when it absorbed Dolphin. The vessel was lost off the Virginia coast in December 2000.

Initially, Nierenberg and company had planned to have their new vessel painted conventional cruise-ship white. But Miami artist Fred Caravetta was asked to prepare several renderings showing the vessel's hull in a number of different solid colors. Nierenberg still remembers the day Caravetta made his presentation. "He went through some colors and nobody was particularly impressed. Then he turned over a sheet of acetate that turned the ship's hull a deep, rich red. Everybody in the room knew immediately that this was it."

In 1986, *StarShip Royale* was supplemented by *StarShip Oceanic*, a vessel whose 1965 maiden voyage as Home Lines *Oceanic* was discussed in chapter 1. Later, *StarShip Majestic* and *StarShip Atlantic* joined the fleet while *StarShip Royale* was sold off, only to return to the Premier fleet under a different guise a few years later. *StarShip Majestic* is also a vessel that was seen earlier as P&O's *Spirit of London* and *Sun Princess* of Princess Cruises. Like *StarShip Oceanic*, *StarShip Atlantic* was a former Home Lines cruise ship, joining Premier shortly after Home Lines itself was absorbed by Holland America Line in 1988.

The company's specialty remained three- and four-night cruises out of Port Canaveral, with package tours available to combine a Premier cruise aboard one of the Big Red Boats with a stay at a Florida hotel and visits to various central Florida attractions. And if imitation is the most sincere form of flattery, then competitive cruise lines have laid some rather heavy flattery on Premier. Where once it was alone in offering cruises out of Port Canaveral, soon it was one of five such lines; and while the Disney organization initially entered a cooperative marketing agreement with Premier allowing the designation of its Big Red Boats as the official cruise ships of Walt Disney World, the partnership was terminated in 1993. Premier turned around and negotiated a new agreement with Warner Brothers, thus allowing cartoon characters like Bugs Bunny and Elmer Fudd to mingle with passengers aboard the Big Red Boat. But if this is unexceptional, what the Disney organization itself did after terminating its agreement with Premier is nothing short of remarkable. It established its own cruise line, designed and built two new 85,000-gross-ton cruise ships, and steamed full-speed ahead into the very market that Premier had quietly pioneered in 1983.

All of this competition at Port Canaveral forced Premier to retrench its operations somewhat. By 1998 there was only a single Big Red Boat in operation, *StarShip Oceanic*. More about the Disney operation later; for now, some interesting twists and turns that Premier has taken in more recent years must be explored.

In early 1997, a corporation called Cruise Holdings purchased Premier. By this time, Nierenberg was no longer associated with the company. Prior to the acquisition, Cruise Holdings had also purchased two other small Caribbean cruise operations, Dolphin Cruise Line and Seawind Cruise Line.

The latter was a one-vessel operation that had gotten underway in 1991 as a joint venture of Swedish and Greek interests; it ran a 1961-built converted

Premier's *OceanBreeze*, a vessel that was built in 1955 at the Harland and Wolff yard in Belfast as *Southern Cross* for Shaw, Savill.

ocean liner called *Seawind Crown* on a lower Caribbean itinerary out of Aruba. Dolphin was formed in 1979 by Greek interests but did not operate its first cruise until 1984. Eventually it grew into a four-vessel company with a fleet that included the 21,010-gross-ton *SeaBreeze I* (formerly Premier's *StarShip Royale*), which ran out of Miami on routine seven-night Caribbean cruises; the 13,007-ton *Dolphin IV*, which provided three- and four-night cruises to the Bahamas; and after 1992, *OceanBreeze*, a rather remarkable vessel which was deployed on a seven-night lower Caribbean itinerary that included a visit to—but not a full transit of—the Panama Canal. (She was seen in chapter 4 as *Azure Seas* of Western Steamship, a company that enjoyed an affiliation with Royal Caribbean.)

Dolphin's fourth vessel, formerly Carnival's *Festivale*, began life as *Transvaal Castle* of Britain's Union-Castle. With the arrival of Carnival's new Fantasy-class vessels in the mid-1990s, Carnival disposed of its initial three "fun ships" and *Festivale* became Dolphin's *IslandBreeze*, at first under the terms of a lease, later by an out-and-out purchase.

In 1997, Cruise Holdings combined its three separate companies—Dolphin, Seawind Cruise, and Premier—under a new brand name called Premier Cruises.

(The original company was known as Premier Cruise Lines.) *StarShip Oceanic* remained painted red, but the rest of the now unified fleet was turned out with very attractive blue hulls. Furthermore, Premier managed to enhance its fleet by acquiring an absolute gem of an ocean liner/cruise ship, Holland America's *Rotterdam* (5), a vessel that HAL chose to retire in late 1997 rather than fit her out with the variety of new safety equipment mandated by international agreements. Premier invested in the new equipment and christened the vessel *Rembrandt*. This created the altogether remarkable situation in 1998 of a six-vessel cruise company, each and every unit of which was powered by steam.

The Premier fleet was deployed on rather expansive itineraries, too. In 1999, for example, while *StarShip Oceanic* continued to offer three- and four-night cruises out of Port Canaveral, *IslandBreeze* was working seven-night cruises in the Canary Islands with most of her passengers being customers of a British package tour company; *SeaBreeze I* was operating out of New York in the summer and out of Montego Bay, Jamaica, in the winter; while *Rembrandt* was offering Mediterranean cruises in summer and various South American itineraries in winter. The Premier fleet, modest as it surely was, was making regular ports of call on four different continents.

OceanBreeze, the one-time *Southern Cross*, was chartered to the Ramada organization in 1999 for work on two-night Bahamas cruises out of Port Everglades as part of a time-share vacation promotion. In early 2000 she was sold outright to Ramada's subsidiary, Imperial Majesty Cruises.

One of the three Dolphin vessels never joined the unified Premier Cruises. This was *Dolphin IV*, which became the sole vessel of a new cruise service that offered split-week cruises out of Port Canaveral under the name Canaveral Cruise Line. *Dolphin IV* has an interesting heritage. She was built in Germany in 1956 as Zim Israel's *Zion*, a transaction that was part of the overall war reparations Germany was required to pay. After Zim Israel departed the passenger steamship business, *Zion* worked for three or four subsequent owners until she came to south Florida as *Dolphin IV* in 1979, first working there for Paquet Cruises and later becoming the initial vessel and namesake of the Dolphin fleet.

In 1993 Dolphin created a separate brand, one that would be mass-market in its orientation, a rung or two up the ladder from the clearly bargain fare that was the specialty of Dolphin itself. Thus was Majesty Cruise Lines created and thus did a newbuilding the company christened *Royal Majesty* arrive in Florida and stake out a claim to the three- and four-night market there. The cruise ship *Royal Majesty* was built in Turku, Finland, at the Warsila yard around the hull of an unfinished car ferry, and she was a delight in every respect. Further expansion of the Majesty brand was planned, but somehow the plans never managed to reach fruition. In the summer of 1995, *Royal Majesty* left Florida and inaugurated a new Boston-Bermuda route, a service the island government was willing to

Majesty Cruise Lines new *Royal Majesty* paid a ceremonial visit to New York in 1992 after cross-ing the North Atlantic from the Finnish shipyard where she was built. In 1997, the vessel was sold to Norwegian Cruise Line and became *Norwegian Majesty*. In 1999 she was lengthened by ninety-two feet to increase her passenger capacity from 1,056 to 1,462.

sanction so long as the vessel confined her visits to the smaller port of St. George's and stayed away from Hamilton.

Boston-Bermuda in summer, coupled with three- and four-night cruises from Miami in winter, became *Royal Majesty's* forte for a number of years, al-though rumors of financial difficulties could never be completely shaken off. The original agreement with Wartsila under which the vessel was purchased and financed had to be renegotiated, for instance.

In June 1995, *Royal Majesty* was involved in an unusual incident that sheds some light on the degree to which contemporary vessel navigation has moved into the high-tech realm. On her way back to Boston from Bermuda, the vessel was under fully automatic control. That is to say a desired arrival time at a sea buoy outside Boston harbor had been programmed into the vessel's onboard computers and the computers then maintained both speed and course to achieve the desired objective.

With respect to vessel position, a satellite-based radionavigation system was employed—global positioning system, or GPS. *Royal Majesty* was also equipped with an older navigational system known as loran C, a redundancy that helped generate an unfortunate measure of confidence on the bridge.

GPS was developed by the U.S. Department of Defense. The system uses a number of orbiting satellites to enable vehicles, vessels, or aircraft to determine their position with startling accuracy. As *Royal Majesty* made her way north from Bermuda for her morning rendezvous outside Boston, everyone assumed the system was working properly and she was maintaining a true and steady course.

But the system was not working properly at all. A simple wire lead had separated from a GPS antenna shortly after the vessel left Bermuda. *Royal Majesty*'s computers thus could not calculate the vessel's true position and as the ship approached the Nantucket area in the dark of night, it was seventeen miles off course to the west. Instead of a heading that would take her safely around Cape Cod, *Royal Majesty* was headed for trouble. She ran softly aground on Rose and Crown Shoal off Nantucket Island and she remained stranded there for a full day until tugboats were able to pull her free and the return voyage to Boston could be completed.

Crown Jewel and *Crown Dynasty* are sister ships that were built for Crown Cruise Line in the early 1990s. *Crown Dynasty,* shown here, became Majesty Cruise Lines *Crown Majesty* briefly in 1998 and later ran for Norwegian Cruise Line as *Norwegian Dynasty.* More recently, the vessel's name reverted to the original *Crown Dynasty.*

The plain and simple lesson this incident taught was this: the use of high-tech automated equipment is well and good, but when a vessel is approaching an area of dangerous shoals, an occasional check of the radar scope and a position check of such old-fashioned and "low-tech" navigational aids as lighthouses is a good idea. A Coast Guard investigator was quoted in the press as saying: "No matter how sophisticated your navigation equipment is, you still have to look out the window."

In 1997, Majesty was finally able to add a second vessel to its fleet, but it was not any kind of growth built on strength and durability. *Crown Dynasty* joined the fleet, was hastily renamed *Crown Majesty* (the letters "*Dyna*" on her hull were simply overpainted with "*Maje*"), and for the 1997 season she picked up the itinerary and the bookings that had already been made for *Crown Dynasty*. That fall, both vessels became part of Norwegian Cruise Line—*Royal Majesty* by purchase and *Crown Majesty* by charter—and Majesty Cruise Lines was history.

After Cruise Holdings combined its three brands into one in 1998, the new Premier Cruises experienced a good deal of financial difficulty; rumors were frequent that the line was about to fold. In 1999, the company turned to an interesting corporate official to help get it back on an even keel. Bruce Nierenberg, the man who founded the original Premier Cruise Lines back in the mid-1980s, was asked to head up the company as president and CEO. Nierenberg accepted the challenge. One of his early moves was to rename the company Premier Cruise Lines and restore its traditional funnel decoration.

Initially, the Nierenberg touch appeared to be working fine; refinancing of the company's debt load improved its operating profile and the growth of the cruise industry itself continued to generate a steady market for the kind of budget fare that was Premier's specialty. Nierenberg also decided to capitalize on the Big Red Boat theme and in late 1999 it was announced that four of the company's vessels were to be designated Big Red Boats, formally renamed as such, and deployed in new markets—New York, Houston, and Los Angeles. *Seawind Crown* was chartered to a cruise operator in Europe, while the one-time Costa vessel *Eugenio C.* was acquired to inaugurate a new Premier service out of New York in the summer and to run seven-night eastern Caribbean cruises out of Tampa in the winter under the new name *The Big Red Boat II*. *StarShip Oceanic* became *The Big Red Boat I* in the spring of 2000, and *IslandBreeze* took over the new Houston service as *The Big Red Boat III*.

Even the one-time *Rotterdam* (5) was scheduled to become part of the new order. As *The Big Red Boat IV*, in late 2000 she was to sail to the West Coast for service out of Los Angeles in the winter and cruises to Alaska in the summer.

Unfortunately, these plans were never fully realized. In the summer of 2000, Premier's creditors reached the sad conclusion that a bargain-basement cruise line operating reconditioned older ships—or, more precisely, *this* bargain-basement cruise line—would never be competitive in the contemporary cruise market. Vessels were seized, some in the midst of cruise itineraries, and the company quietly faded from the scene. Unfortunate as was its ending, the fact remains that Premier Cruise Lines contributed an interesting, colorful chapter to the recent history of the North American cruise industry.

CRYSTAL CRUISES

In talking about cruise companies that market their product to an upscale clientele, the smaller, almost yachtlike vessels often come to mind. Royal Viking Line was clearly an exception to this general perception, and the recent transfer of a one-time Royal Viking vessel, *Royal Viking Sun*, to Seabourn Cruises may help keep that exception alive. But a company that has done even more in the way of deploying larger vessels in the upscale market is a Japanese-owned firm that does business as Crystal Cruises.

Crystal Cruises carried its first passengers in 1990 aboard a new vessel that had been built in Japan by Mitsubishi Heavy Industries and christened *Crystal Harmony*. With a registered gross tonnage of 48,621 and at 790 feet long, *Crystal Harmony* is roughly in the same size category as Celebrity's *Horizon* and *Zenith*. But while each Celebrity vessel has a passenger capacity in excess of 1,600 people, *Crystal Harmony*'s capacity is a far more modest 940.

That probably says it all. *Crystal Harmony* is not a yachtlike luxury vessel in the manner of the first three Seabourn ships or the Sea Goddess vessels. She is a full-size cruise ship that is almost 800 feet from stem to stern. But holding her maximum capacity to 940 passengers ensures that her decks and her public rooms will never be crowded and will always reflect luxury and an upscale tone.

Crystal Harmony proved quite successful, and in 1995 the company supplemented her with a running mate, *Crystal Symphony*. Similar but not totally identical to her older sister, the newer vessel was built at the Kvaerner Masa-Yards in Turku, Finland, as Crystal was quoted a much better price and better terms by the European shipyard. While both vessels have the same passenger capacity, 940, the original vessel includes nineteen inside cabins, while the newer *Crystal Symphony* has none at all. There are also modest differences in the layout of the public rooms aboard the two vessels. Among the passengers who regularly patronize the line, there are supposedly people who are almost passionate in their preference of one ship over the other. Early in the new century, passengers will have a third Crystal vessel to consider when the company adds another newbuilding to its fleet.

The ships sail worldwide itineraries that are the hallmark of an upscale cruise operation. In 2000, for example, *Crystal Symphony* offered a westbound world cruise that began in Los Angeles in late January and concluded in Southampton on May 4. Brochure prices for this 104-day journey ranged from a "low" of $55,295 to a top-of-the-line cost of $180,840. As with most world cruises, passengers could also book segments of the overall voyage, for example, twenty-two days between Cape Town and London or thirty-five days between Los Angeles and Sydney.

Speaking of world cruises, one feature of such voyages is this: A week or two into the voyage, consumption levels of food aboard the vessel decline precipitously. On a cruise of seven nights, or even a cruise as long as two weeks, passengers tend to enjoy themselves in the dining rooms and cafeterias, throwing constraint to the wind. Looking at a much longer cruise, however, after an initial period of indulgence, passengers adopt more modest gastronomic practices.

Cruise companies actually plan around such behavioral restraint when they send provisions to various world ports where a vessel will be resupplied during its voyage. This, of course, suggests another matter that an upscale company like Crystal faces routinely, not just during a once-a-year world cruise. Crystal must constantly reprovision its cruise ships in strange and unusual ports. A mass-market cruise ship working a Caribbean itinerary will take on supplies week after week in Miami or Port Everglades, and smooth working relationships can develop between personnel aboard ship and on shore. Over a year's time, *Crystal Harmony* and *Crystal Symphony* will begin and end cruises in places as diverse as Acapulco, Buenos Aires, Singapore, and Bali. Scheduling the reprovisioning of the Crystal fleet must be done well in advance and in full cognizance of cost implications that are impacted by tariffs and excise taxes, customs regulations, local labor rates, sealift schedules into and out of the ports in question, and myriad other factors.

Consider, for example, the various itineraries that *Crystal Harmony* sailed between January and August in 2000. A twelve-night cruise out of Barbados was followed by a one-way cruise from there to Buenos Aires. Next came Buenos Aires–to–Valparaiso and back again, followed by Buenos Aires north to Port Everglades. A twelve-night Caribbean cruise out of Port Everglades was followed by a cruise through the Panama Canal to Acapulco, and from Acapulco the vessel headed back through the canal to New Orleans. Then came New Orleans–Acapulco, next was Acapulco-Vancouver, and this was followed by five Alaska cruises, most of which began and terminated not in Vancouver, but in San Francisco. *Crystal Harmony* did not put in a full season in Alaska and by late August she was heading west across the Pacific to the Far East and further cruise adventures out of Sydney and Aukland. In late October she headed east on a transpacific voyage that brought her back to the Caribbean for a number of winter offerings.

Such a series of itineraries and a distinct lack of repetition is typical of the offerings one can expect from cruise companies that serve the top end of the market. Loyal customers—and Crystal's customer base is nothing if not loyal—will happily follow the ships wherever they sail and experience new and unique voyages year after year. That, after all, is the very paradigm of an upscale cruise operation.

DISNEY CRUISE LINE

As early as the 1970s, there were continual rumors that large entertainment conglomerates were poised to enter the North American cruise business and capitalize on the growth the industry was on the verge of experiencing. Metro-Goldwyn-Mayer, as one example, was often reported to be mere weeks away from making such an announcement. Despite all the speculation, nothing firm ever materialized.

Because of this history of rumor and inaction, when stories began to circulate in the late 1980s that the Disney organization was beginning to get serious about developing a Florida cruise line to complement the entertainment activities it operated in the Orlando area, lots of people in the cruise industry did not believe it would ever happen. But it did. And when the company's first cruise ship, *Disney Magic*, set sail from Port Canaveral for the Bahamas on its first cruise in July 1998, it represented an absolute high-water mark in the way of a well-financed and carefully planned new cruise venture.

Disney entered the cruise business by constructing not one but two massive 85,000-gross-ton cruise ships at the Fincantieri yard in Italy, ships that on the inside are as modern as tomorrow in every technical way, but from the outside evoke the look and style of more classic ocean liners. The design was executed by Njal Eide of Oslo, following a spirited competition among three major Scandinavian firms. Among designs that the Disney people rejected were proposals that ran the gamut from outrageously futuristic to downright whimsical.

Each ship has a black hull, white superstructure, and twin red stacks, colors that recall many classic ocean liners of yesteryear. Not surprisingly, they are also the haberdashery colors of choice of the world's most famous mouse. And while *Disney Magic* and *Disney Wonder* both feature the typical boxlike hulls that are virtually universal in the contemporary cruise industry, striping along the top of the hull attempts to create an impression of the sheer that was so common a feature of older ocean liners. One thing that both *Disney Magic* and *Disney Wonder* can do that no classic ocean liner ever could do—and more pointedly, would probably never have wanted to do—is play the first seven notes of "When You Wish Upon a Star" on its ship's whistle.

What may be the hallmark of Disney's entry into the cruise business was the degree to which it relied on market research to design and package its product. During early group-focus interviews, many frequent cruise passengers identified the precruise check-in procedure as the least desirable aspect of a typical cruise experience. Disney put its people to work on this and as a result, checking in for a Disney cruise is very different from the norm. The terminal itself has been designed to facilitate boarding. If a passenger is combining a stay at a Walt Disney World hotel or resort with a Disney cruise—something the company earnestly hopes many of its passengers will, in fact, do—the same plastic "room key" that is issued at the hotel will also be used to lock and unlock the cabin aboard ship and to charge onboard purchases while at sea. Indeed the same plastic card is also an admission ticket to whatever Disney entertainment options are included in the vacation package.

Transportation between Walt Disney World and the cruise terminal in Port Canaveral, a new terminal built solely for Disney's use, is provided by a fleet of forty-five custom-designed buses that feature onboard video presentations which prepare passengers for the upcoming cruise. While aboard the vessels, passengers dine in a variety of different restaurants, but one's table mates, and one's wait staff, move from one restaurant to the other to create a sense of continuity.

Another problem that surfaced during the group-focus interviews was the whole business of tendering between ship and shore. People said in very strong terms that they often found it to be unpleasant and sometimes even frightening. Since Disney planned to include a day's stay at a private out-island as part of both its three- and four-night itineraries, tendering appeared to be a necessary evil.

The size and scope of the Disney investment, however, was such that even a "necessary evil" does not have to be tolerated. Instead of a private out-island where passengers are tendered between ship and shore, on Disney's 1,000-acre Castaway Cay in the Bahamas, *Disney Magic* and *Disney Wonder* pull right up to their own pier, allowing passengers to walk ashore. There is even a tram service on the island so passengers need not walk too far to reach dining facilities or entertainment venues on Castaway Cay.

Each of the two initial Disney vessels measures 964 feet long, 106 feet wide, and has a draft of 25 feet, big, but still a size that permits a transit of the Panama Canal. The 964-foot length is actually longer than such post-Panamax cruise ships as *Carnival Destiny* (893 feet) and *Grand Princess* (951 feet). Each Disney ship is powered by five big 16-cylinder Sulzer diesels that drive electric generators; each of two propeller shafts is turned by an electric motor mounted inside the hull. Five electric thrusters—three forward and two aft—help the big ships maneuver in close quarters.

The two Disney vessels feature a very different kind of stern treatment. In place of the squared-off transom sterns that have become so popular on many recent cruise ships, *Disney Magic* and *Disney Wonder* have what might be called a cruiser stern, a style that was derived from heavy naval ships and was once popular on such British-built passenger vessels as Cunard–White Star's *Queen Mary* and *Queen Elizabeth*.

Passenger capacity is listed as 1,750, but this is under the standard industry notation of presuming two people in each of the vessel's 875 cabins. Since many families will travel aboard Disney vessels and more than two passengers will share a cabin, the vessels will often carry passenger loads in excess of "full" capacity, upward, in fact, to a "real" capacity of something in the range of 2,500 passengers. A crew of 920 is needed to minister to the needs of these passengers.

Convincing evidence that the Disney organization had plans for serious expansion of its cruise operation was the top speed for which the two vessels were designed—twenty-four knots. It is difficult to imagine building a cruise ship with twenty-four-knot speed capability if it is intended to assign the vessel to nothing more demanding than three- and four-night cruise service to Nassau and Castaway Cay, itineraries that simply do not require anything remotely this fast. The first newbuilding ever designed for three- and four-night service, Royal Caribbean's *Nordic Empress* of 1990, has a top speed of nineteen knots, for instance. Holland America's *Rotterdam* (6), informally called the *Fast-dam* during its early design phase and, like the Disney twins, built at Fincantieri in Italy, has a twenty-five-knot top speed, something that is regarded as quite fast for a contemporary cruise ship. It is fast, and that means expensive.

The company's first president, Arthur Rodney, was quite outspoken after *Disney Magic* entered service in 1998. "One day we may be in the seven-day market," Rodney said, and then went on to suggest that a fleet of six or seven ships was also a definite possibility someday. Rodney remained silent, though, on exactly what kind of itineraries such an expanded fleet might sail. And then in late 2000, Disney made the first change in its initial operational plan.

One ship, *Disney Wonder*, will remain working three- and four-night split-week cruises, while the other, *Disney Magic*, shifts to a seven-night itinerary, an eastern Caribbean cruise out of Port Canaveral with a stop in Castaway Cay on the way back. Whether the Disney operation remains one of such a scope and style, or whether it expands and moves into even more venturesome cruise markets, will be one of the more interesting things to watch as the cruise industry evolves in the twenty-first century.

WINDSTAR CRUISES

Windstar combines features of an upscale cruise line and a niche-market one. It is different, operating a fleet of "sailing ships" on a variety of itineraries in the Caribbean and the Mediterranean. Windstar does not offer anything even remotely like traditional travel under sail. Its vessels are primarily powered by diesel engines, and while sails are, indeed, hoisted at sea and used as auxiliary power for the ships, the diesel engines ensure that cruise schedules will be met.

Windstar was begun in the mid-1980s by Karl Andren, who is well known in maritime circles as the chief officer of New York's Circle Line, the famous Manhattan Island sightseeing company. In 1987, Holland America Line acquired a 50 percent interest in Windstar; the following year HAL increased its ownership to 100 percent, and early the next year, 1989, Windstar was part of the HAL assets that were acquired by Carnival.

Windstar's first vessel, *Wind Star*, was built in Le Havre, France, by Societe Nouvelle de Ateliers et Chantiers du Havre and delivered in the fall of 1986. Three 6-cylinder Wartsila diesels generate electricity and *Wind Star*'s single screw is turned by an electric motor. She also has four 204-foot masts and her sails are controlled not by seamen scrambling up into the rigging in all kinds of fair and foul weather, but rather by—what else?—computers. While at sea, *Wind Star* often runs on sail power alone, although her diesels must continually operate to supply electricity for other onboard needs. *Wind Star* leans over with the wind to give passengers a bit of the feel of a genuine sailing ship, but never in excess of six degrees.

Wind Star is not a large vessel; her capacity is 148 passengers. All of her 74 staterooms are outside-facing, and all are in the same price category. She includes the amenities one expects on a mass-market or upscale cruise ship: elegant dining room, full air-conditioning, spacious lounge, casino, outdoor swimming pool, and so forth. *Wind Star* also includes a few interesting features that one would not expect to find on a 100,000-gross-ton cruise ship, such as a water sports platform at

Wind Star, shown here in Barcelona, Spain, is the original cruise vessel to sail for Windstar Cruises. Once she leaves port and reaches open water, sails will be set from her four tall masts.

her stern that allows passengers to engage in activities like kayaking and snorkeling, plus an open invitation for passengers to visit the bridge and chat with the ship's officers.

Wind Star was quickly followed by two sister ships, *Wind Song* and *Wind Spirit*, but an option for a fourth vessel was never exercised. Under the management of Holland America Line, Windstar has been operated as a separate cruise brand, although its linkage with HAL is in no way denied. The daily newsletter distributed aboard all Holland America vessels shows the location of other vessels in the company's fleet, for instance, and Windstar vessels are included.

Wind Spirit has a slightly heftier engine than the other two vessels, and it was initially intended that she would operate an Alaskan itinerary in the summer. Because of the mountains surrounding the various Alaskan inlets where cruise ships visit, this did not prove to be a successful deployment for a vessel that relies partly on the wind for its power, and *Wind Spirit* sailed to Alaska for only a single season, 1988.

The Windstar cruise concept proved to be sufficiently successful that it was imitated. The resort consortium popularly known as Club Med built a pair of similar cruise ships—same basic design, same shipyard, five masts rather than four, two propellers instead of one, and capacity for 312 passengers, double the 148 of the three Windstar vessels. *Club Med 1* was built in 1990, *Club Med 2* in 1992. Club Med, though, did not achieve the same success as did Windstar, and in 1997 *Club Med 1* was sold to Windstar and renamed *Wind Surf*.

Windstar is certainly an unusual kind of cruise operation. The total passenger capacity of the company's four current vessels is only 756 passengers, just about enough to fill a typical cruise ship back in the days when 20,000 gross tons was regarded as the industry optimum. But Windstar is a good example of a specialized cruise experience that offers itineraries and experiences that are truly different.

COSTA CROCIERE

Most contemporary cruise companies are relatively new. Carnival inaugurated service in 1972, Royal Caribbean in 1971, Princess in 1964. Some few, though, can trace their roots back to nineteenth-century Europe. Among these is Costa Cruises (Costa Crociere), a mass-market operator whose vessels, itineraries, and overall style give it a very unique character.

At one point, Costa seemed on the way to becoming another imitator of the various North American–oriented companies that saw their primary market as the Caribbean. Before Costa evolved into a Caribbean-oriented cruise company, however, it decided to move in a different direction. It emphasized its European origins and did not try to match the services being offered by the likes of Carnival, Royal Caribbean, or Princess. By century's end, Costa was offering fewer

Caribbean itineraries than it did some years earlier. Instead the Genoa-based company was developing a unique and distinctive specialty all its own. Costa will continue to dispatch one or two vessels to the Caribbean each winter to sail out of Port Everglades, but its specialty and its forte will remain cruise itineraries that visit the many historic seaports of Europe where the company has its roots.

Giacomo Costa started an olive oil business in Italy in 1860, the same year Abraham Lincoln was elected president of the United States. When he died in 1916 he left the business to his three sons, Federico, Enrico, and Eugenio. These three names would later grace a trio of Costa cruise ships.

Sometime after the First World War, the three brothers felt it was time to diversify and expand the family business. And so the brothers began to invest in oceangoing freighters that could deliver olive oil to their various overseas customers.

The end of the Second World War saw the need for a massive sealift of European refugees to new countries, particularly in Latin America. Like Chandris, Home Lines, and Sitmar, Costa moved into this postwar market and began to supplement its freighters with passenger-carrying ships. In some cases, the company simply installed temporary passenger accommodations aboard vessels that were designed to haul cargo. Soon enough, though, Costa was operating regular passenger service between Italy and South America. Interestingly, as early as the 1950s Costa began to supplement its scheduled transatlantic services with leisure-oriented cruises.

Costa's *Franca C.* was running Caribbean cruises out of Port Everglades, Florida, in 1959, well in advance of the emergence of what is today regarded as the contemporary cruise industry. *Franca C.* was no youngster, either, having been launched in Newport News, Virginia, in 1914. At first, *Franca C.* ran out of Port Everglades under charter to a local company known as Atlantic Cruise Lines, an operation founded by Leo Robbins. Costa itself soon took over the operation from Atlantic, and Robbins went on to enjoy a long and successful career with Chandris Lines.

(The career of what was the forty-five-year-old vessel known as *Franca C.* in 1959 was only just beginning. On the day the twentieth century became the twenty-first, she was still in active service as the spry eighty-five-year old *Doulos*, working for an international religious organization and proudly wearing the title of the oldest active oceangoing passenger vessel of all time.)

In 1958, a year before *Franca C.* began running cruise service out of Port Everglades, Costa took delivery of its first passenger newbuilding, a vessel that was christened *Federico C.* to honor the memory of one of the three sons of the company's founder. *Federico C.* would later become Premier's initial vessel, *StarShip Royale,* and still later would return to the same company as *SeaBreeze I.*

As Costa began to devote more of its resources to cruising, additional vessels joined the fleet—some new, some old, some through purchase, others via charter. The family-owned business went public in 1989, and in the early 1990s two French cruise lines, Paquet Cruises and its subsidiary Pearl Cruises, were merged into the Costa operation. Pearl immediately lost its identity in the transaction while Paquet was managed as a separate brand for a number of years.

The 1990s also saw Costa completely upgrade its fleet by investing over a billion dollars in new cruise ships. *Costa Marina* and *Costa Allegra* are among the most unusual vessels in the entire cruise industry. Built on the hulls of one-time containerships, they have an unusual profile that in no way suggests their former status as cargo vessels, but is still quite different from more conventional cruise ships. The two are not identical, either. *Costa Marina* features the same hull geometry and engines as the containership *Axel Johnson* from which she was built. *Costa Allegra* had her hull spliced and lengthened during the conversion process, and new Wartsila diesels were substituted for the Pielstick diesels that powered her when she was the containership *Annie Johnson*.

Costa Riviera is the former Lloyd Triestino ocean liner *Guglielmo Marconi*, a sister ship of *Galileo Galilei*, a vessel that later became *Meridian*, Celebrity's first

Costa Allegra was built as the containership *Annie Johnson* in 1969 and later converted into a cruise ship.

The 1996-built *Costa Victoria* is one of the mainstays of the Costa Crocieri fleet. The cruise ship whose bridge is visible astern of *Costa Victoria* is Airtours/Sun Cruises *Sunbird*, a vessel that originally ran for Royal Caribbean as *Song of America*.

cruise ship. Four newbuildings from the 1990s round out the fleet: *Costa Classica* of 1991, *Costa Romantica* of 1993, *Costa Victoria* of 1996, and *Costa Atlantica* of 2000. *Costa Classica* is scheduled to be stretched from her original 730 feet of length to 894, and from 52,926 gross tons to 79,000. The work is to be done in Great Britain by Cammell-Laird and is being called the largest such alteration ever, not on the sole basis of added length, but because a totally new top deck will also be added, increasing her gross tonnage by almost 50 percent.

A feature that has emerged as a trademark of a Costa cruise ship is the straight funnel, or even several funnels bunched together. Painted yellow and decorated with a large blue "C," it is a design feature that contrasts with the more typical streamlined funnel treatment generally found on contemporary cruise ships. A few non-Costa cruise ships have similar funnels, among them *Crown Princess* and *Regal Princess*, as well as Holland America's *Rotterdam* (6) and *Amsterdam* (3). *Costa Riviera*, the only ship in the current fleet that was neither built new nor substantially rebuilt by Costa, lacks this distinctive company trademark.

The most important development to impact Costa Cruises since the company entered the passenger steamship business after the Second World War happened in 1997, when Costa was purchased by a joint venture of Carnival Corporation and Airtours of Great Britain, a company in which Carnival also holds an interest. In October 2000, Carnival bought out Airtours' share of the company and became sole owner of Costa.

As with other Carnival takeovers such as Holland America Lines and Cunard, the spirit and style of the acquired property has been kept alive and Costa Cruises (Costa Crociere) continues to be marketed and managed as a unique and separate product.

One early benefit of the Carnival/Airtours acquisition of Costa is evident in the look and style of the new 84,000-gross-ton *Costa Atlantica* from Kvaerner Masa-Yards in Finland that joined the fleet in 2000. While the vessel retains the distinctive Costa touch of a straight funnel positioned aft, the basic design of the vessel—its overall lines as well as its below-deck machinery—is patterned after *Carnival Spirit*, the first of a new fleet of Carnival vessels built to Panamax specifications. On the inside, decorations and appointments are all pure Costa. On the outside as well as belowdecks, the new ship is a dramatic statement to the efficiencies that a small company like Costa can realize when its new vessels are designed and built as part of an effort orchestrated by the world's largest cruise company.

MINI CRUISE SHIPS

Throughout the world, diverse fleets of smaller cruise vessels sail itineraries along waterways where larger oceangoing ships are unable to navigate. The rivers of Europe, Africa, and Asia, for example, are home to many different fleets of cruise vessels designed and built to unique specifications mandated by their unusual operating environment. One can book passage along the Rhine, the Danube, the Nile, even the Yangtze, aboard one-, two-, and three-deck cruise ships whose passenger capacity is only a hundred or so, not the several thousand of vessels like *Carnival Destiny, Grand Princess,* or *Voyager of the Seas.*

Similar specialized vessels may also be found in North America. In fact, because of some unusual features of United States maritime law, smaller cruise ships that sail North American itineraries are able to do so while flying the American flag, something quite rare in the world of oceangoing cruise ships.

The U.S. Passenger Vessel Services Act of 1886 is an oft-cited law that prohibits vessels of foreign registry from carrying passengers solely between American ports. Enacted in the nineteenth century as a protectionist measure to keep foreign-flag vessels out of what was then a lucrative U.S. coastwise trade, it has served to define the contemporary oceangoing cruise industry as one that relies almost exclusively on vessels flying foreign flags but whose itineraries may not involve U.S. ports alone. Under the terms of the 1886 legislation, a voyage aboard a foreign-flag vessel may begin and end in a U.S. port so long as it makes at least one intermediate stop in a port not under U.S. jurisdiction, or else makes no stops at all. Other legal requirements stipulate that in order to fly the U.S. flag, a vessel must have been built in a U.S. shipyard and be operated by a U.S. crew.

This 1886 statute is often referred to as "the Jones Act," but such usage is incorrect. The "Jones Act" mandates the use of U.S.-flag vessels in domestic waterborne trade; it is a statute that was enacted in 1920 and applies exclusively to the transport of cargo, not passengers. There is continual talk of amending these laws to allow some measure of coastwise trade by foreign-flag vessels, but they remained unchanged through 2000.

In addition to the Passenger Vessel Services Act of 1886, there is another statutory citation applicable to the world of cruise ships which helps establish a context for the operation of mini cruise ships flying the U.S. flag. It is Title 46, Subpart T, of the Code of Federal Regulations (CFR). Under its provisions, any U.S.-flag passenger vessel with gross registered tonnage less than 100 is subject to significantly reduced crewing requirements than those prevailing on larger ships. U.S.-flag passenger vessels in excess of 100 gross registered tons in either coastwise or oceangoing trade require, at minimum, eleven licensed officers. Vessels that measure less than 100 gross registered tons can get by with as few as two. Because the calculation of gross registered tonnage includes only reve-nue-generating space that is *permanently* enclosed, naval architects have been able to exercise their creativity and design some fair-sized vessels whose formal measurement brings them under the magic mark of 100 gross registered tons. Seemingly interior spaces on such vessels can be enclosed by movable partitions, thus are not "permanently enclosed," and are excluded from the formal calcula-tion.

Put these two legal requirements together—the Passenger Vessel Services Act of 1898 and Title 46, Subpart T, of the CFR—and a situation is created whereby a fleet of almost two dozen mini cruise ships working for a half dozen different companies sail cruise itineraries out of U.S. ports and do so under U.S. registry.

Vessels that fall under the provisions of Title 46, Subpart T, are often re-ferred to informally as "T-boats." Any discussion of T-boats in general and mini cruise ships in particular must begin with the story of World War II veteran Lu-ther Blount, who returned to his Warren, Rhode Island, home after the war and decided to try his hand at the proud old Yankee art of shipbuilding.

Blount Marine, or Blount Industries, as it is sometimes known, is one of the foremost builders of small inland and coastal passenger vessels in the United States. If one visits the Statue of Liberty in New York, travels to the offshore is-lands of Nantucket or Martha's Vineyard, or rides any number of passenger fer-ries or dinner cruisers along waterways from Maine to California, it is more than likely that one has been aboard a vessel (or vessels) turned out by Blount Indus-tries. Blount-built passenger vessels—over three hundred of them—often bear a strong visual similarity to each other, irrespective of the customer who owns and operates the vessel. For purposes of this narrative, though, the most interesting customer of the Blount Marine shipyard is another company founded and owned by Luther Blount himself, a cruise line that has come to be called American Canadian Caribbean Line (ACCL).

Over the years, Blount has designed and built a number of interesting mini cruise ships for ACCL. Furthermore, as the newest and latest Blount designs go to work for his own company, earlier vessels are sold off to other cruise operators with the result being that by the turn of the century, Blount-built mini cruise ships were at work on itineraries from the Caribbean to the Gulf of California, from Lake Erie to Alaska's Inside Passage.

The first true mini cruise ship to operate for what is today called American Canadian Caribbean Line was the 1969-built *Mount Hope.* The success the company achieved with *Mount Hope* soon led to the construction of a slightly larger running mate, *New Shoreham* of 1971. *Mount Hope* was 104 feet long and accommodated thirty-six overnight passengers, while *New Shoreham* measured 125 feet and had a passenger capacity of fifty-two. The two vessels specialized in coastal cruises to northeastern points out of Warren, Rhode Island, during the summer, followed by an autumn migration down the Intracoastal Waterway to Florida and winter cruises there. Come spring, the process would be reversed, and *Mount Hope* and *New Shoreham* headed north again. In later years, ACCL expanded its winter offerings to include visits to any number of interesting Caribbean islands, including trips up and down the Central American coast and into and through the Panama Canal.

The ambiance aboard an ACCL vessel or any other mini cruise ship is decidedly different from that aboard a large, oceangoing cruise liner. Meals are often served family-style, and range from wholesome and hearty to out-and-out gourmet. On a mini cruise ship, though, one never has to worry about whether a given evening's dinner is designated formal, semiformal, or informal; all are decidedly informal. Packing a tuxedo or an evening gown for such a cruise is not only unnecessary, it is downright silly. Furthermore one will look in vain aboard a mini cruise ship for any casinos, discos, or Broadway-style entertainment, much less rock-climbing walls or ice-skating rinks. There is a dining room and a lounge, although often the same general area does double duty and serves as both. Entertainment is usually limited to lectures by authorities knowledgeable on the areas the vessel is about to visit, although a bit of folksinging or similar musical fare is not uncommon. Aboard a mini cruise ship the real entertainment is the cruise itself, as well as the places the vessel visits.

Mini cruise ships will usually tailor their itineraries to accommodate the specialized interests of passengers, be they lighthouse historians, birders, Civil War buffs, or whatever. Most of the ships also have an "open bridge" policy, meaning that passengers can feel free to wander into the pilothouse whenever the spirit moves them and chat with the officer on duty.

American Canadian Caribbean Line's *Grande Mariner* specializes in East Coast cruise itineraries. The vessel is shown here at Alexandria, Virginia, on the Potomac River.

The style of operation encountered in the world of North American mini cruise ships differs in another respect from that normally practiced by oceangoing vessels. The oceangoing ships typically steam overnight from one port of call to the next and spend most days tied up in port. Because much of the attraction of a cruise aboard a smaller vessel is the chance to get an up-close look at sights along an inland waterway, the mini cruise ship pattern usually involves a good deal more travel by day, with the vessel spending the night in port. This gives passengers a chance to wander around town during evening hours and experience a side of port life that passengers traveling aboard larger cruise ships often miss. The reduced crew requirements that apply to T-boats also stipulate that a vessel may not be underway for more than twelve hours a day, a requirement that coincidentally helps establish the style of service these vessels provide. In a port regularly visited by both mini cruise ships and oceangoing vessels, it is not uncommon for the smaller ships to be arriving in port in late afternoon at about the same time larger vessels are preparing for sea.

Two structural features that Luther Blount designed into *Mount Hope* and *New Shoreham* have been repeated on all subsequent cruise vessels ACCL has operated: a bow ramp that gives passengers easy access to beaches and a pilothouse that lowers from its normal position to enable the vessel to pass under low fixed bridges along such restricted waterways as the New York State Barge Canal, successor of the famed Erie Canal.

The bow ramp also provides a glimpse into the kind of service *New Shoreham* and her successors provide. Because of their modest draft, ACCL vessels are often able to maneuver right up onto a sandy beach in a manner not unlike that associated with naval landing craft; there they lower the bow ramp and allow passengers to proceed directly ashore usually without getting their feet wet, but more importantly, without the need for anything so formal as a dock, a wharf, or a fleet of tenders. This feature allows ACCL vessels to visit quiet and exotic beaches that are necessarily off-limits to larger cruise ships. ACCL vessels also include a platform at their aft end that performs a parallel function to the bow ramp, allowing passengers to swim and snorkel directly from the cruise ship, as well as transfer to smaller motorboats for exploration into areas where even a mini cruise ship is too big to navigate.

Following ACCL's success with *New Hope* and *New Shoreham*—names, incidentally, that Luther Blount selected because of their association with early New England coastal steamboats—a number of other companies decided to jump into the fray and compete for the same market that Blount had so successfully staked out. Indeed the early 1980s saw so rapid a proliferation of mini cruise ships and companies that the market was soon overserved; some new entrants left the business as quickly as they entered it.

By the end of the 1990s, a measure of stability had been achieved, with many of the vessels that had originally been built for service along the East Coast of the United States finding a more hospitable and profitable working environment on various itineraries in Alaska. A company known as Alaska Sightseeing/Cruise West, in fact, has emerged as the largest operator of mini cruise ships in the United States. During the summer of 2000, Cruise West was dispatching no fewer than six different mini cruise ships on various Alaskan itineraries, including Luther Blount's *New Shoreham* of 1971, a vessel that has been rechristened *Spirit of Glacier Bay* by her Alaskan owners. Because they fly the U.S. flag and need not incorporate a stopover in a foreign port during a cruise, Alaska Sightseeing/Cruise West can both begin and end its cruises in Alaskan ports such as Juneau and Ketchikan and spend more time poking into glacial inlets and exploring other aspects of the natural beauty of Alaska.

The "West" in Cruise West is familiar in the world of Alaska cruising. Chuck West was the founder of Arctic Alaska Travel Service in 1947, a company that became Westours in 1954. When Westours was purchased by Holland America Line in the 1970s, Chuck West went on to establish Alaska Sightseeing/Cruise West, a company that by the turn of the century was managed by his son, Dick West.

What may be the most interesting of all the mini cruise ships at work in North America today is a vessel that Alaska Sightseeing/Cruise West calls *Spirit of '98*, built in Mobile, Alabama, in 1984 for service along the East Coast as *Pilgrim Belle*. Originally owned by a subsidiary of Hyannis Harbor Tours, a major operator of ferries between Cape Cod and the offshore islands of Nantucket and Martha's Vineyard, *Spirit of '98* is four decks high, includes a passenger elevator, and on the outside looks more like a classic steamboat of yesteryear (complete with a tall funnel) than a modern diesel-powered cruise vessel. By contrast, Blount-built vessels make no effort whatsoever to disguise themselves as anything other than the contemporary motor vessels that they are.

Three other companies operate mini cruise ships in Alaskan waters each summer. Alaska's Glacier Bay Tours and Cruises operates four vessels, three of which once worked for Luther Blount's ACCL. Lindblad Special Expeditions operates two, and Clipper Cruise Line runs one. Both Clipper and Lindblad also operate oceangoing cruise ships that sail under foreign flags but whose passenger capacity and overall size is more in line with the standards of mini cruise ships. The itineraries these foreign-flag vessels work take them to such adventuresome places as the Spice Islands in mid-Pacific, the Galapagos, and even Antarctica.

Clipper Cruise Line annually sends their 1988-built *Yorktown Clipper* to Alaska, while *Nantucket Clipper* of 1984 works the East Coast: northern waters in summer, southern latitudes in the winter. At 257 feet long and with a passenger capacity of 138, *Yorktown Clipper* is the largest of all the T-boats engaged in mini cruise service, even though her gross registered tonnage has been carefully held at 97. Most of the Alaskan mini cruise ships also migrate southward once the

Alaska Sightseeing/Cruise West's *Spirit of '98* is a modern, diesel-powered mini cruise ship. Her external profile recalls coastal steamboats of an older era.

Clipper Cruise Line's *Nantucket Clipper* is another mini cruise ship that specializes in eastern itineraries. Warm summer months find her as far north as the St. Lawrence River; during winter she offers a variety of unusual Caribbean cruises.

summer season is over and spend the winter months sailing itineraries in places like Baja California, with intermediate work along the Columbia River or around San Francisco Bay not uncommon.

One mini cruise ship in North American service that has no need of observing T-boat rules is a sixty-six-passenger vessel working seasonal itineraries up and down the St. Lawrence River. Built in 1981, *Canadian Empress* sails under the Canadian flag and shows a measured gross registered tonnage of 463. The summer of 2000 also saw the return of a U.S.-based mini-cruise operator that was part of the initial expansion of this service category in the 1980s but was unable to sustain its operations the first time around.

American Cruise Lines operated out of Haddam, Connecticut, and by the late 1980s had designed and built three mini cruise ships. Following the 1988 season the company filed for chapter 11 bankruptcy protection, a move that would have allowed it to continue operations while a reorganization plan was put together. In early 1989, though, the chapter 11 process was converted into a chapter 7 filing, and the company had to liquidate its assets.

In 2000 American Cruise Lines was ready to try again. With its original fleet dispersed far and wide, the company designed and built a new mini cruise ship, *American Eagle,* and following her construction at the Salisbury, Maryland, yard of Chesapeake Shipbuilding, she went to work out of Baltimore in late April 2000.

The biggest news on the mini cruise ship front as the twentieth century was ending was the fact that America Classic Voyages, the parent company of Delta Queen Steamboat Company, had formed a new subsidiary called Delta Queen

Coastal Voyages. The company plans to build a fleet of five new 226-passenger coastal vessels that will advance the mini cruise concept to an entirely new level.

The first two vessels are scheduled to be completed by Atlantic Marine in Jacksonville, Florida, in time for the 2001 summer cruise season and will bear the names *Cape May Light* and *Cape Cod Light*. They will be 300 feet long, 50 feet wide, and have a draft of 13 feet, in other words, larger than earlier mini cruise ships. Indeed these newbuildings have not been designed as T-boats at all, since they will measure in the neighborhood of 1,600 gross registered tons. Delta Queen hopes to supplement these first two vessels with three additional ones. Like Cruise West's *Spirit of '98*, the new Delta Queen coastal cruise ships feature an external design that recalls classic steamboats. Unlike the steam-powered stern-wheelers that Delta Queen Steamboat operates along America's inland rivers, though, the new coastal vessels will be diesel powered.

ACCL, however, will forever remain the pioneer in the mini cruise ship field. At the turn of the century the company was operating three new vessels, the 1994-built *Niagara Prince*, an eighty-four-passenger vessel with a length of 174 feet, plus the sister ships *Grande Caribe* of 1997 and *Grande Mariner* of 1998, each of which measures 183 feet from bow to stern and can accommodate 100 passengers.

American Cruise Line reentered the mini cruise business in April 2000. In this photograph, construction of the company's new *American Eagle* is almost complete at the Salisbury, Maryland, yard of Chesapeake Shipbuilding.

A rendering of Delta Queen's new 226-passenger coastal cruise ship. The first two units of the new fleet will be called *Cape Cod Light* and *Cape May Light*.

In the early years of the twentieth century, the New York Central Railroad revolutionized passenger travel between New York and Chicago by dispatching a marvelous new train, the Twentieth Century Limited, up the Hudson Valley, west through the Mohawk Valley, and finally along the southern shores of the Great Lakes to Chicago—"the water level route," as the railroad called it.

By the end of the century, the famous old train was nothing but a memory. Amtrak serves the old route with a train it calls the Lake Shore Limited, but there is still another way to travel the old water level route from the East Coast to Chicago. It is not a fast sixteen-hour overnight trip, such as the Twentieth Century Limited once provided. Luther Blount's *Niagara Prince* requires no less than sixteen *days* to make its way from Warren, Rhode Island, down to New York, up the Hudson to Albany, west through the Mohawk River and the New York State Barge Canal, and finally across the Great Lakes to Chicago, Illinois. But who would ever want to compress such a marvelous trip into sixteen hours?

All in all, the twenty or so mini cruise ships that were at work in North America during the summer season of 2000 provide stateroom accommodations for fewer than 2,000 passengers, less than the overall capacity of many oceangoing cruise ships. But they certainly bring an extraordinary measure of diversity to the North American cruise scene.

DAY CRUISERS

In addition to oceangoing ships, there is another entire category of cruise ships regularly operating out of North American ports. These vessels offer a much shorter sea-going experience, one that is measured in hours, not days.

Ambassador II, a 1975-built vessel that operated in car ferry service for many years in the Baltic and the Mediterranean, is departing Port Canaveral, Florida, in March 2000 for a four-hour cruise to "nowhere" under the banner of Sterling Casino Cruises.

The vessels employed are typically older European car ferries. A company called SeaEscape was a pioneer in this trade, operating vessels on one-day round trips between Miami, Port Everglades, or Port Canaveral and Freeport on Grand Bahama Island. A one-day cruise aboard a SeaEscape vessel usually begins with departure from the mainland at eight o'clock in the morning (sometimes earlier), a six-hour cruise to Freeport, a hurried two hours ashore, then back to Florida, with arrival sometime after ten. Other companies offer similar service on the West Coast between San Diego and Ensenada, Mexico.

While aboard ship, passengers enjoy buffet meals; they can try their luck in the casino, take a dip in the pool, or just relax. For a surcharge, passengers can even have access to a cabin, although most forego the additional expense and spend their day lounging on deck in much the same way passengers once did aboard excursion boats of companies like the Hudson River Day Line.

More recently, the day-cruise business has evolved into one that specializes in even shorter cruises to the ever popular "nowhere." Four- and five-hour trips focused around either lunch or dinner are proving to be attractive, with the casino playing a more prominent role in the whole experience than it does during all-day trips to Freeport or Ensenada.

Over the years, upwards of two dozen vessels have been deployed in day-cruise service out of various North American ports. Given the basic enjoyment that a trip to sea can provide—coupled with the opportunity of "making a killing" in the casino—the day cruiser side of the oceangoing cruise industry seems likely to thrive in the years ahead.

CHAPTER 11

Peter Deilmann Cruises

Managing the Fleet

At some point during virtually every deepwater cruise, passengers are invited to attend a pre- or post-dinner cocktail party that is called something like the Captain's Gala or the Captain's Welcoming Reception. Drinks flow, finger-food is passed around, and the captain takes to the microphone and says a few words to the passengers.

Some cruise ship captains exhibit a definite flair for such presentations and often prove to be better at doing stand-up comedy than the people who have been hired to tell jokes and make passengers laugh during formal evening entertainment. Other captains, of course, are decidedly uncomfortable in such a public role; when it comes to snapping off clever one-liners, they prove that their real talent is vessel navigation.

Key members of the ship's company will typically be introduced during the captain's presentation, often with musical flourishes and drum rolls. These may include the staff captain, the usual title of the officer who is second in command of the vessel; the chief engineer, the expert who oversees the operation of all the ship's machinery; the hotel manager, a person in overall charge of the large staffs who prepare and serve food and beverages, as well as keep passenger cabins shipshape; the ship's doctor, a medical professional who administers to both passengers and crew; the head chef, who generally gets the heartiest applause; and so forth, up to a dozen or more individuals.

Other people who work for cruise companies are never acknowledged or given a round of applause during a Captain's Gala on board ship. These are the people who toil ashore in a cruise company's headquarters and keep the whole enterprise running smoothly. There are few reliable statistics to use to compare the size of a cruise company's staff on shore with the number of people it employs on board its ships. When the new Disney Cruise Line put *Disney Wonder* in service in 1998, the vessel had an onboard staff of 920, while there were 450 people working for the company in various shoreside positions.

Because cruise companies are essentially retail businesses selling a highly perishable product—once an "empty cabin" leaves port on a given cruise, it becomes a lost opportunity that can never be sold—marketing and reservations are extraordinarily critical functions. Marketing sells the product; reservations books the orders.

Marketing includes the same kinds of activities associated with the sale of any retail product: doing market research, preparing and distributing brochures and other materials, retaining ad agencies and other specialized consultants, developing and executing advertising campaigns, preparing seasonal and regional specials of one sort or another, and ensuring that appropriate travel agents are made aware of all that is available.

Some of the larger cruise lines incorporate television commercials into their marketing activities. There are many experienced people within the industry, however, who remain convinced that such efforts serve less to promote one cruise company over another and more to popularize cruise travel itself. People who are so inclined welcome television advertising campaigns, even—and perhaps especially—when they are paid for by the competition.

This is a theory that seems rather plausible, since brand differentiation or the selection of a cruise is not usually made at home while watching television, but rather when a customer sits down across the desk from his or her travel agent. The two factors that weigh most heavily in the final choice of this cruise line over that one, according to the best research on the subject, are the customer's own past cruise experiences and the travel agent's recommendation.

In over 90 percent of cruise bookings, it is the travel agent who calls the cruise line's reservations department and, essentially, makes the sale. The psychology of the relationship between customer and travel agent often creates the impression that the travel agent is working on behalf of the customer. The two, after all, are sitting face-to-face in an office while the cruise line's reservations clerk is a faceless voice on the other end of a telephone line in a corporate facility hundreds or even thousands of miles away.

In fact, of course, it is the travel agent and the cruise company who are in a business partnership with each other and who both stand to gain, financially, if the passenger signs up for a cruise. The fact that potential cruise passengers see travel agents as their allies and do not regard them with the same distrust and even hostility that the public generally harbors toward sales personnel on the retail end of, say, the automobile industry is a benefit of immeasurable worth that the cruise industry currently enjoys, but may seriously underappreciate.

Cruise companies have large reservations offices. Travel agents with anxious and busy clients sitting in their offices do not want to be "put on hold" for indeterminate intervals, so it is important that a cruise line's reservations office be staffed with adequate numbers of trained personnel who answer calls promptly, respond to questions swiftly and accurately, and lock in the sale whenever possible. While precise numbers remain closely held corporate secrets, large cruise lines—Carnival, Royal Caribbean, and Princess—have many hundreds of reservations clerks on duty during the busiest hours.

Royal Caribbean recently did something different in the way of reservations management. While its primary reservations center remains in its Miami headquarters on Dodge Island, in 1997 the company opened a secondary facility in Wichita, Kansas. A whole new set of factors is currently evolving in the business world with respect to where one should locate such "telemarketing" centers: regional wage rates, the quality of a local work force, area unemployment rates, the cost of telephone lines, and real estate values all figure in the equation. Employment at RCI's Wichita center quickly grew to 285 people, and thanks to an expansion of the facility, it is expected to reach 700 by the year 2002.

Royal Caribbean regards its Wichita reservations facility as a backup to its principal Miami facility, but the Midwest center is on-line every day and when a travel agent in Los Angeles or Boston calls to book a reservation aboard *Legend of the Seas*—or aboard Celebrity's *Century* since the same reservations system handles both RCI and its subsidiary—the call may be routed to an agent in Wichita or in Miami. In 1999, RCI estimates that its reservations system handled 6.5 million inquiries, with two-thirds going to Miami, the rest to Wichita. Wichita can even function as RCI's sole reservations center in the event Miami is forced to close for any reason, like a pending hurricane. People from Florida can be relocated to Wichita on a short-term basis to supplement the force permanently assigned there. RCI's Wichita facility also includes the capability to take over fleet management functions should the company's Miami headquarters be under hurricane threat.

An interesting sidelight on the whole marketing and reservations side of cruise line management is block-booking of large quantities of cabins—or even entire vessels—by tour operators. For a number of years, Premier's *IslandBreeze*, later to be renamed *The Big Red Boat III*, operated seven-night cruises from Las Palmas on Grand Canary Island off the west coast of Africa. While Premier dutifully listed the vessel's cruises from there in its regular brochure, in fact the small bargain-basement cruise line with headquarters in Port Canaveral, Florida, considered basing one of its ships in so distant a port as a business risk that it was not prepared to assume alone. Premier had made a prior arrangement with Thomson Travel of Great Britain, a major retailer of packaged tours, and while all business arrangements of the relationship are not known, it was Thomson, not Premier, that primarily saw to the promotion of cruises aboard *IslandBreeze*. More recently, Thomson has prebooked large numbers of cabins aboard Royal Caribbean's *Voyager of the Seas*. But with over fifteen hundred cabins available on this large new vessel, Thomson's block of cabins represents a small percentage of overall accommodations.

Part of a cruise company's reservations operation—or closely related to it—is a department whose sole function is to book air travel for passengers who elect to purchase both the cruise and the travel between home and port as a package. The same office typically handles the booking of hotel stays either before or after the cruise; these are promoted and sold by the cruise line.

Anyone who has ever tried to secure a single airline reservation from one point to another at a specific time and at the cheapest possible price can understand the challenge of booking twenty-five hundred people into and out of south Florida every Sunday of the year to cruise aboard, say, *Carnival Triumph*. And *Carnival Triumph* is but one of fourteen cruise ships Carnival operates, while Carnival Cruise Lines is but one of a half-dozen or more companies offering south Florida departures.

For cruise departures from seaports that feature a reasonable volume of commercial air service, cruise lines prefer to utilize scheduled air service. When a ship begins and ends cruises in a smaller port, one with limited scheduled air traffic (Aruba, for example, or Montego Bay, Jamaica) then charter flights from central cities often make more sense. Renaissance Cruises, many of whose vessels depart from some of the more out-of-the-way harbors on the face of the earth, uses charter aircraft that have been specially decorated with the company logo and look to be "Renaissance Airlines." In any event, arranging airlift to ports of departure is a very demanding aspect of cruise line operations.

For that matter, the work of a cruise company's air department does not necessarily end when flights are booked, tickets printed, and documents sent off to travel agents for delivery to passengers. There remains the ever-present possibility of a departure-day glitch, a cruise industry variation on the dreaded Murphy's Law.

It is a wonderful February Saturday in Miami. Six cruise ships arrive back in port early in the morning with tanned, relaxed, and satisfied passengers, while all over the Northeast and Midwest, frazzled folks looking forward to their own upcoming week under the warm Caribbean sun are calling taxicabs and heading for the airport. Except in Boston, Logan is shut down tight with eight inches of new and heavy snow, the three New York airports are being pelted with sleet and freezing rain, and flight schedules up and down the East Coast are a shambles.

The six ships will sail from Dodge Island that evening, on time if possible, later in the evening if that proves necessary. The air departments of the several cruise lines involved will have worked feverishly all day long to patch together alternate flights to get passengers to Miami or to the vessel's first port of call if no better arrangements can be made. Their work will also entail booking hotel reservations for any nights not spent on board the ship, providing allowances for meals, arranging buses for transfer, and so forth. This particular cruise may be getting off to a rocky and potentially unpleasant start, but passengers must come away from the whole experience with a feeling that the cruise line did everything it possibly could to mitigate their discomfort and disappointment, even in the face of such an uncontrollable development as horrible weather.

Once passengers are aboard ship, the efficient operation of a cruise is something that represents long and hard hours of work by a totally different group of professionals in the cruise company's headquarters. Names, titles, and reporting relationships within the table of organization may vary from one cruise company to another, but a department with the general designation of marine operations includes a number of important functions and elements.

Cruise itineraries must be planned, scheduled, revised, and updated, a task that also involves the company's marketing people. Increasingly common at cruise companies is a new function, an office with a name like total guest satisfaction, which is a kind of ombudsman within the organization working on behalf of cruise passengers. When completely new services are being developed, necessary planning includes site visits to ports in question, meetings with port officials, negotiation of docking arrangements, and assurances that infrastructure is in place to provide adequate and diverse choices in the way of full- and half-day tours to nearby points of interest. If the port is also a place where containers will be shipped to resupply a vessel after it arrives, arrangements must be made to make sure provisioning will take place smoothly. For that matter, even if a new port is not intended to be a place where a cruise ship will be reprovisioned routinely, the port's cargo capabilities must be assessed since supplies may someday be routed to a cruise ship at that port on an emergency basis.

Everything associated with adding a new port to an existing itinerary or developing a totally new and different itinerary must be signed and sealed sufficiently in advance to ensure that promotional materials are prepared and in the hands of travel agents when prospective passengers start to make inquiries, and that can be as early as a year or more before the first departure under the new schedule. Last-minute schedule changes, while sometimes necessary, are never viewed with enthusiasm.

Negotiating docking arrangements in a port or a series of ports where cruise ships routinely call involves one set of problems. An Alaskan itinerary is a good example of this, where the popular ports of Ketchikan, Juneau, and Skagway are already handling large numbers of vessels, and the open slots for newcomers are rather restricted. But the ports themselves are known quantities; their navigational characteristics involve no mysteries, and the only unknown with respect to shore excursions is whether existing tour companies will be able to handle the additional crowds that a new vessel will bring.

A totally different set of challenges is posed when a cruise line decides to send a ship to a port where cruise ships have rarely, if ever, visited. Such was the case in 1998, for example, when Norwegian Cruise Line decided to dispatch its recently acquired *Norwegian Dynasty* on a few Hawaiian cruises at the beginning and the end of the vessel's regular Alaskan season. Because a foreign-flag vessel—*Norwegian Dynasty* was registered in Panama—could not sail an exclusively intra-Hawaiian itinerary without an intermediate call at a port not under U.S. jurisdiction, NCL incorporated a twenty-four-hundred-mile, round-trip deviation to Fanning Island in the middle of a ten-night cruise that both begins and ends in Honolulu. (Fanning Island, a one-time British possession that is now part of the Republic of Kiribati, lies twelve hundred statute miles south of Hawaii.)

Fanning, an unspoiled tropical island, lacks such amenities as air service, so when Mike Pawlus, then serving as NCL's vice president of strategic planning, led an inspection team on a site visit to the proposed port of call, they first had to fly to Easter Island and then travel aboard a single-engine fishing boat across 170 miles of open water to reach Fanning. The boat broke down, Pawlus and his team spent sixty-eight hours at sea, and as he later told the trade journal *Cruise Industry News,* "With six to eight foot swells, our greatest fear was of taking on water and sinking, not whether we had enough food to eat." It all worked out well, though, and NCL is able to schedule a seemingly intra-Hawaiian cruise or two each year by including a diversion to Fanning Island.

Planning itineraries for annual world cruises involves some of this same excitement, since such voyages typically include calls at one or more ports where a company's vessels rarely visit. Many world cruise passengers are steady customers of such journeys, and so it is important that each year's itinerary include a good measure of novelty. A world cruise, in other words, must do more than merely circumnavigate the globe; before a final itinerary is announced, ports must be visited and arrangements made for the planned cruise.

A new port's navigational idiosyncrasies must be examined. *Norwegian Dynasty* never had to be fueled or provisioned at Fanning Island, but operational people planning world cruises must determine where their globe-trotting vessels can be bunkered, where provisions can most easily be shipped and pre-positioned, whether there are acceptable alternatives to the first choices, and whether food products that must necessarily be obtained locally—fresh milk, for instance—are available.

Even without major changes or the excitement of a world cruise, efforts are continually being made to fine-tune itineraries. The marketing people suggest, for example, that if a 5:00 P.M. departure from a given port could be pushed back

Obtaining fuel at various ports a vessel visits is an important task that a cruise line's headquarters staff must arrange.

to 7:00 P.M., more extensive shore excursions could be offered. Operations immediately points out that the later departure will entail higher fuel costs for the faster speeds that will be required to reach the next port at the proper time, and any additional revenue the shore tours might generate will have to be weighed against additional fuel expenses. Word is received from the ship's agent in the port that any departure after 6:00 P.M. will entail premium pay for line handlers to assist in the vessel's departure, while a captain assigned to headquarters for liaison with the fleet reports that the later departure will likely require using a different berth in the port, one that is more difficult to navigate in and out of than the berth the company currently uses and could require the use of tugboats under certain wind and tide conditions. Sometimes, of course, the best itinerary changes are ones that are never made.

Like the air department of a cruise company that does some of its most demanding work on the day flights are delayed and cancelled and alternate arrangements must be made on the spot, so too does marine operations "earn its pay," so to speak, when cruise itineraries must be changed on short notice, such as when a tropical hurricane roars out of the Atlantic and wreaks havoc with cruise schedules from the Caribbean to Canada.

All cruise companies have developed good working relationships with port officials throughout their service area, and they turn first to places they know well when trying to develop an alternative itinerary. But it can still be hectic, and however cooperative a port may want to be, there is often a limit to what can be accomplished, especially on short notice.

Sidestepping hurricanes typically involves heading to the western Caribbean when storms threaten the Atlantic coast, and using the eastern Caribbean as an alternative when a hurricane roars westward past Cuba and heads for the Gulf Coast of Texas or Mexico. An unfortunate situation that substantially reduces options occurs when a cruise ship heads into the western Caribbean to avoid a hurricane that was heading north, only to have the storm change course and follow it there.

Perhaps the most disruptive change that a hurricane can generate is to force a cruise line to terminate a cruise and originate a new one in an unexpected port—Tampa rather than Miami, or Port Canaveral rather than Port Everglades. It is usually better to keep a ship at sea and extend the length of a cruise than to divert it elsewhere and be forced to arrange alternate air or ground transport for passengers, luggage, provisions, even shore personnel.

A popular cruise itinerary that is prone to hurricane disruption is service between New York and Bermuda. Indeed the very first European settlers to land on the island now called Bermuda did so in 1609 when their vessel, the *Sea Venture*, came to grief on underwater reefs surrounding the island chain in the midst of what was undoubtedly a tropical hurricane. The shipwrecked travelers struggled ashore, and while some continued on in the spring to their intended destination—Jamestown, in a new land called Virginia—others remained in Bermuda and became the island's first European residents. It is this incident that William Shakespeare used as the basis of *The Tempest:* "Is the storm overblown? I hid me under the dead mooncalf's gaberdine for fear of the storm."

Cruise lines operating Bermuda service will typically send their vessels north to Canada or even dispatch them south to the Bahamas if the Naval Atlantic Meteorology and Oceanography Center in Norfolk, Virginia, is predicting that a hurricane will either hit Bermuda itself or cut across the sea lanes between New York and Bermuda just as cruise ships are headed that way.

Another aspect of a cruise company's maritime operations that involves both routine and unexpected activity is vessel maintenance. Cruise ships require periodic drydocking, for example. Such visits are negotiated with shipyards and scheduled as far in advance as possible, with all cruise companies seeking to have this work performed during their slack seasons, which are generally spring and fall. But hundreds of cruise ships seeking drydock time at the same time puts a premium on the scheduling of such work. Sometimes a ship will require out-of-service maintenance in a shipyard, but drydocking is not needed; the work can be performed in a "wet dock," as it is sometimes called, which means the ship is simply tied up at a pier. Even relatively new vessels must schedule downtime in shipyards for the performance of work under the terms of their builder's warranties.

Cruise ships working North American itineraries on the East Coast are often drydocked in Jacksonville, Florida; Mobile, Alabama; Norfolk, Virginia; and Baltimore, Maryland. Vancouver, British Columbia, and Portland, Oregon, see a fair volume of cruise work at the start and the end of the summer Alaska season. Cruise companies generate many hundreds of millions of dollars of quality business for North American shipyards each year.

If a ship is to be out of service for a relatively short period—a week to ten days, perhaps—the full hotel staff of waiters and cabin attendants will often stay with the vessel and be put to work on projects in their respective areas of concern, changing out a vessel's linen supply, perhaps, or reworking certain dining room procedures and protocols. A longer stay in a shipyard will normally see the cruise company rotate the hotel staff to other ships in the fleet or to shore leave back home.

Cruise companies wish it would never happen, but vessels sometimes have to be removed from service on short notice for unexpected maintenance or repairs. Accidents, groundings, fires, major mechanical malfunctions, and all kinds of other emergencies can require negotiating with a shipyard for immediate repairs, then calling on the people in reservations to see what they can do about accommodating displaced passengers on alternative cruise departures.

Though not often, an ill wind can sometimes blow a little good. The unexpected cancellation of a week or two of cruises that have less-than-capacity bookings may allow a company to accommodate passengers aboard other not-fully-booked vessels and also to perform maintenance that had been scheduled for a future drydocking, thereby gaining availability of the vessel for fresh bookings during the week when her routine maintenance would have been performed.

A scheduled visit to a shipyard is also a time when vessel modifications that a company has deemed necessary can be made: installation of an additional bow or stern thruster to improve shortcomings in maneuverability, the replacement of certain kitchen equipment that has not been performing up to standards, or even the installation of a small prebuilt module containing some new all-suite accommodations. A continuous responsibility of a cruise company's headquarters staff is to collect comments and recommendations from officers in the fleet, subject them to cost-benefit analysis, and develop a schedule for the implementation of the more investment-worthy vessel improvements. Routine remodeling of cabins and public rooms is also something that happens with a degree of consistency and regularity to ensure that a vessel never starts to look shopworn or threadbare and that older units in the fleet are kept in a comparable condition with a company's newest vessels. The goal is always to accomplish as much work as possible in the shortest time practical so a vessel's out-of-service time is kept to a minimum.

A certain level of maintenance is always going on aboard a cruise ship, even while the vessel remains in service. A cruise ship with a white hull and superstructure can start to look dirty and unkempt very quickly unless touch-up painting is done on a steady basis. When Great Britain was engaged in the Falklands War in 1982, for instance, Cunard's *Queen Elizabeth 2* and P&O's *Canberra* were among the passenger vessels requisitioned for military use. The pair were so used for only three months, but because routine touch-up painting was ignored for the duration, when they returned to England to resume normal service, they both looked quite disheveled.

Nor is in-service maintenance restricted to matters cosmetic. Because contemporary cruise ships have been designed with a good deal of mechanical redundancy, engineering personnel belowdecks can often tear down engines and other mechanical equipment and replace major components even while a vessel continues in cruise service.

In a cruise company's headquarters, another function which is absolutely vital for smooth sailing is that performed by the personnel or human resources department. These are the people who make arrangements for everyone from the captain on the bridge of a ship to the smiling person in the company blazer greeting passengers at the airport to be hired and trained, to report for work when and where they are supposed to, and to receive a pay check for their effort.

Cruise companies hire part-time help for a large number of functions that must be performed ashore to make a passenger's cruise experience a quality one: that greeter at the airport, contractors to transport both passengers and luggage from airport to pier, clerks who collect tickets and check in passengers at the cruise terminal, and lots of people to answer lots of questions that arriving and departing passengers necessarily have. When a cruise company operates continuous itineraries out of regular ports of embarkation, a roster of potential part-time help can be established, and individuals are called for a day's work as needed. When a cruise company expands the scope of its operations, though, and begins to originate cruises in a variety of different world ports—perhaps operating only one or two cruises a year from certain ports—then someone called a ship's agent enters the picture.

Before any ship can enter any foreign port—even for a single day's visit—a ship's agent must be retained in and for that port. The agent handles all kinds of routine business on behalf of the ship and its owner. The ship's agent sees to it that customs and immigration officials are notified of a ship's arrival and keeps them updated if any schedule irregularities develop. The agent makes certain that any provisions intended for the ship have been delivered and that stevedores are available to load supplies aboard. The ship's agent must also be able to assume liability for any damage the ship might do while it is in port. And if a cruise ship is to begin and end a voyage in the agent's port, it is the agent who retains whatever personnel are needed to handle passenger-related tasks and to whose care a quantity of those brightly colored blazers in a variety of sizes will have been shipped weeks before a vessel steams into port.

The cruise company personnel that a passenger sees most, of course, are the various people who work on board. Specialized agencies are usually retained to recruit maritime officers, with many cruise companies preferring to hire deck and engineering staff from a single country. Greece, Norway, and Italy, countries whose maritime traditions began before the dawn of recorded history, provide a heavy percentage of the officers who staff contemporary cruise ships. There is a large volume of paperwork required to make sure the licenses of a company's officers are current in their issuing country and have been properly countersigned by the country where the vessel is registered. A cruise company's personnel department must also make arrangements so deck and engineering personnel are afforded training opportunities to sharpen their skills in the use of new technologies and to become familiar with new regulatory requirements.

The largest component of onboard personnel are the hundreds of people needed to staff the ship's hotel services—waiters, chefs, wine stewards, cabin attendants, bartenders—the list is long. Many of these job categories derive the bulk of their earnings from gratuities left by passengers. Others (kitchen personnel, for example) have no direct contact with passengers, and their compensation is entirely salary. The great bulk of these hires are made in third-world countries and retained under contract provisions that call for a month of shore leave, including air travel home and back, after perhaps six or nine months of onboard service. Agencies of various sorts are routinely used to hire hotel staff and in some cases to conduct rudimentary training as well.

Maintaining a reliable number of employees at a large cruise company is challenging enough, what with routine turnover, in-service training needs, and shore-leave rotation. But with so many cruise companies in such expansive modes—introducing new vessels into the fleet year after year—the business of ensuring that all vessels are adequately and properly staffed is a challenge of serious proportion that company executives must necessarily face on a day-to-day basis.

Although it has not always been the case, at the turn of the new century the trend among cruise lines was to have employees of the cruise line perform a good number of onboard functions that were earlier done by contract personnel. Gambling casinos, for example, were once almost exclusively managed under contract; today they are usually the responsibility of employees of the cruise line itself. The various shops on board cruise ships tend to be run under contract, though, with Greyhound Leisure Service of Miami being a major operator of such shops. (Greyhound is a corporate descendant of the intercity bus company of the same name, although the Miami company of today has no ties with bus operations.) In the past, shipboard food and beverage services were frequently provided by third parties under contract. Some cruise companies, particularly smaller ones, continue to "contract out" these services, but they are more typically performed by people employed by the cruise company itself. An interesting exception to this trend is a recent Royal Caribbean decision to include Johnny Rocket hamburger and malt shops aboard its new vessels, facilities which are operated by Johnny Rocket personnel.

Another exception to the trend of handling things in house is a comprehensive cruise management service offered by a Monte Carlo firm known as V. Ships Leisure, which is the cruise division of a larger corporation called V. Ships. This company is active in a variety of maritime sectors and is a descendant of Sitmar Cruises, the firm that was founded by the Vlasov family in 1938 and sold to P&O/Princess in 1988.

Among past and present cruise company clients of V. Ships Leisure are Commodore Cruise Line, Regency Cruises, Hyundai Merchant Marine, Renaissance, Airtours/Sun Cruises, and Silverseas. The company also has a more complex partnership arrangement with Radisson Seven Seas.

Radisson Seven Seas Cruises is one of several clients that rely on management services supplied by the Monte Carlo–based firm, V. Ships Leisure. The Radisson fleet is made up of a variety of interesting vessels, including the twin-hulled *Radisson Diamond*, shown here in the Estonian port of Tallinn. The vessel in the background is the Tallink car ferry *Georg Ots*.

Cruise companies that retain V. Ships Leisure ordinarily handle their own marketing, sales, and ticketing functions, while the Monte Carlo firm takes care of all operational matters, including hotel services. As part of its partnership with Radisson, V. Ships even helped design and build a new cruise ship—the *Seven Seas Navigator*—and did so in a manner that can only be called unusual.

Radisson wanted to build a small-to-medium-size vessel, and what V. Ships Leisure proposed would probably not work at all for a larger vessel. V. Ships learned of a like-new hull that had been declared surplus in Russia, the *Akademik Nikolay Pilyugin*. Given the temporary name *Blue Sea*, she was towed to T. Mariotti's yard in Genoa, and a vessel that was originally intended to be a submarine-tracking vessel for the Russian navy was repowered, rebuilt, and converted into a new 490-passenger cruise ship. V. Ships had earlier managed a roughly similar conversion project for another of its clients, Swan Hellenic Cruises, whose *Minerva* of 1996 was also built on a one-time Soviet military hull. Radisson's next new-building, a vessel to be called *Seven Seas Mariner*, will be constructed more conventionally at the Chantiers de l'Atlantique yard in St. Nazaire, France, with V. Ships managing the effort from start to finish.

The potential market for the kind of management services that V. Ships Leisure provides would seem, at first blush, to be rather limited with respect to North American cruise companies, where large operations like Carnival, Royal Caribbean, and Princess have developed extensive expertise for handling management functions themselves. Yet Carnival and Princess are both active clients of V. Ships Leisure, with the Monte Carlo firm handling the recruitment of officers who work aboard Carnival ships, as well as all travel arrangements necessary for rotating officers on and off the vessels of Princess Cruises. V. Ships itself has estimated that for every ten officers who are at sea aboard a cruise ship at any given time, five or six additional officers are at one phase or other of vacation rotation.

Another important task that a cruise company's headquarters staff must manage is the acquisition of the tons and *tons* of supplies that its fleet needs to keep sailing, everything from light bulbs and furniture polish to navigational charts and tide tables, from uniforms and table linen to medical equipment and ping-pong balls, from professional journals and office supplies to engine parts and replacement furniture. There is also the food—fresh, frozen, packaged, and canned—which will become the wonderful meals that are such an important part of the total cruise experience. Unlike a land-based resort or a big-city hotel, where an unanticipated shortage of fresh carrots or pancake syrup can be rectified in short order by sending someone out on an errand, if the larder starts to run low aboard ship, the options are usually more restricted. Hence careful planning is critical to ensure that adequate inventories are always on hand.

Cruise companies usually handle their own procurement and remain alert to ways they can reduce costs through more effective practices. Although it did not

Quantities of food are loaded aboard a ship at the start of a cruise.

involve the acquisition of food, Carnival recently decided it could save millions of dollars by eliminating a basket of toiletries that it previously set out in the cabins of all newly arriving passengers. Complaints were forthcoming from passengers, though, and what Carnival did as an alternative was to enter into agreements with the manufacturers of various toiletries whereby instead of Carnival purchasing specially packaged shampoo and other products, it now distributes samples of brand-name merchandise which are supplied by the manufacturers at their expense as a way of advertising.

Contracts for the provision of food are usually let on a six-month basis. When a cruise line must transship provisions to vessels sailing diverse and nonrepetitive itineraries, suppliers will typically deliver food to a company-operated ware-house of one sort or another. With vessels operating out of a given port on a more or less continuous basis, Miami and Port Everglades, for example, procurement contracts often call for delivery directly to the pier on departure day, with con-tract specifications often detailing very narrow time limits to ensure that various suppliers do not all arrive at once.

Food aboard a cruise ship, particularly one operated by a mass-market com-pany, is less the individualized gourmet service so strongly suggested in the bro-chure and more a high-caliber, banquet-style cooking. Given the large numbers of people to be fed, meals are necessarily precooked in quantity, not prepared in-dividually to order, with past experience being a relatively good barometer to es-timate how many people will order beef, how many fish, how many poultry, and therefore how many of each should be prepared for a given meal. The trend in the industry is moving toward purchasing meat, fish, and poultry in precut por-tions to ensure uniformity throughout the dining room and to eliminate the need for meat-cutting aboard ship. With rare exceptions meat, fish, and poultry are delivered frozen.

Food service aboard upscale cruise ships involves a good deal more in the way of individualized food preparation. But upscale cruise companies do not op-erate vessels in the 100,000-gross-ton range, and they certainly do not face the dual challenge of feeding a thousand or more hungry passengers at early-seating dinner and then a similar number at late-seating dinner two hours later.

Food management is an extremely critical function, however, one that can very easily make or break a cruise line in terms of reputation as well as finan-cially, although the two are intimately linked to each other. Those who are re-sponsible for a cruise line's food and beverage services must strive to achieve seemingly contradictory goals: to provide exciting and interesting menu choices that will make repeat passengers out of first-time cruisers, but to do so as eco-nomically as possible. Needless to say, the current state-of-the-art in procure-ment practices for cruise lines—for food and beverage products as well as for other material—involves the very latest in computerized hardware and software to monitor inventories, adjust subsequent orders, detect off-normal situations, advertise contracts in a timely fashion, and conduct all follow-up activities.

Cruise lines are not unwilling to use the power of their purchasing, whether it be for food or for other supplies, to enhance their reputation as "good neigh-bors" in areas where that is important. For example, cruise lines that derive a good deal of their business from visiting islands in the Caribbean like to cultivate working relationships with firms that can supply unique Caribbean products—Jamaican rum, for example, or a certain kind of locally grown produce—presum-ing that island suppliers can deliver dependably and at a competitive price. Stories are told of procurements being let with Caribbean suppliers for a presumably local product, only to learn the supplier was actually acquiring the product in Miami and flying it to the island for delivery.

In any event, the next time one attends a Captain's Gala aboard a cruise ship and a dozen or so members of the ship's company are introduced to the passengers, pause for a moment and think of the many, many people back on shore whose work is just as critical to the success of a cruise as the work of the people being applauded. They deserve a little thanks, too.

CHAPTER 12

Building Cruise Ships

Festival Cruises

The rapid growth of the cruise industry in the last third of the twentieth century could not have happened—and would never have happened to the same degree that it did—had not a strong, vigorous, and competitive shipbuilding industry been available to turn out technically advanced vessels to satisfy the need for newer, bigger, and better ships.

Building passenger ships is intense and complex work. Among shipbuilders, passenger vessels are sometimes said to be "value added" projects. What this expression means is that a cruise ship is not just a hull and a basic propulsion system. A cruise ship involves a complex assortment of internal systems and equipment, elements that have to be designed, constructed or subcontracted, installed, integrated with other systems, and tested before a vessel is completed and ready for service. A modern cruise ship might have upwards of one thousand passenger cabins, six or more separate dining facilities, three or four swimming pools, shopping and entertainment venues, several banks of elevators, places to store and prepare food, cabins and recreational facilities for the crew, a full medical complex, plus equipment to evaporate seawater into freshwater, incinerate garbage and trash, generate electricity, monitor all systems on a continuous basis, maintain communications with the rest of the world, and by no means incidentally, navigate the vessel in fair weather and foul.

Unlike a cargo ship, which by comparison is a powered but largely empty hull, a cruise ship involves all these "value added" components. Warships represent another category of vessels that are referred to as "value added" projects by the shipbuilding community.

Unfortunately, once a shipyard elects to sign contracts for the construction of cruise ships, it is relatively easy for the yard to lose a good deal of money. This is a harsh way of saying that for a shipyard to succeed and become a steady and reliable supplier of quality vessels to the cruise industry, it must successfully master a bewildering set of managerial challenges, and it must do so steadily, consistently, and, of course, profitably.

As the twentieth century was ending, four major European shipyards had emerged as the principal suppliers of the cruise industry's new ships: Finland's Kvaerner Masa-Yards, a company with passenger shipbuilding facilities in both Helsinki and Turku; Germany's Joseph L. Meyer, sometimes called Meyer Werft, located on the River Ems in Papenburg; Italy's Fincantieri, which can build cruise ships in three separate yards at Monfalcone, Trieste, or Marghera; and in France, Chantiers de l'Atlantique in the coastal town of St. Nazaire.

Whether these four firms continue to exercise the same level of market dominance in the future as they have in the recent past, of course, remains to be seen. In 1999, for example, American Classic Voyages contracted with Ingalls Shipbuilding in Pascagoula, Mississippi, for the construction of two 71,000-gross-ton cruise ships with options for two more. The huge five-vessel P&O/Princess order that was announced in May 1999 anticipates the construction of at least two 110,000-gross-ton cruise vessels in Japan by Mitsubishi Heavy Industries. In addition, while it remains correct to identify the four European yards as the source of most of the cruise industry's recent ships, several smaller yards throughout Europe continue to win contracts for the construction of various specialized cruise ships. Might any of these companies emerge—either alone or in partnership with others—to challenge the status currently enjoyed by the likes of Meyer Werft, Fincantieri, and the others for mass-market orders? This, too, is something that only time will tell.

As the new century began, order books at the four major yards remained full, even while Kvaerner was seeking to sell Masa-Yards to a new group of investors. The following table displays the new cruise ships that were delivered to the cruise industry during the year 2000, fourteen new vessels with a combined gross tonnage in excess of 950,000 and with stateroom accommodations for over 18,000 passengers. Assuming, for discussion purposes only, that all fourteen vessels are assigned to typical seven-night cruise itineraries—even though, as a matter of fact, all will not be—these new vessels alone would provide the cruise industry with new capacity for almost a million passengers per year.

Fourteen new deepwater cruise ships in a single year's time was not any kind of statistical aberration, either. Deliveries scheduled for 2001 will likely be in the range of sixteen newbuildings, with at least a dozen and perhaps more in 2002. During 1999, the industry put eleven new vessels in service. Whether this same delivery rate can be sustained on a long-term basis—for a decade or even longer—depends, of course, on how steady the growth of cruising itself remains as the new century progresses.

The building of cruise ships, though, is not something to examine merely at the level of industry statistics. It is very much a business that proceeds at a pace which can be measured one vessel at a time. A more concrete sense of what these general trends mean in real terms may be provided by a look at the Chantiers de l'Atlantique shipyard in the Brittany section of France.

CRUISE SHIP NEWBUILDINGS DELIVERED IN 2000

Ship	Company	Gross tons	Shipyard
R Five	Renaissance	30,200	Chantiers
Ocean Princess	Princess	77,000	Fincantieri
Olympic Voyager	Royal Olympic	25,000	Blohm & Voss
Zaandam	Holland America	65,000	Fincantieri
Costa Atlantica	Costa Crociere	84,000	Kvaerner Masa-Yards
Aurora	P&O	76,000	Meyer Werft
Millennium	Celebrity	91,000	Chantiers
Carnival Victory	Carnival	102,000	Fincantieri
Silver Shadow	Silverseas	25,000	T. Mariotti
Explorer of the Seas	Royal Caribbean	142,000	Kvaerner Masa-Yards
SuperStar Libra	Star	91,000	Meyer Werft
R Six	Renaissance	30,200	Chantiers
Amsterdam	Holland America	61,000	Fincantieri
R Seven	Renaissance	30,200	Chantiers

Source: *Cruise Industry News Quarterly*

ST. NAZAIRE

St. Nazaire is situated about 250 miles southeast of Paris on the north bank of the River Loire, immediately inland from a point where the river empties into the Bay of Biscay. Long famous for its shipbuilding, it was the formation in 1861 of La Compagnie Generale Transatlantique (CGT), a steamship company that English-speaking people generally call the French Line, that set St. Nazaire on its modern shipbuilding course. Because French Line needed a steady source of new vessels for its expanding transatlantic trade, it helped establish a new and modern shipyard in St. Nazaire; its first ocean liner, CGT's *Imperatice Eugenie,* was launched in 1864. The yard that is today called Chantiers de l'Atlantique is part of the French transportation consortium Alstom and is the direct successor of French Line's nineteenth-century venture.

Three important events in St. Nazaire's maritime history deserve mention; two are glorious, one is not. The first happened on October 29, 1932, when CGT's *Normandie* slid down the ways at Chantiers de l'Atlantique into the River Loire. *Normandie* may have been the finest and most magnificent ocean liner of all time, technically as well as aesthetically. Unfortunately, magnificence soon became tragedy; *Normandie* was gutted by fire in New York in February 1942 while being converted for use as an American troopship, the USS *Lafayette*, and she never sailed again.

The second glorious St. Nazaire moment happened on May 11, 1960, when Madame Yvonne de Gaulle christened CGT's *France*, a vessel that was constructed on the same slipway as *Normandie* and can be called the last great superliner designed for traditional transatlantic express service. *France*, of course, was later adapted for cruise service by Knut Kloster and converted into Norwegian Caribbean Line's *Norway*.

Between the launching of *Normandie* in 1932 and *France* in 1960, another defining maritime event (or a series of events) happened in St. Nazaire. The town was occupied by invading Nazi troops on June 21, 1940. Two nights earlier, the partially completed battleship *Jean Bart* quietly slipped away from the Chantiers de l'Atlantique shipyard and successfully steamed to Casablanca to join French forces there. In honor of this heroic escape, an unused drydock at Chantiers de l'Atlantique has been preserved and is still proudly called Ouverage Jean Bart.

Shortly after the Germans marched into St. Nazaire, the Kregsmarine selected the town's harbor as one of six French sites for the construction of concrete submarine pens to service its North Atlantic U-boats. The St. Nazaire facility contained fourteen separate slips and was so sturdily constructed that it proved impervious to Allied ordinance of the day. Its roof, for example, was almost twenty-three feet thick and despite many aerial attacks by the Royal Air Force and the U.S. Eighth Air Force, raids that resulted in heavy losses for the Allies, the German submarine pens in St. Nazaire were largely undamaged. The nearby town of St. Nazaire, however, was not so fortunate; it was completely leveled by Allied air raids and the town's population of forty thousand people were forced to flee into the countryside as exiles. U-boats based in St. Nazaire crossed the North Atlantic and attacked merchant shipping off the East Coast of the United States.

Following Germany's surrender in 1945, residents of St. Nazaire returned to their town and began to rebuild. As a result, the St. Nazaire of today is largely a new and modern metropolis and there is nothing even remotely "old world" about its architecture. One of the few structures to survive the war was the drydock where *Jean Bart* had been constructed. Another was a drydock called Forme Joubert that had been built specifically for *Normandie*. On March 29, 1942, it was the target of a British commando raid undertaken to prevent the use of the facility in the repair of heavy German naval ships such as the battleship *Tirpitz*. Around these two surviving shipyard facilities a new postwar Chantiers de l'Atlantique would be built. As for the German submarine pens in St. Nazaire, they not only survived the war, they are still standing and represent a stark and dramatic reminder of the terrible era when they were built.

During World War II, Germany's Kreigsmarine built a number of heavy concrete submarine pens in French coastal cities to service its Atlantic U-boats. The fourteen-bay facility in St. Nazaire still stands and has recently been converted into a maritime museum.

Today's Chantiers de l'Atlantique shipyard is located on a multiacre site to the east of the town proper. At the northeast corner of St. Nazaire's downtown area one finds the railroad station where fast, electrified trains make the run from the Montparnasse Station in Paris in a little over two and a half hours. Directly across the square from the railway station is the three-story Hotel du Berry, a pleasant and cheerful establishment presided over by the Raymond family. Many people whose travels to St. Nazaire are related to business at Chantiers de l'Atlantique stay at this hotel. The lobby of the du Berry is decorated with renditions of important passenger vessels that sail the world's oceans and were built a mile or so down the road. Visitors to St. Nazaire who fail to sample a *crème brûlée* at the Hotel du Berry are subjecting themselves to senseless deprivation.

BUILDING A MODERN CRUISE SHIP

As a cruise ship operator develops plans and specifications for a new vessel, the selection of a shipyard to construct the newbuilding is, perhaps, the single most critical choice in the entire process. The decision is based on economics, of course, but it is not simply a matter of advertising for bids and awarding to the

The Hotel du Berry in St. Nazaire, where many visitors stay when they have business at the Chantiers de l'Atlantique Shipyard.

low bidder. Complex questions of financing, proposed delivery schedules, and the shipyard's performance with its recent orders must also be factored into the equation. The initial agreement between shipyard and cruise company is usually a nonbinding letter of intent. Under its terms, both parties complete the vessel's design, firm up initial cost estimates, and develop a level of comfort with each other in the way of expectations, delivery schedule, selection of subcontractors, and overall technical capability. Once this phase is satisfactorily completed, a formal contract is executed, a lengthy document that details all aspects of the agreed-upon procurement and that frequently contains an option for an additional vessel or vessels to be ordered within a specified time frame and completed for a specified price. It is a mark of the continued health and vitality of the contemporary cruise industry that options for additional vessels rarely expire and are routinely converted into firm orders. (If cruise companies repeatedly elected *not* to exercise options for additional ships, it would indicate that the boom in cruise ship building had peaked.)

Once the ink is dry on a formal contract, a new vessel's maiden voyage is typically about twenty-four months away. It may be a little more if the design is a completely new one that has never been executed, a little less if the contract is for a vessel similar to one recently completed at the yard. In order to get to the point where a contract can be signed, of course, many months—even years—of preliminary planning and design will already have been expended.

In bygone days, the building of a new ship was a task that was performed on an inclined slipway; both *Normandie* and *France* were so constructed in St. Nazaire, although the slipway where both vessels were built no longer exists and has been converted into an area where modular office facilities are now stacked on top of each other. When a ship was built on a slipway, the initial construction task was laying the keel, a strong and stout steel spine to which riblike frames were then attached. Steel plating was next riveted to the frames, and once a hull reached a certain minimum stage of completion, supporting timbers were removed and the partially completed hull was launched—which is to say gravity was allowed to exercise its influence and the hull slid down the slipway into the water with a mighty and dramatic splash.

While this style of shipbuilding has worked its way into many ordinary expressions of everyday language—for instance, "laying the keel"—as a description of contemporary shipbuilding it is woefully out of date. Today, at a shipyard such as Chantiers de l'Atlantique, vessels are assembled not on inclined slipways but in perfectly level drydocks. Nor does the notion of keel, frames, and plating any longer describe a contemporary vessel, much less how it is built.

The single most important technical change between shipbuilding old-style and shipbuilding today is the fact that the ship's steel sections are now welded together, not riveted. Welding came into its own during the Second World War when massive numbers of new vessels had to be constructed quickly in support of the war effort. Welded construction, once perfected, soon led to preassembling elements of a vessel and subsequently joining them into a finished product in such a way that the welded structure itself became the source of a vessel's strength. Keels and frames and external plating were no longer needed to ensure structural integrity. The term monocoque construction is not commonly heard in shipbuilding circles, but the shift to welded construction in shipyards is very similar, in many ways, to the monocoque designs now common in the construction of aircraft, automobiles, and railway cars.

The second innovation that dictates how Chantiers de l'Atlantique builds ships today is the same instrument that has transformed so many contemporary industries—the computer. Instead of a naval architect producing paper drawings which would be converted into wooden patterns which, in turn, would be used as templates for the cutting of steel, today the shipbuilding process proceeds from idea to hard steel entirely in cyberspace. Furthermore, it is the use of high-speed computers that enables a completed ship's design to be efficiently and effectively broken down into hundreds of subassemblies that are welded together into modules called blocks and brought together for final assembly.

The physical layout of the Chantiers de l'Atlantique shipyard in St. Nazaire helps convey a sense of how ships are constructed; there is an almost "production line" character to the place. One's first impression on entering the yard is of buildings of every shape and size; these house everything from the credit union to the lunch room to offices where engineers and technicians work and facilities for the many subcontractors needed for such major projects as the construction of new vessels. Another impression is of people hurrying all over the place on their appointed rounds, many riding bicycles to save time and shorten distances. Shipyard workers employed by Chantiers de l'Atlantique are dressed in royal blue—blue jumpsuits, blue coveralls, blue jackets and pants. The size of the yard's workforce can vary, but it is generally in the range of four thousand people.

Behind all this action, there is also a basic production sense to the yard's layout that begins with raw material at the western extreme and proceeds eastward, culminating in the finished product.

At the western end of the shipyard is a large field where rolls and sheets and bars of unfinished steel are delivered and maintained in inventory. Two yellow gantry cranes patrol this area, manage the supplies, and deliver steel in needed quantities and qualities to a cutting hall, a building called Panneaux Plans, located to the east of the storage yard. Steel is delivered to the yard by rail; a spur track from a nearby freight yard of SNCF, the French state railway system, leads onto the Chantiers de l'Atlantique property. (Finished products such as machinery, however, usually arrive on flatbed trailer trucks.)

There are two separate production areas in Panneaux Plans where raw steel is cut by fast and efficient computer-directed machines into the thousands of separate parts that a major new cruise ship requires. One of the two cutting areas specializes in flat steel, the other in steel that must be formed and shaped in addition to being cut.

The precision that these cutting machines routinely achieve is one of the most important quality assurances in the entire shipbuilding process. If steel is not cut precisely and to extraordinarily exacting tolerances, the subassemblies that will be welded together with such steel will not measure up to requisite standards and specifications and the whole construction process will be compromised.

Among the first seagoing vessels to use welded construction were certain of the Liberty ships built in American yards during the Second World War. Because welded construction was then new, and because the kind of precision steel-cutting and welding that only computers can guarantee were unknown in the 1940s, welded Liberty ships often had a fatal inclination to break completely in two when battered by strong seas.

An important milestone in a ship's construction on the roughly two-year road from contract signing to maiden voyage is the day when a vessel's first steel is cut; this usually occurs about six months into the process. As steel is cut, it is then welded into various elements of the vessel. Initially these are small and manageable units that can be stored in various places throughout the yard and moved around by trucks, on dollies, or with other specialized transport equipment. Walking around Chantiers de l'Atlantique, one sees acre after acre of such subassemblies. Here is the sharp prow of what will one day become the Millennium-class vessel *Infinity* for Celebrity Cruises; there one sees a funnel adorned with the logo of Renaissance Cruises and identified with the hull number of that company's newbuilding, the 30,200-gross-ton *R Six*. More commonly one sees elements of future cruise ships whose ultimate location and function within a completed vessel is difficult for the untrained eye to discern. Many elements are even positioned in an upside-down orientation, since construction of certain sections can proceed more expeditiously in such a fashion. All are unfinished steel that share a common dull gray color; all are identified with the yard number of the vessel for which they are intended.

Examining hull sections that will eventually form the bottom of a vessel, one sees the innards of the various tanks that will hold hundreds of thousands of gallons of fuel and water—potable water, seawater, and sewage at various stages of treatment. To a landlubber, a tank is usually thought of as an empty container. Because the quantities of fluid that a ship carries represent enormous weight whose shifting can easily affect a vessel's stability, the tanks built into a cruise ship beneath the vessel's lowest deck are fitted with baffles of all sorts to keep product from "sloshing around" and generating unwanted effects.

The cruise ship *R Six* of Renaissance
Cruises under construction at
Chantiers de l'Atlantique.

In any event, as these preassembled elements are joined together to form
larger elements, they necessarily grow bigger and, of course, heavier. This is
when the focus of activity at Chantiers de l'Atlantique shifts to a large area on
the east side of the cutting halls, the place where modular units called blocks are
brought together to create ships.

This is the drydock area. It is big, almost 3,000 feet long and 230 feet wide,
and consists of two separate levels. A lower level is closer to the River Loire; its
floor is actually below the level of the river and necessarily so, since ultimately it
will be flooded so a vessel may be launched. An upper level is inland from this
lower level. The entire drydock, as well as an assembly area immediately adjacent to it, is patrolled by two massive Krupp-built gantry cranes, said to be the
largest in the world and capable, together, of lifting 700-ton loads. As elements

of a ship are welded together into larger blocks in the preassembly area adjacent to the drydock, the cranes hoist the blocks onto the vessel under construction in the drydock.

Another important milestone happens when the first block is lifted by the gantry cranes and positioned in the upper drydock. This is the contemporary equivalent of laying the keel, although cruise ships today do not really have keels in the old-fashioned sense. What happens during this event is that a prefabricated portion of a ship's bottom is lowered into place, often replete with all the symbolic ceremonies long associated with laying the keel. A coin is typically placed under the first steel that is positioned in the drydock; officials from the cruise company, the shipyard, and possibly some of the major suppliers of the vessel's equipment step to the microphone and say a few appropriate words.

(It remains correct to speak of a vessel's bottom-most point as its keel; formal measurements, for instance, speak of a vessel's draft as being the distance from waterline to keel. What contemporary vessels lack is the old-fashioned structural member that was often called a keel, or keelson, a longitudinal structural member incorporated within the framing of a ship to stiffen it, to cite a dictionary definition.)

Celebrity Cruises' new *Millennium* sits in drydock at the Chantiers de l'Atlantique shipyard. The vessel's three thrusters can be seen immediately aft of the bow.

From this point onward, the vessel begins to assume shape and form and identity. Once a ship begins to be fabricated in the drydock, it will only move again when the hull itself is afloat.

The work required to position prefabricated elements of a ship and weld them together has all the complexity of an intricate ballet. Leaving aside the technical and engineering achievement that is required to build separate sections of a vessel that mate up with other sections perfectly and accurately, the moving of such large elements by shipwrights at Chantiers de l'Atlantique requires extraordinary coordination. The gantry crane operators, for example, working in small cockpits atop their machines, cannot even see the point where the new element they are carefully and gently lowering into place joins the hull in the drydock. When the bottom of the new element touches the hull, it will be welded to it; looking down from above, though, the gantry crane operators can see only the top of the section they are lowering. Crane operators are guided by people on the ground giving instructions over two-way radios, and yet their task is to position a new element weighing a hundred tons or more atop the hull in the drydock within tolerances of less than an eighth of an inch.

When the construction process reaches a certain point, a vessel is moved from the upper level of the drydock to the lower level. The hull must be able to float before this can happen. Once the lower level is clear, keel blocks on the floor of the lower level are positioned to handle the shape of the new ship's hull.

Anytime a vessel is placed in drydock, a most important preliminary task is to place keel blocks in such a way that the shape of the particular hull is safely accommodated. Vessels in drydock have been known to tip over, often resulting in fatal accidents and always causing serious damage. Taking proper care in the placement of keel blocks is one important safeguard against such unfortunate mishaps.

Once a hull is moved to the lower level of the drydock, construction continues there, and the first prefabricated elements of another new vessel are hoisted into place on the vacated upper level. Finally, at about the eighteen-month mark following the signing of a contract, a vessel is ready for launching.

LAUNCHING

Unlike older forms of launching where the hull slides down an inclined slipway into the water, construction in a drydock allows a vessel to reach a far more advanced stage of completion before it takes to the water. With slipway launchings, a hull was subjected to severe and unusual forces for several moments during the launch; this mandated that the hull be light in weight when it took to the water. For a few seconds during such a launch, the stern of the vessel would bear much of the force and weight of the entire hull, hence the need to keep the hull as light as possible.

The final phases of construction have begun on Radisson Seven Seas' *Seven Seas Mariner*.

This is not the case, however, with drydock construction, and most cruise ships are only about six months away from their maiden voyage when they are floated out, or launched. By contrast, *France* was almost two years away from entering service when she slid down the ways into the River Loire, *Normandie* closer to three.

At Chantiers de l'Atlantique, float-outs are conducted over weekends; this allows more productive use of shipyard workers' time on weekdays, both before and after the float-out. Typically, the lower level of the drydock will be cleared of all staging, tools, and equipment by departing crews late Friday. Sometime Saturday, valves are opened to flood the lower drydock. Quietly, without notice or ceremony, the new ship floats free of its keel blocks. Then on Sunday, the vessel is moved out of the drydock.

Before this can happen, Chantiers de l'Atlantique workers must roll back the big external sea door of the drydock, a massive steel and concrete structure that keeps the waters of the Loire out of the facility. Since this is a procedure that happens only a few times a year, before the gate is moved, divers are sent down to make certain the path the gate follows is clear of any obstruction. Finally, with the gate pulled into its open position, the new vessel is ready to leave the drydock where it was built.

A number of local tugboats move into the dock. Two go to the head of the new cruise ship to hold it on a steady course, while two others take station off the vessel's stern, secure lines, and begin to exert force. It is a highly charged moment when executives from Chantiers de l'Atlantique and the cruise company who have gathered to watch the event first detect that the vessel is moving—incomplete, unpainted save for the funnel (typically finished off in the new owner's final color scheme), unable to operate under its own power, but taking yet another important step. The tugs carefully maneuver the big vessel to one of the fitting-out berths at Chantiers de l'Atlantique where the final stages of construction will take place. On Monday morning when shipyard workers return from their weekend, they can resume work on the vessel without missing a beat.

One of the advantages of the kind of modular construction that is common in the contemporary shipbuilding industry is that elements of a vessel can be outfitted with all manner of internal equipment before the element is hoisted onto the hull. Wiring and piping, for example, are frequently installed in individual modules and then spliced together after the module is welded into the vessel. Even machinery of various kinds can be installed in modules before they are

New cruise ships are no longer launched by sliding down an inclined way into the sea. Instead the drydock where they were built is flooded, and tugboats ease the new hull into open water.

lifted onto the hull. When a cruise ship under construction reaches the fitting-out basin, it is basically complete; the principal work yet to be performed involves the installation of things like paneling, lighting fixtures, ceilings, furnishings, and other high-visibility components. Plus painting. Plus testing—weeks and weeks of testing.

One of the more interesting aspects of vessel design and construction—indeed it goes to the heart of why cruise ships are said to be value-added projects—involves integrating the work of the naval architect and the engineers with the work of various designers who are responsible for the creative interiors that give a vessel its color and style and character. The naval architect and the engineers, in simple terms, produce a vessel in cold steel with its basic mechanical equipment in place; the designers complement this steel and equipment with wall paneling, drop ceilings, lighting fixtures, and furnishings. When a vessel reaches the fitting-out basin at Chantiers de l'Atlantique, it is primarily the products of the interior designers that remain to be installed.

This is not meant to suggest, however, that the various interior designers are simply "hanging curtains on the windows." They, too, are intimately involved in the entire design process from the outset; they participate in critical meetings, make suggestions to help the process proceed smoothly, and execute their work using computer programs that are integrated with the systems used by the naval architect and the engineers.

A design firm that has been commissioned to develop the decor for a ship's dining room, for instance, might want to suggest changes in the location of serving stations in order to allow certain design themes to be developed. Perhaps the designer feels that passageways linking kitchen and dining room should be relocated for some reason associated with accentuating certain elements of design. Such changes, though, can involve major alterations in electrical wiring, in the placement of equipment, even in the basic structure of the vessel.

Design firms at work on adjacent areas of a cruise ship—a lounge and a casino, for instance—must necessarily work cooperatively to ensure that the themes of the two facilities do not clash or conflict, but meld together seamlessly. The two design firms might eventually conclude that the location of the lounge and the casino should be reversed to achieve some mutually important objectives; this is the kind of interaction that is an important dynamic in the design process, and this is why the various design firms, the naval architect, the shipyard engineers, and professionals from the staff of the cruise company are typically referred to as a design team. The most creative interior design firms in the world will not produce good work for a cruise industry client unless they are able to work effectively in such a team context.

The industry often uses a rule of thumb that indicates what portion of a newbuilding's cost is attributable to what element of its construction. The basic structural steel that defines a ship, from hull to bulkheads to windows, represents 20 percent of total costs. Another 20 percent is accounted for by a vessel's propulsion, navigational, and mechanical systems, everything from main engines to air-conditioning. But a massive 60 percent of a new cruise ship's total cost is attributable to the vessel's interior fittings—the work, essentially, where the interior designers play such a critical role.

Finally, everything is ready. Electrical panels have been energized; equipment has been tested; personnel from the cruise company who have been assigned to St. Nazaire to coordinate with Chantiers de l'Atlantique as well as the shipyard's various subcontractors have made their input; inspectors from the classification society have gone over the vessel from top to bottom; representatives of the United States Coast Guard have paid a preliminary visit so as to facilitate that agency's formal inspection of the vessel when it first reaches a port of U.S. jurisdiction; even technical people from the Panama Canal often travel to St. Nazaire to make any suggestions that might ease a vessel's certification for passage through their waterway. (On one recent St. Nazaire newbuilding, Panama Canal representatives suggested that certain windows on the bridge wings, which had been designed as fixed, be made to open so Panama Canal pilots could stick their heads out for a better view.)

One or two sets of sea trials are critical and take place toward the end of the construction process. A vessel departs St. Nazaire and heads out to sea in the Bay of Biscay, and for a period of days is put through a grueling series of maneuvers to ensure that all equipment as well as the vessel itself performs up to intended specifications. During such trials a cruise ship sails under the tricolor of France, since it is still owned by Chantiers de l'Atlantique and is berthed in a French port. Personnel from the cruise company, including the captain and officers who will soon assume command of the vessel, are always aboard for these trials, of course, carefully noting the performance characteristics the new vessel seems to be exhibiting. Indeed a skeleton staff of captain and key ship's officers are usually in St. Nazaire for the final year or more of a vessel's construction.

Once sea trials have been completed and final structural or mechanical adjustments have been made at the shipyard, the vessel's paint is touched up and the ship's full crew arrives. They begin taking aboard the many tons of equipment and supplies that are needed to make the vessel fully operational. Each person also focuses on whatever aspects of the new ship will be their own particular responsibility. At some shipyards, a ship's crew can live aboard the vessel in the quarters they will later occupy at sea. The policy at Chantiers de l'Atlantique, though, prohibits a ship's crew from living aboard until the vessel has been formally delivered to the cruise company. The crew must stay elsewhere in St. Nazaire and commute to and from the shipyard each day.

DELIVERY

Finally, a low-key ceremony is held forward on the upper deck of a new cruise ship, a ceremony that has been preceded by a more formal exchange of documents and considerations in a businesslike setting ashore. The French flag is flying from the vessel's mainmast as the ceremony begins. It is carefully hauled down and folded, to be replaced by the national ensign of the country where the new vessel will be registered and also the house flag of the cruise line.

And so a newly built cruise ship has been completed and delivered, handed over by Chantiers de l'Atlantique to a customer to whose specifications it has been carefully and meticulously built. The vessel's operational history lies over the horizon and ahead of it. But an important phase of its history has just ended, because over a period of months, a special relationship has developed between the people of St. Nazaire and a cruise ship built there. While the ship is under construction, the people of St. Nazaire look out their windows to check the morning's weather, they see the funnel of a new vessel dominating the eastern skyline, and they come to know this vessel. Breadwinners from families in St. Nazaire head off to work each day to weld and to build and to test the new vessel; indeed it is workers from St. Nazaire who are the first people in the world to walk the decks of a new ship and to learn its unique individuality—which stairway is the best shortcut to the pilothouse, what decks run all the way from bow to stern, how does a certain public room look as afternoon sunlight streams in through windows on the port side. When a cruise ship is floated out of Forme B and moved to one of the fitting-out basins at Chantiers de l'Atlantique, the people of St. Nazaire turn out en masse to participate in the proud event, and no new vessel has ever steamed away from Chantiers de l'Atlantique to join a cruise fleet an ocean away without crowds of townspeople lining the beaches and seawalls and wishing her well.

The Chantiers de l'Atlantique shipyard is one of the four major companies that are supplying newbuildings to the contemporary cruise industry. It is a classic facility where such vessels as *Ile de France* and *Normandie* and *France* were constructed many years ago. It is also a shipyard that withdrew from passenger work for a number of years, then returned with the construction of Holland America's *Nieuw Amsterdam* (3) in 1983. The yard renewed its reputation by turning out such products as *Dreamward* and *Windward* for Norwegian Cruise Line, *Sovereign of the Seas* and *Legend of the Seas* for Royal Caribbean, *Star Princess* for P&O/Princess, and many other fine vessels that work for cruise lines the world over.

The first cruise industry newbuilding to be delivered in the year 2000 was a Chantiers de l'Atlantique product, the 30,200-gross-ton *R Five* of Renaissance Cruises, a vessel that was christened in St. Nazaire as part of the delivery ceremony on the evening of January 29, 2000, in an after-dark ceremony complete with fireworks. The vessel's sponsor was Isabelle Boissier, the spouse of Patrick Boissier, chairman and CEO of the shipyard.

In June of 2000, Chantiers de l'Atlantique delivered GTS *Millennium* to Celebrity Cruises, the first of four sister ships designed to similar specifications as new Project Vantage cruise ships under construction for Royal Caribbean International, Celebrity's parent corporation. The float-out of *Millennium* on a chilly and overcast Sunday afternoon, November 7, 1999, marked a special milestone not only for the new cruise ship and its owner, but also for Chantiers de l'Atlantique.

When a quartet of local tugboats hauled *Millennium* out of the Chantiers de l'Atlantique drydock where she'd been built and maneuvered her down the River Loire for final construction at a fitting-out area known as Bassin C, she became the largest passenger vessel—as measured by gross registered tonnage—ever to be launched in St. Nazaire. This was a distinction that prior to *Millennium* had been held by French Line's legendary *Normandie,* and there were very few in the maritime world who believed that a passenger vessel larger than *Normandie* would ever be built in St. Nazaire.

But records are made to be broken, whether they were set by *Millennium* in 1999 or *Normandie* in 1932. Several months after *Millennium* was floated out, Chantiers de l'Atlantique was awarded a contract by Cunard Line to build its new 150,000-gross-ton *Queen Mary 2.* This vessel will not only exceed *Millennium*

The cruise ship *R Five* of Renaissance Cruises was the first cruise industry newbuilding to be delivered in the year 2000.

in every dimensional respect and become the largest passenger vessel ever built on the banks of the Loire, but *Queen Mary 2* will be the largest passenger vessel ever built anywhere by anybody, exceeding even the 137,276 gross tons of Royal Caribbean's 1999-built *Voyager of the Seas.* One can only wonder, of course, how long *Queen Mary 2* will hold this distinction.

Finally, to give a sense of the time it takes nowadays to build a new cruise ship—as well as to identify some of the important milestones along the way—the following table lays out certain key dates of *Millennium*'s construction. From executing a contract with Celebrity Cruises to turning a completed vessel over to her new owner, Chantiers de l'Atlantique required twenty-seven months and four days.

GTS *MILLENNIUM:* FROM CONTRACT TO MAIDEN VOYAGE

Contract executed	March 18, 1998
First steel cut	November 6, 1998
First block assembled	March 2, 1999
First block in drydock	March 25, 1999
Float to outer drydock	August 15, 1999
Float to fitting-out basin	November 7, 1999
First sea trials	April 7, 2000
Final sea trials	April 21, 2000
Delivery	June 22, 2000
Maiden voyage	July 1, 2000

CHAPTER 13

The Regulatory Environment

Fred Olsen Cruise Lines

Passenger vessels operating in cruise service are subject to a full gamut of rules, regulations, and supervision by a variety of public and private agencies of national and international jurisdiction whose acronyms constitute a veritable "alphabet soup" of initialized jargon. Here is a brief synopsis of the many ways these entities impact the day-to-day operation of a cruise company.

VESSEL SAFETY INSPECTIONS

The United States Coast Guard (USCG) has statutory authority to conduct regular inspections of all U.S.-flag vessels and issue annual certificates of inspection to vessels that pass muster. The standards such vessels must meet are clearly spelled out in a variety of Coast Guard publications and are widely regarded as being the most stringent in the world.

Because the vast majority of cruise ships operating in and out of U.S. ports are of foreign registry, the Coast Guard's rules and regulations do not apply to them. However, the Coast Guard does have the statutory authority to ensure that such vessels are in full conformity with rules and requirements that have been promulgated by the International Convention for the Safety of Life at Sea (SOLAS), a major international treaty that was executed by the world's seafaring nations in London in 1948. SOLAS has been updated over the years and is currently managed by the International Maritime Organization (IMO), an agency that works under the auspices of the United Nations.

The precise protocol being administered by the U.S. Coast Guard, as well as its statutory basis, thus differs between U.S.-flag ships and those of foreign registry. In practical terms, though, the Coast Guard inspects all passenger vessels that call at U.S. ports, regardless of what flag they fly. Vessels are subject to a major annual inspection, supplemented by quarterly follow-up reviews.

Most cruise companies and most cruise ship captains regard the USCG as an agency that is thorough but fair. In virtually all cases, the country in which a vessel is registered will also conduct inspections and safety reviews of vessels flying their flag. Many countries of registry do not conduct such reviews themselves but have empowered agencies known as classification societies to act on their behalf in matters associated with vessel safety.

Foreign-flag vessels are subject to U.S. Coast Guard inspection upon their initial arrival at a U.S. port. With respect to newly constructed cruise ships, Coast Guard inspectors will often travel to the shipyard where a vessel is under construction to conduct preliminary inspections there that will facilitate formal review once the vessel makes its first call at a U.S. port. Because a cruise ship's lifeboats are often used in nonemergency situations to tender passengers ashore from the anchored vessel, in some cases the Coast Guard treats powered lifeboats as separate vessels and subjects them to independent inspection. Seven separate vessels are found in the Coast Guard's inspection index under *Queen Elizabeth 2*, for example. One is a 70,327-gross-ton cruise ship/ocean liner, while the other six are its principal lifeboats and tenders.

If severe deficiencies are discovered during any USCG inspection, they can result in the Coast Guard's refusing to allow the vessel to board passengers in a U.S. port. More typically, deficiencies are less severe and are simply noted; a time frame is established for taking corrective action, and when the vessel is reinspected three months later, the status of any earlier deficiencies is given priority attention. In normal circumstances, the Coast Guard does not conduct "surprise" inspections but schedules them in advance in coordination with the cruise company. Although it remains true that when it inspects a foreign-flag vessel, the Coast Guard is determining its compliance with standards established by a third party—namely, SOLAS—the U.S. Coast Guard has promulgated an extensive set of SOLAS interpretations that represent, in a way, a separate set of regulatory requirements.

To give a sense of the kind of review that USCG inspections involve, the following comments are taken from official Coast Guard reports. They represent relatively minor situations that were quickly and easily corrected before the next follow-up inspection. Because deficiencies of individual vessels are being singled out without citation of full reports, the names of the vessels will not be identified. All sail for major mass-market cruise lines that specialize in the North American market.

- Complete permanent repairs to canopy of lifeboats 7 and 17 where fractured.
- Repaint loadline marks in a contrasting color.
- Install smoke detection and sprinkler system in all refrigeration, food preparation and public restroom spaces.

- Eliminate direct access from stage storeroom to stairway at frame No. 290 to conform with SOLAS 74 (as amended).
- Fuel hoses and nozzles for bunkering tenders do not meet testing, labeling, and back-pressure shutoff nozzle requirements of 33 CFR 154.500. Correct to satisfaction of USCG inspection prior to use of hoses in U.S. waters.
- Light switch and speaker in deck 6 port/forward paint locker are not safe for use in areas containing flammable liquids. Correct to satisfaction of class[ification] society.
- Free up access door for manual fire dampers next to cabin B198.

Again, these are examples intended to show the degree of detail that Coast Guard safety inspections typically entail, with the overall point being that when the USCG examines a vessel, it does not conduct a cursory walk-through. In addition to a thorough physical examination of the vessel from stem to stern, USCG inspections also involve a comprehensive audit of a variety of documents and logs to ensure they are all being maintained in a timely and satisfactory fashion.

SOLAS AND IMO

Mention has been made of the international convention and agreement known by the acronym SOLAS. Prior to the Second World War, efforts to form any kind of international agency for the setting of maritime standards were generally resisted. At the time, it was thought these were matters better left to individual sovereign nations. After the war, with the establishment of the United Nations (UN) and the emergence of a new and more cooperative international environment, old ways of thinking began to change.

Two separate events happened in 1948. In Geneva, Switzerland, a conference convened by the United Nations adopted a convention that established a new international organization that was at first called the Inter-Governmental Maritime Consultative Organization. Later renamed the International Maritime Organization (IMO), it remains an important and active force in setting international maritime standards. IMO is involved with a variety of maritime issues: standards for tanker design, improved safety for fishing vessels, methodologies for measuring gross tonnage, environmental matters, and so forth. As it has been from the outset, IMO is an arm of the UN.

A second important event that took place in 1948 happened in London and it resulted in the drafting of a formal treaty known as the International Convention for the Safety of Life at Sea (SOLAS), a development that was more directly—although not exclusively—focused on passenger vessels. The safety of the lives of crewmembers aboard cargo vessels, for example, is also part of the SOLAS mandate.

SOLAS has been updated and revised several times and its administration and management now resides with IMO. One can even say that the true beginning of SOLAS dates back to a convention signed in London in 1914, which established an international ice patrol in response to the loss of *Titanic* in 1912.

As SOLAS standards apply to the world's passenger ships today, they specify everything from the size, style, and color of graphics used to direct passengers to muster stations, to the kind of deck-level lighting that must be able to function even if a ship's conventional power sources should fail; they include a full complement of technical requirements, details, and specifications in a wide range of areas.

As is common in virtually all industrial sectors, IMO and SOLAS have responded with special urgency when major tragedies raise new concerns about existing safety and operational standards. It was the *Torrey Canyon* disaster in 1967, for example, that focused world attention on the question of oil tanker design and construction, as well as a range of new issues associated with liability for oil spills. The 1987 *Exxon Valdez* disaster was likewise a benchmark event in the development of new standards and procedures.

In the area of passenger vessels, two notable tragedies in recent years—the sinking of the ferry *Estonia* in the Baltic Sea in September 1994 with the loss of 1,049 lives and the capsizing of the ferry *Herald of Free Enterprise* in the English Channel in March 1987 that claimed 189 lives—saw the international maritime community focus its attention on safety issues associated with car ferries equipped with bow doors. A less-well-known tragedy which occurred during this same period involved a vessel, *Scandinavian Star*, that once ran day cruises out of south Florida for SeaEscape. In April 1990, the vessel left Oslo, Norway, bound for Fredkikshavn, on the northern end of Denmark's Jutland peninsula. Shortly after clearing Oslo Fjord and about thirty miles off Faerder light, a fire broke out and quickly spread. The blaze claimed 158 lives and was the single event most responsible for IMO proposing a series of new SOLAS amendments in 1992 designed to render vessels less vulnerable to fire. They were quickly adopted and began to take effect in phases, starting in 1994.

LICENSING OF OFFICERS

The licensing of a ship's officers is a matter that is the responsibility of the country of registry. The Coast Guard has direct responsibility for establishing licensing standards for U.S. flag vessels, while SOLAS requires that all vessels be staffed by competent individuals. Part of USCG's inspection of foreign-flag vessels, therefore, includes a review of the certificates of its personnel, since SOLAS requires that they all be current. Some nations—the Netherlands, for example—mandate that bridge and engineering officers aboard ships flying their flags hold licenses issued by the flag country. One of the "conveniences" associated with flying flags of convenience is that such countries have long been willing to certify maritime licenses issued by virtually any maritime country as valid for working aboard vessels registered in their country.

HEALTH INSPECTIONS

A second U.S. entity that conducts regular inspections of all cruise ships operating in and out of American ports is the Vessel Sanitation Program (VSP), administered by the Centers for Disease Control and Prevention (CDC), which is itself part of the U.S. Department of Health and Human Services (HHS). While the Coast Guard is primarily concerned with matters of safety, structure, and navigation, VSP is on guard to prevent the spread of disease.

A ship is subject to VSP inspection irrespective of its flag of registry, if it visits a U.S. port, carries thirteen or more passengers, and its travels have taken it to a foreign country. VSP staff conduct two unannounced inspections each year with a concentration on six general areas:

- Water supply—how it is stored, distributed and protected;
- Food—its protection during storage, preparation and service;
- The potential for contamination—and what intervention may be necessary;
- Personal hygiene of a ship's crew—detailed reporting is required for certain contagious diseases, especially of a gastro-intestinal sort;
- General cleanliness and physical condition of the ship—with an emphasis on the absence of insects and rodents;
- Training programs—and their effectiveness.

VSP has lengthy criteria and standards against which it evaluates cruise ships. These are detailed in various publications, updated regularly, and provide a good idea of what kind of shipboard conditions the agency is seeking to foster. Like USCG, VSP will dispatch personnel to shipyards where new cruise vessels are under construction for preliminary inspection and consultation.

Formal VSP inspections must result in a vessel's achieving a score of 86 or better for it to be classified as "satisfactory." The inspection methodology involves starting with a perfect score of 100, then subtracting points for any offenses or substandard conditions that are found.

Like Coast Guard safety inspections, VSP reviews are quite thorough. Between 1990 and the first quarter of 2000, the agency conducted 1,359 individual vessel inspections. In 180 cases—13 percent of all inspections—vessels were given unsatisfactory ratings of 85 or less, while in only eight instances were perfect scores of 100 awarded. One vessel, *Crystal Symphony*, managed to earn a perfect score on two separate occasions, while the other six perfect ratings were earned by Celebrity's *Galaxy*, *Century*, and *Mercury*, Carnival's *Fantasy* and *Elation*, and Windstar's *Wind Spirit*.

The following citations are taken from VSP inspection reports on vessels that received not only satisfactory ratings, but also rather high numerical scores—95 or better. To the uninitiated, the deficiencies may sound foreboding. In fact they represent vessels whose overall health conditions are substantially above average. As was the case with citations from USCG safety reports, the vessels involved will not be identified.

- *Site:* Lido/buffet pantry. *Violation:* Carved decorative watermelons were stored on several different shelves over ready to eat foods. *Recommendation:* Provide a dedicated shelving unit or store these items below ready to eat foods to reduce the potential of cross contamination. No points deducted.
- *Site:* Lido/pot washing area. *Violation:* A trolley of soiled pots and pans was stored in front of a fixed shelving unit of clean items. *Recommendation:* Provide additional storage space for soiled pots and pans in this area. One point deducted.
- *Site:* Room service pantry. *Violation:* The bulkhead on the clean end of the dishwashing machine and the air conditioning duct cover had a large amount of condensation present. *Recommendation:* Ventilation systems shall be adequately designed to remove a large percentage of the hot humid air in food service areas to prevent workers from perspiring profusely and to prevent the accumulation of condensation on deckheads. No points deducted.
- *Site:* Specialty galley. *Violation:* The doors on the pizza oven were corroded on the inside. *Recommendation:* Food-contact and ice-contact surfaces must be constructed of materials that are nontoxic, smooth, corrosion-resistant, nonabsorbent and durable under conditions of normal use. No points deducted.
- *Site:* Hot galley. *Violation:* There were no catch pans for the drip channels on the grills; the channels have an overflow that drains onto the deck. *Recommendation:* Provide catch pans below the overflows to prevent spillage on the deck. One point deducted.

As was also the case with safety issues under the Coast Guard's jurisdiction, the point in citing these specific violations is to give a sense of the level of detail that is involved in the regular inspections of cruise ships conducted by the Vessel Sanitation Program of the Centers for Disease Control and Prevention.

An area of parallel concern in both USCG and VSP reviews involves medical issues and medical records. The Coast Guard is interested in shipboard injuries or illnesses that may be the result of unsafe conditions; the Vessel Sanitation Program wants to know about any outbreaks of disease. VSP, for example, is totally intolerant of any failure to report gastrointestinal epidemics and has often levied a maximum penalty of five points for improper record-keeping in this important area.

Once in a while, cruise companies will throw up their hands in frustration over seemingly conflicting demands levied by USCG and VSP. Recently, for example, the Coast Guard issued an interpretation of SOLAS that said as a fire-prevention measure, there must be a certain minimum distance between the top of freezers and refrigerators and the ceiling above them. At the same time, though, VSP was mandating that such equipment be elevated above the deck by a certain distance as a technique for avoiding likely breeding grounds for insects and rodents.

Both mandates probably make sense, but having to "squeeze" a stainless steel refrigerator or freezer so it can conform to both standards is obviously impossible. Inspection protocols remain an active issue, of course, and though the implementation of their recommendation is not always easy, it must be done.

ENVIRONMENTAL COMPLIANCE

Compared to the unspeakable environmental devastation that was caused by such vessels as the *Torrey Canyon* in 1967 or the *Exxon Valdez* in 1987, cruise ships are good neighbors to the environment they inhabit, and they have a record to prove it. Not too many years ago, though, a cruise ship passenger taking a late-night stroll around the promenade deck with a portable video recorder at the ready captured a scene that has haunted the industry ever since—the unlawful throwing overboard of plastic bags full of garbage in complete contravention of prevailing environmental rules, standards, and sensibilities. This was quickly followed by cases of cruise ships discharging oily wastes into open ocean waters in violation of applicable law, with appropriate fines and penalties levied for such behavior.

The entire maritime world has moved from a position just a few decades ago where it was felt that the ocean was fully capable of absorbing the discharge of just about anything—oil, sewage, solid wastes—to a situation where more stringent standards prevail, even if they are occasionally violated. Indeed when the world's seafaring community began to address questions of pollution in the wake of the *Torrey Canyon* disaster, it was quickly recognized that routine maritime practices then regarded as standard procedures—cleaning empty tankers with seawater and discharging the wash into the sea, for example—represented a greater threat to the environment than did an occasional, albeit dramatic and newsworthy, one-time accident.

The environmental requirements vessels must meet include statutes enacted by various countries for their own territorial waters, plus the international standards known as MARPOL that have been developed under the aegis of the International Convention for the Prevention of Pollution from Ships.

Environmental requirements and specifications mandated by MARPOL enjoy all the force of international law.

If there is one clear and unequivocal mandate under MARPOL it is this: no plastics may be discharged at sea—nowhere, not ever. For other waste, from paper products to food to sewage, there are detailed protocols that must be observed by various combinations of compacting, incinerating, recycling, treatment, and, in some cases, retention for disposition on shore. Sewage aboard ship is euphemistically identified as "gray water" and "black water," the latter being the effluent from toilets. Both black water and gray water must be treated and either discharged at sea or into sewer systems on shore within specified time limits. When sewage is discharged at sea, MARPOL mandates in nontechnical terms that it must have been treated to such a degree that its purity exceeds that of the ocean into which it is discharged. Both the Coast Guard and the Vessel Sanitation Program undertake detailed examinations of a vessel's logs and records during their inspections to ensure that MARPOL standards are being met.

CLASSIFICATION SOCIETIES

Maritime organizations known as classification societies play a very important role in maintaining a safe and secure shipboard environment. The best known of the several classification societies is the British-based Lloyd's Register of Shipping, a name that applies both to the organization itself and to its annual three-volume publication that provides an up-to-date listing of the world's merchant fleet. Other classification societies include the American Bureau of Shipping in the United States, Bureau Veritas in France, Det Norske Veritas in and for Scandinavian countries, as well as a number of others. There is even a general organization to which classification societies themselves belong—the International Association of Classification Societies, IACS, which was founded in 1968.

There is an important link between the work of classification societies and the issuing of marine insurance. Seen historically, classification societies began as an arm of the insurance industry and were established to inspect vessels in a reasonably independent manner so insurance could be written confidently. Because proper insurance coverage is an economic *sine qua non* for all shipping companies, classification societies still play such a role in certifying the general seaworthiness of vessels, as well as the degree to which they have been built in conformity with applicable SOLAS standards, itself a requirement for the issuing of marine insurance.

More recently, the role played by classification societies has substantially expanded. The relatively small countries whose flags are regarded as flags of convenience by the world cruise industry—Panama, the Bahamas, and Liberia, primarily—do not have sophisticated vessel inspection capability of their own. Instead, they have contracted with classification societies to handle all inspection procedures on their behalf, a development that has brought an important element of consistency and professionalism to the determination that any given vessel is seaworthy and is in conformity with all appropriate SOLAS standards, irrespective of the flag that it flies.

For a vessel classified by Lloyd's Register of Shipping, the inspection process begins during the design phase, long before any steel is cut. It continues not only during the construction process—Lloyd's has personnel assigned, permanently, to the world's major shipyards—but also at intervals throughout the life of the vessel. It is Lloyd's, for example, that conducts very precise measurements to determine where a vessel's various load lines should be located. Centered around the so-called Plimsoll mark, load lines specify how much of the hull may safely remain submerged under a set of specified conditions. A vessel can tolerate maximum load under conditions described as "tropical: saltwater." The load then decreases, in increments, through a series of intermediate stages such as "tropical: freshwater" until it reaches the most restricted load limit found on any vessel. It is ominous, especially when one reflects on the fact that transatlantic steamship service was once such an important year-round avenue of world commerce. The load limit inscribed on the side of oceangoing merchant ships specifies that "winter: North Atlantic" (usually abbreviated WNA) is the service that is most restrictive as to the load the vessel may carry. It is also Lloyd's Register—or whatever classification society is being used—that conducts the final and formal measurement of a vessel to determine its gross registered tonnage.

Lloyd's Register is a large organization. It has a network of 240 offices throughout the world and its staff numbers in excess of 1,600 technical personnel. Together with parallel classification societies in other countries, its work has helped create a more uniform maritime climate throughout the world.

THE NATIONAL TRANSPORTATION SAFETY BOARD

The National Transportation Safety Board (NTSB) is an arm of the U.S. government whose charter is to investigate all civil aviation accidents in the United States and significant accidents in other modes of transportation—railroad, highway, pipeline, and maritime. Established in 1967, NTSB is typically on the scene of major transportation accidents within hours, gathering evidence and trying to determine what went wrong.

NTSB has conducted investigations of a number of cruise ship accidents because even though most vessels are of foreign registry, they are subject to Coast Guard inspection, they board passengers in United States ports, and so forth.

NTSB's strength has long been its independence. It is not part of the United States Department of Transportation and is not part of the regulatory apparatus of the federal government. It is an autonomous agency staffed by trained and qualified professionals who are free to investigate and reach conclusions based on evidence, and evidence alone.

The NTSB has a long history of findings and recommendations that it has made over the years. As a result, many people in the transportation industry believe that the board has shown an unfortunate tendency to conduct new investigations in a manner that seeks to substantiate its own earlier recommendations. Indeed the volume of recommendations that the board has made over the years constitutes a kind of de facto regulatory presence in the aviation industry, the railroad industry, and the maritime world, even though NTSB does not have statutory authority to issue formal regulations.

The NTSB has become a highly visible presence at most transportation disasters, conducting news conferences at the site and releasing selected information to the public as soon as it is available. Perhaps mounting criticism of the agency would lessen if NTSB itself assumed a less visible posture in front of the television cameras and returned to its earlier practice of letting the evidence do the talking.

Although professionals in the maritime industry can easily—and perhaps even rightly—chafe under this or that specific regulatory dictate or interpretation, the cold fact is that the shipboard environment is a highly vulnerable one that demands the very highest standards if it is to remain safe, secure, *and* profitable. The U.S. Coast Guard may chide a vessel because a single fire door is not working properly. Yet on the vessel's next cruise, that door may be called on to contain a blaze, thereby helping to ensure that the lives of all the ship's passengers are not put at risk.

The regulatory climate within which the contemporary cruise industry has grown and prospered is certainly more stringent than the one that prevailed in 1965 when *Yarmouth Castle* caught fire and went down with the loss of ninety souls. It does not seem unreasonable to suggest that the success which the contemporary cruise industry has experienced is related in some direct and incontrovertible way to the more demanding regulatory environment in which it now operates.

Cunard Line

Epilogue

The growth of the contemporary cruise industry in the final decades of the twentieth century was a success story whose proportions were utterly unimaginable in the days after jet aircraft revolutionized transoceanic travel and old-line steamship companies began to fall by the wayside. Who could possibly have predicted that the likes of Carnival and Royal Caribbean and Princess would emerge in the way that they have, or that by the end of the century, they and their competitors would be welcoming eager cruise passengers aboard their vessels at a rate approaching seven million a year? When Cunard Line's RMS *Queen Elizabeth*, the world's largest ocean liner, was withdrawn from transatlantic service in 1968, who would have dared suggest that her 83,673 gross tons would one day be eclipsed by passenger vessels whose gross tonnage would be in excess of 100,000? Is there anyone who might have been relaxing along Miami's Government Cut in the late 1960s and watching Eastern Steamship's *Ariadne* head out to sea with three hundred passengers aboard who could possibly have dreamed that *Voyager of the Seas* would one day follow the very same course with over three *thousand* passengers ready to enjoy a cruise vacation?

The key to the industry's future, of course, is the degree to which its growth can be sustained. The most optimistic statistic that can be cited to argue for the continuation of growth on a long-term basis is the fact that among the 270 million or more people who call the United States home, only 5 percent have ever taken a cruise vacation. Repeat business among people who have already taken a cruise is important, but the potential for growth among those who have not yet enjoyed a cruise vacation is nothing less than enormous.

This is not to say that there will not be bumps along the road; every healthy industry has them. Among the potentially troubling issues that the cruise industry must address or manage to avoid are these:

- The recent growth of the cruise industry has taken place during a time of unprecedented world prosperity. What will happen to the industry's steady growth rate, and who will fill all the new cabins in all the new cruise ships, if an economic downturn should occur?
- What strategies will emerge to deal with the problem of airlift capacity in and out of such places as Miami, Fort Lauderdale, and even Vancouver? Basing cruise vessels in ports that might today be regarded as unconventional is one possibility. Another might be the design of a new generation of faster cruise ships, vessels that could accomplish seven-night itineraries from ports where generous airlift capacity is readily available but today's vessels are too slow to exploit.
- Will the industry's safety and security record remain as good as, or better than, it has been in recent years? Because video cameras are as popular today as box cameras were in the 1930s, any mishap whatsoever is guaranteed to wind up on somebody's "eleven o'clock news." In 1999, stories surfaced of sexual assaults aboard certain cruise ships. The shipboard environment is so totally different and unforgiving that any safety and security shortcomings, actual or perceived, are quite capable of eroding customer confidence in the industry's product.
- How will the industry's relationship with travel agents change as the Internet plays an even more active role in routine commercial transactions? Shopping for a cruise vacation is a style of purchase that would seem to be made-to-order for wholesale shifting to the world of "e-commerce." Several cruise lines have already developed procedures for travel agents to make reservations for their clients via the Internet, but what will happen if passengers are able to book cruises themselves? Shifts of this sort can bring unanticipated consequences; up to now, the cruise industry has seen its years of greatest growth with independent travel agents serving as the point-of-sale for over 90 percent of its bookings.
- Will new governmental initiatives emerge that will collectively impact the industry and dim its prospects for the future? Might new safety mandates, or passenger taxes, or environmental requirements, or navigational restrictions be enacted that would restrict growth and reduce earnings?
- The balance between overall industry capacity and actual cruise bookings is very critical but also very delicate. If the gap between the two starts to widen, it could quickly lead to a situation where a cruise company offers discount prices to ensure that its vessels sail with maximum passengers. Such discounts can be sound business if used to fill berths that would otherwise be vacant in slack seasons. But if berths remain empty during what should be peak traffic periods, discounting can quickly erode a company's anticipated revenue base.

These are the kinds of issues that the industry's leaders must address to the best of their ability today, then pass along their solutions to successors for fine-tuning and continued attention.

Perhaps the most unsettling question of all—clearly one that many industries only wish they were facing—is this: what can an industry whose growth between 1965 and 2000 was in *excess of one thousand percent* reasonably expect to achieve over the next thirty-five years?

It will certainly be fascinating to see how this question is answered.

Celebrity Cruises

APPENDIX A

Cruise Ship Fleet Rosters

The following rosters provide technical data and information about passenger vessels used in North American cruise service. The rosters do not include each and every vessel that ever offered such service, merely those of the principal companies whose primary orientation is or was the North American cruise market. Rosters are arranged alphabetically by fleet and are restricted, roughly, to the final third of the twentieth century, 1965 through 2000. In the case of cruise companies that were established within this time frame, the rosters endeavor to identify all vessels that sailed in any company's service. In the case of older steamship lines that date back to the days of transoceanic service and survived to play an important role in the cruise era, only vessels primarily identified with cruising are included. Older steamship companies that offered only a token amount of cruise service during their final years prior to abandoning passenger operations outright are not included at all. There is an admitted degree of arbitrariness to such exclusion or inclusion. Dates of service are shown following the names of cruise companies that are no longer in operation.

As was the case in the text, cruise companies based in Europe or Asia who occasionally operate out of North American ports have been included, but on a somewhat random basis. In other cases, for example, Airtours of Great Britain and Star Cruises of Malaysia, contemporary companies with virtually no operational links to North America have been included in the roster because these lines provided interesting "second careers" for a number of notable vessels whose earlier service was critical to the development of the cruise industry in North America. Vessels that operated for more than one company are included under each company for which they ran. Within a given fleet, vessels are usually listed in the order in which they joined that fleet.

Certain vessel statistics can and do vary over the years, even in the absence of major refitting or rebuilding. The number of passengers a vessel may carry, for

243

example, and even a vessel's gross registered tonnage might be different from one year to the next. To the maximum extent possible, data in the following rosters describe a vessel at the time it began to operate for the cruise line under which it is listed.

For ease and convenience, dimensional data have been rounded to the nearest foot. Minor variations between this roster and other published sources can often be explained by such rounding coupled with conversion from metric values, the almost universal standard of measurement today in international maritime circles.

The identification of "previous name(s)" and/or "subsequent name(s)" likely means that a vessel enjoyed a career with another company either before or after its service with the company in whose fleet it is shown. Such companies are often identified in notes.

The category "owner" can often generate confusion. For a variety of business purposes, maritime operating companies will often register the vessels in their fleets under the names of separate corporations. Such subsidiary companies are rarely, if ever, identified to the general public, who continue to regard vessels as "owned" by the more popular operating companies they have come to know and whose brochures they avidly read. (Passengers will often find the names of these subsidiary companies amid the small print on their cruise tickets and contracts.)

It is also common for the formal ownership of vessels to be transferred from one subsidiary company to another during tenure with a given fleet; no effort has been made to identify such purely internal transactions. There have even been instances when in selling a vessel to another company, a cruise line transfers the subsidiary company that holds nominal title to the vessel to the new owner along with the ship. In identifying previous and/or subsequent owners of a vessel, the popular names of operating cruise lines are generally shown, not the names of such subsidiary corporations.

In some instances, cruise companies do not own the vessels they operate, but hold them under the provisions of charters, or leases. While every short-term chartering arrangement in the cruise industry between 1965 and 2000 is not reflected in the following rosters, an effort has been made to include transactions that extended over long periods of time or that might otherwise be regarded as important.

"Flag" indicates the country of registry. In the case of vessels registered in the United States, the vessel's official number is displayed in parentheses. Identification of more than one flag indicates a shift in the country of registry during service with the fleet in question.

"Gross tons," more properly "gross registered tonnage," is a common measurement not of a merchant vessel's weight, but of its overall size, with one hundred cubic feet of permanently enclosed revenue-generating space being held to equal one gross ton. There have been published accounts claiming that, with cruise ships, space dedicated to storage and quarters for the crew are excluded from the calculation of revenue-generating space. This is not correct. The engine room and areas used for the carrying of fuel and water are excluded, but crews' quarters, as well as freezers and lockers where food and supplies are stored, are incorporated into the calculation of revenue-generating space, and, therefore, of gross registered tonnage.

The three values shown under "dimensions" provide measurements, in rounded feet, of the overall or extreme length of a vessel's hull, the breadth of the hull, and the vessel's maximum draft. Alternate vessel dimensions may cite waterline length, length between perpendiculars, registered length, molded breadth, molded depth, or registered depth. Discrepancies between published information can often be resolved by further inquiry about which dimensional data are, in fact, being cited.

"Place built" indicates the city where the shipyard that built the vessel in question is located. In the item identified as "shipyard," the number in parentheses that follows the name of a shipyard indicates the hull number by which the vessel was known during construction at that yard.

Under "engines" will be found a description of the main engines that power a vessel. With respect to diesel engines, the most common style of contemporary cruise ship power, information is provided on the number of engines, the number of cylinders in each engine, as well as the manufacturer and model number, if available. Separate engines used solely for the generation of onboard electric current are not identified.

"Propulsion" is a general category that describes how power produced by the main engine(s) is used to propel the vessel, with most designations being self-explanatory. "Other equipment" identifies such items as bow and stern thrusters, bow or stern ramps, and so forth.

As is common in the cruise industry, "passenger capacity" refers not to the absolute maximum number of people who can legally, or even comfortably, book passage aboard a given vessel, but rather to the number a vessel carries assuming two passengers per cabin, with appropriate adjustments for single-berth cabins, should a vessel happen to have any. While this results in the often self-serving statistical situation of a given ship—or even an entire company—operating with a passenger load in excess of 100 percent capacity, it is the common way passenger capacity is identified in the industry. In cases where a vessel's passenger capacity does not follow this convention but is expressed as the total number of available berths, an asterisk follows the number.

Passenger capacity is rarely constant over the life of a ship. New cabins are added; separate cabins are combined into suites; passenger accommodations are converted into quarters for the crew, and vice versa. Cruise ship brochures may use the term "pax," a maritime shorthand expression for passengers.

The rosters are divided into three extremely unequal parts. Part 1 displays current and historical information about the vessels of fifty-three major cruise companies, present and past. Part 2 identifies eight North American companies that operate so-called mini cruise ships. Roster information in this part differs slightly from the information in Part 1 in that it is restricted to a one-time snapshot of vessels that were in operation for such companies during the summer of 2000 and, therefore, lacks some of the historical dimension found in Part 1. Part 3 displays information about a dozen classic ocean liners from bygone years so contrasts may be drawn between such vessels and contemporary cruise ships.

Information in the rosters is primarily taken from annual editions of *Lloyd's Register of Shipping* plus selected trade journals of the maritime industry such as *Marine Engineering, Cruise Industry News,* and *Fairplay.* Also helpful, particularly in tracking down elusive bits of information, were *Great Passenger Ships of the World* (6 volumes) and *Great Passenger Ships of the World Today* by Arnold Kludas, *Cruise Ships of the World* by Nicholas T. Cairis, *Pictorial Encyclopedia of Ocean Liners* by William H. Miller, Jr., and *The Atlantic Liners: 1925–1970* by Frederick Emmons. Peter T. Eisele's "Guide to Cruise Ships," published regularly in the historical journal *Steamboat Bill,* was invaluable. Information provided by the cruise lines themselves in the form of brochures, postings on Internet Web sites, and in some cases, individual letters, e-mails, and telephone calls, helped to answer many questions. For vessels enrolled in the United States, *Merchant Vessels of the United States* as well as the annual *Register* of the American Bureau of Shipping were consulted.

Finally, any roster or other compilation of data and information about so dynamic and changing an activity as that of the contemporary cruise industry will necessarily become dated very quickly. As a benchmark, the following tables are proposed as current for the summer cruise season of 2000, although certain anticipated developments beyond this time are indicated as likely to develop.

Part 1—Major Cruise Companies, Past and Present

ADMIRAL CRUISES (1986–1989)

Name	*Emerald Seas*	*Azure Seas*	*Stardancer*
Previous name(s)	USS *General W.P. Richardson* *LaGuardia* *Leilani* *President Roosevelt* *Atlantis*	*Southern Cross* *Calypso I* *Calypso*	*Scandinavia*
Subsequent name(s)	*Sapphire Seas* *Ocean Explorer I*	*OceanBreeze*	*Viking Serenade*
Owner	Eastern Steamship Lines, Inc.	Western Steamship Lines, Inc.	Sundance Cruises Corp.
Flag	Panama	Panama	Bahamas
Gross tons	18,927	14,673	26,747
Dimensions (feet)	623 × 76 × 27	604 × 78 × 25	608 × 89 × 23
Year built	1944	1955	1981
Place built	Kearny, N.J.	Belfast, Northern Ireland	Nantes, France
Shipyard	Federal Shipbuilding (No. 276)	Harland & Wolff (No. 1,498)	Dubigeon-Normandie (No. 164)
Engines	4 steam turbines	4 steam turbines	2 9-cyl. B&W 9L55GFCA diesels
Propulsion	Geared, twin screw	Geared, twin screw	Geared, twin screw, controllable pitch
Other equipment			2 bow thrusters, 2 stern doors and ramps
Passenger capacity	756*	821*	1,606*
Notes	1	2	3

Notes

1. Acquired from Chandris by Eastern Steamship, a predecessor of Admiral, in 1972; sold to Ambassador Cruises in 1992.
2. Acquired from Ulysses Line by Western Steamship, a predecessor of Admiral, in 1980; sold to Dolphin Cruise Line in 1992.
3. Built as car ferry; acquired from DFDS by Sundance Cruises, a predecessor of Admiral, in 1985; conveyed to Royal Caribbean in 1990.

* Total number of available berths

AIRTOURS/SUN CRUISES

Name	*Carousel*	*Seawing*	*Sundream*
Previous name(s)	*Nordic Prince*	*Southward*	*Song of Norway*
Subsequent name(s)			
Owner	Airtours PLC	Airtours PLC	Airtours PLC
Flag	Bahamas	Bahamas	Bahamas
Gross tons	22,945	16,710	22,945
Dimensions (feet)	635 × 79 × 21	536 × 75 × 21	637 × 79 × 21
Year built	1971	1971	1970

Continued

AIRTOURS/SUN CRUISES—*Continued*

Name	*Carousel*	*Seawing*	*Sundream*
Place built	Helsinki, Finland	Riva, Italy	Helsinki, Finland
Shipyard	Wartsila (No. 393)	Cantieri Navali del Tirreno e Riuniti (No. 288)	Wartsila (No. 392)
Engines	4 9-cyl. Sulzer 92H40/48 diesels	4 10-cyl. Fiat diesels	4 9-cyl. Sulzer 92H40/48 diesels
Propulsion	Geared, twin screw, controllable pitch	Geared, twin screw, controllable pitch	Geared, twin screw, controllable pitch
Other equipment	2 bow thrusters	Bow thruster	2 bow thrusters
Passenger capacity	1,040	798	1,038
Notes	1	2	3

Name	*Sunbird*
Previous name(s)	*Song of America*
Subsequent name(s)	
Owner	Airtours PLC
Flag	Norway
Gross tons	37,584
Dimensions (feet)	703 × 93 × 17
Year built	1982
Place built	Helsinki, Finland
Shipyard	Wartsila (No. 431)
Engines	4 8-cyl. Sulzer 8ZL40/48 diesels
Propulsion	Geared, twin screw, controllable pitch
Other equipment	2 bow thrusters
Passenger capacity	1,600
Notes	4

Notes

1. Acquired from Royal Caribbean in 1995.
2. Acquired from Norwegian Cruise Line in 1994.
3. Acquired from Royal Caribbean in 1996.
4. Acquired from Royal Caribbean in 1998.

AMERICAN FAMILY CRUISES (1993–1994)

Name	*American Adventure*	*"American Pioneer"*
Previous name(s)	*Guglielmo Marconi* *Costa Riviera*	*Eugenio C.* *Eugenio Costa*
Subsequent name(s)	*Costa Riviera*	*Eugenio Costa* *Edinburg Castle* *The Big Red Boat II*
Owner	Costa Armatori, S.p.A.	Costa Armatori, S.p.A.
Flag	Italy	Italy

Name	*American Adventure*	*"American Pioneer"*
Gross tons	28,137	32,753
Dimensions (feet)	701 × 94 × 28	713 × 96 × 28
Year built	1963	1966
Place built	Monfalcone, Italy	Monfalcone, Italy
Shipyard	Adriatico (No. 1,863)	Adriatico (No. 1,884)
Engines	4 steam turbines	4 steam turbines
Propulsion	Geared, twin screw	Geared, twin screw
Other equipment		
Passenger capacity	984	844
Notes	1	2

Notes

1. Chartered from Costa in 1993; returned to Costa in 1994.

2. Was to have been chartered from Costa in 1994. American Family Cruises ceased operations before vessel joined fleet; was never formally enrolled as *American Pioneer*.

AMERICAN HAWAII CRUISE LINE

Name	*Independence*	*Constitution*	*Liberte*
Previous name(s)	*Independence*	*Constitution*	*Brasil*
	Oceanic Independence	*Oceanic Constitution*	*Volendam*
	Sea Luck		*Monarch Sun*
	Oceanic Independence		*Volendam*
			Island Sun
Subsequent name(s)			*Canada Star*
			Queen of Bermuda
			Enchanted Seas
			Universe Explorer
Owner	Great Independence Ship Co.	American Global Line, Inc.	American Hawaii Cruises (Panama), Inc.
Flag (Off. No.)	U.S. (261147)	U.S. (262027)	Panama
Gross tons	20,220	20,269	23,680
Dimensions (feet)	683 × 89 × 30	683 × 89 × 30	617 × 88 × 27
Year built	1950	1951	1958
Place built	Quincy, Mass.	Quincy, Mass.	Pascagoula, Miss.
Shipyard	Bethlehem Steel (No. 1,618)	Bethlehem Steel (No. 1,619)	Ingalls (No. 467)
Engines	4 steam turbines	4 steam turbines	4 steam turbines
Propulsion	Geared, twin screw	Geared, twin screw	Geared, twin screw
Other equipment			
Passenger capacity	750	950	715*
Notes	1	2	3

Notes

1. Built for American Export Line; acquired in 1980 after long layup.

2. Built for American Export Line; acquired in 1981 after long layup. Retired in 1996; lost (sunk) en route to ship breakers in 1997.

3. Acquired in 1985; sold to Orley Shipping Company for charter to Bermuda Star Line in 1987.

*Total number of available berths.

BAHAMA CRUISE LINE (1974–1990)
INCLUDING BERMUDA STAR LINE

Name	*Freeport I*	*Veracruz I*	*Freeport II*
Previous name(s)	*Freeport*	*Theodor Herzl*	*Patricia*
		Carnivale	*Ariadne*
		Freeport	
Subsequent name(s)	*Freeport*	*Sun Ambassador*	*Bon Vivant*
	Svea Star	*The Fiesta*	*Ariane*
	Caribe		*Empress Katerina*
	Caribe Bremen		*Empress 65*
	Scandinavian Sun		
	Balanga Queen		
	Discovery Sun		
Owner	Miami Terminal	Bahama Cruise Line,	Bon Vivant Cruises,
	Transport Co.	Inc.	Inc.
Flag	Liberia	Panama	Liberia
Gross tons	10,488	9,914	6,644
Dimensions (feet)	441 × 71 × 18	488 × 65 × 21	454 × 58 × 19
Year built	1968	1957	1951
Place built	Lubeck, West Germany	Hamburg, West Germany	Newcastle, U.K.
Shipyard	Orenstein-Koppel	Deutsche Werft (No. 697)	Swan, Hunter & Wigham
	(No. 658)		Richardson (No. 1,884)
Engines	2 16-cyl. Pielstick	4 steam turbines	3 steam turbines
	16PC2V-406 diesels		
Propulsion	Geared, twin screw,	Geared, twin screw	Geared, single screw
	controllable pitch		
Other equipment,	Bow thruster, stern door	Converted passenger/cargo	
special features		vessel	
Passenger capacity	350*	571*	329
Notes	1	2	3

Name	*Bermuda Star*	*Canada Star*
Previous name(s)	*Argentina*	*Brasil*
	Veendam	*Volendam*
	Brasil	*Monarch Sun*
	Monarch Star	*Volendam*
		Island Sun
		Liberte
Subsequent name(s)	*Enchanted Isle*	*Queen of Bermuda*
	Commodore Hotel	*Enchanted Seas*
	Enchanted Isle	*Universe Explorer*
Owner	Billingshurst Shipping,	Orley Shipping Co., Ltd.
	Ltd.	
Flag	Panama	Panama
Gross tons	14,208	13,680
Dimensions (feet)	598 × 88 × 27	598 × 88 × 27
Year built	1958	1958
Place built	Pascagoula, Miss.	Pascagoula, Miss.

Name	Bermuda Star	Canada Star
Shipyard	Ingalls Shipbuilding (No. 468)	Ingalls Shipbuilding (No. 467)
Engines	4 steam turbines	4 steam turbines
Propulsion	Geared, twin screw	Geared, twin screw
Other equipment		
Passenger capacity	713	693
Notes	4	5

Notes

1. Conveyed to Birka Line in 1973.
2. Acquired from Freeport Cruise Lines in 1985; conveyed to Festival Shipping and Tourist Enterprises, Ltd. in 1990.
3. Chartered from Chandris from 1972 to 1974.
4. Acquired from Holland America Line in 1984; conveyed to Commodore Cruise Line in 1990.
5. Acquired in 1987; conveyed to Commodore Cruise Line in 1990.
*Total number of available berths.

CAPE CANAVERAL CRUISE LINE

Name	Dolphin IV
Previous name(s)	Zion
	Amelia de Mello
	Ithaca
Subsequent name(s)	
Owner	The Kosmas Group
Flag	Panama
Gross tons	12,091
Dimensions (feet)	502 × 65 × 28
Year built	1956
Place built	Hamburg, West Germany
Shipyard	Deutsche Werft (No. 691)
Engines	2 steam turbines
Propulsion	Geared, single screw
Other equipment	
Passenger capacity	588
Notes	1

Notes

1. Acquired from Dolphin Cruise Line in 1998; removed from service in 2000.

CARNIVAL CRUISE LINES

Name	Mardi Gras	Carnivale	Festivale
Previous name(s)	Empress of Canada	Empress of Britain	Transvaal Castle
		Queen Anna Maria	S.A. Vaal
Subsequent name(s)	Olympic	Fiesta Marina	IslandBreeze
	Star of Texas	Olympic	The Big Red Boat III
	Apollon	The Topaz	
	Olympic 2004		
	Apollon		

Continued

CARNIVAL CRUISE LINES—*Continued*

Name	*Mardi Gras*	*Carnivale*	*Festivale*
Owner	Carnival Cruise Lines	Fairweather Corp.	Festivale Maritime, Inc.
Flag	Panama; Bahamas	Panama	Panama; Bahamas
Gross tons	18,261	18,952	26,632
Dimensions (feet)	650 × 87 × 29	640 × 85 × 29	760 × 90 × 32
Year built	1961	1956	1961
Place built	Newcastle, U.K.	Glasgow, Scotland	Clydebank, Scotland
Shipyard	Vickers-Armstrongs (No. 171)	Fairfield (No. 731)	John Brown (No. 720)
Engines	6 steam turbines	6 steam turbines	4 steam turbines
Propulsion	Geared, twin screw	Geared, twin screw	Geared, twin screw
Other equipment			Bow thruster
Passenger capacity	906	950	1,146
Notes	1	2	3

Name	*Tropicale*	*Holiday*	*Jubilee*
Previous name(s)			
Subsequent name(s)			
Owner	Tropicale Cruises, Inc.	Sunbury Assets	Jubilee Cruises, Inc.
Flag	Liberia	Panama; Bahamas	Panama; Bahamas
Gross tons	36,674	46,052	47,262
Dimensions (feet)	672 × 87 × 23	727 × 92 × 26	737 × 93 × 25
Year built	1981	1985	1987
Place built	Aalborg, Denmark	Aalborg, Denmark	Malmo, Sweden
Shipyard	Aalborg Vaerft (No. 234)	Aalborg Vaerft (No. 246)	Kockums Shipyard (No. 596)
Engines	2 7-cyl. Sulzer 7RND68M diesels	2 7-cyl. Sulzer 7RND68M diesels	2 7-cyl. Sulzer 7RND68M diesels
Propulsion	Geared, twin screw, controllable pitch	Geared, twin screw, controllable pitch	Geared, twin screw, controllable pitch
Other equipment	Bow thruster	2 bow thrusters	2 bow thrusters
Passenger capacity	1,022	1,452	1,486
Notes			

Name	*Celebration*	*Fantasy*	*Ecstasy*
Previous name(s)			
Subsequent name(s)			
Owner	Celebration Cruise, Inc.	Carnival Corp.	Carnival Corp.
Flag	Liberia	Liberia	Liberia
Gross tons	47,262	70,367	70,367
Dimensions (feet)	733 × 93 × 25	855 × 103 × 26	859 × 103 × 26
Year built	1987	1990	1991
Place built	Malmo, Sweden	Helsinki, Finland	Helsinki, Finland
Shipyard	Kockums Shipyard (No. 597)	Masa-Yards (No. 479)	Kvaerner Masa-Yards (No. 480)
Engines	2 7-cyl. Sulzer 7RLB66 diesels	4 12-cyl. Sulzer 12ZAV40S and 2 8-cyl. Sulzer 8ZAL40S diesels	4 12-cyl. Sulzer 12ZAV40S and 2 8-cyl. Sulzer 8ZAL40S diesels

Name	*Celebration*	*Fantasy*	*Ecstasy*
Propulsion	Geared, twin screw, controllable pitch	Electric drive, twin screw, controllable pitch	Electric drive, twin screw, controllable pitch
Other equipment	2 bow thrusters	3 bow thrusters, 3 stern thrusters	3 bow thrusters, 3 stern thrusters
Passenger capacity	1,486	2,048	2,044
Notes		4	4

Name	*Sensation*	*Fascination*	*Imagination*
Previous name(s)			
Subsequent name(s)			
Owner	Carnival Corp.	Carnival Corp.	Carnival Corp.
Flag	Panama; Bahamas	Panama; Bahamas	Panama; Bahamas
Gross tons	70,367	70,367	70,367
Dimensions (feet)	859 × 103 × 26	859 × 103 × 26	859 × 103 × 26
Year built	1993	1994	1995
Place built	Helsinki, Finland	Helsinki, Finland	Helsinki, Finland
Shipyard	Kvaerner Masa-Yards (No. 484)	Kvaerner Masa-Yards (No. 487)	Kvaerner Masa-Yards (No. 488)
Engines	4 12-cyl. Sulzer 12ZAV40S and 2 8-cyl. Sulzer 8ZAL40S diesels	4 12-cyl. Sulzer 12ZAV40S and 2 8-cyl. Sulzer 8ZAL40S diesels	4 12-cyl. Sulzer 12ZAV40S and 2 8-cyl. Sulzer 8ZAL40S diesels
Propulsion	Electric drive, twin screw, controllable pitch	Electric drive, twin screw, controllable pitch	Electric drive, twin screw, controllable pitch
Other equipment	3 bow thrusters, 3 stern thrusters	3 bow thrusters, 3 stern thrusters	3 bow thrusters, 3 stern thrusters
Passenger capacity	2,048	2,040	2,040
Notes	4	4	4

Name	*Inspiration*	*Elation*	*Paradise*
Previous name(s)			
Subsequent name(s)			
Owner	Carnival Corp.	Carnival Corp.	Carnival Corp.
Flag	Panama; Bahamas	Panama	Panama
Gross tons	70,367	70,390	70,390
Dimensions (feet)	859 × 103 × 26	859 × 103 × 26	859 × 103 × 26
Year built	1996	1998	1998
Place built	Helsinki, Finland	Helsinki, Finland	Helsinki, Finland
Shipyard	Kvaerner Masa-Yards (No. 489)	Kvaerner Masa-Yards (No. 491)	Kvaerner Masa-Yards (No. 494)
Engines	4 12-cyl. Sulzer 12ZAV40S and 2 8-cyl. Sulzer 8ZAL40S diesels	6 12-cyl. Wartsila 12V38 diesels	6 12-cyl. Wartsila 12V38 diesels
Propulsion	Electric drive, twin screw, controllable pitch	2 Azipod electric pod-propulsion units	2 Azipod electric pod-propulsion units
Other equipment	3 bow thrusters, 3 stern thrusters	3 bow thrusters	3 bow thrusters
Passenger capacity	2,040	2,040	2,040
Notes	4	4	4, 5

Continued

CARNIVAL CRUISE LINES—*Continued*

Name	*Carnival Destiny*	*Carnival Triumph*	*Carnival Victory*
Previous name(s)			
Subsequent name(s)			
Owner	Futura Cruises, Inc.	Utopia Cruises, Inc.	
Flag	Panama; Bahamas	Panama; Bahamas	Panama
Gross tons	101,353	101,509	101,509
Dimensions (feet)	893 × 117 × 27	893 × 117 × 27	893 × 117 × 27
Year built	1997	1999	2000
Place built	Monfalcone, Italy	Monfalcone, Italy	Monfalcone, Italy
Shipyard	Fincantieri (No. 5,941)	Fincantieri (No. 5,979)	Fincantieri
Engines	4 16-cyl. Sulzer 16ZAV40S and 2 12-cyl. Sulzer 12ZAV40S diesels	4 16-cyl. Sulzer 16ZAV40S and 2 12-cyl. Sulzer 12ZAV40S diesels	4 16-cyl. Sulzer 16ZAV40S and 2 12-cyl. Sulzer 12ZAV40S diesels
Propulsion	Electric drive, twin screw, controllable pitch	Electric drive, twin screw, controllable pitch	Electric drive, twin screw, controllable pitch
Other equipment	3 bow thrusters, 3 stern thrusters	3 bow thrusters, 3 stern thrusters	3 bow thrusters, 3 stern thrusters
Passenger capacity	2,640	2,758	2,758
Notes	6, 7	7	7

Name	*Carnival Spirit*	*Carnival Pride*	*Carnival Conquest*
Previous name(s)			
Subsequent name(s)			
Owner			
Flag			
Gross tons	84,000	84,000	110,000
Dimensions (feet)	957 × 106	957 × 106	953 × 117 × 27
Year built	2001	2001	2002
Place built	Helsinki, Finland	Helsinki, Finland	Monfalcone, Italy
Shipyard	Kvaerner Masa-Yards (No. 499)	Kvaerner Masa-Yards	Fincantieri
Engines	6 9-cyl. Wartsila 9L46 diesels	6 9-cyl. Wartsila 9L46 diesels	4 16-cyl. Sulzer 16ZAV40S and 2 12-cyl. Sulzer 12ZAV40S diesels
Propulsion	2 Azipod electric pod-propulsion units	2 Azipod electric pod-propulsion units	Electric drive, twin screw, controllable pitch
Other equipment			3 bow thrusters, 3 stern thrusters
Passenger capacity	2,112	2,112	2,974
Notes			7, 8

Name	*Carnival Legend*	*Carnival Glory*	*Carnival Valor*
Previous name(s)			
Subsequent name(s)			
Owner			

Name	*Carnival Legend*	*Carnival Glory*	*Carnival Valor*
Flag			
Gross tons	84,000	110,000	110,000
Dimensions (feet)	957 × 106	953 × 117 × 27	953 × 117 × 27
Year built	2002	2003	2004
Place built	Helsinki, Finland	Monfalcone, Italy	Monfalcone, Italy
Shipyard	Kvaerner Masa-Yards	Fincantieri	Fincantieri
Engines	6 9-cyl. Wartsila 9L46 diesels	4 16-cyl. Sulzer 16ZAV40S and 2 12-cyl. Sulzer 12ZAV40S diesels	4 16-cyl. Sulzer 16ZAV40S and 2 12-cyl. Sulzer 12ZAV40S diesels
Propulsion	2 Azipod electric pod-propulsion units	Electric drive, twin screw, controllable pitch	Electric drive, twin screw, controllable pitch
Other equipment		3 bow thrusters, 3 stern thrusters	3 bow thrusters, 3 stern thrusters
Passenger capacity	2,112	2,974	2,974
Notes		7, 8	7, 8

Name	*Carnival Miracle*
Previous name(s)	
Subsequent name(s)	
Owner	
Flag	
Gross tons	84,000
Dimensions (feet)	957 × 106
Year built	2004
Place built	Helsinki, Finland
Shipyard	Kvaerner Masa-Yards
Engines	6 9-cyl. Wartsila 9L46 diesels
Propulsion	2 Azipod electric pod-propulsion units
Other equipment	
Passenger capacity	2,112
Notes	

Notes

1. Acquired from Canadian Pacific in 1971; sold to Epirotiki Lines in 1993. While owned by Canadian Pacific, gross tonnage was 27,284.

2. Originally owned by Canadian Pacific; purchased from Greek Line in 1975; transferred to Carnival-controlled Fiesta Cruise Line in 1992; sold to Epirotiki Lines in 1994. While owned by Canadian Pacific, gross tonnage was 25,516.

3. Originally operated for Union-Castle Line; acquired from South African Marine Corporation in 1977; leased to Premier Cruise Lines in 1996 and later sold to same company. While owned by Union-Castle, gross tonnage was 32,697.

4. One of eight Fantasy-class vessels.

5. Smoking not permitted by either passengers or crew aboard this vessel.

6. World's first passenger vessel to exceed 100,000 gross tons.

7. Post-Panamax vessel; will not fit through the Panama Canal.

8. Slightly larger version of Destiny-class.

CELEBRITY CRUISES

Name	*Meridian*	*Horizon*	*Zenith*
Previous name(s)	*Galileo Galilei* *Galileo*		
Subsequent name(s)	*Sun Vista*		
Owner	Fourth Transoceanic Shipping Co., Ltd.	Fantasia Cruising, Inc.	Fantasia Cruising, Inc.
Flag	Bahamas	Liberia	Liberia
Gross tons	17,634	46,811	47,255
Dimensions (feet)	702 × 94 × 28	682 × 95 × 24	682 × 95 × 24
Year built	1963	1990	1992
Place built	Monfalcone, Italy	Papenburg, Germany	Papenburg, Germany
Shipyard	Cantieri Riuniti dell'Adriatico (No. 1,862)	Meyer Werft (No. 619)	Meyer Werft (No. 620)
Engines	4 steam turbines	2 9-cyl. MAN 9L40/54 diesels and 2 6-cyl. MAN 6L40/54 diesels	2 9-cyl. MAN 9L40/54 diesels and 2 6-cyl. MAN 6L40/54 diesels
Propulsion	Geared, twin screw	Geared, twin screw, controllable pitch	Geared, twin screw, controllable pitch
Other equipment		2 bow thrusters	2 bow thrusters, 1 stern thruster
Passenger capacity	1,106	1,354	1,375
Notes	1		

Name	*Century*	*Galaxy*	*Mercury*
Previous name(s)			
Subsequent name(s)			
Owner	Blue Sapphire Marine, Inc.	Esker Marine Shipping	Seabrook Maritime, Inc.
Flag	Liberia	Liberia	Panama
Gross tons	70,606	77,713	77,713
Dimensions (feet)	815 × 105 × 25	866 × 106 × 26	866 × 106 × 26
Year built	1995	1996	1997
Place built	Papenburg, Germany	Papenburg, Germany	Papenburg, Germany
Shipyard	Meyer Werft (No. 637)	Meyer Werft (No. 638)	Meyer Werft (No. 639)
Engines	2 9-cyl. MAN 9L48/60 diesels and 2 6-cyl. MAN 6L48/60 diesels	2 9-cyl. MAN 9L48/60 diesels and 2 6-cyl. MAN 6L48/60 diesels	2 9-cyl. MAN 9L48/60 diesels and 2 6-cyl. MAN 6L48/60 diesels
Propulsion	Geared, twin screw, controllable pitch	Geared, twin screw, controllable pitch	Geared, twin screw, controllable pitch
Other equipment	3 bow thrusters, 2 stern thrusters	3 bow thrusters, 2 stern thrusters	3 bow thrusters, 2 stern thrusters
Passenger capacity	1,750	1,870	1,870
Notes			

Name	*Millennium*	*Infinity*	*Summit*
Previous name(s)			
Subsequent name(s)			
Owner			
Flag	Liberia	Liberia	Liberia
Gross tons	90,228	91,000	91,000
Dimensions (feet)	965 × 105 × 26	965 × 105 × 26	965 × 105 × 26
Year built	2000	2001	2001
Place built	St. Nazaire, France	St. Nazaire, France	St. Nazaire, France
Shipyard	Chantiers de l'Atlantique (No. R-31)	Chantiers de l'Atlantique (No. S-31)	Chantiers de l'Atlantique (No. T-31)
Engines	2 GE LM2500+ gas turbines	2 GE LM2500+ gas turbines	2 GE LM2500+ gas turbines
Propulsion	2 Mermaid electric pod-propulsion units	2 Mermaid electric pod-propulsion units	2 Mermaid electric pod-propulsion units
Other equipment	3 bow thrusters	3 bow thrusters	3 bow thrusters
Passenger capacity	1,950	1,950	1,950
Notes	2		

Name	Newbuilding
Previous name(s)	
Subsequent name(s)	
Owner	
Flag	Liberia
Gross tons	91,000
Dimensions (feet)	965 × 105 × 26
Year built	2002
Place built	St. Nazaire, France
Shipyard	Chantiers de l'Atlantique (No. U-31)
Engines	2 GE LM2500+ gas turbines
Propulsion	2 Mermaid electric pod-propulsion units
Other equipment	3 bow thrusters
Passenger capacity	1,950
Notes	

Notes

1. Sold to Sun Cruises in 1997.

2. World's first cruise ship to be powered by gas-turbine engines.

CHANDRIS (1959–1995)
Chandris Lines, Chandris Cruises, and Chandris Fantasy Cruises are included.
See separate listing for Celebrity Cruises.

Name	*Patris*	*Romantica*	*Brittany*
Previous name(s)	*Bloemfontein Castle*	*Fort Townshend* *Al Amir Saud* *Mansour*	*Bretagne*

Continued

CHANDRIS (1959–1995)—*Continued*

Name	*Patris*	*Romantica*	*Brittany*
Subsequent name(s)	*Mediterranean Island* *Mediterranean Star*		
Owner	Greek Australian Line, SA	Marifortuna Navigation	Europe-Australia Line, Ltd.
Flag	Greece	Greece	Greece
Gross tons	16,259	3,743	16,644
Dimensions (feet)	595 × 76 × 29	326 × 41 × 25	581 × 73 × 26
Year built	1950	1936	1952
Place built	Belfast, Northern Ireland	Glasgow, Scotland	St. Nazaire, France
Shipyard	Harland & Wolff (No. 1,421)	Blythswood Shipbuilding	Chantiers de l'Atlantique (No. X-12)
Engines	2 8-cyl. B&W diesels	3-cyl. triple-expansion reciprocating steam	2 steam turbines
Propulsion	Geared, twin screw	Single screw	Geared, twin screw
Other equipment	Side doors		
Passenger capacity	1,036	200	1,290
Notes	1	2	3

Name	*Ellinis*	*Australis*	*Regina*
Previous name(s)	*Lurline*	*America* USS *West Point* *America*	*Panama* USS *James Parker* *Panama* *President Hoover* *Regina*
Subsequent name(s)		*America* *Italis* *Noga* *Alferdoss* *American Star*	
Owner	Australia Line, SA	Okeania, SA	International Cruises, SA
Flag	Greece	Panama	Greece; Panama
Gross tons	18,564	26,315	10,153
Dimensions (feet)	642 × 79 × 28	723 × 94 × 33	494 × 64 × 26
Year built	1932	1940	1939
Place built	Quincy, Mass.	Newport News, Va.	Quincy, Mass.
Shipyard	Bethlehem Steel (No. 1,447)	Newport News Shipbuilding (No. 369)	Bethlehem Steel (No. 1,467)
Engines	4 steam turbines	6 steam turbines	4 steam turbines
Propulsion	Geared, twin screw	Geared, twin screw	Geared, twin screw
Other equipment			
Passenger capacity	800*	1,046*	650*
Notes	4	5	6

Name	*Queen Frederica*	*Amerikanis*	*Britanis*
Previous name(s)	*Malolo* *Matsonia* *Atlantic*	*Kenya Castle*	*Monterey* *Matsonia* *Lurline*
Subsequent name(s)			*Belofin I*

Name	*Queen Frederica*	*Amerikanis*	*Britanis*
Owner	National Hellenic American Line	Fifth Transoceanic Shipping Co., Ltd.	Ajax Navigation Co.
Flag	Greece	Greece; Panama	Greece; Panama
Gross tons	16,435	19,905	18,254
Dimensions (feet)	582 × 82 × 29	577 × 74 × 26	631 × 79 × 28
Year built	1927	1952	1932
Place built	Philadelphia, Pa.	Belfast, Northern Ireland	Quincy, Mass.
Shipyard	Wm. Cramp & Sons (No. 509)	Harland & Wolff (No. 1,432)	Bethlehem Steel (No. 1,441)
Engines	8 steam turbines	6 steam turbines	4 steam turbines
Propulsion	Geared, twin screw	Geared, twin screw	Geared, twin screw
Other equipment			
Passenger capacity	1,079*	640	926
Notes	7	8	9

Name	*Atlantis*	*Romanza*	*Regina Magna*
Previous name(s)	USS *General W.P. Richardson* *LaGuardia* *Leilani* *President Roosevelt*	*Huascaran* *Beaver Brae* *Aurelia*	*Pasteur* *Bremen*
Subsequent name(s)	*Emerald Seas* *Sapphire Seas* *Ocean Explorer I*	*Romantica*	*Saudi Phil I* *Filipinas Saudi I*
Owner	Solon Navigation, SA	Armadores Romanza, SA	International Cruises, SA
Flag	Greece	Panama	Greece
Gross tons	18,936	7,537	23,801
Dimensions (feet)	623 × 76 × 27	487 × 60 × 22	697 × 90 × 31
Year built	1944	1939	1938
Place built	Kearny, N.J.	Hamburg, Germany	St. Nazaire, France
Shipyard	Federal Shipbuilding (No. 276)	Blohm & Voss (No. 518)	Chantiers de l'Atlantique (No. R-8)
Engines	4 steam turbines	3 9-cyl. MAN diesels	4 steam turbines
Propulsion	Geared, twin screw	Electric drive, single screw	Geared, quadruple screw
Other equipment			
Passenger capacity	756*	730	751*
Notes	10	11	12

Name	*Bon Vivant*	*The Victoria*	*Galileo*
Previous name(s)	*Patricia* *Ariadne* *Freeport II*	*Dunnottar Castle* *Victoria*	*Galileo Galilei*
Subsequent name(s)	*Ariane* *Empress 65* *Empress Katerina*	*Princesa Victoria*	*Meridian* *Sun Vista*
Owner	Bon Vivant Cruises, Inc.	Phaidon Navigation, SA	Fourth Transoceanic Shipping Co., Ltd.
Flag	Liberia	Panama	Panama

Continued

CHANDRIS(1959–1995)—*Continued*

Name	*Bon Vivant*	*The Victoria*	*Galileo*
Gross tons	6,644	14,917	18,083
Dimensions (feet)	454 × 58 × 19	68 × 72 × 26	702 × 94 × 28
Year built	1951	1936	1963
Place built	Newcastle, U.K.	Belfast, Northern Ireland	Monfalcone, Italy
Shipyard	Swan, Hunter & Wigham Richardson (No. 1,884)	Harland & Wolff (No. 859)	Cantieri Riuniti dell' Adriatico (No. 1,862)
Engines	3 steam turbines	2 7-cyl. Fiat diesels	2 steam turbines
Propulsion	Geared, single screw	Geared, twin screw	Geared, twin screw
Other equipment			
Passenger capacity	239	831*	1,106
Notes	13	14	15

Name	*Azur*
Previous name(s)	*Eagle*
Subsequent name(s)	*The Azur*
Owner	Nouvelle Compagnie de Paquebots
Flag	France
Gross tons	13,965
Dimensions (feet)	466 × 74 × 18
Year built	1971
Place built	Nantes, France
Shipyard	Dubigeon-Normandie, SA (No. 123)
Engines	2 12-cyl. Pielstick 12PC3V-480 diesels
Propulsion	Geared, twin screw, controllable pitch
Other equipment	Stern door and ramp
Passenger capacity	688
Notes	16

Notes

1. Acquired from Union-Castle Line in 1959; sold to Karageorgis Lines in 1979.

2. Acquired from Saudi Arabian interests in 1960; laid up in 1977.

3. Acquired from Transports Maritimes in 1961; laid up in 1977.

4. Acquired from Matson Lines in 1963; laid up in 1980; scrapped in 1987.

5. Acquired from United States Lines in 1964; sold to America Cruise Line, a short-lived venture, in 1978; reacquired by Chandris later that same year and laid up in 1979; sold to Far Eastern interests in 1980.

6. Acquired from American President Lines in 1964; laid up in 1979; scrapped in 1985.

7. Acquired from Home Lines in 1965; laid up in 1973; scrapped in 1978.

8. Acquired from Union-Castle Line in 1967; chartered to Costa from 1983 to 1984; removed from service and laid up about 1995.

9. Acquired from Matson Lines in 1970; sold about 1995.

10. Acquired from American President Lines in 1970; sold to Eastern Steamship in 1972.

11. Acquired from Cogedar Line in 1970; sold to Cyprus interests in 1990.

12. Acquired from Hapag-Lloyd in 1971; laid up in 1974; sold to Philippine interests in 1977.

13. Acquired from Eastern Steamship in 1972; chartered to Freeport Cruise Lines from 1972 to 1974; assigned to Chandris-controlled Bon Vivant Cruises in 1974; laid up in 1978; sold to Cyprus interests in 1989.

14. Acquired from Incres Lines in 1975; sold to Cyprus interests in 1993.

15. Acquired from Lloyd Triestino by charter in 1981; charter converted to purchase in 1983; conveyed to Chandris-controlled Celebrity Cruises in 1990.

16. Acquired from Azur Transportation by charter in 1987; conveyed to Festival Cruises in 1994.

*Total number of available berths.

COMMODORE CRUISE LINE

Name	*Princesa Leopoldina*	*Boheme*	*Bolero*
Previous name(s)			
Subsequent name(s)	*Coral Princess*	*Freewinds*	*Scandinavica*
	Cora Princess		*Bolero*
	Coral Princess		*Jupiter*
			Crucero Express
Owner	Companhia de Navegacao Lloyd Brasileiro	Wallenius Bremen G.m.b.H. & Co.	Fred Olsen & Co.
Flag	Brazil	West Germany; Bahamas	Norway
Gross tons	9,696	9,866	11,344
Dimensions (feet)	478 × 61 × 18	441 × 69 × 18	464 × 72 × 18
Year built	1962	1968	1972
Place built	Bilbao, Spain	Abo, Finland	Nantes, France
Shipyard	Cia. Euskalduna de Const. (No. 156)	Wartsila (No. 1,161)	Dubigeon-Normandie (No. 133A)
Engines	2 8-cyl. B&W 8-50VTBF-110 diesels	2 8-cyl. Sulzer 8RD56 diesels	2 12-cyl. Pielstick 12PC3V-480 diesels
Propulsion	Geared, twin screw	Geared, twin screw, controllable pitch	Geared, twin screw
Other equipment	Side door	Bow thruster	2 bow thrusters, bow and stern doors
Passenger capacity	500	500	872*
Notes	1	2	3

Name	*Caribe*	*Caribe*	*Enchanted Isle*
Previous name(s)	*Freeport*	*Olympia*	*Argentina*
	Freeport I		*Veendam*
	Freeport		*Brasil*
	Svea Star		*Monarch Star*
			Bermuda Star
			Enchanted Isle
			Commodore Hotel
Subsequent name(s)	*Caribe Bremen*	*Caribe I*	
	Scandinavian Sun	*Regal Empress*	
	Balanga Queen		
	Discovery Sun		
Owner	Bremer Schiffahrtsgesellschaft G.m.b.A. & Co.	Olympia Caribbean Shipping Co.	Almira Enterprises, Inc.
Flag	West Germany	Panama	Panama
Gross tons	9,963	14,533	23,395
Dimensions (feet)	441 × 72 × 18	610 × 79 × 28	617 × 84 × 28

Continued

COMMODORE CRUISE LINE—*Continued*

Name	*Caribe*	*Caribe*	*Enchanted Isle*
Year built	1968	1953	1958
Place built	Lubeck, West Germany	Glasgow, Scotland	Pascagoula, Miss.
Shipyard	Orenstein-Koppel (No. 658)	Alexander Stephen & Sons (No. 636)	Ingalls (No. 468)
Engines	2 16-cyl. Pielstick 16 PC2V-406 diesels	4 12-cyl. Deutz RBV12M40 diesels	4 steam turbines
Propulsion	Geared, twin screw	Geared, twin screw	Geared, twin screw
Other equipment	Bow thruster, bow and stern doors	Bow thruster	
Passenger capacity	736*	875	725
Notes	4	5	6

Name	*Enchanted Seas*	*Enchanted Capri*	*Enchanted Sun*
Previous name(s)	*Brasil* *Volendam* *Monarch Sun* *Island Sun* *Liberte* *Canada Star* *Queen of Bermuda*	*Azerbaydzhan* *Arkadiya* *Island Holiday*	*Castalia* *Stena America* *Scandinavian Saga* *Pride of San Diego* *Tropic Star II* *Stena Arcadia* *Emerald Empress* *Sofia*
Subsequent name(s)	*Universe Explorer*		
Owner	Azure Investments	Norsong Shipping Ltd.	Viejas Enterprises
Flag	Panama	Bahamas	Bahamas
Gross tons	22,162	15,410	5,259
Dimensions (feet)	617 × 84 × 28	513 × 72 × 19	433 × 65 × 17
Year built	1958	1975	1974
Place built	Pascagoula, Miss.	Turku, Finland	Kynossoura, Greece
Shipyard	Ingalls (No. 467)	Wartsila (No. 1,221)	Kynossoura Dockyard Co.
Engines	4 steam turbines	2 18-cyl. Pielstick 18PC2-2V-400 diesels	2 8-cyl. Atlas-MaK Maschinenbau 8M551AK diesels
Propulsion	Geared, twin screw	Geared, twin screw, controllable pitch	Geared, twin screw
Other equipment		Bow door and ramp, side door and ramp, hull strengthened for ice conditions	Stern doors
Passenger capacity	688	460	264
Notes	7	8	9

Notes

1. Chartered from Brasilian Coastal Line in 1963.

2. Chartered from Wallenius in 1968; charter later converted to purchase; sold to International Association of Scientologists in 1986.

3. Operated summer car ferry route between Portland, Maine, and Yarmouth, Nova Scotia, from 1973 to 1976. Used in south Florida cruise service by Commodore during winter months on an irregular basis from 1973 to 1976.

4. Acquired from Svea Line in 1976; conveyed to DFDS Seaways in 1980.

5. Purchased from Greek Line in 1981, following seven-year layup; conveyed to Regal Cruise Line in 1993. Originally steam powered; converted to diesel by Commodore in 1983.

6. Acquired when Commodore merged with Bermuda Star Line in 1990.

7. Acquired when Commodore merged with Bermuda Star Line in 1990; vessel began operating under charter to World Explorer Cruises as *Universe Explorer* in 1996.

8. Acquired from Ukraine interests in 1998.

9. Acquired in 1999 for short-lived day-cruise service; laid up in 2000.

*Total number of available berths.

COSTA CROCIERI

Name	*Franca C.*	*Daphne*	*Federico C.*
Previous name(s)	*Medina* *Roma*	*Port Sydney*	
Subsequent name(s)	*Doulos*	*Switzerland*	*Royale* *Starship Royale* *SeaBreeze I*
Owner	Costa Armatori, S.p.A.	Independent Continental Lines, Ltd.	Costa Armatori, S.p.A.
Flag	Italy	Panama	Italy
Gross tons	6,822	9,436	20,416
Dimensions (feet)	428 × 55 × 18	533 × 70 × 29	606 × 79 × 29
Year built	1914	1955	1958
Place built	Newport News, Va.	Wallsend, U.K.	Genoa, Italy
Shipyard	Newport News Shipbuilding (No. 176)	Swan, Hunter & Wigham Richardson (No. 1,827)	Ansaldo (No. 1,516)
Engines	6-cyl. Fiat diesel	2 6-cyl. Doxford diesels	4 steam turbines
Propulsion	Single screw	Geared, twin screw	Geared, twin screw
Other equipment			
Passenger capacity	552	500*	840
Notes	1	2	3

Name	*Carla C.*	*Enrico C.*	*Eugenio C.*
Previous name(s)	*Flandre*	*Provence*	
Subsequent name(s)	*Carla Costa* *Pallas Athena*	*Enrico Costa* *Symphony* *Aegean II*	*Eugenio Costa* *Edinburgh Castle* *The Big Red Boat II*
Owner	Costa Armatori, S.p.A.	Costa Armatori, S.p.A.	Costa Armatori, S.p.A.
Flag	Italy	Italy	Italy
Gross tons	19,975	13,607	32,753
Dimensions (feet)	600 × 80 × 28	579 × 73 × 25	713 × 96 × 28
Year built	1952	1950	1966
Place built	Dunkirk, France	Newcastle, U.K.	Monfalcone, Italy
Shipyard	Antiers et Chantiers de France (No. 206)	Swan, Hunter & Wigham Richardson (No. 1,874)	Adriatico (No. 1,884)
Engines	8 steam turbines	6 steam turbines	4 steam turbines
Propulsion	Geared, twin screw	Geared, twin screw	Geared, twin screw
Other equipment			
Passenger capacity	754*	1,198*	844
Notes	4	5	6

Continued

COSTA CROCIERI—*Continued*

Name	*Columbus C.*	*Italia*	*Bianca C.*
Previous name(s)	*Kungsholm* *Europa*		*Marechal Petain* *La Marseillaise* *Arosa Sky*
Subsequent name(s)		*Ocean Princess* *Sea Prince* *Sea Prince V* *Princesa Oceania* *Sapphire*	
Owner	Independent Continental Lines, Ltd.	Crociere d'Oltremare S.p.A.	Giacomo Costa Fu Andrea
Flag	Panama	Italy	Italy
Gross tons	21,513	12,219	18,427
Dimensions (feet)	600 × 77 × 26	489 × 70 × 21	594 × 76 × 26
Year built	1953	1967	1944/1949
Place built	Vlissingen, Sweden	Trieste, Italy	La Ciotat, France
Shipyard	N.V. Koninklijke Maats. Schelde (No. 273)	Cantieri Navali Riuniti Feiszegi (No. 76)	Societe Provencale de Construction Navale (No. 161)
Engines	2 8-cyl. B&W diesels	2 9-cyl. Sulzer 9RD56 diesels	3 11-cyl. Sulzer diesels
Propulsion	Geared, twin screw	Twin screw	Triple screw
Other equipment			
Passenger capacity	785*	500	1,252
Notes	7	8	9

Name	*Flavia*	*Fulvia*	*Danae*
Previous name(s)	*Media*	*Oslofjord*	*Port Melbourne* *Therisos Express*
Subsequent name(s)	*Flavian* *Lavia*		*Anar* *Starlight Princess* *Baltica* *Princess Danae*
Owner	Costa Armatori, S.p.A.	Norwegian American Line	Independent Continental Lines, Ltd.
Flag	Italy	Norway	Liberia
Gross tons	15,465	16,923	9,603
Dimensions (feet)	556 × 70 × 30	577 × 72 × 27	532 × 70 × 25
Year built	1947	1949	1955
Place built	Clydebank, Scotland	Amsterdam, Netherlands	Belfast, Northern Ireland
Shipyard	John Brown (No. 629)	Netherlands Dock & Shipbuilding (No. 410)	Harland & Wolff (No. 1,483)
Engines	4 steam turbines	2 7-cyl. Stork diesels	2 6-cyl. B&W 6-75VYF-150/50 diesels
Propulsion	Geared, twin screw	Twin screw	Twin screw
Other equipment			
Passenger capacity	850	646	412
Notes	10	11	12

Name	*Costa Riviera*	*Costa Allegra*	*Costa Marina*
Previous name(s)	*Guglielmo Marconi*	*Annie Johnson* *Regent Moon* *Alexandra*	*Axel Johnson* *Regent Sun* *Italia*
Subsequent name(s)	*American Adventure* *Costa Riviera*		
Owner	Costa Armatori, S.p.A.	Prestige Cruises NV	Prestige Cruises NV
Flag	Italy	Liberia	Liberia
Gross tons	28,137	28,430	25,558
Dimensions (feet)	701 × 94 × 28	616 × 85 × 27	571 × 85 × 27
Year built	1963	1969	1969
Place built	Monfalcone, Italy	Turku, Finland	Turku, Finland
Shipyard	Adriatico (No. 1,863)	Wartsila (No. 1,170)	Wartsila (No. 1,169)
Engines	4 steam turbines	4 6-cyl. Wartsila 6R46 diesels	2 16-cyl. Pielstick 16PC2V-400 and 2 12-cyl. Pielstick 12PC2V-400 diesels
Propulsion	Geared, twin screw	Geared, twin screw, controllable pitch	Geared, twin screw, controllable pitch
Other equipment		2 bow thrusters	Bow thruster
Passenger capacity	984	820	776
Notes	13	14	14

Name	*Costa Classica*	*Costa Romantica*	*Costa Playa*
Previous name(s)			*Finlandia* *Finnstar* *Innstar* *Pearl of Scandinavia* *Ocean Pearl* *Pearl*
Subsequent name(s)			*Oriental Pearl*
Owner	Prestige Cruises NV	Prestige Cruises NV	Prestige Cruises NV
Flag	Liberia	Liberia	Bahamas
Gross tons	52,926	53,049	12,704
Dimensions (feet)	730 × 108 × 25	723 × 101 × 25	502 × 66 × 18
Year built	1991	1993	1967
Place built	Venice, Italy	Venice, Italy	Helsinki, Finland
Shipyard	Fincantieri (No. 5,877)	Fincantieri (No. 5,899)	Wartsila (No. 383)
Engines	4 8-cyl. Sulzer 8ZAL40S diesels	4 8-cyl. Sulzer 8ZAL40S diesels	4 9-cyl. Sulzer 9ZH40/48 diesels
Propulsion	Geared, twin screw, controllable pitch	Geared, twin screw, controllable pitch	Geared, twin screw, controllable pitch
Other equipment	2 bow thrusters	2 bow thrusters, 1 stern thruster	2 bow thrusters, stern door and ramp
Passenger capacity	1,308	1,356	512
Notes	15		16

Name	*Costa Victoria*	*"Costa Olympia"*	*Costa Atlantica*
Previous name(s)			
Subsequent name(s)		*Norwegian Sky*	

Continued

COSTA CROCIERI—*Continued*

Name	*Costa Victoria*	*"Costa Olympia"*	*Costa Atlantica*
Owner	Prestige Cruises NV		
Flag	Liberia		Italy
Gross tons	75,166		86,000
Dimensions (feet)	830 × 118 × 26	830 × 118 × 26	966 × 106 × 27
Year built	1996		2000
Place built	Bremen, Germany	Bremen, Germany	Helsinki, Finland
Shipyard	Vulkan Werft (No. 107)	Vulkan Werft (No. 108)	Kvaerner Masa-Yards
Engines	3 6-cyl. MAN 6L58/64 and 3 7-cyl. MAN 7L58/64 diesels		6 9-cyl. Wartsila 9L46 diesels
Propulsion	Electric drive, twin screw, controllable pitch		2 Azipod electric pod-propulsion units
Other equipment	3 bow thrusters, 2 stern thrusters		
Passenger capacity	1,928		2,114
Notes		17	

Name	Newbuilding
Previous name(s)	
Subsequent name(s)	
Owner	
Flag	
Gross tons	86,000
Dimensions (feet)	966 × 106 × 27
Year built	2003
Place built	Helsinki, Finland
Shipyard	Kvaerner Masa-Yards
Engines	6 9-cyl. Wartsila 9L46 diesels
Propulsion	2 Azipod electric pod-propulsion units
Other equipment	
Passenger capacity	2,114
Notes	

Notes

1. Acquired via bankruptcy auction in 1952; steam engine removed and replaced by diesel; sold to Operation Mobilisation in 1977. Thought to be oldest oceangoing passenger vessel of all time. Still in service in 2000.
2. Chartered from Carras Cruises in 1979; purchased in 1985. Conveyed to Prestige Cruises in 1990; returned to Costa shortly afterward; chartered to Swiss interests in 1996 with an option to purchase.
3. First Costa passenger newbuilding; sold to Premier Cruises in 1983.
4. Acquired from French Line in 1968; chartered to Princess Cruises from 1968 to 1970. Steam engines removed and replaced by two 20-cylinder Stork-Werkspoor diesels in 1974. Sold to Epirotiki Lines in 1992.
5. Acquired from Transports Maritimes in 1965; sold to Starlauro Cruises in 1994.
6. Was to have been assigned to American Family Cruises in 1994 and renamed *American Pioneer*, but transfer never occurred. Sold to Liberian interests in 1994, but remained under charter to Costa through 1996; sold to Lowline in 1996.
7. Acquired from North German Lloyd in 1980; scrapped in 1985.
8. Acquired in 1973 following earlier charter to Princess Cruises; sold to Ocean Cruise Line in 1983.
9. Acquired from Arosa Line in 1958; lost to fire in 1961.

10. Chartered from Cogedar Line in 1968; charter converted to purchase in 1969; sold to C.Y. Tung Group in 1982.

11. Chartered from Norwegian-American Line in 1969; lost to explosion and fire in 1970.

12. Chartered from Delian Cruises in 1979; sold to Equinox Enterprises in 1992.

13. Built for Lloyd Triestino and sister ship of *Meridian* that ran for Celebrity Cruises; acquired by Costa in 1983. Chartered to Costa-controlled American Family Cruises in 1993; returned to Costa in 1994.

14. Built as containership; initial effort by Regency Cruises to convert into cruise ship not realized. Conversion completed under Costa auspices in early 1990s.

15. Was scheduled for stretching during winter of 2000–01 at Cammell Laird, Birkenhead, U.K.; new dimensions will be 78,000 gross tons, 870 feet long, with passenger capacity of 2,012. Project will add a full deck to the vessel in addition to new midsection and is thus being called the largest stretching effort ever. Speed will be increased to twenty-three knots by adding a Siemens-Schottel pod-propulsion unit to the vessel's original twin-screw system. New schedule has moved the work to the winter of 2001–02.

16. Built as car ferry for Baltic Sea service; converted to cruise ship in 1978; conveyed to Costa in 1995, following Costa's takeover of Paquet Cruises.

17. Vessel never delivered to Costa and never formally enrolled as *Costa Olympia* (see text); completed by Norwegian Cruise Line as *Norwegian Sky*.

*Total number of available berths.

CROWN CRUISE LINE (1984–1997)

Name	*Viking Princess*	*Crown Del Mar*	*Crown Monarch*
Previous name(s)	*Ilmatar*	*Las Palmas de Gran Canaria*	
Subsequent name(s)	*Palm Beach Princess*	*D. Juan*	*Nautican* *Walrus*
Owner	Crown Cruise Line SA	Maritima Albatros SA	Cruceros de Valencia SA
Flag	Panama	Panama	Panama
Gross tons	6,421	16,292	15,271
Dimensions (feet)	421 × 54 × 15	429 × 63 × 18	494 × 68 × 19
Year built	1964	1967	1990
Place built	Helsinki, Finland	Valencia, Spain	Valencia, Spain
Shipyard	Wartsila (No. 375)	Union Naval (No. 94)	Union Naval (No. 185)
Engines	2 16-cyl. and 1 12-cyl. Sulzer diesels	2 6-cyl. B&W 7-62VT2BF-90 diesels	4 9-cyl. Normo BRM-9 diesels
Propulsion	Geared, triple screw, controllable pitch	Geared, twin screw, controllable pitch	Geared, twin screw, controllable pitch
Other equipment	Bow thruster, side door, hull strengthened for ice conditions	Bow thruster, converted RO/RO vessel	2 bow thrusters
Passenger capacity	346	487	560
Notes	1	2	3

Name	*Crown Jewel*	*Crown Dynasty*
Previous name(s)		
Subsequent name(s)	*SuperStar Gemini*	*Crown Majesty* *Norwegian Dynasty* *Crown Dynasty*
Owner	Crown Jewel, Inc.	Crown Dynasty, Inc.
Flag	Panama	Panama
Gross tons	19,093	19,093
Dimensions (feet)	537 × 74 × 18	537 × 74 × 18
Year built	1992	1993

Continued

CROWN CRUISE LINE (1984–1997)—*Continued*

Name	*Crown Jewel*	*Crown Dynasty*
Place built	Valencia, Spain	Valencia, Spain
Shipyard	Union Naval (No. 197)	Union Naval (No. 198)
Engines	4 8-cyl. Wartsila 8R32E diesels	4 8-cyl. Wartsila 8R32E diesels
Propulsion	Geared, twin screw, controllable pitch	Geared, twin screw, controllable pitch
Other equipment	2 bow thrusters	2 bow thrusters
Passenger capacity	820	820
Notes	4	5

Notes

1. Acquired in 1984; sold to Deerbrooke Investments, Inc. in 1977. Vessel primarily assigned to day cruises during tenure with Crown.

2. Acquired from Sol Lines in 1988; sold to Spanish interests about 1992.

3. Sold to Far Eastern interests in 1994.

4. Sold to Star Cruises in 1995.

5. Conveyed to Majesty Cruise Line in 1997. (See second entry for Crown Cruise Line.)

CROWN CRUISE LINE
Company established in 1999 as subsidiary of Commodore Cruise Lines. Because of ownership linkages, could be regarded as a restoration of the Crown Cruise Lines that was in operation 1984–1997.

Name	*Crown Dynasty*
Previous name(s)	*Crown Dynasty*
	Crown Majesty
	Norwegian Dynasty
Subsequent name(s)	
Owner	Crown Dynasty, Inc.
Flag	Panama
Gross tons	19,093
Dimensions (feet)	537 × 74 × 18
Year built	1993
Place built	Valencia, Spain
Shipyard	Union Naval (No. 198)
Engines	4 8-cyl. Wartsila 8R32E diesels
Propulsion	Geared, twin screw, controllable pitch
Other equipment	2 bow thrusters
Passenger capacity	820
Notes	1

Notes

1. Acquired from Crown Dynasty, Inc., in 1999 following charter to Norwegian Cruise Line; acquisition initially charter, later converted to purchase.

CRYSTAL CRUISES
INCLUDING NYK LINE

Name	*Crystal Harmony*	*Crystal Symphony*	*Asuka*
Previous name(s)			
Subsequent name(s)			
Owner	Crystal Ship, Ltd.	Crystal Ship, Ltd.	NYK Line
Flag	Bahamas	Bahamas	Japan
Gross tons	48,621	51,044	28,717
Dimensions (feet)	790 × 105 × 25	781 × 99 × 25	623 × 81 × 25
Year built	1990	1995	1991
Place built	Nagasaki, Japan	Turku, Finland	Nagasaki, Japan
Shipyard	Mitsubishi (No. 2,100)	Kvaerner Masa-Yards (No. 1,323)	Mitsubishi (No. 2,050)
Engines	4 8-cyl. MAN 8L58/64 diesels	6 9-cyl. Sulzer 9ZAL40S diesels	2 7-cyl. MAN 7L 58/64 diesels
Propulsion	Electric drive, twin screw, controllable pitch	Electric drive, twin screw, controllable pitch	Geared, twin screw, controllable pitch
Other equipment	2 bow thrusters	2 bow thrusters, 1 stern thruster	Bow thruster
Passenger capacity	940	940	584
Notes			

CUNARD LINE
See Appendix A, Part 3, for data and information about several earlier Cunard vessels.

Name	*Carmania*	*Franconia*	*Queen Elizabeth 2*
Previous name(s)	*Saxonia*	*Ivernia*	
Subsequent name(s)	*Leonid Soninov*	*Fyodor Shalyapin* *Feodor Shalyapin*	
Owner	Cunard Line, Ltd.	Cunard Line, Ltd.	Cunard Line, Ltd.
Flag	U.K.	U.K.	U.K.
Gross tons	21,370	21,406	65,863
Dimensions (feet)	608 × 80 × 29	608 × 80 × 29	963 × 105 × 33
Year built	1954	1955	1969
Place built	Clydebank, Scotland	Clydebank, Scotland	Clydebank, Scotland
Shipyard	John Brown (No. 692)	John Brown (No. 693)	John Brown (No. 736) (see note)
Engines	4 steam turbines	4 steam turbines	4 steam turbines
Propulsion	Geared, twin screw	Geared, twin screw	Geared, twin screw, controllable pitch
Other equipment			2 bow thrusters
Passenger capacity	612		1,800
Notes	1	2	3

Name	*Cunard Adventurer*	*Cunard Ambassador*	*Cunard Countess*
Previous name(s)			
Subsequent name(s)	*Sunward II* *Triton*	*Linda Clausen* *Procyon* *Raslyn*	*Awani Dream* *Olympic Countess*

Continued

CUNARD LINE—*Continued*

Name	*Cunard Adventurer*	*Cunard Ambassador*	*Cunard Countess*
Owner	Cunard Line, Ltd.	Cunard Cruise Ships, Ltd.	Cunard Cruise Ships, Ltd.
Flag	U.K.	U.K.	Bahamas
Gross tons	14,151	14,160	17,593
Dimensions (feet)	486 × 72 × 19	486 × 72 × 19	537 × 75 × 19
Year built	1971	1972	1976
Place built	Rotterdam, Netherlands	Rotterdam, Netherlands	Copenhagen, Denmark
Shipyard	Rotterdam Drydock (No. 329)	N.V. Mch. & Schps. (No. 666)	A/S Burmeister & Wain (No. 858)
Engines	4 12-cyl. Stork-Werkspoor 12TM410 diesels	4 12-cyl. Stork-Werkspoor 12TM410 diesels	4 7-cyl. B&W 7U50HU diesels
Propulsion	Geared, twin screw, controllable pitch	Geared, twin screw, controllable pitch	Geared, twin screw, controllable pitch
Other equipment	Bow thruster	Bow thruster	Bow thruster
Passenger capacity	832	800	750
Notes	4	5	6

Name	*Cunard Princess*	*Sagafjord*	*Caronia*
Previous name(s)	*Cunard Conquest*		*Vistafjord*
Subsequent name(s)	*Rhapsody*	*Gripsholm* *Saga Rose*	
Owner	Cunard Cruise Ships, Ltd.	Cunard Line, Ltd.	Cunard Steamship Co., Ltd.
Flag	Bahamas	Bahamas	Bahamas; U.K.
Gross tons	17,496	24,474	24,492
Dimensions (feet)	537 × 75 × 19	620 × 80 × 27	628 × 82 × 27
Year built	1977	1965	1973
Place built	Copenhagen, Denmark	La Seyne, France	Newcastle, U.K.
Shipyard	A/S Burmeister & Wain (No. 859)	Forges & Ch. de la Mediterranee (No. 1,366)	Swan, Hunter & Wigham Richardson (No. 39)
Engines	4 7-cyl. B&W 7U50HU diesels	2 9-cyl. Sulzer 9RD68 diesels	2 9-cyl. Sulzer 9RD68 diesels
Propulsion	Geared, twin screw, controllable pitch	Geared, twin screw	Geared, twin screw
Other equipment	Bow thruster	Bow thruster	Bow thruster
Passenger capacity	810	588	736
Notes	7	8	9

Name	*Sea Goddess I*	*Sea Goddess II*	*Royal Viking Sun*
Previous name(s)			
Subsequent name(s)	*Seabourn Goddess I*	*Seabourn Goddess II*	*Seabourn Sun*
Owner	Norwegian Cruises, Ltd	Norwegian Cruises, Ltd.	Cunard Line, Ltd.
Flag	Isle of Man, U.K.	Isle of Man, U.K.	Bahamas
Gross tons	4,253	4,200	37,845
Dimensions (feet)	344 × 58 × 14	344 × 58 × 14	669 × 106 × 24
Year built	1984	1985	1988
Place built	Helsinki, Finland	Helsinki, Finland	Turku, Finland
Shipyard	Wartsila (No. 466)	Wartsila (No. 467)	Wartsila (No. 1,296)

Name	Sea Goddess I	Sea Goddess II	Royal Viking Sun
Engines	2 12-cyl. Wartsila 12V22HF diesels	2 12-cyl. Wartsila 12V22HF diesels	4 8-cyl. Sulzer 8ZAL40S diesels
Propulsion	Geared, twin screw, controllable pitch	Geared, twin screw, controllable pitch	Geared, twin screw, controllable pitch
Other equipment	Bow thruster	Bow thruster	2 bow thrusters
Passenger capacity	120	120	740
Notes	10	10	11

Name	Queen Mary 2
Previous name(s)	
Subsequent name(s)	
Owner	
Flag	U.K.
Gross tons	150,000
Dimensions (feet)	1131 × 135
Year built	2003
Place built	St. Nazaire, France
Shipyard	Chantiers de l'Atlantique
Engines	4 diesels, 2 gas turbines
Propulsion	4 Mermaid electric pod-propulsion units
Other equipment	
Passenger capacity	2,800
Notes	12

Notes

1. Sold to Black Sea Shipping Co. in 1973.

2. Sold to Black Sea Shipping Co. in 1973.

3. Built at the one-time John Brown yard in Clydebank. By 1969, however, John Brown was part of Upper Clyde Shipbuilders, Ltd. Over winter of 1986–87, vessel converted to diesel-electric power at Lloyd Werft in Bremerhaven, West Germany, with nine 9-cylinder MAN 9L58/64 diesels and electric drive; gross tonnage increased to 70,327.

4. Sold to Norwegian Caribbean Line in 1977.

5. Caught fire in 1974; sold to Danish interests and converted to livestock carrier.

6. Sold to Awani Cruise Line in 1997.

7. Sold to Gramerco International in 1995.

8. Acquired from Norwegian-American Line in 1983; sold to Saga Holidays in 1996.

9. Acquired from Norwegian-American Line in 1983.

10. Acquired from Sea Goddess Cruises in 1986; conveyed to Seabourn Cruise Line in 1999.

11. Acquired from Royal Viking Line in 1994; conveyed to Seabourn Cruise Line in 1999.

12. Post-Panamax vessel; will not fit through the Panama Canal.

DELTA QUEEN STEAMBOAT COMPANY
INCLUDING DELTA QUEEN COASTAL CRUISES

Name	Delta Queen	Mississippi Queen	American Queen
Previous name(s)	Delta Queen USS YFB-56		
Subsequent name(s)			

Continueud

DELTA QUEEN STEAMBOAT COMPANY—*Continued*

Name	*Delta Queen*	*Mississippi Queen*	*American Queen*
Owner	Delta Queen Steamboat Co.	Great Ocean Cruise Line	Delta Queen Steamboat Co.
Flag (Off. No.)	U.S. (225875)	U.S. (574200)	U.S. (1030765)
Gross tons	1,650	3,364	3,707
Dimensions (feet)	285 × 60 × 9	379 × 68 × 8	419 × 89 × 8
Year built	1926	1976	1995
Place built	Stockton, Calif.	Jeffersonville, Ind.	Amelia, La.
Shipyard	(See note)	Jeffboat (No. 2,999)	McDermott Shipyard (No. 296)
Engines	2 1-cyl. cross-compound steam engines	2 2-cyl. tandem-compound steam engines	2 2-cyl. tandem-compound steam engines
Propulsion	44-ton stern-wheel	73-ton stern-wheel	45-ton stern-wheel
Other equipment		Bow thruster	2 fully azimuthal Z-drive bow thrusters
Passenger capacity	174	416*	436
Notes	1		2

Name	*Columbia Queen*	*Cape May Light*	*Cape Cod Light*
Previous name(s)	*Capitol Queen*		
Subsequent name(s)			
Owner	Delta Queen Steamboat Co.	Ocean Development Co.	Ocean Development Co.
Flag (Off. No.)	U.S. (1023608)	U.S. (1103209)	U.S. (1103208)
Gross tons	1,390	1,580	1,580
Dimensions (feet)	218 × 60 × 12	300 × 50 × 13	300 × 50 × 13
Year built	1994	2001	2001
Place built	Jennings, La.	Jacksonville, Fla.	Jacksonville, Fla.
Shipyard	Leevac Shipyards	Atlantic Marine	Atlantic Marine
Engines	2 12-cyl. Cummins KTA38M2 diesels	2 Caterpillar 3616B diesels	2 Caterpillar 3616B diesels
Propulsion	Twin screw	Twin Schottel Z-drives	Twin Schottel Z-drives
Other equipment	Bow thruster	Bow thruster	Bow thruster
Passenger capacity	161	226	226
Notes	3	4	4

Notes

1. Hull built at Isherwood in Glasgow, Scotland; disassembled for shipment to California. Engines built in Dumbarton, Scotland; paddle-wheel shafts and cranks built in Germany at Krupp Iron Works. Acquired by Greene Line, corporate predecessor of Delta Queen Steamboat in 1946.

2. Powered by steam engines salvaged from the steam dredge *Kennedy*. Additional power provided by twin Z-drive thrusters.

3. Built as gaming boat for service in Missouri but never completed; acquired by Delta Queen Steamboat in 1999; brought to West Coast aboard oceangoing barge and converted to overnight cruise vessel at Nicholas Brothers, Freeland, Washington.

4. Initial vessels of a new fleet of coastal cruise ships. Ocean Development Co. is a wholly owned subsidiary of American Classic Voyages, parent corporation of Delta Queen Coastal and Delta Queen Steamboat. It was formed to manage construction of the new vessels and may not continue to serve as formal owner once operation begins in 2001.

*Total number of available berths.

DISNEY CRUISE LINE

Name	*Disney Magic*	*Disney Wonder*
Previous name(s)		
Subsequent name(s)		
Owner	Disney Cruise Line Management, Ltd.	Disney Cruise Line Services, Ltd.
Flag	Bahamas	Bahamas
Gross tons	83,338	83,308
Dimensions (feet)	964 × 106 × 25	964 × 106 × 25
Year built	1998	1999
Place built	(see note)	Maghera, Italy
Shipyard	Fincantieri (No. 5,989)	Fincantieri (No. 5,990)
Engines	5 16-cyl. Sulzer 16ZAV40S diesels	5 16-cyl. Sulzer 16ZAV40S diesels
Propulsion	Electric drive, twin screw	Electric drive, twin screw
Other equipment	3 bow thrusters, 2 stern thrusters	3 bow thrusters, 2 stern thrusters
Passenger capacity	1,750	1,750
Notes	1	

Notes

1. Forward section of vessel built in Maghera, Italy, and aft section in Trieste; completion in Maghera.

DOLPHIN CRUISE LINE (See Premier Cruise Line)

EASTERN STEAMSHIP (1954–1986)

When company initiated cruise service out of south Florida in 1954, it was called Eastern Shipping Corporation; name was changed to Eastern Steamship Lines in 1962.

Name	*Evangeline*	*Yarmouth*	*Bahama Star*
Previous name(s)		*Yarmouth* *Yarmouth Castle* *Queen of Nassau* *Yarmouth Castle*	*Boringuen* *Puerto Rico* *Arosa Star*
Subsequent name(s)	*Yarmouth Castle*	*San Andres* *Elizabeth A.*	*La Jenelle*
Owner	McCormick Shipping	McCormick Shipping	McCormick Shipping
Flag	Panama	Panama	Panama
Gross tons	5,002	5,002	7,114
Dimensions (feet)	379 × 56 × 20	379 × 56 × 20	466 × 60 × 24
Year built	1927	1927	1931
Place built	Philadelphia, Pa.	Philadelphia, Pa.	Quincy, Mass.
Shipyard	Wm. Cramp & Sons	Wm. Cramp & Sons (No. 518)	Bethlehem Steel (No. 1,432)
Engines	4 steam turbines	4 steam turbines	3 steam turbines
Propulsion	Geared, twin screw	Geared, twin screw	Geared, single screw
Other equipment			
Passenger capacity	350*	365*	735
Notes	1	2	3

Continued

EASTERN STEAMSHIP (1954–1986)—*Continued*

Name	*Ariadne*	*New Bahama Star*	*Emerald Seas*
Previous name(s)	*Patricia*	*Jerusalem* *Miami*	USS *General W.P.* *Richardson* *LaGuardia* *Leilani* *President Roosevelt* *Atlantis*
Subsequent name(s)	*Freeport* *Bon Vivant* *Ariane* *Empress 65* *Empress Katerina*	*Bahama Star* *Bonaire Star*	*Sapphire Seas* *Ocean Explorer I*
Owner	Ares Shipping Corp.	Bahama Shipping Corp.	Eastern Steamship Lines
Flag	Liberia	Liberia	Panama
Gross tons	6,644	8,312	18,927
Dimensions (feet)	454 × 58 × 19	488 × 65 × 21	623 × 76 × 27
Year built	1951	1957	1944
Place built	Newcastle, U.K.	Hamburg, West Germany	Kearny, N.J.

Shipyard	Swan, Hunter & Wigham
	   Richardson (No. 1,884)
		Deutsche Werft, A.G.
		   (No. 717)
			Federal Shipbuilding
			   (No. 276)

Engines	3 steam turbines	4 steam turbines	4 steam turbines
Propulsion	Geared, single screw	Geared, twin screw	Geared, twin screw
Other equipment			
Passenger capacity	329	573*	1,084*
Notes	4	5	6

Notes

1. Acquired from Eastern Steamship Lines in 1954; sold to Yarmouth Steamship in 1964.

2. Acquired from Eastern Steamship Lines in 1954; sold to Yarmouth Steamship in 1962. Was last vessel built by Wm. Cramp & Sons.

3. Acquired from Arosa Line in 1959; retired in 1968; wrecked while being prepared for assignment as shoreside hotel in California in 1970.

4. Acquired from Hamburg America Line in 1961; sold to Chandris in 1972.

5. Acquired in 1968 following charter operation for Peninsular and Occidental; retired in 1978; lost (sunk) en route to Taiwan scrap yard in 1979. In 1972 was last vessel to originate a cruise from old piers in downtown Miami.

6. Acquired from Chandris in 1972; conveyed to corporate successor, Admiral Cruises, in 1986.

*Total number of available berths

FESTIVAL CRUISES
Company is marketed in North America as First European Cruises.

Name	*The Azur*	*Flamenco*	*Bolero*
Previous name(s)	*Eagle* *Azur*	*Spirit of London* *Sun Princess* *Starship Majestic* *Southern Cross*	*Starward*

Name	*The Azur*	*Flamenco*	*Bolero*
Subsequent name(s)			
Owner	Azur Transportation, Inc.	Flamenco Transportation	Mediterranean Transportation, Inc.
Flag	Panama	Bahamas	Panama
Gross tons	9,159	17,042	15,781
Dimensions (feet)	466 × 74 × 18	536 × 81 × 21	525 × 75 × 22
Year built	1971	1972	1968
Place built	Nantes, France	Genoa, Italy	Bremerhaven, West Germany
Shipyard	Dubigeon-Normandie SA (No. 123)	Cantieri Navali del Tirreno e Riuniti (No. 290)	A.G. Weser Werk (No. 935)
Engines	2 12-cyl. Pielstick 12 PC3V-480 diesels	4 10-cyl. Fiat C420.10L diesels	2 16-cyl. MAN 16V40/54 diesels
Propulsion	Geared, twin screw, controllable pitch	Geared, twin screw, controllable pitch	Geared, twin screw, controllable pitch
Other equipment	Converted car ferry	Bow thruster	Bow thruster; converted passenger-RO/RO cargo vessel
Passenger capacity	720	784	802
Notes	1	2	3

Name	*Mistral*	*European Vision*	*European Dream*
Previous name(s)			
Subsequent name(s)			
Owner	Auxilliaire Maritime J3ISA		
Flag	Wallis and Futuna Islands (France)		
Gross tons	47,276	58,600	
Dimensions (feet)	709 × 95 × 23		
Year built	1999	2001	2002
Place built	St. Nazaire, France	St. Nazaire, France	St. Nazaire, France
Shipyard	Chantiers de l'Atlantique (No. J-31)	Chantiers de l'Atlantique (No. V-31)	Chantiers de l'Atlantique
Engines	4 12-cyl. Wartsila 12V38 diesels		
Propulsion	Electric drive, twin screw		
Other equipment		2 Mermaid electric pod-propulsion units	2 Mermaid electric pod-propulsion units
Passenger capacity	1,196	1,566	1,566
Notes			

Notes

1. Acquired from Chandris in 1994.

2. Acquired from C.T.C. Cruises in 1998.

3. Acquired from Norwegian Cruise Line in 1997.

FLAGSHIP CRUISES (1972–1978)

Name	*Sea Venture*	*Island Venture*	*Kungsholm*
Previous name(s)			
Subsequent name(s)	*Pacific Princess*	*Island Princess*	*Sea Princess*
		Hyundai Pungak-Ho	*Victoria*
Owner	K/S Sea Venture A/S and Co.	K/S Cruise Venture A/S and Co.	Flagship Cruises, Ltd.
Flag	Norway	Norway	Liberia
Gross tons	19,903	19,907	18,174
Dimensions (feet)	554 × 81 × 23	554 × 81 × 23	660 × 87 × 28
Year built	1971	1972	1966
Place built	Rheinstahl, West Germany	Rheinstahl, West Germany	Clydebank, Scotland
Shipyard	Nordseewerke (No. 411)	Nordseewerke (No. 414)	John Brown (No. 728)
Engines	2 10-cyl. Fiat C420.10L diesels	2 10-cyl. Fiat C420.10L diesels	2 9-cyl. Gotaverken 760/1500VGS9 diesels
Propulsion	Geared, twin screw, controllable pitch	Geared, twin screw, controllable pitch	Geared, twin screw
Other equipment	Bow thruster	Bow thruster	Bow thruster
Passenger capacity	750	750	750
Notes	1	2	3

Notes

1. Sold to P&O/Princess in 1975.
2. Leased to Princess Cruises in 1972; purchased by P&O/Princess in 1974.
3. Acquired from Swedish American Line in 1975; sold to P&O Cruises in 1978.

FURNESS BERMUDA LINE (1919–1966)

Name	*Queen of Bermuda*	*Ocean Monarch*
Previous name(s)		
Subsequent name(s)		*Varna*
		Riviera
		Reina del Mar
Owner	Furness-Withy, Ltd.	Furness-Withy, Ltd.
Flag	U.K.	U.K.
Gross tons	22,575	13,824
Dimensions (feet)	580 × 77 × 27	516 × 72 × 24
Year built	1933	1951
Place built	Barrow, U.K.	Newcastle, U.K.
Shipyard	Vickers-Armstrongs (No. 681)	Vickers-Armstrongs (No. 119)
Engines	2 steam turbines	4 steam turbines
Propulsion	Electric drive, quadruple screw	Geared, twin screw
Other equipment		
Passenger capacity	1,466	430*
Notes	1	2

Notes

1. Served as both armed cruiser and troop transport during Second World War. Addition of a new bow increased vessel's length to 591 feet in 1961; scrapped in 1966.
2. Sold to Bulgarian interests about 1965.
*Total number of available berths.

GERMAN ATLANTIC LINE (1958–1974)

Name	*Hanseatic*	*Hanseatic*	*Hamburg*
Previous name(s)	*Empress of Japan* *Empress of Scotland* *Scotland*	*Shalom*	
Subsequent name(s)		*Doric* *Royal Odyssey* *Regent Sun* *Sun*	*Hanseatic* *Maksim Gorkiy*
Owner	Hamburg-Atlantic Line	Hanseatic Schiffahrts G.m.b.H.	Deutsche Atlantik Line
Flag	West Germany	West Germany	West Germany
Gross tons	30,030	25,320	24,981
Dimensions (feet)	667 × 84 × 32	628 × 82 × 27	638 × 87 × 27
Year built	1930	1964	1968
Place built	Glasgow, Scotland	St. Nazaire, France	Hamburg, West Germany
Shipyard	Fairfield Shipbuilding (No. 634)	Chantiers de l'Atlantique (No. Z-21)	Deutsche Werft (No. 997)
Engines	6 steam turbines	4 steam turbines	4 steam turbines
Propulsion	Geared, twin screw	Geared, twin screw	Geared, twin screw
Other equipment			
Passenger capacity	1,274*	1,090*	790*
Notes	1	2	3

Notes

1. Acquired from Canadian Pacific in 1958; scrapped following 1966 fire.
2. Acquired from Zim Israel Navigation Company in 1967; sold to Home Lines in 1973.
3. Sold to Black Sea Steamship Company about 1974.
*Total number of available berths.

HAPAG-LLOYD CRUISES

Hapag-Lloyd was formed by the merger of two German steamship lines with long transatlantic histories, Hamburg American Line and North German Lloyd. Only North German Lloyd resumed transatlantic passenger service following the Second World War.

Name	*Europa*	*Europa*	*Hanseatic*
Previous name(s)	*Kungsholm*		*Society Adventurer*
Subsequent name(s)	*Columbus C.*	*SuperStar Aires*	
Owner	Hapag-Lloyd A.G.	m.s. "Europa" der Breschag Bremer Schiffsvercharterungs	Hapag-Lloyd Cruiseship Management, G.m.b.H.
Flag	West Germany	West Germany; Germany	Bahamas
Gross tons	21,514	37,012	8,378

Continued

HAPAG-LLOYD CRUISES—*Continued*

Name	*Europa*	*Europa*	*Hanseatic*
Dimensions (feet)	600 × 77 × 26	655 × 94 × 28	403 × 59 × 15
Year built	1953	1981	1991
Place built	Vlissingen, Sweden	Bremen, West Germany	Rauma, Finland
Shipyard	N/V Koninklijke Maars. Schelde (No. 273)	Bremer Vulkan (No. 1,001)	Rauma Yards (No. 306)
Engines	2 8-cyl. B&W diesels	2 9-cyl. MAN K7SZ70/125B diesels	2 8-cyl. MaK 8M453C diesels
Propulsion	Geared, twin screw	Geared, twin screw, controllable pitch	Geared, twin screw, controllable pitch
Other equipment		Bow thruster	Bow thruster, hull strengthened for ice conditions
Passenger capacity	843*	632	188
Notes	1	2	3

Name	*Bremen*	*C. Columbus*	*Europa*
Previous name(s)	*Frontier Spirit*		
Subsequent name(s)			
Owner	J.G. Maritime, Ltd.	Conti I. Kreuzfahrt G.m.b.H.	Hapag-Lloyd
Flag	Bahamas	Bahamas	Bahamas
Gross tons	6,752	14,903	28,600
Dimensions (feet)	366 × 57 × 15	476 × 85 × 17	651 × 79 × 19
Year built	1990	1997	1999
Place built	Kobe, Japan	Wismar, Germany	Helsinki, Finland
Shipyard	Mitsubishi Heavy Industries (No. 1,182)	MTW Schiffswerft G.m.b.H. (No. 451)	Kvaerner Masa-Yards (No. 495)
Engines	2 8-cyl. Daihatsu 8DKM-32L diesels	4 6-cyl. Wartsila 6R32 diesels	2 7-cyl. MAN/B&W 7L40/54 diesels;2 8-cyl. MAN/B&W8:40/54 diesels
Propulsion	Geared, twin screw, controllable pitch	Geared, twin screw, controllable pitch	2 Azipod electric pod-propulsion units
Other equipment	Bow thruster	2 bow thrusters	2 bow thrusters
Passenger capacity	164	394	408*
Notes	4		

Name	*Astra II*
Previous name(s)	*Golden Odyssey*
Subsequent name(s)	
Owner	Astra II Shipping, Ltd.
Flag	Bahamas
Gross tons	6,757
Dimensions (feet)	427 × 64 × 17
Year built	1974
Place built	Helsingor, Denmark
Shipyard	Helsingor Vaerft A/S (No. 404)

Name	Astra II
Engines	2 12-cyl. Atlas-MaK 12M551AK diesels
Propulsion	Geared, twin screw
Other equipment	2 bow thrusters
Passenger capacity	460
Notes	5

Notes

1. Acquired from Swedish-American Line in 1975; sold to Costa Crocieri in 1980.

2. Sold to Star Cruises in 1997 but leased back to Hapag-Lloyd through June 1999.

3. Acquired from Hanseatic Cruises in 1996.

4. Acquired in 1993.

5. Acquired by charter in 1994.

*Total number of available berths.

HOLLAND AMERICA LINE

Name	Statendam (4)	Rotterdam (5)	Prinsendam
Previous name(s)			
Subsequent name(s)	Rhapsody	Rembrandt	
	Regent Sun		
	Sea Harmony		
Owner	Holland America Line	M.V. Mailship Rotterdam	N.V. Prinsendam
Flag	Netherlands	Netherlands	Netherlands
Gross tons	24,294	38,647	8,566
Dimensions (feet)	642 × 81 × 28	749 × 94 × 30	427 × 63 × 20
Year built	1957	1959	1973
Place built	Rotterdam, Netherlands	Rotterdam, Netherlands	Hardinxvled, Netherlands
Shipyard	Wilton-Fijenoord (No. 753)	Rotterdam Drydock (No. 300)	N.V. Scheepswerft (No. 606)
Engines	4 steam turbines	6 steam turbines	4 8-cyl. Stork-Werkspoor TM410 diesels
Propulsion	Geared, twin screw	Geared, twin screw	Geared, twin screw, controllable pitch
Other equipment			Bow thruster
Passenger capacity	740	1,456	374
Notes	1	2	3

Name	Veendam (2)	Volendam (2)	Nieuw Amsterdam (3)
Previous name(s)	Argentina	Brasil	
Subsequent name(s)	Brasil	Monarch Sun	Patriot
	Monarch Star	Volendam	
	Veendam	Island Sun	
	Bermuda Star	Liberte	
	Enchanted Isle	Canada Star	
	Commodore Hotel	Queen of Bermuda	
	Enchanted Isle	Enchanted Seas	
		Universe Explorer	

Continued

HOLLAND AMERICA LINE

Name	*Veendam* (2)	*Volendam* (2)	*Nieuw Amsterdam* (3)
Owner	N.V. Veendam	N.V. Volendam	HAL Antillen NV
Flag	Netherlands	Netherlands	Netherlands
Gross tons	23,372	23,372	33,930
Dimensions (feet)	598 × 88 × 27	598 × 88 × 27	704 × 89 × 25
Year built	1958	1958	1983
Place built	Pascagoula, Miss.	Pascagoula, Miss.	St. Nazaire, France
Shipyard	Ingalls Shipbuilding (No. 468)	Ingalls Shipbuilding (No. 467)	Chantiers de l'Atlantique (No. V-27)
Engines	4 steam turbines	4 steam turbines	2 7-cyl. Sulzer 7RLB66 diesels
Propulsion	Geared, twin screw	Geared, twin screw	Geared, twin screw, controllable pitch
Other equipment			2 bow thrusters, 1 stern thruster
Passenger capacity	713	693	1,214
Notes	4	5	6

Name	*Noordam* (3)	*Westerdam* (2)	*Statendam* (5)
Previous name(s)		*Homeric*	
Subsequent name(s)			
Owner	Holland America Cruises NV	HAL Antillen NV	HAL Nederland NV
Flag	Netherlands	Netherlands	Netherlands
Gross tons	33,933	53,872	55,451
Dimensions (feet)	704 × 89 × 24	798 × 98 × 24	719 × 101 × 25
Year built	1984	1986	1993
Place built	St. Nazaire, France	Papenburg, West Germany	Monfalcone, Italy
Shipyard	Chantiers de l'Atlantique (No. X-27)	Meyer Werft (No. 610)	Fincantieri (No. 5,881)
Engines	2 7-cyl. Sulzer 7RLB66 diesels	2 10-cyl. B&W 10L55GB diesels	2 12-cyl. Sulzer 12ZAV40S and 3 8-cyl. Sulzer 8ZAL40S diesels
Propulsion	Geared, twin screw, controllable pitch	Geared, twin screw, controllable pitch	Electric drive, twin screw, controllable pitch
Other equipment	2 bow thrusters, 1 stern thruster	2 bow thrusters, 1 stern thruster	2 bow thrusters, 1 stern thruster
Passenger capacity	1,214	1,476	1,266
Notes		7	

Name	*Maasdam* (4)	*Ryndam* (3)	*Veendam* (4)
Previous name(s)			
Subsequent name(s)			
Owner	HAL Nederland NV	HAL Nederland NV	Wind Surf, Ltd.
Flag	Netherlands	Netherlands	Bahamas
Gross tons	55,451	55,451	55,451
Dimensions (feet)	719 × 101 × 25	719 × 101 × 25	719 × 101 × 25

Name	*Maasdam* (4)	*Ryndam* (3)	*Veendam* (4)
Year built	1993	1994	1996
Place built	Monfalcone, Italy	Monfalcone, Italy	Marghera, Italy
Shipyard	Fincantieri (No. 5,882)	Fincantieri (No. 5,883)	Fincantieri (No. 5,954)
Engines	2 12-cyl. Sulzer 12ZAV40S and 3 8-cyl. Sulzer 8ZAL40S diesels	2 12-cyl. Sulzer 12ZAV40S and 3 8-cyl. Sulzer 8ZAL40S diesels	2 12-cyl. Sulzer 12ZAV40S and 3 8-cyl. Sulzer 8ZAL40S diesels
Propulsion	Electric drive, twin screw, controllable pitch	Electric drive, twin screw, controllable pitch	Electric drive, twin screw, controllable pitch
Other equipment	2 bow thrusters, 1 stern thruster	2 bow thrusters, 1 stern thruster	2 bow thrusters, 1 stern thruster
Passenger capacity	1,266	1,266	1,266
Notes			

Name	*Rotterdam* (6)	*Volendam* (3)	*Zaandam*
Previous name(s)			
Subsequent name(s)			
Owner	Holland America Tours	HAL Antillen NV	
Flag	Netherlands	Netherlands	Netherlands
Gross tons	59,652	60,906	60,906
Dimensions (feet)	780 × 106 × 26	781 × 106 × 26	781 × 106 × 26
Year built	1997	1999	2000
Place built	Marghera, Italy	Marghera, Italy	
Shipyard	Fincantieri (No. 5,980)	Fincantieri (No. 6,035)	Fincantieri
Engines	5 12-cyl. Sulzer 12ZAV40S diesels	5 12-cyl. Sulzer 12ZAV40S diesels	5 12-cyl. Sulzer 12ZAV40S diesels
Propulsion	Electric drive, twin screw, controllable pitch	Electric drive, twin screw, controllable pitch	Electric drive, twin screw, controllable pitch
Other equipment	2 bow thrusters, 2 stern thrusters	2 bow thrusters, 2 stern thrusters	2 bow thrusters, 2 stern thrusters
Passenger capacity	1,318	1,440	1,440
Notes			

Name	*Amsterdam* (3)	Newbuilding	Newbuilding
Previous name(s)			
Subsequent name(s)			
Owner			
Flag	Netherlands Antilles		
Gross tons	61,000	84,000	84,000
Dimensions (feet)	780 × 106 × 26	Length, 951	Length, 951
Year built	2000	2002	2003
Place built		Marghera, Italy	Marghera, Italy
Shipyard	Fincantieri	Fincantieri	Fincantieri
Engines	5 12-cyl. Sulzer diesels	Diesels and gas turbine	Diesels and gas turbine
Propulsion	2 Azipod electric pod-propulsion units	Pod-propulsion units	Pod-propulsion units
Other equipment	2 bow thrusters		
Passenger capacity	1,380	1,800	1,800
Notes			

Continued

HOLLAND AMERICA LINE—*Continued*

Name	Newbuilding	Newbuilding	Newbuilding
Previous name(s)			
Subsequent name(s)			
Owner			
Flag			
Gross tons	84,000	84,000	84,000
Dimensions (feet)	Length, 951	Length, 951	Length, 951
Year built	2003	2004	2005
Place built	Marghera, Italy	Marghera, Italy	Marghera, Italy
Shipyard	Fincantieri	Fincantieri	Fincantieri
Engines	Diesels and gas turbine	Diesels and gas turbine	Diesels and gas turbine
Propulsion	Pod-propulsion units	Pod-propulsion units	Pod-propulsion units
Other equipment			
Passenger capacity	1,800	1,800	1,800
Notes			

Notes

1. Sold to Paquet Cruises in 1981.

2. Sold to Premier Cruises in 1997.

3. Lost (sunk following fire)in the Gulf of Alaska in 1980.

4. Built for Moore-McCormick Lines; acquired in 1971 following three-year layup. Taken out of service in 1974. Conveyed to Monarch Cruise Lines in 1977; reverted to HAL when Holland America took over Monarch in 1978. Conveyed to Bermuda Star Line in 1984.

5. Built for Moore-McCormick Lines; acquired in 1971 following three-year layup. Taken out of service in 1974. Conveyed to Monarch Cruise Lines in 1975; reverted to HAL when Holland America took over Monarch in 1978. Conveyed to Island Sun Navigation Corp. in 1984.

6. Sold to United States Lines in 2000.

7. Acquired from Home Lines in 1988. Lengthened to dimensions shown from 1988 to 1989. (See Home Lines roster for dimensions prior to lengthening.)

HOME LINES (1949–1987)

Name	*Atlantic*	*Homeric*	*Doric*
Previous name(s)	*Malolo*	*Mariposa*	*Shalom*
	Matsonia		*Hanseatic*
Subsequent name(s)	*Queen Frederica*		*Royal Odyssey*
			Regent Sun
			Sun
Owner	Home Lines, Inc.	Home Lines, Inc.	Home Lines, Inc.
Flag	Greece	Panama	Panama
Gross tons	21,239	18,503	25,320
Dimensions (feet)	582 × 83 × 29	638 × 80 × 27	628 × 82 × 27
Year built	1927	1931	1964
Place built	Philadelphia, Pa.	Quincy, Mass.	St. Nazaire, France
Shipyard	Wm. Cramp & Sons (No. 509)	Bethlehem Steel (No. 1,440)	Chantiers de l'Atlantique (No. Z-21)
Engines	8 steam turbines	6 steam turbines	4 steam turbines
Propulsion	Geared, twin screw	Geared, twin screw	Geared, twin screw
Other equipment			
Passenger capacity	1,178*	704*	836

Name	*Atlantic*	*Homeric*	*Doric*
Notes	1	2	3

Name	*Oceanic*	*Atlantic*	*Homeric*
Previous name(s)			
Subsequent name(s)	*Royale Oceanic* *StarShip Oceanic* *The Big Red Boat I*	*StarShip Atlantic* *Melody*	*Westerdam*
Owner	Home Lines, Inc.	Home Lines, Inc.	Home Lines, Inc.
Flag	Panama	Liberia	Panama
Gross tons	39,241	19,337	42,092
Dimensions (feet)	782 × 97 × 28	672 × 90 × 46	669 × 98 × 24
Year built	1965	1982	1986
Place built	Monfalcone, Italy	La Seyne, France	Papenburg, West Germany
Shipyard	Cantieri Riuniti dell'Adriatico (No. 1,876)	CNIM (No. 1,432)	Meyer Werft (No. 610)
Engines	4 steam turbines	2 10-cyl. GMT B600-10L diesels	2 10-cyl. B&W 10L55GB diesels
Propulsion	Geared, twin screw	Geared, twin screw, controllable pitch	Geared, twin screw, controllable pitch
Other equipment		Bow thruster	2 bow thrusters
Passenger capacity	1,600	1,179*	1,030
Notes	4	5	6

Notes

1. Acquired from Matson Line in 1948; sold to Chandris in 1965.

2. Originally owned by Matson Line; acquired in 1953 following layup after World War II service as a troopship; damaged by fire in 1973 and scrapped in 1974.

3. Acquired from German Atlantic Line in 1973; sold to Royal Cruise Line in 1981.

4. Sold to Premier Cruises in 1985.

5. Sold to Holland America Line in 1988, but never operated for HAL; sold to Premier Cruise Lines.

6. Sold to Holland America Line in 1988.

*Total number of available berths.

IMPERIAL MAJESTY CRUISE LINE

Name	*OceanBreeze*
Previous name(s)	*Southern Cross* *Calypso I* *Calypso* *Azure Seas*
Subsequent name(s)	
Owner	
Flag	Liberia
Gross tons	14,673
Dimensions (feet)	604 × 78 × 25
Year built	1955

Continued

IMPERIAL MAJESTY CRUISE LINE—*Continued*

Name	*OceanBreeze*
Place built	Belfast, Northern Ireland
Shipyard	Harland & Wolff
	(No. 1,498)
Engines	2 steam turbines
Propulsion	Geared, twin screw
Other equipment	
Passenger capacity	734
Notes	1

Notes

1. Acquired from Premier by charter in 1999; lease converted to purchase in 2000.

INCRES LINE (1950–1975)

Name	*Nassau*	*Victoria*
Previous name(s)	*Mongolia*	*Dunnottar Castle*
	Rimutaka	
	Europa	
Subsequent name(s)	*Acapulco*	*The Victoria*
		Princesa Victoria
Owner	Incres Steamship Co., Ltd.	Incres Steamship Co., Ltd.
Flag	Liberia	Liberia
Gross tons	15,043	14,917
Dimensions (feet)	573 × 72 × 30	573 × 72 × 26
Year built	1923	1936
Place built	Newcastle, U.K.	Belfast, Northern Ireland
Shipyard	Armstrong, Whitworth, Ltd. (No. 964)	Harland and Wolff (No. 959)
Engines	6 steam turbines	2 B&W diesels
Propulsion	Geared, twin screw	Geared, twin screw
Other equipment		
Passenger capacity	410	831*
Notes	1	2

Notes

1. Acquired from New Zealand Shipping Company in 1950; sold to Cia. Naviera Turistica Mexicana for cruise service between Los Angeles and Mexico in 1961.
2. Acquired from Union-Castle Line in 1958; B&W diesels replaced by Fiat diesels in 1959; sold to Chandris in 1975.

* Total number of available berths.

MAJESTY CRUISE LINE (1992–1997)

Name	*Royal Majesty*	*Crown Majesty*
Previous name(s)		*Crown Dynasty*
Subsequent name(s)	*Norwegian Majesty*	*Norwegian Dynasty*
		Crown Dynasty

Name	*Royal Majesty*	*Crown Majesty*
Owner	Compania Naviera S.A.	Crown Dynasty, Inc.
Flag	Bahamas	Panama
Gross tons	32,396	19,089
Dimensions (feet)	568 × 89 × 20	537 × 74 × 18
Year built	1992	1993
Place built	Turku, Finland	Valencia, Spain
Shipyard	Kvaerner Masa-Yards (No. 1,312)	Union Naval de Levante (No. 198)
Engines	4 6-cyl. Wartsila 6R46 diesels	4 8-cyl. Wartsila 8R32E diesels
Propulsion	Geared, twin screw, controllable pitch	Geared, twin screw, controllable pitch
Other equipment	2 bow thrusters	2 bow thrusters
Passenger capacity	1,056	820
Notes	1	2

Notes

1. Intended to be car ferry, but completed as cruise ship; conveyed to Norwegian Cruise Line in 1997.

2. Chartered from Effjohn International in 1997; lease transferred to Norwegian Cruise Line in 1997.

MEDITERRANEAN SHIPPING CRUISES

Name	*Melody*	*Monterey*	*Symphony*
Previous name(s)	*Atlantic* *StarShip Atlantic*	*Free State Mariner*	*Provence* *Enrico C.* *Enrico Costa*
Subsequent name(s)			*Aegean II*
Owner	Westria Holdings, Inc.	Compania Naviera Panocean, SA	Navitalia S.r.I.
Flag	Panama	Panama	Italy
Gross tons	35,143	20,046	16,741
Dimensions (feet)	672 × 90 × 46	564 × 76 × 29	579 × 73 × 25
Year built	1982	1952	1950
Place built	La Seyne, France	Sparrows Point, Md.	Wallsend, U.K.
Shipyard	CNIM (No. 1,432)	Bethlehem Steel (No. 4,507)	Swan, Hunter & Wigham Richardson, Ltd. (No. 1,874)
Engines	2 10-cyl. GMT B600.10L diesels	2 steam turbines	2 16-cyl. Wartsila 16V32 diesels
Propulsion	Geared, twin screw, controllable pitch	Geared, single screw	Geared, twin screw, controllable pitch
Other equipment	Bow thruster		Bow thruster
Passenger capacity	1,064	639	664
Notes	1	2	3

Continued

MEDITERRANEAN SHIPPING CRUISES—*Continued*

Name	*Rhapsody*
Previous name(s)	*Cunard Conquest*
	Cunard Princess
Subsequent name(s)	
Owner	Gramerco International
Flag	Panama
Gross tons	16,852
Dimensions (feet)	537 × 75 × 19
Year built	1974
Place built	Copenhagen, Denmark
Shipyard	A/S Burmeister & Wain (No. 859)
Engines	4 7-cyl. B&W 7U50HU diesels
Propulsion	Geared, twin screw, controllable pitch
Other equipment	Bow thruster
Passenger capacity	810
Notes	4

Notes

1. Acquired from Premier in 1997.

2. Converted into passenger vessel from Mariner-class cargo ship *Free State Mariner;* acquired about 1994.

3. Acquired from Costa in 1994; conveyed to Golden Sun Cruises about 1997.

4. Chartered from Paquet in 1995.

MISCELLANEOUS VESSELS

Name	*Nili*	*Bilu*	*Viking Princess*
Previous name(s)			*Lavoisier*
			Riviera Prima
Subsequent name(s)	*Jamaica Queen*	*Dan*	
	Nili	*El Greco*	
		Saudi Moon	
		Golden Sky	
		Vergina	
		Mir	
Owner	Nili-Somerfin Car Ferries, Ltd.	Bilu-Somerfin Car Ferries, Ltd.	A/S Sigline
Flag	Israel	Israel	Norway
Gross tons	7,851	6,445	12,812
Dimensions (feet)	450 × 62 × 17	419 × 61 × 17	537 × 65 × 22
Year built	1965	1964	1950
Place built	Glasgow, Scotland	Hoboken, Belgium	St. Nazaire, France
Shipyard	Fairfield Shipbuilding	S.A. Cockerill-Ougree (No. 810)	At. & Ch. de la Loire
Engines	2 6-cyl. Sulzer diesels	2 7-cyl. Fiat 600.7S diesels	2 8-cyl. Sulzer diesels
Propulsion	Geared, twin screw	Geared, twin screw	Geared, twin screw

Name	*Nili*	*Bilu*	*Viking Princess*
Other equipment	Bow thruster; RO/RO	Bow thruster; RO/RO	
Passenger capacity	544*	362	
Notes	1	2	3

Name	*Florida*	*Achille Lauro*
Previous name(s)		*Willem Ruys*
Subsequent name(s)	*Le Palais Flottant*	
Owner	Blue Steamship Company	Starlauro S.p.A.
Flag	Liberia	Italy
Gross tons	4,956	23,629
Dimensions (feet)	388 × 57 × 20	643 × 82 × 29
Year built	1931	1946
Place built	Newport News, Va.	Flushing, Netherlands
Shipyard	Newport News Shipbuilding	De Schelde NV (No. 214)
Engines	4 steam turbines	8 8-cyl. Sulzer diesels
Propulsion	Geared, twin screw	Geared, twin screw
Other equipment		
Passenger capacity	500*	1,097*
Notes	4	5

Notes

1. See chapter 3; operated in south Florida cruise service by Arison Shipping in 1966.

2. See chapter 3; operated in south Florida cruise service about 1966.

3. See chapter 1; lost to fire on April 8, 1966.

4. Operated by Peninsular and Occidental Steamship Lines; initially ran between Miami and Havana; operated some cruise service to the Bahamas in early1960s; retired in 1966 and scrapped in 1968.

5. Vessel laid down in 1939; little work done until after Second World War. Taken over by terrorists on October 7, 1985, between Alexandria and Port Said; one passenger murdered.

*Total number of available berths.

NORWEGIAN-AMERICAN LINE (1910–1983)

Name	*Oslofjord*	*Bergensfjord*	*Sagafjord*
Previous name(s)			
Subsequent name(s)	*Fulvia*	*De Grasse*	*Gripsholm*
		Rasa Sayang	*Saga Rose*
		Golden Moon	
Owner	Den Norske Amerikalinje A/S	Den Norske Amerikalinje A/S	Den Norske Amerikalinje A/S
Flag	Norway	Norway	Norway
Gross tons	16,844	18,739	24,002
Dimensions (feet)	577 × 72 × 27	578 × 72 × 28	620 × 80 × 27
Year built	1949	1956	1965
Place built	Amsterdam, Netherlands	Wallsend-on-Tyne, U.K.	La Seyne, France
Shipyard	Netherlands Dock & Shipbuilding (No. 410)	Swan, Hunter & Wigham Richardson (No. 1,849)	Forges & Ch. de la Mediterranee (No. 1,366)

Continued

NORWEGIAN-AMERICAN LINE (1910–1983)—*Continued*

Name	*Oslofjord*	*Bergensfjord*	*Sagafjord*
Engines	2 7-cyl. Stork diesels	2 8-cyl. Stork diesels	2 9-cyl. Sulzer 9RD68 diesels
Propulsion	Geared, twin screw	Geared, twin screw	Geared, twin screw
Other equipment			Bow thruster
Passenger capacity		878	789
Notes	1	2	3

Name	*Vistafjord*
Previous name(s)	
Subsequent name(s)	*Caronia*
Owner	Den Norske Amerikalinje A/S
Flag	Norway
Gross tons	24,292
Dimensions (feet)	628 × 82 × 27
Year built	1973
Place built	Newcastle, U.K.
Shipyard	Swan, Hunter & Wigham Richardson (No. 39)
Engines	2 9-cyl. Sulzer 9RD68 diesels
Propulsion	Geared, twin screw
Other equipment	Bow thruster
Passenger capacity	600
Notes	3

Notes

1. Chartered to Greek Line in 1967; chartered to Costa in 1968; lost to fire in 1970.

2. Conveyed to French Line in 1971.

3. Conveyed to Cunard Line in 1983.

NORWEGIAN CRUISE LINE

Company began operations in 1966 as Norwegian Caribbean Line.
Name changed to Norwegian Cruise Line in 1987.

Name	*Sunward*	*Starward*	*Skyward*
Previous name(s)			
Subsequent name(s)	*Ile de Beaute*	*Bolero*	*Shangri-la World*
	Grand Flotel		*Asean World*
	Saudi Moon I		*Fantasy World*
	Ocean Spirit		*Continental World*
	Scandinavian Song		*Leisure World*
	Santiago de Cuba		
	The Empress		
Owner	Kloster Rederi R/A	Kloster Cruise Ltd.	Kloster Cruise Ltd.
Flag	Norway	Norway; Bahamas	Norway; Bahamas
Gross tons	8,666	16,107	16,254
Dimensions (feet)	457 × 68 × 17	525 × 75 × 22	525 × 75 × 22

Name	*Sunward*	*Starward*	*Skyward*
Year built	1966	1968	1969
Place built	Bergen, Norway	Bremerhaven, West Germany	Bremerhaven, West Germany
Shipyard	A/S Bergens MV (No. 455)	A.G. Weser Werk (No. 935)	A.G. Weser Werk (No. 942)
Engines	2 12-cyl. B&W 12-42VT2BF-90 diesels	2 16-cyl. MAN V16V40/54 diesels	2 16-cyl. MAN V16V40/54 diesels
Propulsion	Geared, twin screw	Geared, twin screw, controllable pitch	Geared, twin screw, controllable pitch
Other equipment	Bow thruster, stern door and ramp	Bow thruster, side door, stern door and ramp	Bow thruster
Passenger capacity	540*	736	728
Notes	1	2	3

Name	*Southward*	*Norway*	*Sunward II*
Previous name(s)		*France*	*Cunard Adventurer*
Subsequent name(s)	*Seawing*		*Triton*
Owner	Kloster Cruise Ltd.	Norwegian Cruise Line	Kloster Cruise Ltd.
Flag	Norway; Bahamas	Norway; Bahamas	Bahamas
Gross tons	16,607	76,049	14,110
Dimensions (feet)	536 × 75 × 21	1035 × 111 × 34	486 × 72 × 19
Year built	1971	1961	1971
Place built	Riva, Italy	St. Nazaire, France	Rotterdam, Netherlands
Shipyard	Cantieri Navali del Tirreno e Riuniti (No. 288)	Chantiers de l'Atlantique (No. G-19)	Rotterdam Drydock (No. 329)
Engines	4 10-cyl. Fiat diesels	4 steam turbines	4 12-cyl. Stork-Werkspoor 12TM410 diesels
Propulsion	Geared, twin screw, controllable pitch	Twin screw	Geared, twin screw, controllable pitch
Other equipment	Bow thruster, converted passenger/RO-RO cargo	3 bow thrusters, 2 stern thrusters	2 bow thrusters
Passenger capacity	727	2,032	832*
Notes	4	5	6

Name	*Westward*	*Sunward*	*Seaward*
Previous name(s)	*Royal Viking Star*	*Royal Viking Sky*	
Subsequent name(s)	*Star Odyssey*	*Birka Queen*	*Norwegian Sea*
	Black Watch	*Golden Princess*	
		SuperStar Capricorn	
		Hyundai Keumkang	
Owner	Kloster Cruise Ltd.	Kloster Cruise Ltd.	Norwegian Cruise Line
Flag	Bahamas	Bahamas	Bahamas
Gross tons	28,492	20,078	42,276
Dimensions (feet)	674 × 83 × 25	675 × 83 × 24	709 × 107 × 23
Year built	1972	1973	1988

Continued

NORWEGIAN CRUISE LINE—*Continued*

Name	*Westward*	*Sunward*	*Seaward*
Place built	Helsinki, Finland	Helsinki, Finland	Turku, Finland
Shipyard	Wartsila (No. 395)	Wartsila (No. 396)	Wartsila (No. 1,294)
Engines	4 9-cyl. Sulzer 9ZH40/48 diesels	4 9-cyl. Sulzer 9ZH40/48 diesels	4 8-cyl. Sulzer 8ZAL40S diesels
Propulsion	Geared, twin screw, controllable pitch	Geared, twin screw, controllable pitch	Geared, twin screw, controllable pitch
Other equipment	2 bow thrusters	2 bow thrusters	2 bow thrusters
Passenger capacity	794	740	1,548
Notes	7	8	

Name	*Dreamward*	*Windward*	*Leeward*
Previous name(s)			*Viking Saga* *Sally Albatross*
Subsequent name(s)	*Norwegian Dream*	*Norwegian Wind*	*SuperStar Taurus*
Owner	Norwegian Cruise Line	Norwegian Cruise Line	Crown Jewel, Inc.
Flag	Bahamas	Bahamas	Panama
Gross tons	39,217	39,277	25,611
Dimensions (feet)	624 × 95 × 23	624 × 95 × 23	521 × 83 × 23
Year built	1992	1993	1980
Place built	St. Nazaire, France	St. Nazaire, France	Turku, Finland
Shipyard	Chantiers de l'Atlantique (No. C-30)	Chantiers de l'Atlantique (No. D-30)	Wartsila (No. 1,247)
Engines	2 8-cyl. MAN 8L40.54 diesels and 2 6-cyl. MAN 6L40/54 diesels	2 8-cyl. MAN 8L40.54 diesels and 2 6-cyl. MAN 6L40/54 diesels	4 12-cyl. Pielstick 12PC2-5V-400 diesels
Propulsion	Geared, twin screw, controllable pitch	Geared, twin screw, controllable pitch	Geared, twin screw, controllable pitch
Other equipment	2 bow thrusters	2 bow thrusters	2 bow thrusters; see note
Passenger capacity	1,242	1,246	950
Notes	9	9	10

Name	*Norwegian Crown*	*Norwegian Majesty*	*Norwegian Dynasty*
Previous name(s)	*Crown Odyssey*	*Royal Majesty*	*Crown Dynasty* *Crown Majesty*
Subsequent name(s)	*Crown Odyssey*		*Crown Dynasty*
Owner	Norwegian Cruise Line	Norwegian Cruise Line	Crown Dynasty, Inc.
Flag	Bahamas	Bahamas	Panama
Gross tons	34,242	32, 396	19,093
Dimensions (feet)	616 × 96 × 24	568 × 89 × 20	537 × 74 × 18
Year built	1988	1992	1993
Place built	Papenburg, West Germany	Turku, Finland	Valencia, Spain
Shipyard	Meyer Werft (No. 616)	Kvaerner Masa-Yards (No. 1,312)	Union Naval de Levante (No. 198)
Engines	2 6-cyl. Krupp MaK 6M35 diesels, 2 8-cyl. Krupp MaK 8M601AK diesels	4 6-cyl. Wartsila 6R46 diesels	4 8-cyl. Wartsila 8R32E diesels

Name	*Norwegian Crown*	*Norwegian Majesty*	*Norwegian Dynasty*
Propulsion	Geared, twin screw, controllable pitch	Geared, twin screw, controllable pitch	Geared, twin screw, controllable pitch
Other equipment	2 bow thrusters	2 bow thrusters	2 bow thrusters
Passenger capacity	1,052	1,056	820
Notes	11	12	13

Name	*Norwegian Star*	*Aida*	*Norwegian Sky*
Previous name(s)	*Royal Viking Sea* *Royal Odyssey*		See note
Subsequent name(s)	*SuperStar Capricorn*		
Owner	Actinor Cruise, AS	Norwegian Cruise Line	Norwegian Cruise Line
Flag	Bahamas	Liberia	Bahamas
Gross tons	28,018	38,531	77,104
Dimensions (feet)	674 × 89 × 25	634 × 107 × 20	848 × 106 × 26
Year built	1973	1996	1999
Place built	Helsinki, Finland	Turku, Finland	Bremen, Germany
Shipyard	Wartsila (No. 397)	Kvaerner Masa-Yards (No. 1,337)	Vulkan Werft (No. 108)
Engines	4 9-cyl. Sulzer 9ZH40/48 diesels	4 6-cyl. MAN-B&W 6L48/60 diesels	3 6-cyl. MAN 6L58/64 and 3 7-cyl. MAN 7L58/64 diesels
Propulsion	Geared, twin screw, controllable pitch	Electric drive, twin screw, controllable pitch	Electric drive, twin screw, controllable pitch
Other equipment	2 bow thrusters	2 bow thrusters	3 bow thrusters, 2 stern thrusters
Passenger capacity	798	1,186	2,002
Notes	14	15	16

Name	*Norwegian Sun*	Newbuilding
Previous name(s)		See note
Subsequent name(s)		
Owner		
Flag	Bahamas	
Gross tons	77,104	91,000
Dimensions (feet)	853 × 108 × 26	961 × 106
Year built	2001	2002
Place built	Bremerhaven, Germany	Papenburg, Germany
Shipyard	Lloyd Werft	Meyer Werft
Engines	Diesel	
Propulsion	Electric drive, twin screw, controllable pitch	
Other equipment		
Passenger capacity		2,300
Notes		17

Notes

1. Transferred from Klosters Sunward Ferries, Ltd. in 1966; sold to French interests in 1973.

2. Sold to Festival Cruises in 1997.

Continued

NORWEGIAN CRUISE LINE—*Continued*

3. Chartered to Far Eastern interests in 1992; charter converted to sale about 1995.

4. Sold to Airtours in 1994.

5. Built for French Line; acquired after five-year layup in 1979. Gross registered tonnage in 1979 was 66,348.

6. Acquired from Cunard in 1977; transferred to Epirotiki in 1991 with full sale completed in 1994.

7. Acquired from Royal Viking Line in 1991; transferred to Royal Cruise Line in 1994.

8. Acquired from Royal Viking Line in 1991; sold to Birka Line in early 1990s, with short-term lease back to NCL.

9. Stretched at Lloyd Werft in Bremerhaven, West Germany, in 1998, with new dimensions as follows: 50,760 gross registered tons, 754 feet long, passenger capacity of 1,748. Stretching procedure reduced draft from 23 feet to 22.

10. Built as Baltic Sea car ferry; leased by NCL from 1995 through 1999.

11. Acquired from Royal Cruise Line in 1995; conveyed to NCL-controlled Orient Line in 1999.

12. Purchased from Majesty Cruise Line in 1997. Stretched at Lloyd Werft in Bremerhaven, West Germany, in 1999, with new dimensions as follows: 40,876 gross registered tons, 680 feet long, passenger capacity of 1,462.

13. Leased by NCL from 1998 to 1999.

14. Acquired in 1997; later transferred to NCL-controlled Norwegian Capricorn Line. Acquired by Star Cruises in 2000.

15. Acquired in 1998; never operated for NCL but was leased back to previous owner, Arkona Touristik. Resold to Arkona Touristik in 1999. (Arkona Touristik later established a new cruise company in partnership with P&O Cruises that was called Aida Cruises.)

16. Hull constructed in Bremen, West Germany, at Vulkan Werft and was intended to be Costa Crociere's *Costa Olympia*. Work suspended in October 1996 when yard went bankrupt. Hull acquired by NCL and completed at Lloyd Werft in Bremerhaven as *Norwegian Sky*.

17. Vessel was ordered by Star Cruises with the intention it would become *SuperStar Scorpio*. When Star Cruises acquired NCL, it was announced vessel would be assigned to NCL when it is completed in 2002.

*Total number of available berths.

ORIENT LINES

Name	*Marco Polo*	*Crown Odyssey*
Previous name(s)	*Aleksandr Pushkin*	*Crown Odyssey*
		Norwegian Crown
Subsequent name(s)		
Owner	Fiducia Shipping Co. SA	Norwegian Cruise Line
Flag	Bahamas	Bahamas
Gross tons	22,080	34,250
Dimensions (feet)	578 × 77 × 27	616 × 96 × 24
Year built	1965	1988
Place built	Wismar, East Germany	Papenburg, West Germany
Shipyard	Mathias-Thesen Werft (No. 126)	Meyer Werft (No. 616)
Engines	2 7-cyl. Sulzer 7RND76 diesels	2 6-cyl. Krupp MaK 6M35 diesels and 2 8-cyl. Krupp MaK 8M601MK diesels
Propulsion	Geared, twin screw	Geared, twin screw, controllable pitch
Other equipment	Bow thruster, side doors	2 bow thrusters
Passenger capacity	850	1,052
Notes	1	2

Notes

1. Acquired from Baltic Shipping Company in 1991.

2. Conveyed from Norwegian Cruise Line in 2000.

P&O CRUISES
INCLUDING P&O HOLIDAY CRUISES

Name	*Arcadia*	*Oriana*	*Canberra*
Previous name(s)			
Subsequent name(s)			
Owner	P&O Steam Navigation Co.	P&O Lines	P&O Lines
Flag	U.K.	U.K.	U.K.
Gross tons	29,735	41,923	45,733
Dimensions (feet)	721 × 91 × 31	804 × 97 × 31	820 × 104 × 33
Year built	1954	1960	1961
Place built	Clydebank, Scotland	Barrow-in-Furness, U.K.	Belfast, Northern Ireland
Shipyard	John Brown (No. 675)	Vickers-Armstrongs (No. 1,061)	Harland & Wolff (No 1,621)
Engines	6 steam turbines	Steam turbines	2 steam turbines
Propulsion	Geared, twin screw	Geared, twin screw	Electric drive, twin screw
Other equipment			Bow thruster
Passenger capacity	1,410*	2,134	1,706
Notes	1	2	3

Name	*Spirit of London*	*Fair Princess*	*Fairstar*
Previous name(s)		*Carinthia* *Fairland* *Fairsea*	*Oxfordshire*
Subsequent name(s)	*Sun Princess* *Starship Majestic* *Southern Cross* *Flamenco*	*Regent Isle* *Fair Princess*	*Ripa*
Owner	P&O Lines, Ltd.	P&O Holidays, Ltd.	Fairstar Shipping Corp.
Flag	U.K.	Liberia	Liberia
Gross tons	17,370	24,799	21,619
Dimensions (feet)	536 × 81 × 21	608 × 80 × 29	609 × 78 × 28
Year built	1972	1956	1957
Place built	Genoa, Italy	Clydebank, Scotland	Glasgow, Scotland
Shipyard	Cantieri Navali del Tirreno e Riuniti (No. 290)	John Brown (No. 699)	Fairfield Shipbuilding (No. 775)
Engines	4 10-cyl. Fiat C420.10L diesels	4 steam turbines	4 steam turbines
Propulsion	Geared, twin screw, controllable pitch	Geared, twin screw	Geared, twin screw
Other equipment			
Passenger capacity	876	962	976
Notes	4	5	6

Name	*Sea Princess*	*Oriana*	*Arcadia*
Previous name(s)	*Kungsholm*		*Star Princess*
Subsequent name(s)	*Victoria*		

Continued

P&O CRUISES—*Continued*

Name	*Sea Princess*	*Oriana*	*Arcadia*
Owner	P&O Lines, Ltd.	P&O Steam Navigation Co.	P&O Steam Navigation Co.
Flag	U.K.	U.K.	U.K.
Gross tons	27,670	69,153	63,524
Dimensions (feet)	660 × 87 × 28	853 × 106 × 26	806 × 106 × 27
Year built	1966	1995	1989
Place built	Clydebank, Scotland	Papenburg, Germany	St. Nazaire, France
Shipyard	John Brown (No. 728)	Meyer Werft (No. 636)	Chantiers de l'Atlantique (No. B-29)
Engines	2 9-cyl. Gotaverken 760/1500VGS9 diesels	2 9-cyl. MAN 9L58/64 and 2 6-cyl. MAN 6L58/64 diesels	4 8-cyl. MAN 8L58/64 diesels
Propulsion	Geared, twin screw	Geared, twin screw, controllable pitch	Electric drive, twin screw
Other equipment	Bow thruster	3 bow thrusters, 1 stern thruster	2 bow thrusters, 1 stern thruster
Passenger capacity	778	1,828	1,470
Notes	7		8

Name	*Aurora*	*Pacific Sky*	Newbuilding
Previous name(s)		*Fairsky* *Sky Princess*	
Subsequent name(s)			
Owner	P&O Cruises	P&O Holidays, Ltd.	
Flag	U.K.	U.K.	U.K.
Gross tons	76,152	46,078	109,000
Dimensions (feet)	886 × 106 × 26	787 × 92 × 26	951 × 118 × 26
Year built	2000	1984	
Place built	Papenburg, Germany	La Seyne, France	Monfalcone, Italy
Shipyard	Meyer Werft (No. 640)	CNIM Shipyards (No. 1,436)	Fincantieri
Engines	4 14-cyl. MAN 14V48/60 diesels	4 steam turbines	6 16-cyl. Sulzer 16ZAV40S diesels
Propulsion	Electric drive, twin screw	Geared, twin screw	Electric drive, twin screw
Other equipment	3 bow thrusters, 1 stern thruster	Bow thruster	3 bow thrusters, 3 stern thrusters
Passenger capacity	1,840	1,212	2,600
Notes		9	10

Notes

1. Scrapped in 1979.

2. Sold to Japanese interests in 1986; converted to museum ship.

3. Withdrawn from service in 1997; scrapped.

4. Conveyed to P&O-controlled Princess Cruises in 1974.

5. Acquired when Sitmar Cruises was purchased by P&O in 1988 and assigned to P&O-controlled Princess Cruises; was to have been sold to Regency Cruises in 1995 to become *Regent Isle*, but sale was never finalized. Conveyed to P&O Holiday Cruises in 1997.

6. Acquired when Sitmar Cruises was purchased by P&O in 1988; only vessel to retain Sitmar name while in P&O service. Withdrawn from service in 1997.

7. Acquired from Flagship in 1978. Operated as *Sea Princess* for both P&O and Princess Cruises.

8. Conveyed from P&O-controlled Princess Cruises in 1997.

9. Scheduled to be conveyed from P&O-controlled Princess Cruises in late 2000.

10. Post-Panamax vessel; will not fit through the Panama Canal.

* Total number of available berths.

PACIFIC FAR EAST LINE (1971–1980)

Name	*Mariposa*	*Monterey*
Previous name(s)	*Pine Tree Mariner*	*Free State Mariner*
Subsequent name(s)	*Jin Pang*	
	Queen of Jin Jiang	
	Henge Li	
Owner	American World Line, Inc.	American Maritime Holdings
Flag (Off. No.)	U.S. (265137)	U.S. (264687)
Gross tons	14,799	14,799
Dimensions (feet)	563 × 70 × 29	564 × 76 × 29
Year built	1953	1952
Place built	Quincy, Mass.	Sparrows Point, Md.
Shipyard	Bethlehem Steel (No. 1,624)	Bethlehem Steel (No. 4,507)
Engines	2 steam turbines	2 steam turbines
Propulsion	Geared, single screw	Geared, single screw
Other equipment		
Passenger capacity	365*	365*
Notes	1	2

Notes

1. Converted into passenger vessel from Mariner-class cargo ship *Pine Tree Mariner* in 1956. Acquired from Matson Line in 1971; sold to Far Eastern interests in 1980.

2. Converted into passenger vessel from Mariner-class cargo ship *Free State Mariner* in 1956. Acquired from Matson Line in 1971; conveyed to Aloha Pacific Cruises for further operation under U.S. flag in 1980. Later acquired by Mediterranean Shipping Cruises.

*Total number of available berths.

PAQUET (1860–1993)

Company founded in 1860 as a Mediterranean shipping enterprise. Activity in North American cruise markets began in 1960s but was not continuous. Acquired by Costa Crociere in 1993, although some operation under Paquet flag in subsequent years.

Name	*Mermoz*	*Renaissance*	*Massalia*
Previous name(s)	*Jean Mermoz*		
Subsequent name(s)		*Homeric Renaissance*	*Stena Baltica*
		World Renaissance	*Island Fiesta*
		Awani Dream	*Scandinavian Star*
		World Renaissance	*Candi*
			Regal Voyager

Continued

PAQUET (1860–1993)—*Continued*

Name	*Mermoz*	*Renaissance*	*Massalia*
Owner	Chargeurs Savamo	Nouvelle Compagnie de Paquebots	Nouvelle Compagnie de Paquebots
Flag	France; Bahamas	France	France
Gross tons	13,804	11, 724	10,513
Dimensions (feet)	531 × 65 × 21	492 × 69 × 20	465 × 72 × 18
Year built	1957	1966	1971
Place built	St. Nazaire, France	St. Nazaire, France	Nantes, France
Shipyard	Chantiers de l'Atlantique (No. D-17)	Chantiers de l'Atlantique (No. D-23)	Dubigeon-Normandie (No. 124)
Engines	2 6-cyl. B&W 7-62VTBF-115 diesels	2 6-cyl. B&W 6-62VT2BF-90 diesels	2 16-cyl. Pielstick 16PC2V-400 diesels
Propulsion	Geared, twin screw	Geared, twin screw	Geared, twin screw, controllable pitch
Other equipment		Side door	2 bow thrusters, stern door and ramp, bow door and ramp
Passenger capacity	556	528	230
Notes	1	2	3

Name	*Azur*	*Dolphin IV*	*Rhapsody*
Previous name(s)	*Eagle*	*Zion* *Amelia de Mello* *Ithaca*	*Statendam*
Subsequent name(s)	*The Azur*		*Regent Star* *Sea Harmony*
Owner	Nouvelle Compagnie de Paquebots	Cia. de Vapores Realma, S.A.	Arctus Investment, Inc.
Flag	France	Panama	Bahamas
Gross tons	11,609	6,695	24,413
Dimensions (feet)	465 × 74 × 18	502 × 65 × 28	642 × 81 × 26
Year built	1971	1956	1957
Place built	Nantes, France	Hamburg, West Germany	Schiedam, Netherlands
Shipyard	Dubigeon-Normandie (No. 123)	Deutsche Werft (No. 691)	Wilton-Fijenoord (No. 753)
Engines	2 12-cyl. Pielstick 12PC3V-480 diesels	2 steam turbines	4 steam turbines
Propulsion	Geared, twin screw, controllable pitch	Geared, single screw	Twin screw
Other equipment	Stern door and ramp		
Passenger capacity	688	588	650*
Notes	4	5	6

Name	*Ocean Pearl*	*Rhapsody*
Previous name(s)	*Finlandia* *Finnstar* *Innstar* *Pearl of Scandinavia*	*Cunard Conquest* *Cunard Princess*

Name	*Ocean Pearl*	*Rhapsody*
Subsequent name(s)	*Pearl*	
	Costa Playa	
	Oriental Pearl	
Owner	Sodimarit S.A.	Gramerco International Corp.
Flag		Panama
Gross tons	12,704	16,852
Dimensions (feet)	502 × 66 × 18	537 × 75 × 20
Year built	1967	1974
Place built	Helsinki, Finland	Copenhagen, Denmark
Shipyard	Wartsila (No. 383)	A/S Burmeister & Wain (No. 859)
Engines	4 9-cyl. Sulzer 9ZH40/48 diesels	4 7-cyl. B&W 7U50HU diesels
Propulsion	Geared, twin screw, controllable pitch	Geared, twin screw, controllable pitch
Other equipment	2 bow thrusters, stern door and ramp	Bow thruster
Passenger capacity	512	810
Notes	7	8

Notes

1. Acquired from Fabre Line in 1965; conveyed to Louis Cruises about 1999.

2. Acquired from Cie Francaise de Nav. in 1970; conveyed to Epirotiki in 1977.

3. Conveyed to Stena in 1984.

4. Acquired from Eagle Ferries Division of P&O Lines in 1975; converted from car ferry to cruise ship in 1981; conveyed to Azur Transportation for charter to Chandris in 1987.

5. Acquired from Greek interests in 1978; jointly managed by Paquet and Ulysses Line; conveyed to Dolphin in 1984.

6. Acquired from Holland America Line in 1981; chartered to Westours for summer season in 1983; conveyed to Regency Cruises in 1986.

7. Acquired from Ocean Cruise Line in 1990 when Ocean merged with Paquet; conveyed to Costa Crociere in 1995, following latter's acquisition of Paquet in 1993.

8. Acquired from Cunard in 1995; chartered to Mediterranean Shipping Cruises in 1995.

*Total number of available berths.

PREMIER CRUISE LINES (1984–2000)
INCLUDING DOLPHIN CRUISE LINE AND SEAWIND CRUISE LINE

Premier Cruise Lines inaugurated service in 1984, Dolphin Cruise Line in the same year, Seawind Cruise Line in 1991. In 1997, all three were combined into a unified operation under the name Premier Cruises. Company later renamed Premier Cruise Lines; all service suspended in late 2000.

Name	*Royale*	*StarShip Majestic*	*StarShip Atlantic*
Previous name(s)	*Federico C.*	*Spirit of London*	*Atlantic*
		Sun Princess	
Subsequent name(s)	*StarShip Royale*	*Southern Cross*	*Melody*
	SeaBreeze I	*Flamenco*	
Owner		Premier Cruise Lines, Ltd.	Premier Cruise Lines, Ltd.

Continued

PREMIER CRUISE LINES (1984–2000)—*Continued*

Name	*Royale*	*StarShip Majestic*	*StarShip Atlantic*
Flag	Panama	Bahamas	Liberia
Gross tons	21,010	17,370	35,143
Dimensions (feet)	606 × 79 ×29	535 × 75 × 21	672 × 90 × 46
Year built	1958	1972	1982
Place built	Genoa, Italy	Genoa, Italy	La Seyne, France
Shipyard	Ansaldo (No. 1,516)	Cantieri Navali del Tirreno e Riuniti (No. 290)	CNIM Shipyards (No. 1,432)
Engines	4 steam turbines	4 10-cyl. Fiat C420.10L diesels	2 10-cyl. Grandi Motori Trieste B600.10L diesels
Propulsion	Geared, twin screw	Geared, twin screw, controllable pitch	Geared, twin screw, controllable pitch
Other equipment		Bow thruster	Bow thruster
Passenger capacity		760	1,098
Notes	1, 2	1, 3	1, 4

Name	*StarShip Oceanic*	*Seawind Crown*	*Dolphin IV*
Previous name(s)	*Oceanic* *Royale Oceanic*	*Infante Dom Henrique* *Vasco Da Gama*	*Zion* *Amelia de Mello* *Ithaca*
Subsequent name(s)	*The Big Red Boat I*		
Owner	Premier Cruise Lines, Ltd.	Cruise Corp., Ltd.	
Flag	Bahamas	Panama	Panama
Gross tons	38,772	23,145	12,091
Dimensions (feet)	782 × 97 × 28	642 × 84 × 27	502 × 65 × 28
Year built	1965	1961	1956
Place built	Monfalcone, Italy	Hoboken, Belgium	Hamburg, West Germany
Shipyard	Cantieri Riuniti dell'Adriatico (No. 1,876)	Cockerill-Ougree (No. 814)	Deutsche Werft (No. 691)
Engines	4 steam turbines	2 steam turbines	2 steam turbines
Propulsion	Geared, twin screw	Geared, twin screw	Geared, single screw
Other equipment		2 bow thrusters	
Passenger capacity	1,180	654	
Notes	1, 5	6	7

Name	*SeaBreeze I*	*OceanBreeze*	*IslandBreeze*
Previous name(s)	*Federico C.* *Royale* *StarShip Royale*	*Southern Cross* *Calypso I* *Calypso* *Azure Seas*	*Transvaal Castle* *S.A. Vaal* *Festivale*
Subsequent name(s)			*The Big Red Boat III*

Name	*SeaBreeze I*	*OceanBreeze*	*IslandBreeze*
Owner	Compania de Vapores Seabreeze SA	Oceanbreeze, Ltd.	Festivale Maritime, Inc.
Flag	Panama	Panama	Bahamas
Gross tons	21,010	20,204	31,793
Dimensions (feet)	606 × 79 × 29	604 × 78 × 25	760 × 90 × 32
Year built	1958	1955	1961
Place built	Genoa, Italy	Belfast, Northern Ireland	Clydebank, Scotland
Shipyard	Ansaldo (No. 1,516)	Harland & Wolff (No. 1,498)	John Brown (No. 720)
Engines	4 steam turbines	2 steam turbines	4 steam turbines
Propulsion	Geared, twin screw	Geared, twin screw	Geared, twin screw
Other equipment			Bow thruster
Passenger capacity	770	734	1,146
Notes	8	9	10

Name	*Rembrandt*	*The Big Red Boat II*
Previous name(s)	*Rotterdam* (5)	*Eugenio C.* *Eugenio Costa* *Edinburgh Castle*
Subsequent name(s)		
Owner	Holland America Cruises NV	Lowline (PSV) Ltd.
Flag	Bahamas	U.K.
Gross tons	39,674	32,753
Dimensions (feet)	748 × 94 × 30	713 × 96 × 28
Year built	1959	1966
Place built	Rotterdam, Netherlands	Monfalcone, Italy
Shipyard	Rotterdam Drydock (No. 300)	Adriatico (No. 1,884)
Engines	6 steam turbines	4 steam turbines
Propulsion	Geared, twin screw	Geared, twin screw
Other equipment		
Passenger capacity	1,074	844
Notes	11	12

Notes

1. One of the original "Big Red Boats."

2. Acquired from Costa by Premier in 1983; sold by Premier to Dolphin in 1989.

3. Acquired from Princess Cruises in 1988; conveyed to C.T.C. Cruises in 1995.

4. Acquired from Home Lines in 1988; conveyed to Mediterranean Shipping Cruises in 1997.

5. Acquired from Home Lines in 1985.

6. Acquired by Seawind Cruise Line from Trans World Cruises in 1991; conveyed to Spanish interests in 2000.

7. Acquired from Paquet in 1984; conveyed to Cape Canaveral Cruise Line in 1998.

8. Lost off the Virginia coast in 2000.

9. Acquired by Dolphin Cruise Line from Western Cruise Line in 1992; conveyed to Imperial Majesty Cruise Line in 1999.

10. Leased by Dolphin Cruise Line from Carnival in 1996; lease later converted to purchase.

11. Acquired from Holland America Line in 1997.

12. Acquired from Lowline by charter in 1999.

PRINCESS CRUISES

Name	*Princess Patricia*	*"Princess Italia"*	*"Princess Carla"*
Previous name(s)		*Italia*	*Flandre*
			Carla C.
Subsequent name(s)		*Ocean Princess*	*Carla C.*
		Sea Prince	*Carla Costa*
		Sea Prince V	*Pallas Athena*
		Princesa Oceania	
		Sapphire	
Owner	Canadian Pacific Railway	Crociere d'Oltremare, S.p.A.	Costa Armatori, S.p.A.
Flag	Canada	Italy	Italy
Gross tons	6,062	12,218	19,975
Dimensions (feet)	374 × 56 × 16	489 × 70 × 21	600 × 80 × 28
Year built	1949	1967	1952
Place built	Glasgow, Scotland	Trieste, Italy	Dunkirk, France
Shipyard	Fairfield (No. 730)	Cantieri Navali Riuniti, Feiszegi (No. 76)	Ateliers et Chantiers de France (No. 206)
Engines	2 steam turbines	2 9-cyl. Adriatico diesels	8 steam turbines
Propulsion	Electric drive, twin screw	Geared, twin screw	Geared, twin screw
Other equipment			
Passenger capacity	N/A	550	995
Notes	1	2	3

Name	*Pacific Princess*	*Island Princess*	*Sun Princess*
Previous name(s)	*Sea Venture*	*Island Venture*	*Spirit of London*
Subsequent name(s)		*Hyundai Pungak-Ho*	*Starship Majestic*
			Southern Cross
			Flamenco
Owner	P&O Lines, Ltd.	P&O Lines, Ltd.	P&O Lines, Ltd.
Flag	U.K.	U.K.	U.K.
Gross tons	19,903	19,907	17,370
Dimensions (feet)	554 × 81 × 23	554 × 81 × 23	535 × 75 × 21
Year built	1971	1972	1972
Place built	Rheinstahl, West Germany	Rheinstahl, West Germany	Riva, Italy
Shipyard	Nordseewerke (No. 411)	Nordseewerke (No. 414)	Cantieri Navali del Tirreno e Riuniti (No. 290)
Engines	4 10-cyl. Fiat C420.10SS diesels	4 10-cyl. Fiat C420.10L diesels	4 10-cyl. Fiat C420.10L diesels
Propulsion	Geared, twin screw, controllable pitch	Geared, twin screw, controllable pitch	Geared, twin screw, controllable pitch
Other equipment	Bow thruster	Bow thruster	Bow thruster
Passenger capacity	640	640	736
Notes	4	5	6

Name	*Dawn Princess*	*Fair Princess*	*Golden Princess*
Previous name(s)	*Sylvania*	*Carinthia*	*Royal Viking Sky*
	Fairwind	*Fairland*	*Sunward*
	Sitmar Fairwind	*Fairsea*	*Birka Queen*
Subsequent name(s)	*Princess*	*Regent Isle*	*SuperStar Capricorn*
	Albatros	*Fair Princess*	*Hyundai Keumkang*
Owner	Sitmar Cruises, Inc.	Sitmar Cruises, Inc.	Birka Cruise Ltd.
Flag	Liberia	Liberia	Bahamas
Gross tons	24,803	16,627	28,388
Dimensions (feet)	608 × 80 × 29	608 × 80 × 29	583 × 83 × 24
Year built	1957	1956	1973
Place built	Clydebank, Scotland	Clydebank, Scotland	Helsinki, Finland
Shipyard	John Brown (No. 700)	John Brown (No. 699)	Wartsila (No. 396)
Engines	4 steam turbines	4 steam turbines	4 9-cyl. Wartsila 92H40/48 diesels
Propulsion	Geared, twin screw	Geared, twin screw	Geared, twin screw, controllable pitch
Other equipment			2 bow thrusters
Passenger capacity	890	962	830
Notes	7	8	9

Name	*Sky Princess*	*Star Princess*	*Sea Princess*
Previous name(s)	*Fairsky*		*Kungsholm*
Subsequent name(s)	*Pacific Sky*	*Arcadia*	*Victoria*
Owner	P&O Lines, Ltd.	Cosedia Marine, Inc.	Investors in Industry plc
Flag	Liberia; U.K.	Liberia	U.K.
Gross tons	46,087	63,524	27,670
Dimensions (feet)	787 × 92 × 26	804 × 106 × 27	660 × 87 × 28
Year built	1984	1989	1966
Place built	La Seyne, France	St. Nazaire, France	Clydebank, Scotland
Shipyard	CNIM Shipyards (No. 1,436)	Chantiers de l'Atlantique (No. B-29)	John Brown (No. 728)
Engines	4 steam turbines	4 MAN 8-cyl. 8L58/64 diesels	2 9-cyl. Gotaverken 760/1500VGS9 diesels
Propulsion	Geared, twin screw	Electric drive, twin screw	Twin screw
Other equipment	Bow thruster	2 bow thrusters	Bow thruster
Passenger capacity	1,212	1,621	778
Notes	10	11	12

Name	*Royal Princess*	*Crown Princess*	*Regal Princess*
Previous name(s)			
Subsequent name(s)			
Owner	P&O Lines, Ltd.	Astramar, S.p.A.	Astramar, S.p.A
Flag	U.K.	Liberia; Bermuda (U.K.)	Liberia; U.K.
Gross tons	44,588	69,845	69,845
Dimensions (feet)	756 × 106 × 25	833 × 105 × 27	833 × 105 × 27
Year built	1984	1990	1991
Place built	Helsinki, Finland	Monfalcone, Italy	Monfalcone, Italy
Shipyard	Wartsila (No. 464)	Fincantieri (No. 5,839)	Fincantieri (No. 5,840)

Continued

PRINCESS CRUISES—*Continued*

Name	*Royal Princess*	*Crown Princess*	*Regal Princess*
Engines	4 6-cyl. Pielstick 6PC4-2L570 diesels	4 8-cyl. MAN 8L58/64 diesels	4 8-cyl. MAN 8L58/64 diesels
Propulsion	Geared, twin screw, controllable pitch	Electric drive, twin screw	Electric drive, twin screw
Other equipment	2 bow thrusters	2 bow thrusters	2 bow thrusters
Passenger capacity	1,260	1,590	1,596
Notes		13	13

Name	*Sun Princess*	*Dawn Princess*	*Sea Princess*
Previous name(s)			
Subsequent name(s)			
Owner	Astramar, S.p.A.	Fairline Shipping International Corp.	Princess Cruises Liberia, Inc.
Flag	Liberia; U.K.	Liberia; U.K.	Liberia; U.K.
Gross tons	77,441	77,441	77,449
Dimensions (feet)	857 × 106 × 27	857 × 106 × 27	857 × 106 × 27
Year built	1995	1997	1998
Place built	Monfalcone, Italy	Monfalcone, Italy	Monfalcone, Italy
Shipyard	Fincantieri (No. 5,909)	Fincantieri (No. 5,955)	Fincantieri (No. 5,998)
Engines	4 16-cyl. Sulzer 16ZAV40S diesels	4 16-cyl. Sulzer 16ZAV40S diesels	4 16-cyl. Sulzer 16ZAV40S diesels
Propulsion	Electric drive, twin screw	Electric drive, twin screw	Electric drive, twin screw
Other equipment	2 bow thrusters, 2 stern thrusters	2 bow thrusters, 2 stern thrusters	2 bow thrusters, 2 stern thrusters
Passenger capacity	1,950	1,950	2,022
Notes			

Name	*Grand Princess*	*Ocean Princess*	*Golden Princess*
Previous name(s)			
Subsequent name(s)			
Owner	Fairline Shipping International Corp.	O.P. Shipping Corp., Ltd.	
Flag	Liberia; Bermuda (U.K.)	U.K.	U.K.
Gross tons	108,806	77,499	109,000
Dimensions (feet)	951 × 118 × 26	857 × 106 × 27	951 × 118 × 26
Year built	1998	2000	2001
Place built	Monfalcone, Italy	Monfalcone, Italy	Monfalcone, Italy
Shipyard	Fincantieri (No. 5,956)	Fincantieri (No. 6,044)	Fincantieri
Engines	6 16-cyl. Sulzer 16ZAV40S diesels	4 16-cyl. Sulzer 16ZAV40S diesels	6 16-cyl. Sulzer 16ZAV40S diesels
Propulsion	Electric drive, twin screw	Electric drive, twin screw	Electric drive, twin screw
Other equipment	3 bow thrusters, 3 stern thrusters	2 bow thrusters, 2 stern thrusters	3 bow thrusters, 3 stern thrusters
Passenger capacity	2,600	2,022	2,600
Notes	14		14

Name	Star Princess	Coral Princess	Island Princess
Previous name(s)			
Subsequent name(s)			
Owner			
Flag			
Gross tons	88,000	109,000	88,000
Dimensions (feet)		951 × 118 × 26	
Year built	2002	2002	2003
Place built	St. Nazaire, France	Monfalcone, Italy	St. Nazaire, France
Shipyard	Chantiers de l'Atlantique	Fincantieri	Chantiers de l'Atlantique
Engines	Diesel and gas turbine	6 16-cyl. Sulzer 16ZAV40S diesels	Diesel and gas turbine
Propulsion	Electric drive	Electric drive, twin screw	Electric drive
Other equipment		3 bow thrusters, 3 stern thrusters	
Passenger capacity	1,950	2,600	1,950
Notes		14	

Name	Diamond Princess	Sapphire Princess
Previous name(s)		
Subsequent name(s)		
Owner		
Flag		
Gross tons	113,000	113,000
Dimensions (feet)		
Year built	2003	2004
Place built	Nagasaki, Japan	Nagasaki, Japan
Shipyard	Mitsubishi	Mitsubishi
Engines	4 diesels, 1 gas turbine	4 diesels, 1 gas turbine
Propulsion		
Other equipment	3 bow thrusters, 3 stern thrusters	3 bow thrusters, 3 stern thrusters
Passenger capacity		
Notes	14	14

Notes

1. See text; leased from Canadian Pacific from 1964 to 1966 and never owned by Princess.

2. Leased from Italian interests from 1966 to 1973 and never owned by Princess. While commonly referred to as *Princess Italia*, vessel was never formally so enrolled.

3. Leased from Costa from 1968 to 1970 and never owned by Princess. While commonly referred to as *Princess Carla*, vessel was never formally so enrolled.

4. Purchased from Flagship in 1975.

5. Leased from Flagship in 1972; lease converted to purchase in 1974; sold to Hyundai Merchant Marine in 1999.

6. Conveyed to Princess by P&O in 1974; sold to Premier Cruises in 1988.

7. Acquired from Sitmar in 1988; sold to V. Ships in 1993.

8. Acquired from Sitmar in 1988; sold to Regency Cruises in 1995; reacquired by P&O in 1995.

9. Chartered from Birka Line in 1993; charter concluded and vessel conveyed to Star Cruises in 1997.

10. Acquired from Sitmar in 1988; conveyed to P&O Cruises in 2000.

11. Conveyed to P&O Cruises in 1997.

12. Acquired from Flagship by P&O Cruises in 1978. Vessel operated for both Princess and P&O Cruises as *Sea Princess*.

13. See text; designed by Sitmar and acquired in 1988 while still under construction.

14. Post-Panamax vessel; will not fit through the Panama Canal.

RADISSON SEVEN SEAS CRUISES

Name	*Song of Flower*	*Radisson Diamond*	*Paul Gauguin*
Previous name(s)	*Fernhill* *Begonia* *Explorer Starship*		
Subsequent name(s)			
Owner	Radisson Seven Seas Cruises	Radisson Seven Seas Cruises	Copropriete du Navire Paul Gauguin
Flag	Bahamas	Bahamas	Wallis and Futuna Islands (France)
Gross tons	8,282	20,295	19,170
Dimensions (feet)	409 × 53 × 15	420 × 103 × 26	513 × 71 × 17
Year built	1986	1992	1997
Place built	Kristiansand, Norway	Rauma, Finland	St. Nazaire, France
Shipyard	Kristiansands M/V (No. 220)	Finnyards OY (No. 310)	Chantiers de l'Atlantique (No. G-31)
Engines	2 10-cyl. Wichmann WX28V10 diesels	2 8-cyl. Wartsila 8R32E and 2 6-cyl. Wartsila 6R32E diesels	2 9-cyl. MAN B&W 9L33/40 and 2 6-cyl. MAN B&W 6L32/40 diesels
Propulsion	Geared, twin screw, controllable pitch	Geared, twin screw, controllable pitch	Electric drive, twin screw
Other equipment		Built with SWATH technology, twin hulls and 4 stabilizers	Bow thruster, stern thruster
Passenger capacity	170	354	320
Notes	1		

Name	*Seven Seas Navigator*	*Seven Seas Mariner*
Previous name(s)	(See note)	
Subsequent name(s)		
Owner	Finship Italy, S.r.l.	
Flag	Bahamas	
Gross tons	28,550	46,000
Dimensions (feet)	560 × 81 × 21	709 × 93 × 21
Year built	1999	2001
Place built	Genoa, Italy	St. Nazaire, France
Shipyard	T. Mariotti (No. 6,125)	Chantiers de l'Atlantique
Engines	4 8-cyl. Wartsila 8L-38 diesels	
Propulsion	Geared, twin screw, controllable pitch	
Other equipment	2 bow thrusters	
Passenger capacity	550	720
Notes	2	

Notes

1. Acquired from Fearnley and Egar A/S in 1989.

2. Launched in 1991 at Admiralty Yards in St. Petersburg, Russia, as the submarine tracking vessel *Akademik Nikolay Pilyugin* (hull no. 2,510) but never completed as a Soviet warship. Towed to T. Mariotti yard in Genoa in 1997 bearing temporary name *Blue Sea* and completed as cruise ship in 1999.

REGAL CRUISES

Name	**Regal Empress**
Previous name(s)	*Olympia*
	Caribe
	Caribe I
Subsequent name(s)	
Owner	Regal Cruises, Ltd.
Flag	Bahamas
Gross tons	21,909
Dimensions (feet)	610 × 79 × 28
Year built	1953
Place built	Glasgow, Scotland
Shipyard	Alexander Stephen & Sons (No. 636)
Engines	2 12-cyl. Deutz RBV12M540 diesels
Propulsion	Geared, twin screw
Other equipment	2 bow thrusters
Passenger capacity	
Notes	1

Notes

1. Built as *Olympia* for Greek Line's transatlantic service; originally powered by four steam turbines geared to twin screws, later converted to diesel. Acquired from Commodore Cruise Lines in 1993.

REGENCY CRUISES (1984–1995)

Name	**Regent Sun**	**Regent Star**	**Regent Sea**
Previous name(s)	*Shalom*	*Statendam*	*Gripsholm*
	Hanseatic	*Rhapsody*	*Samantha*
	Doric		*Navarino*
	Royal Odyssey		
Subsequent name(s)	*Sun*	*Sea Harmony*	*Sea*
Owner	Regsun Holding, Ltd.	Shining Cruises SA	Ridan Investment Trust
Flag	Bahamas	Bahamas	Panama; Bahamas
Gross tons	17,884	24,413	15,294
Dimensions (feet)	628 × 82 × 27	642 × 81 × 26	631 × 82 × 28
Year built	1964	1957	1957
Place built	St. Nazaire, France	Schiedam, Netherlands	Genoa, Italy
Shipyard	Chantiers de l'Atlantique (No. Z-21)	Wilton-Fijenoord (No. 753)	Ansaldo S.p.A. (No. 1,500)
Engines	4 steam turbines	2 16-cyl. Pielstick 16PC2V-400 and 2 12-cyl. Pielstick 12PC2V-400 diesels	2 9-cyl. Gotaverken diesels
Propulsion	Geared, twin screw	Geared, twin screw, controllable pitch	Geared, twin screw
Other equipment	Bow thruster	Bow thruster	

Continued

REGENCY CRUISES (1984–1995)—*Continued*

Name	*Regent Sun*	*Regent Star*	*Regent Sea*
Passenger capacity	836	914	684
Notes	1	2	3

Name	*Regent Rainbow*	*Regent Spirit*	*Regent Jewel*
Previous name(s)	*Santa Rosa*	*Anna Nery*	*Canguro Verde*
	Pacific Sun	*Danaos*	*Durr*
	Diamond Island	*Constellation*	*Ionian Harmony*
		Morning Star	*Sun Fiesta*
Subsequent name(s)	*The Emerald*	*Salamis Glory*	*Regent Calypso*
			Calypso
Owner	North River Overseas SA	Ridgeway Shipping SA	N/A
Flag	Bahamas	Bahamas	Bahamas
Gross tons	24,851	10,392	11,162
Dimensions (feet)	583 × 84 × 27	492 × 66 × 18	444 × 63 × 18
Year built	1958	1962	1968
Place built	Newport News, Va.	Pula, Yugoslavia	Castellammare, Italy
Shipyard	Newport News Ship building (No. 521)	Brodogradiliste (No. 237)	Italcantieri (No. 645)
Engines	4 steam turbines	2 7-cyl. B&W 7-50VTBF-110 diesels	2 12-cyl. Wartsila 12V32D diesels
Propulsion	Geared, twin screw	Geared, twin screw	Geared, twin screw, controllable pitch
Other equipment			Bow thruster, stern thruster, stern door and ramp
Passenger capacity	960	422	594
Notes	4	5	6

Name	*"Regent Isle"*
Previous name(s)	*Carinthia*
	Fairland
	Fairsea
	Fair Princess
Subsequent name(s)	*Fair Princess*
Owner	
Flag	Bahamas
Gross tons	21,947
Dimensions (feet)	608 × 80 × 29
Year built	1956
Place built	Clydebank, Scotland
Shipyard	John Brown (No. 699)
Engines	4 steam turbines
Propulsion	Geared, twin screw
Other equipment	
Passenger capacity	890
Notes	7

Notes

1. Acquired from Royal Cruise Line in 1988; conveyed to Premier Cruises after Regency ceased operations in 1995 but never operated by Premier.

2. Acquired by Regency in the late 1980s; laid up when Regency ceased operations in 1995.

3. Purchased from Italian interests in 1984; acquired by Cerberus Corporation after Regency ceased operations in 1995 but remained out of service.

4. Acquired in 1992; conveyed to Louis Cruise Lines after Regency ceased operations in 1995.

5. Acquired in 1992; conveyed to Salmis Lines after Regency ceased operations in 1995.

6. Last vessel to operate in cruise service for Regency. Acquired in 1993; conveyed to Jule Cruises when Regency ceased operations in 1995.

7. Acquired from P&O Lines in 1995 but never operated by Regency; returned to P&O after Regency ceased operations that same year.

RENAISSANCE CRUISES

The first eight Renaissance vessels are generally identified by the company's name and a Roman numeral, while the final eight vessels are called *R One, R Two,* etc. In *Lloyd's Register,* vessels of both classes are identified as *Renaissance One, Renaissance Two,* etc.

Name	*Renaissance*	*Renaissance II*	*Renaissance III*
Previous name(s)			
Subsequent name(s)	*Renaissance I* *The Mercury*	*The Neptune*	*Galapagos Explorer*
Owner	Renaissance Cruises, Inc.	Renaissance Cruises, Inc.	Renaissance Cruises (Antigua), Ltd.
Flag	Liberia	Liberia	Liberia
Gross tons	4,077	4,077	4,077
Dimensions (feet)	290 × 51 × 13	290 × 51 × 13	288 × 49 × 13
Year built	1989	1990	1988/1990
Place built	La Spezia, Italy	La Spezia, Italy	La Spezia, Italy
Shipyard	Cantieri Navale Ferrari (No. 43)	Cantieri Navale Ferrari (No. 44)	Cantieri Navale Ferrari (No. 45)
Engines	2 12-cyl. Alpha 12V28/32 diesels	2 12-cyl. Alpha 12V28/32 diesels	2 12-cyl. Alpha 12V28/32 diesels
Propulsion	Geared, twin screw, controllable pitch	Geared, twin screw, controllable pitch	Geared, twin screw, controllable pitch
Other equipment	Bow thruster	Bow thruster	Bow thruster
Passenger capacity	100	100	100
Notes	1	2	3

Name	*Renaissance IV*	*Renaissance V*	*Renaissance VI*
Previous name(s)			
Subsequent name(s)	*Clelia II*	*Hanseatic Renaissance* *Renaissance V* *Sun Viva I* *MegaStar Sagittarius*	*Sun Viva II* *MegaStar Capricorn*
Owner	Renaissance Cruises (Antigua), Ltd.	Renaissance Cruises (Antigua), Ltd.	Renaissance Cruises (Antigua), Ltd.
Flag	Liberia	Liberia	Liberia
Gross tons	4,077	4,200	4,200
Dimensions (feet)	297 × 50 × 13	296 × 50 × 13	297 × 50 × 13
Year built	1990	1991	1991

Continued

RENAISSANCE CRUISES—*Continued*

Name	*Renaissance IV*	*Renaissance V*	*Renaissance VI*
Place built	La Spezia, Italy	Marina di Carrare, Italy	Marina di Carrare, Italy
Shipyard	Cantieri Navale Ferrari (No. 46)	Nuovi Cantieri Apuania (No. 1,144)	Nuovi Cantieri Apuania (No. 1,145)
Engines	2 12-cyl. Alpha 12V28/32 diesels	2 8-cyl. MAN 8L28/32 diesels	2 8-cyl. MAN 8L28/32 diesels
Propulsion	Geared, twin screw, controllable pitch	Geared, twin screw, controllable pitch	Geared, twin screw, controllable pitch
Other equipment	Bow thruster	Bow thruster	Bow thruster
Passenger capacity	100	120	114
Notes	4	5	6

Name	*Renaissance VII*	*Renaissance VIII*	*Aegean I*
Previous name(s)	*Renaissance VII* *Regina Renaissance*		*Narcis* *Alkyon* *Aegean Dolphin* *Dolphin* *Aegean Dolphin*
Subsequent name(s)			*Ocean Explorer II*
Owner	Renaissance Cruises (Antigua), Inc.	Renaissance Cruises (Antigua), Inc.	Golden Sun Cruises
Flag	Liberia	Liberia	Greece
Gross tons	4,280	4,200	11,563
Dimensions (feet)	297 × 50 × 13	297 × 50 × 13	461 × 68 × 22
Year built	1991	1991	1973
Place built	Marina di Carrare, Italy	La Spezia, Italy	Galatz, Romania
Shipyard	Nuovi Cantieri Apuania (No. 1,146)	Nuovi Cantieri Apuania (No. 1,147)	Santierul Naval S.A. Galatz (No. 617)
Engines	2 8-cyl. MAN 8L28/32 diesels	2 8-cyl. MAN 8L28/32 diesels	2 14-cyl. Pielstick 14 PO2V-400 diesels
Propulsion	Geared, twin screw, controllable pitch	Geared, twin screw, controllable pitch	Geared, twin screw, controllable pitch
Other equipment	Bow thruster	Bow thruster	
Passenger capacity	114	114	576
Notes			7

Name	*R One*	*R Two*	*R Three*
Previous name(s)			
Subsequent name(s)			
Owner	Renaissance Cruises (Liberia), Inc.	Renaissance Cruises (Liberia), Inc.	
Flag	Liberia	Liberia	Gibraltar
Gross tons	30,277	30,277	30,277
Dimensions (feet)	594 × 84 × 20	594 × 84 × 20	594 × 84 × 20
Year built	1998	1999	1999
Place built	St. Nazaire, France	St. Nazaire, France	St. Nazaire, France
Shipyard	Chantiers de l'Atlantique (No. H-31)	Chantiers de l'Atlantique (No. I-31)	Chantiers de l'Atlantique

Name	R One	R Two	R Three
Engines	4 12-cyl. Wartsila 12 V32 diesels	4 12-cyl. Wartsila 12 V32 diesels	4 12-cyl. Wartsila 12 V32 diesels
Propulsion	Electric drive, twin screw, controllable pitch	Electric drive, twin screw, controllable pitch	Electric drive, twin screw, controllable pitch
Other equipment	2 bow thrusters	2 bow thrusters	2 bow thrusters
Passenger capacity	702	700	684
Notes			

Name	R Four	R Five	R Six
Previous name(s)			
Subsequent name(s)			
Owner		Renaissance Cruises (Liberia), Inc.	
Flag	Gibraltar	Liberia	Liberia
Gross tons	30,277	30,277	30,200
Dimensions (feet)	594 × 84 × 20	594 × 84 × 20	594 × 84 × 20
Year built	1999	2000	2000
Place built	St. Nazaire, France	St. Nazaire, France	St. Nazaire, France
Shipyard	Chantiers de l'Atlantique (No. O-31)	Chantiers de l'Atlantique (No. P-31)	Chantiers de l'Atlantique (No. Q-31)
Engines	4 12-cyl. Wartsila 12 V32 diesels	4 12-cyl. Wartsila 12 V32 diesels	4 12-cyl. Wartsila 12 V32 diesels
Propulsion	Electric drive, twin screw, controllable pitch	Electric drive, twin screw, controllable pitch	Electric drive, twin screw, controllable pitch
Other equipment	2 bow thrusters	2 bow thrusters	2 bow thrusters
Passenger capacity	702	702	684
Notes			

Name	R Seven	R Eight
Previous name(s)		
Subsequent name(s)		
Owner		
Flag	Liberia	Liberia
Gross tons	30,200	30,200
Dimensions (feet)	594 × 84 × 20	594 × 84 × 20
Year built	2000	2001
Place built	St. Nazaire, France	St. Nazaire, France
Shipyard	Chantiers de l'Atlantique (No. Y-31)	Chantiers de l'Atlantique (No. Z-31)
Engines	4 12-cyl. Wartsila 12 V32 diesels	4 12-cyl. Wartsila 12 V32 diesels
Propulsion	Electric drive, twin screw, controllable pitch	Electric drive, twin screw, controllable pitch
Other equipment	2 bow thrusters	2 bow thrusters
Passenger capacity	684	684
Notes		

Notes

1. Conveyed to Universal Cruises (Singapore) in 1998.

2. Conveyed to Universal Cruises (Singapore) in 1998.

Continued

RENAISSANCE CRUISES—*Continued*

3. Conveyed to Enchanted Islands Corp. in 1997.
4. Conveyed to Golden Seas Cruises in 1996.
5. Conveyed to Sun Cruises (Malaysia) in 1997.
6. Conveyed to Sun Cruises (Malaysia) in 1998.
7. Leased from Golden Sun Cruises from 1997 to 1998.

ROYAL CARIBBEAN INTERNATIONAL
Company began operations in 1970 as Royal Caribbean Cruise Line. Name changed to Royal Caribbean International about 1997.

Name	*Song of Norway*	*Nordic Prince*	*Sun Viking*
Previous name(s)			
Subsequent name(s)	*Sundream*	*Carousel*	*SuperStar Sagittarius*
			Hyundai Pongnae
Owner	Sameiet m.s. Song of Norway	Sameiet Nordic Prince	Sameiet m.s. Sun Viking
Flag	Norway	Norway	Norway
Gross tons	18,416	18,436	18,559
Dimensions (feet)	552 × 79 × 21	552 × 79 × 21	563 × 79 × 21
Year built	1970	1971	1972
Place built	Helsinki, Finland	Helsinki, Finland	Helsinki, Finland
Shipyard	Wartsila (No. 392)	Wartsila (No. 393)	Wartsila (No. 394)
Engines	4 9-cyl. Sulzer 92H40/48 diesels	4 9-cyl. Sulzer 92H40/48 diesels	4 9-cyl. Sulzer 92H40/48 diesels
Propulsion	Geared, twin screw, controllable pitch	Geared, twin screw, controllable pitch	Geared, twin screw, controllable pitch
Other equipment	Bow thruster	Bow thruster	Bow thruster
Passenger capacity	876	876	714
Notes	1	2	3

Name	*Song of America*	*Sovereign of the Seas*	*Viking Serenade*
Previous name(s)			*Scandinavia*
			Stardancer
Subsequent name(s)	*Sunbird*		
Owner	Song of America, Ltd.	Sovereign of the Seas, Ltd.	Viking Serenade, Inc.
Flag	Norway	Norway	Liberia
Gross tons	37,584	73,129	40,132
Dimensions (feet)	703 × 93 × 17	880 × 106 × 25	608 × 89 × 23
Year built	1982	1987	1981
Place built	Helsinki, Finland	St. Nazaire, France	Nantes, France
Shipyard	Wartsila (No. 431)	Chantiers de l'Atlantique (No. A-29)	Dubigeon-Normandie (No. 164)
Engines	4 8-cyl. Sulzer 8ZL40/48 diesels	4 9-cyl. Pielstick 9PC20L400 diesels	2 9-cyl. B&W 9L55GFCA diesels
Propulsion	Geared, twin screw, controllable pitch	Geared, twin screw, controllable pitch	Geared, twin screw, controllable pitch
Other equipment	2 bow thrusters	2 bow thrusters	2 bow thrusters

Name	Song of America	Sovereign of the Seas	Viking Serenade
Passenger capacity	1,402	2,276	2,104
Notes	4		5

Name	Nordic Empress	Monarch of the Seas	Majesty of the Seas
Previous name(s)			
Subsequent name(s)			
Owner	Nordic Empress, Ltd.	Monarch of the Seas, Inc.	Majesty of the Seas, Inc.
Flag	Liberia	Norway	Norway
Gross tons	48,563	73,941	73,941
Dimensions (feet)	623 × 100 × 25	880 × 106 × 25	880 × 106 × 25
Year built	1990	1991	1992
Place built	St. Nazaire, France	St. Nazaire, France	St. Nazaire, France
Shipyard	Chantiers de l'Atlantique (No. G-29)	Chantiers de l'Atlantique (No. A-30)	Chantiers de l'Atlantique (No. B-30)
Engines	2 12-cyl. Wartsila 12V32 and 2 8-cyl. Wartsila 8R32 diesels	4 9-cyl. Pielstick 9PC20L400 diesels	4 9-cyl. Pielstick 9PC20L400 diesels
Propulsion	Geared, twin screw, controllable pitch	Geared, twin screw, controllable pitch	Geared, twin screw, controllable pitch
Other equipment	2 bow thrusters, 1 stern thruster	2 bow thrusters	2 bow thrusters
Passenger capacity	1,600	2,354	2,354
Notes	6		

Name	Legend of the Seas	Splendour of the Seas	Grandeur of the Seas
Previous name(s)			
Subsequent name(s)			
Owner	G.I.E. Cruise Vision One	G.I.E. Cruise Vision Two	Grandeur of the Seas, Inc.
Flag	Liberia	Norway	Liberia
Gross tons	69,130	69,130	73,817
Dimensions (feet)	867 × 105 × 24	867 × 105 × 24	916 × 106 × 25
Year built	1995	1996	1996
Place built	St. Nazaire, France	St. Nazaire, France	Helsinki, Finland
Shipyard	Chantiers de l'Atlantique (No. A-31)	Chantiers de l'Atlantique (No. B-31)	Kvaerner Masa-Yards (No. 492)
Engines	5 12-cyl. Wartsila 12V46 diesels	5 12-cyl. Wartsila 12V46 diesels	4 12-cyl. MAN 12V48/60 diesels
Propulsion	Electric drive, twin screw	Electric drive, twin screw	Electric drive, twin screw
Other equipment	2 bow thrusters, 1 stern thruster	2 bow thrusters, 1 stern thruster	2 bow thrusters, 1 stern thruster
Passenger capacity	1,750	1,750	1,950
Notes			

Name	Rhapsody of the Seas	Enchantment of the Seas	Vision of the Seas
Previous name(s)			
Subsequent name(s)			
Owner	Rhapsody of the Seas, Inc.	Enchantment of the Seas, Inc.	Vision of the Seas, Inc.
Flag	Norway	Norway	Liberia

Contineud

ROYAL CARIBBEAN INTERNATIONAL—*Continued*

Name	*Rhapsody of the Seas*	*Enchantment of the Seas*	*Vision of the Seas*
Gross tons	78,491	74,136	78,491
Dimensions (feet)	915 × 106 × 25	916 × 106 × 25	915 × 106 × 25
Year built	1997	1997	1998
Place built	St. Nazaire, France	Helsinki, Finland	St. Nazaire, France
Shipyard	Chantiers de l'Atlantique (No. E-31)	Kvaerner Masa-Yards (No. 493)	Chantiers de l'Atlantique (No. F-31)
Engines	4 12-cyl. MAN 12V48/60 diesels	4 12-cyl. MAN 12V48/60 diesels	4 12-cyl. Wartsila 12V46C diesels
Propulsion	Electric drive, twin screw	Electric drive, twin screw	Electric drive, twin screw
Other equipment	2 bow thrusters, 1 stern thruster	2 bow thrusters, 1 stern thruster	2 bow thrusters, 1 stern thruster
Passenger capacity	2,000	1,950	2,000
Notes			

Name	*Voyager of the Seas*	*Explorer of the Seas*	*Adventure of the Seas*
Previous name(s)			
Subsequent name(s)			
Owner	Voyager of the Seas, Inc.		
Flag	Liberia		
Gross tons	137,276	137,000	142,000
Dimensions (feet)	1,020 × 126 × 29	1,020 × 126 × 29	1,020 × 126 × 29
Year built	1999	2000	2003
Place built	Turku, Finland	Turku, Finland	Turku, Finland
Shipyard	Kvaerner Masa-Yards (No. 1,344)	Kvaerner Masa-Yards	Kvaerner Masa-Yards
Engines	6 12-cyl. Wartsila 12V46C diesels	6 12-cyl. Wartsila 12V46C diesels	6 12-cyl. Wartsila 12V46C diesels
Propulsion	3 Azipod electric pod-propulsion units	3 Azipod electric pod-propulsion units	3 Azipod electric pod-propulsion units
Other equipment	4 bow thrusters	4 bow thrusters	4 bow thrusters
Passenger capacity	3,118	3,114	3,114
Notes	7	7	7

Name	*Radiance of the Seas*	*Brilliance of the Seas*	Project Vantage Newbuilding
Previous name(s)			
Subsequent name(s)			
Owner			
Flag			
Gross tons	85,000	85,000	85,000
Dimensions (feet)	965 × 105 × 26	965 × 105 × 26	965 × 105 × 26
Year built	2001	2002	2003
Place built	Papenburg, Germany	Papenburg, Germany	Papenburg, Germany
Shipyard	Meyer Werft	Meyer Werft	Meyer Werft
Engines	2 GE LM 2500+ gas turbines	2 GE LM 2500+ gas turbines	2 GE LM 2500+ gas turbines

Name	*Radiance of the Seas*	*Brilliance of the Seas*	Project Vantage Newbuilding
Propulsion	2 Azipod electric pod-propulsion units	2 Azipod electric pod-propulsion units	2 Azipod electric pod-propulsion units
Other equipment			
Passenger capacity			
Notes			

Name	Project Vantage Newbuilding	Project Voyager Newbuilding	Project Voyager Newbuilding
Previous name(s)			
Subsequent name(s)			
Owner			
Flag			
Gross tons	85,000	142,000	142,000
Dimensions (feet)	965 × 105 × 26	1,020 × 126 × 29	1,020 × 126 × 29
Year built	2004	2002	2003
Place built	Papenburg, Germany	Turku, Finland	Turku, Finland
Shipyard	Meyer Werft	Kvaerner Masa-Yards	Kvaerner Masa-Yards
Engines	2 GE LM 2500+ gas turbines	6 12-cyl. Wartsila 12V46C diesels	6 12-cyl. Wartsila 12V46C diesels
Propulsion	2 Azipod electric pod-propulsion units	3 Azipod electric pod-propulsion units	3 Azipod electric pod-propulsion units
Other equipment		4 bow thrusters	4 bow thrusters
Passenger capacity		3,114	3,114
Notes		7	7

Notes

1. In 1977 vessel was lengthened to 635 feet; gross tonnage increased to 22,945 and passenger capacity expanded to 1,082. Sold to Airtours in 1996.

2. In 1980 vessel was lengthened to 637 feet; gross tonnage increased to 23,149 and passenger capacity expanded to 1,040. Sold to Airtours in 1995.

3. Sold to Star Cruises in 1997.

4. Sold to Airtours in 1998.

5. See text; acquired from Admiral Cruises in 1988.

6. See text; although delivered to RCCL as *Nordic Empress*, vessel was designed and ordered by Admiral Cruises and was to have been called *Future Seas*.

7. Post-Panamax vessel; will not fit through the Panama Canal.

ROYAL CRUISE LINE (1974–1996)

Name	*Golden Odyssey*	*Royal Odyssey*	*Crown Odyssey*
Previous name(s)		*Shalom* *Hanseatic* *Doric*	
Subsequent name(s)	*Astra II*	*Regent Sun* *Sun*	*Norwegian Crown* *Crown Odyssey*
Owner	Castellana Maritime, Inc.	Lido Maritime, Inc.	Royal Cruise Line, Ltd.
Flag	Greece	Greece	Bahamas

Continued

ROYAL CRUISE LINE (1974–1996)—*Continued*

Name	*Golden Odyssey*	*Royal Odyssey*	*Crown Odyssey*
Gross tons	10,500	17,884	34,242
Dimensions (feet)	427 × 64 × 17	628 × 82 × 27	616 × 96 × 24
Year built	1974	1964	1988
Place built	Helsingor, Denmark	St. Nazaire, France	Papenburg, West Germany
Shipyard	Helsingor Vaerft A/S (No. 404)	Chantiers de l'Atlantique (No. Z-21)	Meyer Werft (No. 616)
Engines	2 12-cyl. Atlas MaK 12M551AK diesels	4 steam turbines	2 6-cyl. Krupp MaK 6M35 diesels, 2 8-cyl. Krupp MaK 8M601AK diesels
Propulsion	Geared, twin screw	Geared, twin screw	Geared, twin screw, controllable pitch
Other equipment	2 bow thrusters	Bow thruster	2 bow thrusters
Passenger capacity	474	725*	1,052
Notes	1	2	3

Name	*Royal Odyssey*	*Star Odyssey*	*Queen Odyssey*
Previous name(s)	*Royal Viking Sea*	*Royal Viking Star Westward*	*Royal Viking Queen*
Subsequent name(s)	*Norwegian Star SuperStar Capricorn*	*Black Watch*	*Seabourn Legend*
Owner	Kloster Cruise, Ltd.	Kloster Cruise, Ltd.	Kloster Cruise, Ltd.
Flag	Bahamas	Bahamas	Bahamas
Gross tons	28,018	21,848	9,961
Dimensions (feet)	674 × 83 × 24	674 × 83 × 25	443 × 67 × 17
Year built	1973	1972	1992
Place built	Helsinki, Finland	Helsinki, Finland	Bremerhaven, Germany
Shipyard	Wartsila (No. 397)	Wartsila (No. 395)	AS Othes (No. 1,071)
Engines	4 9-cyl. Sulzer 9ZH40/48 diesels	4 9-cyl. Sulzer 9ZH40/48 diesels	2 12-cyl. Normo KVMB-12 and 2 8-cyl. Normo KRMB-8 diesels
Propulsion	Geared, twin screw, controllable pitch	Geared, twin screw, controllable pitch	Geared, twin screw, controllable pitch
Other equipment	2 bow thrusters	2 bow thrusters	Bow thruster
Passenger capacity	536	802	212
Notes	4	5	6

Notes

1. Conveyed to Hapag-Lloyd in 1994.
2. Acquired from Home Lines in 1981; sold to Regency Cruises in 1988.
3. Conveyed to Norwegian Cruise Line in 1995.
4. Acquired from Royal Viking Line in 1991; conveyed to Norwegian Cruise Line in 1996.
5. Acquired from Norwegian Cruise Line in 1994; conveyed to Fred Olsen Cruises in 1996.
6. Vessel built to same specifications as the original Seabourn fleet; conveyed to Seabourn in 1996.
*Total number of available berths.

ROYAL VIKING LINE (1972–1994)

Name	*Royal Viking Star*	*Royal Viking Sky*	*Royal Viking Sea*
Previous name(s)			
Subsequent name(s)	*Westward*	*Sunward*	*Royal Odyssey*
	Star Odyssey	*Birka Queen*	*Norwegian Star*
	Black Watch	*Golden Princess*	*SuperStar Capricorn*
		SuperStar Capricorn	
		Hyundai Keumkang	
Owner	K/S Det Bergenske D/S	Det Nordenfjeldske D/S	Det Nordenfjeldske D/S
Flag	Norway; Bahamas	Norway; Bahamas	Norway; Bahamas
Gross tons	21,848	21,891	21,897
Dimensions (feet)	583 × 83 × 24	583 × 83 × 24	583 × 83 × 24
Year built	1972	1973	1973
Place built	Helsinki, Finland	Helsinki, Finland	Helsinki, Finland
Shipyard	Wartsila (No. 395)	Wartsila (No. 396)	Wartsila (No. 397)
Engines	4 9-cyl. Wartsila 9ZH40/48 diesels	4 9-cyl. Wartsila 9ZH40/48 diesels	4 9-cyl. Wartsila 9ZH40/48 diesels
Propulsion	Geared, twin screw, controllable pitch	Geared, twin screw, controllable pitch	Geared, twin screw, controllable pitch
Other equipment	2 bow thrusters	2 bow thrusters	2 bow thrusters
Passenger capacity	539	536	536
Notes	1	2	3

Name	*Royal Viking Sun*	*Royal Viking Queen*
Previous name(s)		
Subsequent name(s)	*Seabourn Sun*	*Queen Odyssey*
		Seabourn Legend
Owner	Kloster Cruise, Ltd.	Kloster Cruise, Ltd.
Flag	Bahamas	Bahamas
Gross tons	37,845	9,961
Dimensions (feet)	669 × 95 × 24	443 × 67 × 17
Year built	1988	1992
Place built	Turku, Finland	Bremerhaven, Germany
Shipyard	Wartsila (No. 1,298)	AS Othes (No. 1,071)
Engines	4 8-cyl. Sulzer 8ZAL40S diesels	2 12-cyl. Normo KVMB-12 and 2 8-cyl. Normo KRMB-8 diesels
Propulsion	Geared, twin screw, controllable pitch	Geared, twin screw, controllable pitch
Other equipment	2 bow thrusters	Bow thruster
Passenger capacity	760	212
Notes	4	5

Notes

1. In 1981 vessel was lengthened to 674 feet; gross tonnage increased to 28,221 and passenger capacity expanded to 758. Conveyed to Norwegian Cruise Line in 1991.

2. In 1983 vessel was lengthened to 674 feet; gross tonnage increased to 28,078 and passenger capacity expanded to 812. Conveyed to Norwegian Cruise Line in 1991.

Continued

ROYAL VIKING LINE (1972–1994)—*Continued*

3. In 1983 vessel was lengthened to 674 feet; gross tonnage increased to 28,018 and passenger capacity expanded to 812. Conveyed to Royal Cruise Line in 1991.
4. Sold to Cunard in 1994.
5. Built to same specifications as original Seabourn fleet. Sold to Royal Cruise Line in 1991.

SEABOURN CRUISE LINE

Name	*Seabourn Pride*	*Seabourn Spirit*	*Seabourn Legend*
Previous name(s)			*Royal Viking Queen*
			Queen Odyssey
Subsequent name(s)			
Owner	Seabourne Cruise Line, Ltd.	Seabourne Cruise Line, Ltd.	Seabourne Cruise Line, Ltd.
Flag	Norway	Norway	Norway
Gross tons	9,975	9,975	9,961
Dimensions (feet)	439 × 67 × 16	439 × 67 × 16	443 × 67 × 17
Year built	1988	1989	1992
Place built	Bremerhaven, Germany	Bremerhaven, Germany	Bremerhaven, Germany
Shipyard	Schichau Seebeckwerft AG (No. 1,065)	Schichau Seebeckwerft AG (No. 1,070)	AS Othes (No. 1,071)
Engines	2 12-cyl. Normo KVMB-12 and 2 8-cyl. Normo KRMB-8 diesels	2 12-cyl. Normo KVMB-12 and 2 8-cyl. Normo KRMB-8 diesels	2 12-cyl. Normo KVMB-12 and 2 8-cyl. Normo KRMB-8 diesels
Propulsion	Geared, twin screw, controllable pitch	Geared, twin screw, controllable pitch	Geared, twin screw, controllable pitch
Other equipment	Bow thruster	Bow thruster	Bow thruster
Passenger capacity	204	204	204
Notes			1

Name	*Seabourn Goddess I*	*Seabourn Goddess II*	*Seabourn Sun*
Previous name(s)	*Sea Goddess I*	*Sea Goddess II*	*Royal Viking Sun*
Subsequent name(s)			
Owner	Cunard White Star Ltd.		Cunard White Star Ltd.
Flag	Bahamas	Bahamas	Bahamas
Gross tons	4,253	4,260	37,845
Dimensions (feet)	344 × 58 × 14	344 × 48 × 14	669 × 95 × 24
Year built	1984	1985	1988
Place built	Helsinki, Finland	Helsinki, Finland	Turku, Finland
Shipyard	Wartsila (No. 466)	Wartsila (No. 467)	Wartsila (No. 1,298)
Engines	2 12-cyl. Wartsila 12V22HF diesels	2 12-cyl. Wartsila 12V22HF diesels	4 8-cyl. Sulzer 8ZAL40S diesels
Propulsion	Geared, twin screw, controllable pitch	Geared, twin screw, controllable pitch	Geared, twin screw, controllable pitch
Other equipment	Bow thruster	Bow thruster	2 bow thrusters
Passenger capacity	116	116	740
Notes	2	2	2

Notes

1. Built to same specifications as *Seabourn Pride* and *Seabourn Spirit* (see text, chapter 8); acquired from Royal Cruise Line in 1996.
2. Acquired from Cunard Line in 1999.

SEAWIND CRUISE LINE (See Premier Cruise Lines)

SILVERSEAS CRUISES

Name	*Silver Cloud*	*Silver Wind*	*Silver Shadow*
Previous name(s)			
Subsequent name(s)			
Owner	Coimar S.p.A.	Coimar S.p.A.	
Flag	Bahamas	Bahamas	Bahamas
Gross tons	16,927	16,927	28,255
Dimensions (feet)	511 × 70 × 18	511 × 70 × 18	597 × 82 × 20
Year built	1994	1994	2000
Place built	Viareggio, Italy	Viareggio, Italy	Viareggio, Italy
Shipyard	Societa Esercizio Cantieri (No. 775)	Societa Esercizio Cantieri (No. 776)	Societa Esercizio Cantieri
Engines	2 6-cyl. Wartsila 6R46 diesels	2 6-cyl. Wartsila 6R46 diesels	Wartsila diesels
Propulsion	Geared, twin screw, controllable pitch	Geared, twin screw, controllable pitch	
Other equipment	2 bow thrusters	2 bow thrusters,1 stern thruster	2 bow thrusters
Passenger capacity	296	296	388
Notes	1	1	1

Name	*Silver Whisper*
Previous name(s)	
Subsequent name(s)	
Owner	
Flag	
Gross tons	25,000
Dimensions (feet)	597 × 82 × 20
Year built	2000
Place built	Viareggio, Italy
Shipyard	Societa Esercizio Cantieri
Engines	
Propulsion	
Other equipment	2 bow thrusters
Passenger capacity	388
Notes	1

Notes

1. T. Mariotti prime contractor for all four Silverseas vessels; vessels completed at Mariotti's Genoa yard. Hulls built and launched in Viareggio, as indicated.

SITMAR (1971–1988)

Inclusive dates shown are for Sitmar Cruises, Inc. See text, chapter 5, for additional information about Sitmar, the Vlasov Group, and V. Ships. See roster entry for Princess Cruises for details about three new-buildings designed by Sitmar but completed and delivered after company was acquired by P&O/Princess.

Name	*Fairstar*	*Fairland*	*Sitmar Fairwind*
Previous name(s)	*Oxfordshire*	*Carinthia*	*Sylvania*
Subsequent name(s)	*Ripa*	*Fairsea*	*Fairwind*
		Fair Princess	*Dawn Princess*
		Regent Isle	*Albatros*
		Fair Princess	
Owner	Fairstar Shipping Corp.	Fairsea Shipping Corp.	Fairwinds Shipping Corp.
Flag	Liberia	Liberia	Liberia
Gross tons	21,619	16,627	16,667
Dimensions (feet)	609 × 78 × 28	608 × 80 × 29	608 × 80 × 29
Year built	1957	1956	1957
Place built	Glasgow, Scotland	Clydebank, Scotland	Clydebank, Scotland
Shipyard	Fairfield Shipbuilding (No. 775)	John Brown (No. 699)	John Brown (No. 700)
Engines	4 steam turbines	4 steam turbines	4 steam turbines
Propulsion	Geared, twin screw	Geared, twin screw	Geared, twin screw
Other equipment			
Passenger capacity	1,870*	850	1,020*
Notes	1	2	2

Name	*Fairsky*	*Fairsky*
Previous name(s)	*Principe Perfeito*	
Subsequent name(s)	*Vera*	*Sky Princess*
	Marianna IX	*Pacific Sky*
	Marianna 9	
Owner		Sitmar Cruises, Inc.
Flag	(See note)	Liberia
Gross tons	19,393	46,314
Dimensions (feet)	625 × 79 × 26	787 × 92 × 26
Year built	1961	1984
Place built	Newcastle, U.K.	La Seyne, France
Shipyard	Swan, Hunter & Wigham Richardson (No. 1,974)	CNIM Shipyards (No. 1,436)
Engines	4 steam turbines	4 steam turbines
Propulsion	Geared, twin screw	Geared, twin screw
Other equipment		
Passenger capacity	880	1,212
Notes	3	4

Notes

1. Acquired from Bibby Line in 1964; became full-time cruise ship in 1973. Conveyed to P&O in 1988 but retained Sitmar-oriented name *Fairstar*.

2. Acquired from Cunard in 1968; conveyed to P&O/Princess in 1988.

3. Acquired from Global Transportation in 1979 but never operated in cruise service for Sitmar; sold to Greek interests in 1982.

4. Conveyed to P&O/Princess in 1988.

*Total number of available berths.

STAR CRUISES

Name	Langkapuri Star Aquarius	Star Pisces	MegaStar Aries
Previous name(s)	Athena Star Aquarius	Kalypso	Lady Sara Aurora II
Subsequent name(s)			
Owner	Star Aquarius, Ltd.	Star Pisces, Ltd.	Megastar Aries, Ltd.
Flag	Panama	Panama	Panama
Gross tons	40,022	40,053	3,264
Dimensions (feet)	580 × 95 × 20	580 × 95	270 × 46 × 12
Year built	1989	1990	1991
Place built	Turku, Finland	Turku, Finland	Luebeck, Germany
Shipyard	Wartsila (No. 1,297)	Masa-Yards (No. 1,298)	Flender Werft (No. 648)
Engines	4 9-cyl. Sulzer 9ZAL40S diesels	4 9-cyl. Sulzer 9ZAL40S diesels	2 16-cyl. Motoren Werke Mannheim TBD604BV16 diesels
Propulsion	Geared, twin screw	Geared, twin screw	Geared, twin screw, controllable pitch
Other equipment	2 bow thrusters	2 bow thrusters	Bow thruster
Passenger capacity	1,712*	2,165*	64
Notes	1	1	2

Name	MegaStar Taurus	SuperStar Capricorn	SuperStar Gemini
Previous name(s)	Lady Diana Lady D. Aurora I	Royal Viking Sky Sunward Birka Queen Sunward Golden Princess	Crown Jewel
Subsequent name(s)		Hyundai Keumkang	
Owner	Megastar Taurus IOM, Ltd.	Superstar Capricorn, Ltd.	Superstar Gemini, Ltd.
Flag	Panama	Panama	Panama
Gross tons	3,264	28,388	19,093
Dimensions (feet)	270 × 46 × 12	674 × 83 × 24	537 × 74 × 18
Year built	1991	1973	1992
Place built	Luebeck, Germany	Helsinki, Finland	Valencia, Spain
Shipyard	Flender Werft (No. 647)	Wartsila (No. 396)	Union Naval (No. 197)
Engines	2 16-cyl. Motoren Werke Mannheim TBD604BV16 diesels	4 9-cyl. Wartsila 9ZH40/48 diesels	4 8-cyl. Wartsila 8R32E diesels
Propulsion	Geared, twin screw, controllable pitch	Geared, twin screw, controllable pitch	Geared, twin screw, controllable pitch
Other equipment	Bow thruster	2 bow thrusters	2 bow thrusters
Passenger capacity	70	804	820
Notes	2	3	4

Name	SuperStar Sagittarius	SuperStar Leo	SuperStar Virgo
Previous name(s)	Sun Viking		
Subsequent name(s)	Hyundai Bongnae		

Continued

STAR CRUISES—*Continued*

Name	*SuperStar Sagittarius*	*SuperStar Leo*	*SuperStar Virgo*
Owner	Actinor Cruise II, SA	Superstar Leo, Ltd.	Superstar Virgo, Ltd.
Flag	Panama	Panama	Panama
Gross tons	18,455	75,338	75,338
Dimensions (feet)	563 × 79 × 21	881 × 106 × 27	881 × 106 × 27
Year built	1972	1998	1999
Place built	Helsinki, Finland	Papenburg, Germany	Papenburg, Germany
Shipyard	Wartsila (No. 394)	Meyer Werft (No. 646)	Meyer Werft (No. 647)
Engines	4 9-cyl. Sulzer 92H40/48 diesels	4 14-cyl. MAN-B&W 14V 48/60 diesels	4 14-cyl. MAN-B&W 14V 48/60 diesels
Propulsion	Geared, twin screw, controllable pitch	Electric drive, twin screw	Electric drive, twin screw
Other equipment	Bow thruster	Bow thruster	Bow thruster
Passenger capacity	762	1,964	2,000
Notes	5		

Name	*SuperStar Aries*	*SuperStar Libra*	*"SuperStar Scorpio"*
Previous name(s)	*Europa*		
Subsequent name(s)			See note
Owner	Megastar Asia, Ltd.		
Flag	Panama		
Gross tons	37,012	91,000	91,000
Dimensions (feet)	655 × 94 × 28	961 × 106	961 × 106
Year built	1981	2001	2002
Place built	Bremen, Germany	Papenburg, Germany	Papenburg, Germany
Shipyard	Bremer Vulkan (No. 1,001)	Meyer Werft	Meyer Werft
Engines	2 9-cyl. MAN K7SZ70/125B diesels		
Propulsion	Geared, twin screw, controllable pitch		
Other equipment	Bow thruster		
Passenger capacity	632	2,300	2,300
Notes	6		7

Name	*SuperStar Taurus*	*MegaStar Capricorn*	*MegaStar Sagittarius*
Previous name(s)	*Viking Saga*	*Renaissance VI*	*Renaissance V*
	Sally Albatross	*Sun Viva II*	*Hanseatic Renaissance*
	Leeward		*Renaissance V*
			Sun Viva I
Subsequent name(s)			
Owner			
Flag	Panama		
Gross tons	25,611	4,200	4,200

Name	SuperStar Taurus	MegaStar Capricorn	MegaStar Sagittarius
Dimensions (feet)	521 × 83 × 23	297 × 50 × 13	296 × 50 × 13
Year built	1980	1991	1991
Place built	Turku, Finland	Marina di Carrare, Italy	Marina di Carrare, Italy
Shipyard	Wartsila (No. 1,247)	Nuovi Cantieri Apuania (No. 1,145)	Nuovi Cantieri Apuania (No. 1,144)
Engines	4 12-cyl. Pielstick 12PC2-5V-400 diesels	2 8-cyl. MAN 8L28/32 diesels	2 8-cyl. MAN 8L28/32 diesels
Propulsion	Geared, twin screw, controllable pitch	Geared, twin screw, controllable pitch	Geared, twin screw, controllable pitch
Other equipment	2 bow thrusters	Bow thruster	Bow thruster
Passenger capacity	950	100	100
Notes	8	9	9

Name	SuperStar Capricorn	SuperStar Sagittarius	SuperStar Capricorn
Previous name(s)	Royal Viking Sea Royal Odyssey Norwegian Star		
Subsequent name(s)			
Owner			
Flag	Bahamas		
Gross tons	28,018	112,000	112,000
Dimensions (feet)	674 × 89 × 25	1,042 × 117	1,042 × 117
Year built	1973	2003	2004
Place built	Helsinki, Finland	Papenburg, Germany	Papenburg, Germany
Shipyard	Wartsila (No. 397)	Meyer Werft	Meyer Werft
Engines	4 9-cyl. Sulzer 9ZH40/48 diesels		
Propulsion	Geared, twin screw, controllable pitch		
Other equipment	2 bow thrusters		
Passenger capacity	798	3,000	3,000
Notes	10	11	11

Notes

1. Former car ferry; acquired from Viking Line in 1993.

2. Acquired from New Frontier Cruise Line in 1994.

3. Acquired from Princess Cruises in 1997; conveyed to Hyundai Marine in 1998.

4. Acquired from Crown Cruise Line in 1995.

5. Acquired from Royal Caribbean in 1997; chartered to Hyundai Marine in 1999

6. Purchased from Hapag-Lloyd in 1997; leased back to Hapag through 1999; was to have been called *SuperStar Europe*.

7. Although the name *SuperStar Scorpio* was originally announced for this vessel, the cruise ship will likely be assigned to Norwegian Cruise Line when completed in 2002 and named accordingly; see text, chapter 6.

8. Acquired from Effjohn International in 1999.

9. Acquired from Sun Cruises in 2000.

10. Acquired from Norwegian Cruise Line in 2000.

11. Post-Panamax vessel; will not fit through the Panama Canal.

*Total number of available berths.

SUNDANCE CRUISES (1984–1986)

Name	*Sundancer*	*Stardancer*
Previous name(s)	*Svea Cornoa*	*Scandinavia*
Subsequent name(s)	*Pegasus*	*Viking Seranade*
Owner	Johnson Line A/B	Sundance Cruise Corp.
Flag	Sweden	Bahamas
Gross tons	12,576	26,747
Dimensions (feet)	502 × 72 × 19	608 × 89 × 23
Year built	1974	1981
Place built	Nantes, France	Nantes, France
Shipyard	Dubigeon-Normandie (No. 141)	Dubigeon-Normandie (No. 164)
Engines	4 12-cyl. Pielstick 12PC2V-400 diesels	2 9-cyl. B&W 9L55GFCA diesels
Propulsion	Geared, twin screw	Geared, twin screw, controllable pitch
Other equipment	Bow thruster, bow door and ramp, stern door and ramp	2 bow thrusters, stern door and ramp
Passenger capacity	800*	1,606*
Notes	1	2

Notes

1. Acquired from Svea Line in 1984; seriously damaged early in first season of service; sold to Epirotiki in 1984.
2. Acquired from DFDS in 1985; conveyed to Admiral Cruises via merger in 1985.
*Total number of available berths.

SWEDISH AMERICAN LINE (1915–1975)

Name	*Kungsholm*	*Gripsholm*	*Kungsholm*
Previous name(s)			
Subsequent name(s)	*Europa* *Columbus C.*	*Samantha* *Navarino* *Regent Sea*	*Sea Princess* *Victoria*
Owner	A/B Svenska Amerika Linien	A/B Svenska Amerika Linien	A/B Svenska Amerika Linien
Flag	Sweden	Sweden	Sweden
Gross tons	21,141	23,191	26,678
Dimensions (feet)	600 × 77 × 27	631 × 82 × 27	660 × 87 × 28
Year built	1953	1957	1966
Place built	Vlissingen, Sweden	Genoa, Italy	Clydebank, Scotland
Shipyard	N.V. Koninklijke Maats. Schelde (No. 273)	Ansaldo S.p.A. (No. 1,500)	John Brown (No. 728)
Engines	2 8-cyl. B&W diesels	2 9-cyl. Gotaverken diesels	2 9-cyl. Gotaverken 760/1500VGS9 diesels
Propulsion	Geared, twin screw	Geared, twin screw	Geared, twin screw
Other equipment			Bow thruster
Passenger capacity	802	842	750
Notes	1	2	3

1. Conveyed to North German Lloyd in 1964.
2. Conveyed to Karageorgis Line in 1975.
3. Conveyed to Flagship Cruises in 1975.

UNITED STATES LINES

United States Lines, a subsidiary of American Classic Voyages, initiated cruise service in the Hawaiian Islands in late 2000. Company has no corporate ties to the United States Lines that once operated transatlantic passenger liners.

Name	*Patriot*	Newbuilding	Newbuilding
Previous name(s)	*Nieuw Amsterdam* (3)		
Subsequent name(s)			
Owner			
Flag	U.S.	U.S.	U.S.
Gross tons	33,930	72,000	72,000
Dimensions (feet)	704 × 89 × 25	840 × 106 × 26	840 × 106 × 26
Year built	1983	2003	2004
Place built	St. Nazaire, France	Pascagoula, Miss.	Pascagoula, Miss.
Shipyard	Chantiers de l'Atlantique (No. V-27)	Ingalls Shipbuilding	Ingalls Shipbuilding
Engines	2 7-cyl. Sulzer 7RLB66 diesels	4 8-cyl. Wartsila 8L46C diesels	4 8-cyl. Wartsila 8L46C diesels
Propulsion	Geared, twin screw, controllable pitch	2 Mermaid electric pod-propulsion units	2 Mermaid electric pod-propulsion units
Other equipment	2 bow thrusters, 1 stern thruster	3 bow thrusters	3 bow thrusters
Passenger capacity	1,214	1,900	1,900
Notes	1	2	

1. Acquired from Holland America Line in 2000.
2. Will be first oceangoing passenger vessel built in the United States in forty years.

WEST LINE LTD. (1967–1972)

Name	*Polar Star*	*West Star*
Previous name(s)	*Wappen von Hamburg* *Delos*	*Cabo Izarra*
Subsequent name(s)	*Pacific Star* *Xanadu* *Expex* *Faithful*	*Donna Montserrat* *Xing Hu*
Owner	West Line, Ltd.	Westours, Inc.
Flag	Canada; Panama	Liberia
Gross tons	2,599	3,658
Dimensions (feet)	272 × 43 × 22	344 × 52 × 26
Year built	1955	1966
Place built	Hamburg, West Germany	Cadiz, Spain

Contniued

WEST LINE LTD. (1967–1972)—*Continued*

Name	*Polar Star*	*West Star*
Shipyard	Steinwerder Industrien AG (No. 786)	Societe Espanola de Construction Navale, SA (No. 120)
Engines	4 12-cyl. Maybach diesels	2 9-cyl. B&W diesels
Propulsion	Geared, twin screw	Geared, twin screw
Other equipment		
Passenger capacity	155	220
Notes	1	2

Notes

1. Acquired in 1967; sold to Xanadu Cruises of Seattle for Alaska service in 1972.

2. Acquired from Spanish interests after brief cruising career in south Florida in 1970; sold to Philippine interests in 1975.

WINDSTAR CRUISES

Name	*Wind Star*	*Wind Song*	*Wind Spirit*
Previous name(s)			
Subsequent name(s)			
Owner	Windstar Cruises, Ltd.	Windstar Cruises, Ltd.	Windstar Cruises, Ltd.
Flag	Bahamas	Bahamas	Bahamas
Gross tons	5,703	5,350	5,736
Dimensions (feet)	440 × 51 × 14	440 × 51 × 14	440 × 51 × 14
Year built	1985	1986	1985
Place built	LeHavre, France	LeHavre, France	LeHavre, France
Shipyard	Societe Nouvelle de Ateliers du Havre (No. 269)	Societe Nouvelle de Ateliers du Havre (No. 273)	Societe Nouvelle de Ateliers du Havre (No. 271)
Engines	3 6-cyl. Wartsila 6R22 diesels	3 6-cyl. Wartsila 6R22 diesels	3 6-cyl. Wartsila 6R32E diesels
Propulsion	Electric drive, single screw	Electric drive, single screw	Electric drive, single screw
Other equipment	Four masts with computer-controlled sails, bow thruster	Four masts with computer-controlled sails, bow thruster	Four masts with computer-controlled sails, bow thruster
Passenger capacity	148	148	148
Notes			

Name	*Wind Surf*
Previous name(s)	*Club Med 1*
Subsequent name(s)	
Owner	Carnival Corp.
Flag	Bahamas
Gross tons	14,745
Dimensions (feet)	613 × 66 × 16
Year built	1990
Place built	LeHavre, France

Name	Wind Surf
Shipyard	Societe Nouvelle de Ateliers du Havre (No. 274)
Engines	4 6-cyl. Wartsila 6R32 diesels
Propulsion	Electric drive, twin screw
Other equipment	Five masts with computer-controlled sails, bow thruster, stern thruster
Passenger capacity	312
Notes	1

Notes

1. Acquired from Club Med Cruises in 1997.

YARMOUTH STEAMSHIP COMPANY (1965–1967)

Name	Yarmouth Castle	Yarmouth
Previous name(s)	*Evangeline*	*Yarmouth* *Yarmouth Castle* *Queen of Nassau* *Yarmouth Castle*
Subsequent name(s)		*San Andres* *Elizabeth A.*
Owner	Chadade Steamship Co.	Yarmouth Steamship Co., Inc.
Flag	Panama	Panama
Gross tons	5,002	5,002
Dimensions (feet)	379 × 56 × 20	379 × 56 × 20
Year built	1927	1927
Place built	Philadelphia, Pa.	Philadelphia, Pa.
Shipyard	Wm. Cramp & Sons	Wm. Cramp & Sons (No. 518)
Engines	4 steam turbines	4 steam turbines
Propulsion	Geared, twin screw	Geared, twin screw
Other equipment		
Passenger capacity	365*	350*
Notes	1	2

Notes

1. Acquired from Eastern Steamship in 1964; lost to fire in 1966 (see text, chapter 1).

2. Acquired from Eastern Steamship in 1962; sold to Greek interests in 1967. Was last vessel built by Wm. Cramp & Sons.

*Total number of available berths.

Part 2—The North American Fleet of
Mini Cruise Ships in the Summer of 2000

ALASKA'S GLACIER BAY TOURS AND CRUISES

Name	*Wilderness Discoverer*	*Executive Explorer*	*Wilderness Explorer*
Previous name(s)	*Mayan Prince*		*Mount Hope* *Arkansas Explorer* *Viking Explorer*
Flag (Off. No.)	U.S. (952722)	U.S. (697964)	U.S. (520611)
Gross tons	95	93	98
Dimensions (feet)	172 × 39 × 6	96 × 37 × 11	104 × 21 × 8
Year built	1992	1986	1969
Place built	Warren, R.I.	Freeland, Wash.	Warren, R.I.
Shipyard	Blount Industries	Nicholas Bros. (No. S-81)	Blount Industries
Engines & propulsion	Twin diesels, geared, twin screw	2 16-cyl. Deutz diesels, geared, twin screw	Twin diesels, geared, twin screw
Other equipment	Bow ramp	Catamaran hull	
Passenger capacity	88	49	36
Notes	1		1

Name	*Wilderness Adventurer*
Previous name(s)	*Caribbean Prince*
Flag (Off. No.)	U.S. (664136)
Gross tons	89
Dimensions (feet)	156 × 36 × 6
Year built	1983
Place built	Warren, R.I.
Shipyard	Blount Industries (No. LB-250)
Engines & propulsion	2 12-cyl. GM 12V-71 diesels, geared, twin screw
Other equipment	Bow ramp
Passenger capacity	76
Notes	1

ALASKA SIGHTSEEING/CRUISE WEST

Name	*Spirit of Glacier Bay*	*Spirit of Alaska*	*Spirit of Discovery*
Previous name(s)	*New Shoreham I* *Glacier Bay Explorer*	*Pacific Northwest Explorer*	*Independence* *Columbia* *Spirit of Glacier Bay*
Flag (Off. No.)	U.S. (534100)	U.S. (628951)	U.S. (574958)
Gross tons	97	97	94
Dimensions (feet)	125 × 28 × 7	143 × 28 × 8	166 × 37 × 8

Name	*Spirit of Glacier Bay*	*Spirit of Alaska*	*Spirit of Discovery*
Year built	1971	1980	1976
Place built	Warren, R.I.	Warren, R.I.	Boothbay Harbor, Maine
Shipyard	Blount Industries	Blount Industries (No. AP-234)	Eastern Shipbuilding
Engines & propulsion	2 12-cyl. GM 12V71N diesels, geared, twin screw	2 12-cyl. Caterpillar 3412 diesels, geared, twin screw	2 8-cyl. Caterpillar 3508 diesels, geared, twin screw
Other equipment	Bow ramp		
Passenger capacity	52	82	82
Notes	1		

Name	*Spirit of Columbia*	*Spirit of '98*	*Spirit of Endeavor*
Previous name(s)	*New Shoreham II*	*Pilgrim Belle* *Colonial Explorer* *Victorian Empress*	*Newport Clipper* *Sea Spirit*
Flag (Off. No.)	U.S. (614006)	U.S. (677464)	U.S. (661485)
Gross tons	98	96	95
Dimensions (feet)	143 × 28 × 7	192 × 40 × 9	217 × 37 × 9
Year built	1979	1984	1983
Place built	Warren, R.I.	Mobile, Ala.	Jeffersonville, Ind.
Shipyard	Blount Industries (No. NS-225)	Bender Shipyard	Jeffboat (No. 82-2542)
Engines & propulsion	2 12-cyl. GM 12V71N diesels, geared, twin screw	2 12-cyl. Caterpillar 3512 diesels, geared, twin screw	2 12-cyl. Caterpillar 3512 diesels, geared, twin screw
Other equipment	Bow ramp	Bow thruster	
Passenger capacity	72	99	107
Notes	1		

AMERICAN CANADIAN CARIBBEAN LINE

Name	*Niagara Prince*	*Grande Caribe*	*Grande Mariner*
Previous name(s)			
Flag (Off. No.)	U.S. (1027834)	U.S. (1052604)	U.S. (1066911)
Gross tons	95	94	97
Dimensions (feet)	174 × 40 × 6	183 × 40 × 7	183 × 40 × 7
Year built	1994	1997	1998
Place built	Warren, R.I.	Warren, R.I.	Warren, R.I.
Shipyard	Blount Industries (No. LB-287)	Blount Industries	Blount Industries
Engines & propulsion	Twin diesels, geared, twin screw	Twin diesels, geared, twin screw	2 MAN D2842LE diesels, geared, twin screw
Other equipment	Bow ramp, retractable pilothouse, bow thruster	Bow ramp, retractable pilothouse, bow thruster	Bow ramp, retractable pilothouse, bow thruster
Passenger capacity	84	100	100
Notes			

AMERICA WEST STEAMBOAT COMPANY

Name	*Queen of the West*
Previous name(s)	
Flag (Off. No.)	U.S. (1033572)
Gross tons	92
Dimensions (feet)	230 × 50
Year built	1995
Place built	Freeland, Wash.
Shipyard	Nichols Brothers
Engines & propulsion	
Other equipment	
Passenger capacity	163
Notes	

AMERICAN CRUISE LINES

Name	*American Eagle*
Previous name(s)	
Flag (Off. No.)	U.S. (1088888)
Gross tons	1,148
Dimensions (feet)	170 × 40 × 7
Year built	2000
Place built	Salisbury, Md.
Shipyard	Chesapeake Shipbuilding
Engines & propulsion	Twin Caterpillar diesels, geared, twin screw
Other equipment	Bow thruster
Passenger capacity	49
Notes	

CLIPPER CRUISE LINE

Name	*Nantucket Clipper*	*Yorktown Clipper*	*Clipper Adventurer*
Previous name(s)			*Admiral Lazarev* *Alla Tarasova*
Flag (Off. No.)	U.S. (677685)	U.S. (928931)	Bahamas
Gross tons	96	97	4,364
Dimensions (feet)	173 × 37 × 12	257 × 43 × 8	330 × 54 × 14
Year built	1984	1988	1975
Place built	Jeffersonville, Ind.	Green Cove Springs, Fla.	Kraljevoca, Yugoslavia
Shipyard	Jeffboat (No. 82-2543)	First Coast Shipbuilding (No. 001)	Brodogradiliste Titovo (No. 408)
Engines & propulsion	2 12-cyl. GM 12V92 diesels, geared, twin screw	2 8-cyl. Caterpillar 3508DITA diesels, geared, twin screw	2 8-cyl. B&W 8-35VF-62 diesels, geared, twin screw, controllable pitch
Other equipment			
Passenger capacity	100	138	122
Notes			

Name	Clipper Odyssey
Previous name(s)	Oceanic Grace
	Oceanic Odyssey
Flag (Off. No.)	Bahamas
Gross tons	5,218
Dimensions (feet)	338 × 51 × 14
Year built	1989
Place built	Tsu, Japan
Shipyard	Nippon Kokan K.K.
	(No. 112)
Engines & propulsion	2 16-cyl. Wartsila
	16V22HF diesels,
	geared, twin screw,
	controllable pitch
Other equipment	Bow thruster
Passenger capacity	120
Notes	

LINDBLAD SPECIAL EXPEDITIONS

Name	Sea Bird	Sea Lion	Caledonian Star
Previous name(s)	Majestic Explorer	Great Rivers Explorer	Marburg
			North Star
Flag (Off. No.)	U.S. (644046)	U.S. (648350)	Bahamas
Gross tons	99	99	3,095
Dimensions (feet)	136 × 31 × 11	136 × 31 × 11	295 × 46 × 21
Year built	1982	1982	1966
Place built	Freeland, Wash.	Freeland, Wash.	Bremerhaven, Germany
Shipyard	Nicholas Brothers Boat Builders (No. S-62)	Nicholas Brothers Boat Builders (No. S-63)	A.G. Weser Werk Seebeck (No. 917)
Engines & propulsion	Twin diesel, geared, twin screw	Twin diesel, geared, twin screw	2 8-cyl. MaK 8M582AK diesels, geared, twin screw
Other equipment			Converted fish factory stern trawler
Passenger capacity	88	74	110
Notes			

Name	Polaris
Previous name(s)	Oresund
	Lindblad Polaris
Flag (Off. No.)	Ecuador
Gross tons	2,214
Dimensions (feet)	238 × 43 × 14
Year built	1964
Place built	Aalborg, Denmark
Shipyard	Aalborg Vaerft, AS
	(No. 55)

Continued

LINDBLAD SPECIAL EXPEDITIONS—*Continued*

Name	*Polaris*
Engines & propulsion	2 6-cyl. diesels, geared, twin screw
Other equipment	Hull strengthened for ice conditions
Passenger capacity	80
Notes	

ST. LAWRENCE CRUISE LINE

Name	*Canadian Empress*
Previous name(s)	
Flag (Off. No.)	Canada
Gross tons	463
Dimensions (feet)	108 × 30 × 5
Year built	1981
Place built	Gananoque, Ontario
Shipyard	Algan Shipyard (No. 35)
Engines & propulsion	2 6-cyl. Volvo Penta TAMD120B diesels, geared, twin screw
Other equipment	Bow thruster
Passenger capacity	66
Notes	

Notes

1. Vessel originally ran for American Canadian Caribbean Line.

Part 3—A Dozen Historic Ocean Liners

Name	*Andrea Doria*	*Aquitania*	*Caronia*
Previous name(s)			
Subsequent name(s)			*Columbia*
			Caribia
Owner/Operator	Italian Line	Cunard Line	Cunard-White Star Line
Flag	Italy	U.K.	U.K.
Gross tons	29,083	45,647	34,172
Dimensions (feet)	700 × 90 × 30	901 × 97	715 × 91 × 32
Year built	1953	1914	1948
Place built	Genoa, Italy	Clydebank, Scotland	Clydebank, Scotland
Shipyard	S. A. Ansaldo (No. 918)	John Brown (No. 409)	John Brown (No. 635)
Engines	6 steam turbines	4 steam turbines	6 steam turbines
Propulsion	Geared, twin screw	Direct drive, quadruple screw	Geared, twin screw
Other equipment			
Passenger capacity	1,241*	3,230*	932*
Notes	1	2	3

Name	*Ile de France*	*Mauretania*	*Nieuw Amsterdam* (2)
Previous name(s)			
Subsequent name(s)	*Furanzu Maru*		
Owner/Operator	French Line	Cunard Line	Holland America Line
Flag (Off. No.)	France	U.K.	Netherlands
Gross tons	43,153	31,938	36,667
Dimensions (feet)	791 × 91	790 × 88	759 × 88 × 32
Year built	1927	1907	1938
Place built	St. Nazaire, France	Newcastle, U.K.	Rotterdam, Netherlands
Shipyard	Chantiers de l'Atlantique (No. R-5)	Swan, Hunter & Wigham Richardson (No. 735)	Rotterdam Drydock (No. 200)
Engines	Steam turbines	6 steam turbines	8 steam turbines
Propulsion	Geared, quadruple screw	Direct drive, quadruple screw	Geared, twin screw
Other equipment			
Passenger capacity	1,786*	2,165*	1,187*
Notes	4	5, 6	7

Name	*Normandie*	*Queen Elizabeth*	*Queen Mary*
Previous name(s)			
Subsequent name(s)	USS *Lafayette*	*Seawise University*	
Owner/Operator	French Line	Cunard-White Star Line	Cunard-White Star Line
Flag	France	U.K.	U.K.
Gross tons	83,423	83,673	81,235
Dimensions (feet)	1,028 × 119 × 37	1,031 × 110 × 39	1,018 × 118 × 39
Year built	1935	1940	1936
Place built	St. Nazaire, France	Clydebank, Scotland	Clydebank, Scotland
Shipyard	Chantiers de l'Atlantique (No. T-6)	John Brown (No. 552)	John Brown (No. 534)
Engines	4 steam turbines	16 steam turbines	16 steam turbines
Propulsion	Electric drive, quadruple screw	Geared, quadruple screw	Geared, quadruple screw
Other equipment			
Passenger capacity	1,972*	2,283*	2,139*
Notes	5, 8, 9	8, 10	5, 8, 11

Name	*Rex*	*Titanic*	*United States*
Previous name(s)			
Subsequent name(s)			
Owner/Operator	Italian Line	White Star Line	United States Lines
Flag (Off. No.)	Italy	U.K.	U.S. (263934)
Gross tons	51,062	46,329	53,329
Dimensions (feet)	880 × 96	882 × 92 × 34	917 × 102 × 39
Year built	1932	1912	1952
Place built	Genoa, Italy	Belfast, Northern Ireland	Newport News, Va.
Shipyard	Ansaldo (No. 296)	Harland & Wolff (No. 401)	Newport News S/B (No. 488)
Engines	Steam turbines	2 4-cyl. triple-expansion steam reciprocating and 1 steam turbine	4 steam turbines
Propulsion	Geared, quadruple screw	Triple screw	Geared, quadruple screw

Name	Rex	Titanic	United States
Other equipment			
Passenger capacity	2,358*	2,603*	1,928*
Notes	5, 12	13	5, 14

Notes

1. In service from 1953 to 1956; lost off Nantucket Island after collision with Swedish American's *Stockholm*.

2. In service from 1914 to 1949; scrapped in 1950. Last four-stack transatlantic liner; served as cruiser and then troop-ship during First World War and as troopship during Second World War.

3. In service from 1947 to 1967.

4. In service from 1927 to 1958; scrapped in 1959. Served as troopship during Second World War.

5. At one time vessel held "Blue Riband" for fastest transatlantic crossing.

6. In service from 1907 to 1935. Service for Royal Navy during First World War.

7. In service from 1938 to 1973; scrapped in 1974. Served as troopship during Second World War.

8. Vessel could not fit through the Panama Canal.

9. In service from 1935 to 1940; lost to fire while being converted into troopship USS *Lafayette* in New York in 1942.

10. Troopship service from 1941 to 1945; commercial service from 1946 to 1968; lost to fire while being converted into a floating university in Hong Kong in 1971.

11. In service from 1936 to 1967; converted to shoreside hotel in Long Beach, California. Served as troopship during Second World War.

12. In commercial service from 1932 to 1939; sunk by Royal Air Force in 1944; raised and scrapped in 1947.

13. In service in 1912; lost to collision with iceberg on maiden voyage in 1912.

14. In service from 1952 to 1969; since 1969 laid up pending disposition.

*Total number of available berths.

APPENDIX B

Cruise Ship Locations and Itineraries: July 4, 2000

Sterling Casino Lines

The following tables provide information about the operations of the contemporary cruise industry by showing the locations of 156 vessels at high noon, local time, on Tuesday, July 4, 2000. Fleets are presented in alphabetical order; operators of mini cruise ships are clustered separately at the end.

The information is self-explanatory. A cruise identified with the name of a single port—for example, a seven-night eastern Caribbean cruise from Miami—refers to an itinerary that begins and ends in the same place. If two ports are shown—for instance, a twelve-night cruise from Dover to Copenhagen—the itinerary begins in one city and ends in another.

The information is taken primarily from schedules and itineraries published in advance by the cruise companies. It has been supplemented with any variations from announced itineraries that are known to have occurred. Under the heading "status," a vessel may be identified as "approaching port." This indicates the vessel was expected to dock within an hour or so of high noon; it does not refer to a vessel's next port of call. The expression "in port" does not necessarily mean a vessel was docked in the harbor; in some instances, a vessel could have been at anchor, and passengers were transferred to shore by tender.

Vessels shown as "under construction" do not represent the industry's full backlog of newbuildings. Rather they are vessels whose construction was in the final stage on July 4, 2000, with delivery anticipated roughly before December 31, 2000.

AIRTOURS/SUN CRUISES

Vessel	Status	Cruise
Carousel	In port: Naples, Italy	7-night Mediterranean cruise from Palma, Majorca
Seawing	At sea	7-night Greek island cruise from Limassol, Cyprus
Sunbird	In port: Civitavecchia, Italy	7-night Mediterranean cruise from Palma, Majorca
Sundream	In port: Alesund, Norway	14-night North Cape cruise from Southampton

AMERICAN HAWAII CRUISE LINE

Vessel	Status	Cruise
Independence	In port: Kahului, Hawaii	7-night Hawaii cruise from Honolulu

CAPE CANAVERAL CRUISE LINE

Vessel	Status	Cruise
Dolphin IV	Approaching port: Key West, Fla.	4-night Bahamas cruise from Port Canaveral

CARNIVAL CRUISE LINES

Vessel	Status	Cruise
Carnival Destiny	In port: Halifax, Nova Scotia	5-night Canada cruise from New York
Carnival Triumph	At sea	7-night western Caribbean cruise from Miami
Celebration	At sea	7-night western Caribbean cruise from New Orleans
Ecstasy	In port: Key West, Fla.	4-night western Caribbean cruise from Miami
Elation	At sea	7-night Mexico cruise from Los Angeles
Fantasy	In port: Nassau, Bahamas	4-night Bahamas cruise from Port Canaveral
Fascination	In port: Dominica, West Indies	7-night southern Caribbean cruise from San Juan
Holiday	In port: Catalina Island, Calif.	4-night Mexico cruise from Los Angeles
Imagination	In port: Ocho Rios, Jamaica	5-night western Caribbean cruise from Miami
Inspiration	In port: Antigua, West Indies	7-night southern Caribbean cruise from San Juan
Jubilee	At sea	7-night Alaska cruise from Seward to Vancouver
Paradise	In port: Cozumel, Mexico	7-night western Caribbean cruise from Miami

Vessel	Status	Cruise
Sensation	In port: Grand Cayman, Cayman Islands	7-night western Caribbean cruise from Tampa
Tropicale	At sea	5-night western Caribbean cruise from Tampa
Carnival Victory	Monfalcone, Italy	Under construction

CELEBRITY CRUISES

Vessel	Status	Cruise
Century	In port: San Juan, Puerto Rico	7-night eastern Caribbean cruise from Port Everglades
Galaxy	At sea: cruising Hubbard Glacier	7-night Alaska cruise from Vancouver
Horizon	In port: St. George's, Bermuda	7-night Bermuda cruise from New York
Mercury	In port: Skagway, Alaska	7-night Alaska cruise from Vancouver to Seward
Millennium	At sea	14-night Baltic cruise from Amsterdam
Zenith	In port: Hamilton, Bermuda	7-night Bermuda cruise from New York
Infinity	St. Nazaire, France	Under construction

COMMODORE CRUISES

Vessel	Status	Cruise
Enchanted Capri	In port: Cozumel, Mexico	5-night western Caribbean cruise from New Orleans
Enchanted Isle	Approaching port: Grand Cayman, Cayman Islands	7-night western Caribbean cruise from New Orleans
Universe Explorer (operating for World Explorer Cruises)	In port: Seward, Alaska	14-night Alaska cruise from Vancouver

COSTA CROCIERI

Vessel	Status	Cruise
Costa Allegra	In port: Funchal, Madeira Island, Portugal	11-night Canary Island cruise from Genoa
Costa Atlantica	In port: Katakolon, Greece	7-night Mediterranean cruise from Venice
Costa Classica	In port: Bari, Italy	7-night Mediterranean cruise from Venice
Costa Marina	In port: Stockholm, Sweden	7-night Baltic cruise from Copenhagen
Costa Riviera	In port: Cannes, France	7-night Mediterranean cruise from Genoa
Costa Romantica	In port: Helsinki, Finland	11-night Baltic cruise from Amsterdam
Costa Victoria	In port: Palermo, Sicily	7-night Mediterranean cruise from Genoa

CROWN CRUISE LINE

Vessel	Status	Cruise
Crown Dynasty	At sea	7-night Bermuda cruise from Philadelphia

CRYSTAL CRUISES

Vessel	Status	Cruise
Crystal Harmony	In port: Sitka, Alaska	11-night Alaska cruise from Vancouver
Crystal Symphony	In port: Stockholm, Sweden	12-night Baltic cruise from Stockholm to Dover

CUNARD LINE

Vessel	Status	Cruise
Caronia	In port: Hamburg, West Germany	12-night Norwegian fjord cruise from Hamburg to Dover
Queen Elizabeth 2	In port: New York, N.Y.	4-night "tall ships" cruise from New York

DELTA QUEEN STEAMBOAT COMPANY

Vessel	Status	Cruise
American Queen	In port: Prairie de Chien, Wisc.	6-night Mississippi River cruise from St. Paul to St. Louis
Columbia Queen	Cruising Columbia River	7-night Columbia River cruise from Portland, Oregon
Delta Queen	In port: St. Louis, Mo.	7-night Mississippi River cruise from New Orleans to St. Louis
Mississippi Queen	In port: St. Louis, Mo.	7-night Mississippi River cruise from New Orleans to St. Louis

DISNEY CRUISE LINE

Vessel	Status	Cruise
Disney Magic	In port: Nassau, Bahamas	4-night Bahamas cruise from Port Canaveral
Disney Wonder	In port: Castaway Cay, Bahamas	4-night Bahamas cruise from Port Canaveral

FESTIVAL CRUISES

Vessel	Status	Cruise
Bolero (operating for First Cruise)	Under charter	17-night Mediterranean cruise from Palma

Vessel	Status	Cruise
Flamenco	In port: Geiranger, Norway	7-night Norway fjord cruise from Kiel, Germany
Mistral	In port: Santorini, Greece	7-night Aegean cruise from Venice
The Azur	At sea	12 night eastern Mediterranean cruise from Genoa

HAPAG-LLOYD

Vessel	Status	Cruise
Astra II	In port: Lerwick, Shetland Islands, Scotland	17-night North Atlantic cruise from Bremerhaven
Bremen	In port: Ærø Island, Denmark	11-night Baltic cruise from Hamburg
C. Columbus	In port: Hammerfest, Norway	12-night North Cape cruise from Kiel, Germany
Europa	In port: Gravdal Island, Norway	14-night North Cape cruise from Kiel to Hamburg
Hanseatic	In port: Stockholm, Sweden	12-night Baltic cruise from Hamburg

HOLLAND AMERICA LINE

Vessel	Status	Cruise
Maasdam (4)	In port: Tallinn, Estonia	7-night Baltic cruise from Stockholm
Nieuw Amsterdam (3)	At sea: cruising Hubbard Glacier	7-night Alaska cruise from Vancouver
Noordam (3)	At sea	10-night Mediterranean cruise from Civitavecchia to Istanbul
Rotterdam (6)	At sea	12-night Baltic cruise from Copenhagen to Dover
Ryndam (3)	At sea: cruising Glacier Bay	7-night Alaska cruise from Seward to Vancouver
Statendam (5)	In port: Ketchikan, Alaska	7-night Alaska cruise from Vancouver to Seward
Veendam (4)	At sea	7-night Alaska cruise from Vancouver
Volendam (3)	At sea	7-night Alaska cruise from Vancouver
Westerdam (2)	In port: Skagway, Alaska	7-night Alaska cruise from Vancouver
Zaandam (3)	In port: San Juan, Puerto Rico	7-night eastern Caribbean cruise from Port Everglades
Amsterdam	Monfalcone, Italy	Under construction

IMPERIAL MAJESTY CRUISE LINE

Vessel	Status	Cruise
OceanBreeze	In port: Nassau, Bahamas	2-night Bahamas cruise from Port Everglades

NORWEGIAN CRUISE LINE

Vessel	Status	Cruise
Norway	In port: Philipsburg, St. Maarten, West Indies	7-night eastern Caribbean cruise from Miami
Norwegian Dream	At sea: transit of Kiel Canal	12-night Baltic cruise from Dover, England
Norwegian Majesty	In port: St. George's, Bermuda	7-night Bermuda cruise from Boston
Norwegian Sea	Approaching port: Cancun, Mexico	7-night western Caribbean cruise from Houston
Norwegian Sky	In port: Haines, Alaska	7-night Alaska cruise from Seattle
Norwegian Star (operating for Norwegian Capricorn Line)	At sea	7-night Great Barrier cruise from Sydney to Cairns
Norwegian Wind	At sea	7-night Alaska cruise from Vancouver

ORIENT LINES

Vessel	Status	Cruise
Crown Odyssey	In port: Istanbul	7-night Mediterranean cruise from Istanbul to Civitavecchia
Marco Polo	At sea	7-night Norway fjord cruise from Copenhagen

P&O CRUISES
INCLUDING P&O HOLIDAY CRUISES

Vessel	Status	Cruise
Arcadia	In port: Gibraltar, U.K.	13-night Mediterranean cruise from Southampton
Aurora	In port: Nynashamn, Sweden	13-night Baltic cruise from Southampton
Fair Princess (operating for P&O Holiday Cruises)	At sea: cruising Boulari-Havannah Passage	10-night South Pacific cruise from Sydney
Oriana	At sea	12-night Mediterranean cruise from Southampton
Victoria	At sea	13-night North Cape cruise from Southampton

PREMIER CRUISE LINES

Vessel	Status	Cruise
The Big Red Boat I	In port: Nassau, Bahamas	4-night Bahamas cruise from Port Canaveral
The Big Red Boat II	At sea	7-night Canada cruise from New York

Vessel	Status	Cruise
The Big Red Boat III	At sea	7-night western Caribbean cruise from Houston
Rembrandt (operating for Didion World Cruises)	At sea	3-night cruise to "nowhere" from Baltimore
SeaBreeze I	In port: Halifax, Nova Scotia	5-night Canada cruise from Boston
Seawind Crown (operating for Pullmantur)	At sea	7-night Mediterranean cruise from Barcelona

PRINCESS CRUISES

Vessel	Status	Cruise
Crown Princess	In port: St. Petersburg , Russia	10-night Baltic cruise from Copenhagen
Dawn Princess	At sea	7-night Alaska cruise from Vancouver to Seward
Grand Princess	At sea	12-night Mediterranean cruise from Barcelona to Istanbul
Ocean Princess	In port: Skagway, Alaska	7-night Alaska cruise from Seward to Vancouver
Pacific Princess	In port: Hamilton, Bermuda	7-night Bermuda cruise from New York
Regal Princess	Approaching port: Juneau, Alaska	7-night Alaska cruise from Vancouver
Royal Princess	In port: Isafjordhur, Iceland	18-night Atlantic cruise from Dover
Sea Princess	In port: Juneau, Alaska	7-night Alaska cruise from Vancouver to Seward
Sky Princess	In port: Skagway, Alaska	11-night Alaska cruise from San Francisco
Sun Princess	At sea	7-night Alaska cruise from Seward to Vancouver
Golden Princess	Monfalcone, Italy	Under construction

RADISSON SEVEN SEAS CRUISES

Vessel	Status	Cruise
Paul Gauguin	In port: Bora-Bora, French Polynesia	7-night South Seas cruise from Tahiti
Radisson Diamond	In port: St. Petersburg, Russia	11-night Baltic cruise from Dover to Stockholm
Seven Seas Navigator	In port: Juneau, Alaska	11-night Alaska cruise from Vancouver to Seward
Song of Flower	In port: Portree, Isle of Skye, Scotland	9-night British Isles cruise from Rouen to Edinburgh

REGAL CRUISES

Vessel	Status	Cruise
Regal Empress	In port: St. John, New Brunswick	5-night Canada cruise from New York

ROYAL CARIBBEAN INTERNATIONAL

Vessel	Status	Cruise
Enchantment of the Seas	In port: Cozumel, Mexico	7-night western Caribbean cruise from Port Everglades
Grandeur of the Seas	Approaching port: San Juan, Puerto Rico	7-night eastern Caribbean cruise from Miami
Legend of the Seas	In port: Civitavecchia, Italy	7-night Mediterranean cruise from Barcelona
Majesty of the Seas	In port: Nassau, Bahamas	4-night Bahamas cruise from Miami
Monarch of the Seas	In port: St. Johns, Antigua, West Indies	7-night southern Caribbean cruise from San Juan
Nordic Empress	In port: Kings Wharf, Bermuda	7-night Bermuda cruise from New York
Rhapsody of the Seas	In port: Skagway, Alaska	7-night Alaska cruise from Vancouver
Sovereign of the Seas	At anchor: Coco Cay, Bahamas	4-night Bahamas cruise from Port Canaveral
Splendour of the Seas	In port: Harwich, England	12-night Baltic cruise from Harwich
Viking Serenade	In port: San Diego, Calif.	4-night Mexico cruise from Los Angeles
Vision of the Seas	At sea	7-night Alaska cruise from Vancouver
Voyager of the Seas	In port: Labadee, Haiti	7-night western Caribbean cruise from Miami
Explorer of the Seas	Turku, Finland	Under construction

SEABOURN CRUISE LINE

Vessel	Status	Cruise
Seabourn Legend	At sea	14-night cruise from Lisbon to Amsterdam
Seabourn Pride	In port: Molde, Norway	14-night Norwegian fjord cruise from Copenhagen to London
Seabourn Spirit	In port: Mykonos, Greece	14-night Greek island cruise from Piraeus
Seabourn Goddess I	At sea: cruising Tyrrhenian Sea	7-night Mediterranean cruise from Piraeus to Civitavecchia
Seabourn Goddess II	In port: Porto Cervo, Sardinia, Italy	7-night Mediterranean cruise from Civitavecchia to Nice
Seabourn Sun	Approaching port: Visby, Sweden	14-night Baltic cruise from Copenhagen

SILVERSEAS CRUISES

Vessel	Status	Cruise
Silver Cloud	In port: Piraeus, Greece	14-night Mediterranean cruise from Piraeus to Monte Carlo
Silver Wind	At sea	7-night Baltic cruise from Copenhagen to Stockholm
Silver Shadow	Genoa, Italy	Under construction

WINDSTAR CRUISES

Vessel	Status	Cruise
Wind Star	In port: Port Vendres, France	7-night Mediterranean cruise from Barcelona to Nice
Wind Song	In port: Rhodes, Greece	7-night cruise from Athens to Istanbul
Wind Spirit	In port: Rhodes, Greece	7-night cruise from Istanbul to Athens
Wind Surf	At sea	7-night Mediterranean cruise from Civitavecchia to Venice

(The following cruise companies operate primarily smaller vessels. Their itineraries are more flexible than those of larger oceangoing vessels; thus port visits need not necessarily follow preestablished schedules, and schedules themselves are often quite flexible.)

ALASKA'S GLACIER BAY TOURS AND CRUISES

Vessel	Status	Cruise
Executive Explorer	Cruising: Glacier Bay National Park, Alaska	7-night Alaska cruise from Ketchikan to Juneau
Wilderness Adventurer	Cruising	6-night Alaska adventure cruise from Juneau
Wilderness Discoverer	In port: Skagway, Alaska	6-night Alaska cruise from Juneau
Wilderness Explorer	Cruising: Icy Strait, Alaska	5-night Alaska cruise from Juneau to Glacier Bay

ALASKA SIGHTSEEING/CRUISE WEST

Vessel	Status	Cruise
Spirit of Alaska	Cruising: Misty Fjords	7-night Alaska cruise from Juneau to Ketchikan
Spirit of Columbia	Cruising: College Fjord	4-night Alaska cruise from Whittier
Spirit of Discovery	Cruising: Glacier Bay	7-night Alaska cruise from Ketchikan to Juneau
Spirit of Endeavor	Cruising: Frederick Sound	7-night Alaska cruise from Juneau to Seattle
Spirit of Glacier Bay	In port: Cordova, Alaska	4-night Alaska cruise from Whittier
Spirit of '98	Approaching port: Ketchikan, Alaska	7-night Alaska cruise from Seattle to Juneau

AMERICAN CANADIAN CARIBBEAN LINE

Vessel	Status	Cruise
Grand Caribe	Cruising: Saguenay River	12-night St. Lawrence cruise from Ottawa to Rocky Harbor, Nfld.
Grand Mariner	Approaching St. Peters Canal, Nova Scotia	16-night Canada cruise from Quebec to Warren, R.I.
Niagara Prince	Approaching port: Wyandotte, Mich.	16-night Erie Canal cruise from Warren, R.I. to Chicago

AMERICAN CRUISE LINE

Vessel	Status	Cruise
American Eagle	Cruising: New York Harbor	7-night Hudson River cruise from Haddam, Conn.

AMERICA WEST STEAMBOAT COMPANY

Vessel	Status	Cruise
Queen of the West	Cruising: Snake River	7-night Columbia River cruise from Portland

CLIPPER CRUISE LINE

Vessel	Status	Cruise
Clipper Adventurer	In port: Dover, England	11-night Baltic cruise from St. Petersburg to Dover
Clipper Odyssey	At sea off Chirpoy Island	11-night cruise from Petropavlovsk, Russia, to Kobe, Japan
Nantucket Clipper	Cruising	St. Lawrence–Great Lakes area
Yorktown Clipper	Cruising	7-night Alaska cruise from Ketchikan to Juneau

LINDBLAD SPECIAL EXPEDITIONS

Vessel	Status	Cruise
Caledonian Star	In port: Orkney Islands	12-night British Isles cruise from Dover to Leith, Scotland
Sea Bird	At sea	7-night Alaska cruise from Sitka to Juneau
Sea Lion	In port: Petersburg, Alaska	7-night Alaska cruise from Sitka to Juneau
Polaris	Cruising Galapagos Islands	7-night Galapagos cruise from Quito to Guayaquil, Ecuador

ST. LAWRENCE CRUISE LINES, INC.

Vessel	Status	Cruise
Canadian Empress	In port: Montreal, Quebec	6-night St. Lawrence cruise from Kingston to Quebec City

Norweigian Cruise Line

Bibliography

The literature dealing with cruise ships falls into a variety of categories. The titles listed are by no means exhaustive, but they do provide adequate suggestions for further reading and research.

GENERAL WORKS ON PASSENGER VESSELS

Cairis, Nicholas T. *Cruise Ships of the World.* London: Pegasus, 1989.

Dunn, Laurence. *Passenger Liners.* London: Adlard Coles, 1961, 1965.

Eisele, Peter T. "Cruise Ships for the Eighties." *Steamboat Bill* 159 (1981): 155–64.

Emmons, Frederick. *The Atlantic Liners: 1925–70.* New York: Drake, 1972.

Kludas, Arnold. *Great Passenger Ships of the World.* 6 volumes, translated by Charles Hodges and Keith Lewis. Wellingborough, U.K.: Patrick Stephens, 1975–1986.

———. *Great Passenger Ships of the World Today.* Translated by Keith P. Lewis. Somerset, U.K.: Patrick Stephens, 1992.

Maxtone-Graham, John. *Crossing & Cruising.* New York: Scribners, 1992.

———. *Liners to the Sun.* New York: Macmillan, 1985.

———. *The Only Way to Cross.* New York: Macmillan, 1972.

Miller, William H., Jr. *Pictorial Encyclopedia of Ocean Liners, 1860–1994.* New York: Dover, 1995.

———. *Modern Cruise Ships: 1965–1990.* New York: Dover, 1992.

———. *Great Cruise Ships and Ocean Liners from 1954 to 1986.* New York: Dover, 1988.

Moody, Bert. *Ocean Ships.* Shepperton, U.K.: Ian Allan, 1964.

STUDIES OF INDIVIDUAL CRUISE COMPANIES AND VESSELS

Basar, Joseph. *"Song of America."* *Steamboat Bill* 166 (1983): 105–12.

Braynard, Frank O., and William H. Miller, Jr. *Picture History of the Cunard Line: 1840–1990.* New York: Dover, 1991.

Cudahy, Brian J., *Around Manhattan Island and Other Maritime Tales of New York.* (New York: Fordham University Press, 1997) Chapter 6, "From Ambrose Light to Five Fathom Hole" is a history of passenger service between New York and Bermuda.

———, "From *Southern Cross* to *OceanBreeze.*" *Steamboat Bill* 231 (Fall 1999): 191–6.

Dalkmann, H. A., and A. J. Schoonderbeek. *One Hundred and Twenty-Five Years of Holland America Line.* Edinburgh: Pentland, 1998.

Dawson, Philip. *"Canberra": In the Wake of a Legend.* London: Conway Maritime Press, 1997.

———. *British Superliners of the Sixties: A Design Appreciation of the "Oriana," "Canberra," and "QE2."* London: Conway Maritime Press, 1990.

Eisele, Peter T. *"'Norway'*—Superliner Transformed." *Steamboat Bill* 155 (1980): 155–66.

Eliseo, Maurizio. *The Sitmar Liners & the V Ships.* London: Carmania Press, 1998.

Eliseo, Maurizio, and Paolo Piccione. *The Costa Liners.* London: Carmania Press, 1997.

Fox, William A. *"'Amerikanis'* Sails On." *Steamboat Bill* 201 (1992): 25–34.

Heminway, John. *"Disney Magic": The Launching of a Dream.* New York: Hyperion, 1998.

Kolltveit, Bard, and John Maxtone-Graham. *Under Crown and Anchor: Royal Caribbean Cruise Line, the First Twenty-five Years.* Miami: OnBoard Media, 1995.

Lloyd, Harvey. *Voyages of the Royal Vikings.* San Francisco: Royal Viking Line, 1985.

Maxtone-Graham, John. *Cunard: 150 Glorious Years.* London: David and Charles, 1989.

Miller, Laurence. "Cruise Ship on Trial: Putting *'Jubilee'* Through Her Paces." *Steamboat Bill* 179 (1986): 184–8.

Miller, William H. *Going Dutch: The Holland America Line Story.* London: Carmania Press, 1998.

———. *The Chandris Liners.* London: Carmania, 1993.

Miller, William H., and Luis Miguel Correia. *SS "Canberra" of 1961.* Lisbon: Liner Books, 1997.

Plowman, Peter. "The Sitmar Story." *Steamboat Bill* 179 (1986): 164–72.

Warwick, Ronald W. *"QE2."* New York: Norton, 1985 and 1999.

THE CRUISE INDUSTRY

Bannerman, Gary. *Cruise Ships: The Inside Story.* Sidney, B.C.: Saltaire, 1976.

Dickinson, Bob, and Andy Vladimir. *Selling the Sea: An Inside Look at the Cruise Industry.* New York: Wiley, 1997.

Kloster, Knut U. *Cruise-farten og det amerikanske marked.* Bergen, Norway: Skipsfartsokonomisk institttt, 1979.

U.S. Department of Commerce. *Analysis of the North American Cruise Industry.* Washington, D.C.: U.S. Department of Commerce, 1980.

REGISTERS

American Bureau of Shipping (ABS). *Register of the American Bureau of Shipping.* New York: ABS, annually.

Eacott, Maggie, ed. *Fairplay World Shipping Directory: 1998–99.* Surrey, U.K.: Fairplay Publications Ltd., 1998.

Lloyd's Register. *Lloyd's Register of Shipping.* London: Lloyd's Register, annually. (This is the standard reference work for vessel data and information.)

United States Coast Guard. *Merchant Vessels of the United States.* Washington, D.C.: U.S. Coast Guard. (Published annually from the late 1880s through 1980; then in 1982 and 1989. More up-to-date information is or will soon be available in electronic format.)

INAUGURAL BOOKS

This is a unique category of work: commemorative volumes published at the time a new cruise ship is introduced into service. They are intended for distribution to passengers and guests at a vessel's christening, to travel agents, and so forth. In some cases such books are the work of a single author; in other cases, specific chapters are prepared by various specialists. While these books typically are not released to the general public or cataloged by the Library of Congress, they are valuable and can often be obtained through specialized maritime booksellers. Following is a random selection from a variety of cruise companies:

Carnival Cruise Lines. *"Carnival Destiny."* Miami: Carnival Cruise Lines, 1996.

————. *The SuperLiner "Ecstasy."* Miami: Carnival Cruise Lines, 1991.

Maxtone-Graham, John. *From Song to Sovereign.* Stamford, Conn.: Cruise Passenger Network, 1988.

Miller, Bill. *"Costa Victoria."* Miami: OnBoard Media, 1996.

Peninsular and Oriental Steam Navigation Company. *"Star Princess" Inauguration.* London: P&O Steam Navigation Company, 1989.

Sbarsky, Sherry Lorber. *"Mercury."* Miami: OnBoard Media, 1997.

PERIODICALS

Unless noted otherwise, all of the following were still being published in the year 2000:

Cruise Industry News Quarterly, professional journal of the cruise industry.

Cruise News Daily, subscription newsletter available over the Internet at
 www.cruisenewsdaily.com.

Cruise Travel, monthly magazine for cruise travelers, with considerable treatment of ships and cruise industry matters.

Fairplay, biweekly news magazine of the world shipping industry.

International Cruise and Ferry Review, professional journal for the operators of
 deepwater passenger vessels.

Maritime Reporter and Engineering News, news magazine of the maritime industry, with emphasis on North America.

Ocean and Cruise News, issued monthly by the World Ocean & Cruise Liner Society.

Professional Mariner, bimonthly publication that describes itself as "the journal
 of professional seamanship"; includes objective accounts of cruise-ship
 mishaps.

Ships and the Sea, issued between 1950 and 1959 by Kalmbach Publishing Company; originally called *Ships and Sailing*.

Ships Monthly, magazine for ship enthusiasts; emphasis on Britain and Europe
 but worldwide in scope.

Steamboat Bill, quarterly journal of the Steamship Historical Society of America.

MISCELLANEOUS ITEMS

Albion, Robert Greenhalgh. *Naval and Maritime History: an Annotated Bibliogra-
 phy*. Mystic, Conn.: Munson Institute, 1972. (Although this work largely
 predates the rise of the modern cruise industry, it is a standard maritime
 bibliographical resource.)

Brown, Alexander Crosby. "Inferno on the *'Yarmouth Castle.'*" In *The Good Ships
 of Newport News*, 195–227. Cambridge, Md.: Tidewater Publishers, 1976.

Brown, Carl Raymond. "The Peninsular & Occidental Steamship Company—Fifty Years of Service." *Steamboat Bill* 58 (1956): 25–30.

Campbell, Anne. *Fielding's Guide to Worldwide Cruises*. Redondo Beach, Calif.:
 Fielding Worldwide, annually. (One of many cruise guides geared to the
 needs of prospective passengers.)

"Classification Societies," *Fairplay* 307 (September 8, 1988): 8-14.

Eisele, Peter T. "Guide to Cruise Ships." *Steamboat Bill*. (Published annually,
 although the issue in which the guide appears can vary from year to year.)

Heinz, Karl, and Michael Schmeelke. *German U-Boat Bunkers Today and Yesterday*. Atglen, Pa.: Schiffer, 1999.

Johnson, Arthur L. "No Fire Bell in the Night." *Steamboat Bill* 131 (1974):
 141–8. (Excellent account of the loss of *Yarmouth Castle*.)

Miller, Willis H. "America's Junior Cruise Ships." *Steamboat Bill* 179 (1986):
 173–9.

Netherland-Brown, Carl. *Biscayne Bay Pilots and the Port of Miami.* Miami: Biscayne Bay Pilots, 1988.

Rachline, Michel. *The Sage of Chantiers de l'Atlantique Shipyard.* Paris: Albin Michel, 1991.

Reed Travel Group, *Official Cruise Guide.* Secaucus, N.J.: Reed Publishing, annually. (A guide published primarily for travel agents and other professionals.)

Seward, Herbert L. *Safety of Life at Sea: Report on the "Yarmouth Castle" Disaster.* Washington, D.C.: Government Printing Office, 1966. (Report to the Committee on Merchant Marine and Fisheries, U.S. House of Representatives, pursuant to House Resolution 151, 89th Congress.)

Macmillan Travel. *The Unofficial Guide to Cruises.* New York: Macmillan Travel, annually. (One of many cruise guides geared to the needs of prospective passengers.)

Holland America Line

Index

GENERAL INDEX

Ships are indexed separately in Vessel Index following General Index.

VESSEL INDEX